The Seven Altar Thrones of Genesis 1:1

by
John-James of the House of Flores.®

Foreword by
David Mathews

CCB Publishing
British Columbia, Canada

The Seven Altar Thrones of Genesis 1:1

Copyright ©2021 by John-James of the House of Flores.®
ISBN-13   978-1-77143-487-4
First Edition

Library and Archives Canada Cataloguing in Publication
Title: The seven altar thrones of Genesis 1:1 / by John-James of the House of Flores.® ;
foreword by David Mathews.
Names: John-James of the House of Flores.®, author.
Identifiers: Canadiana (print) 20210220090 | Canadiana (ebook) 20210220651
| ISBN 9781771434874 (softcover) | ISBN 9781771434881 (PDF)
Subjects: LCSH: Bible. Genesis, I—Language, style. | LCSH: Bible. Genesis, I—Criticism, Textual.
| LCSH: Hebrew language—Grammar.
Classification: LCC BS1235.52 .J64 2021 | DDC 222/.11077—dc23

All Scriptural quotes are from the 1987 version of the KJV Bible and are in the Public Domain.

All other authors' quotes or materials written or otherwise contained herein are quoted by permission and/or are in the Public Domain.

All images contained herein are reproduced by permission from the copyright holder or are in the Public Domain.

Cover artwork credit: © Simon Wong
Email: simon-wong@live.co.uk / Website: www.simon-wong.co.uk

The Hebrew fonts contained within are from BibleWorks.
"BWHEBB, BWHEBL, BWTRANSH [Hebrew]; BWGRKL, BWGRKN, and BWGRKI [Greek] PostScript® Type 1 and TrueType fonts Copyright ©1994-2013 BibleWorks, LLC. All rights reserved. These Biblical Greek and Hebrew fonts are used with permission and are from BibleWorks (www.bibleworks.com).

Extreme care has been taken by the author to ensure that all information presented in this book is accurate and up to date at the time of publishing. Neither the author nor the publisher can be held responsible for any errors or omissions. Additionally, neither is any liability assumed for damages resulting from the use of the information contained herein.

All rights reserved. No part of this publication may be reproduced, stored in a retrieval system or transmitted in any form or by any means, electronic, mechanical, photocopying, recording or otherwise without the express written permission of the author, except in the case of excerpts used in brief reviews or publications.

For information regarding written permission or for author interviews please contact:
shepherd John-James of the House of Flores.®
c/o 1050 Sunnyview Road, NE
P.O. Box 7379
Salem, OR   97351
www.remnantoftruth.net

Publisher: CCB Publishing
                  British Columbia, Canada
                  www.ccbpublishing.com

Dedication

To my Savior and King Yahshua HaMashiach:

Special thank you to you my King, for making this even possible with someone who didn't even like to read at one time long ago. You placed this desire and hunger in me as you are the manifested Word and Creator of all wisdom and knowledge, who made this even possible. You have deposited a piece of yourself in my spirit. Thank you to my beautiful and selfless wife, best friend and lifelong companion Rochelle Denise Flores. I want to honor you my love for sacrificing so much time of your own so I could complete this task along with many other demands. You and I have walked this out together and will continue to press forward as our King and Redeemer has given us a place to always stand upon!

Acknowledgements

First and foremost, I would like to thank my Abba Elohim and His Son Yahshua HaMashiach who made this all possible. If my life was not arrested from death, I would not be here writing this book. I would like to thank my beloved wife and best friend Rochelle Denise Flores, for her sacrificial and ongoing support I needed, especially from her, to complete this task. To listen to your voice Rochelle at the times of compiling this into a Book, singing and worshipping throughout the house, strengthened and encouraged me more than you will ever know, I love you still with all my life.

I would like to thank all of my children and grandchildren: Jeremiah, Ashley, Johannah, Judah, Jedidiah and my son-in-law Eli'sha Cruz, you all have been a part to this journey in ministry. You all have supported me in a way you haven't realized. Listening and watching you all grow into powerful worship leaders was part of the motivation and determination, which assisted the completion to this Book. This was a strength for me knowing you are not wayward, but on the narrow path of truth and righteousness.

Also, I would like to thank my good brother who has stood by me as I wrote this book. You saw all the challenges and knowing the struggles that come with leadership and sacrifice, one of my best friends and mentors, as well as a spiritual father, Pastor John-David of the honorable House of Mathews. Pastor David Mathews helped me with the battle field of editing this work, which I'm grateful for his wisdom. A special thank you and huge hug to Pastor Brittney-Michelle Scott for assisting in the editing as well and encouragement to this compelling work. I would like to thank my good friends and extended family, the House of O'Brien's and Westfalls.

I would like to thank one of my best friends John-William of the Clan of Robertson who begun a special journey hand and hand with me and my family with many tears, storms and struggles. Thank you, my beloved brother, for believing in me and being a strength more than you will ever know, you're a true son of righteousness. Thank you, my beloved brother Mark of the honorable House, of Terrazone, Richard Terrazone and countless others. "Nothing broken, nothing missing." I would like to say a special thank you to a very special family that took me in as their own son, when I was 16 years old. This is where it all first began in a seed form in my life. You transformed and re-establishing my life from a suicidal crossroads into a road of life and meaning, my spiritual father and mother Johnny and Wanda Crawford. I honor you with all my heart and soul.

Thanks to my natural father and mother John Joseph and Joyce Ann Flores who were handpicked by God/Elohim Himself to bring me here. Thank you to all my sisters, brother and cousins I had many Bible studies with that were pieces to this journey. Thank you for all who have stood and even the ones who departed before the time, you all played a role in keeping me steadfast and focused.

I would like to give a huge thank you to Simon Wong, who did the impeccable art work for my Book Cover. One of the best in the business if I might say.

May this Altar Throne revelation minister to everyone who open the pages thereof. May you know the importance of The Altar and the unbreakable bond it has on all of Creation, as well as, all pertaining to your life. May all who read this book come to the place of knowing our Righteous King Yahshua HaMashiach, aka Jesus Christ, more than ever before. If this is the first time coming to know Him, may you be empowered with the truths that walk out from the pages of this book. May you be bound to His matchless and unfailing love that speaks to you from His Sacred Place, The Altar Thrones of Genesis 1:1. Shalom everyone and I pray you will enjoy the secrets embedded in the Beginning, before there was even a foundation of the world - The Seven Altar Thrones of Genesis 1:1.

Disclaimer

This book is compiled to reveal to the reader the mysteries that have been embedded in the ancient text of our Scriptures. Therefore, I have been given a task to convey to you, the reader, the revelation of these Seven Eternal and Everlasting Altars, which all we know have been created. In my 25+ years of ministry I have discovered once I come to something that seems to be the greatest revelation of Scripture, I then discover I have only scratched the surface to this masterpiece. The Sages say that this is an impossible task to accomplish in one lifetime. Just when we think we have learned all there is to learn, we then discover we have only just begun. Though I am not an expert by any means or, a Theologian, I am a persistent and determined scriptural archeologist who can stand side-by-side with the most experienced expositors today because of my desire and love for the Word of Elohim.

In this Book, there are many references to Bible verses used. Yet, not all are locked into a specific translation with the exception of a few. Some of the Scripture quotes are from the 1987 King James Version, which are on the public domain. Any other transliterations are the Author's own.

What my intent, as the Author of this compelling and at times riveting work, has done was return to the original language of the scrolls, connecting many ideas defined by certain words, which only expand their meaning without changing the message or context of what is written. Also, I have gleaned from the Strong's

Greek, Etymological Hebrew Dictionaries, Edenics and Hebrew Number Sequences hidden within the text for expanding the learning spectrum for everyone. As you will discover from this book, there has been a hidden message in Genesis 1:1, which the entirety of Scripture agrees with, emanating these truths.

Without the Altar and without The Place of the Altar, Creation itself would not have existed because The Altar activates The Word. Altars are Bridges and Platforms where the Spiritual and the Natural make contact. I will not make a claim to being an expert in the Hebrew and Greek language, or any of the scrolls for that matter, but the languages do speak for themselves. Therefore, the conclusion to the revelation of Genesis 1:1, regarding the Seven Hebrew words, stand as the Seven Eternal and Everlasting Altars. Each one of them are in agreement with what was scribed thousands of years ago, regarding Biblical History. There is much to question, challenge and ponder; and yet this book is not near an exhaustive or complete revelation of the Beginning of beginnings. May the reader use this not as a final say so, but as a platform expanding their own journey of the Scriptures.

~shepherd John-James of the House of Flores.®

Contents

Foreword by David Mathews xiii

Introduction xv

Chapter 1: The Seven Altar Thrones of Genesis 1:1 1

Chapter 2: בראשית ~ The Altar Throne of
Beginnings – B'resheet 30

Chapter 3: ברא ~ The Altar Throne, Creations
Origins – Bara 59

Chapter 4: אלהים ~ The Altar Throne of Creative
Powers – Elohim 95

Chapter 5: את ~ The Altar Throne of The Word,
The High-Priest of Genesis 1:1 114

Chapter 6: השמים ~ The Altar Throne of The Heavens –
Shamayim, The Kingdom of Righteousness ... 135

Chapter 7: ואת ~ The Altar Throne of Dominion, Royal
Power on Earth – The Earth's Loftiest Altar,
The Adamah Altar 214

Chapter 8: הארץ ~ The Altar Throne of The Earth,
Your Kingdom Reign – HaAretz 275

Hebrew Alef Bet Numerical and Ordinal Value Chart 298

Glossary 299

Foreword

We are told that all Scripture is inspired of YHVH and profitable for doctrine, for reproof, correction and instruction in righteousness. It is this benchmark called Scripture that we measure ourselves by. How closely we adhere to its standards and the level of our understanding becomes the true portrait that is our lives and whether it is framed in the Likeness of the Creator.

Be that as it may, what if there were depths and heights in His Word that remain yet to explore? After all, His ways and His thoughts are higher than ours. If this is plausible, perhaps the barely scratched surface of our Scriptural knowledge can be expanded, stretched beyond the confines of the staid schools of divinity where doctrine and dogma suffice for the profession!

If you are a Truth-Seeker, then we've just opened the floodgates to an inexhaustible possibility wherein the scope of the Creator's mind and His Divine Will could in all good consciousness be far more ascertainable and thus, applicable in the lives of those who would dare to press the envelope!

As I write this Foreword, we are literally trembling in anticipation, knowing that in all likelihood we have in our hands just such an instrument! The Author of this book (Dare I say, this Living Being now revealed in written form) has plunged into the depths of the Language of Creation – Hebrew – and has taken those same inspired Scriptures and pulled back the curtain of theology, religion, scholarly bias, and the tired, old, patented answers and exposed for the first time in my 37-years of ministry an embedded picture of the true Salvific Plan of Genesis revealing both the Creator Himself and our Messiah in a measure that is sure to leave the reader with his mouth agape!

You will see for the first time why the Earth mirrors the Image of the Heavenly Throne Room! The necessity for the Altar of Redemption that is entwined within the revelation of the 7-Branched Menorah, depicted in both the heavens and the earth! You will find that Man's beginning and his End are eternally woven together upon the Altars of Creation!

You will understand at this most crucial hour in history, the greatest deception known to man is about to be unleashed upon the Religious masses! You will not falter when all the eschatological prophecies of building a man-made, counterfeit 3rd-Temple altar [the construction of which will galvanize the world bringing Judaism, Christianity and Islam to the brink of cavernous divide like has never been known] takes center stage in the conflict of the ages - and you dear Reader will know the Truth and this Truth will make you free!

This Book, this Divinely timed inoculation against the lying signs and wonders of the greatest enemy of the Altar - awaits you! Let the journey begin!

By David Mathews

Introduction

- **Hebrews 1:1** Elohim, who at many times and in different ways spoke in time past unto the fathers by the prophets, Heb 1:2 Has in these last days spoken unto us by The Son, who he appointed heir of all things, by whom also he made the worlds;

- John 1:1 <u>In the beginning</u> was <u>the Word</u>, and <u>the Word</u> was with Elohim, and <u>the Word</u> was Elohim. John 1:2 <u>The same</u> was <u>in the beginning</u> with Elohim. John 1:3 All things <u>were made by him</u>; and without <u>him</u> was not anything made that was made.

There has always been a Place, a Platform and Altar which The Word continually manifest and is known by all. There is a matchless power which has been unfolding throughout the ages. We have a King soon to arrive, who has ascended to the Highest of The Thrones in The Loftiest Heavens. Will you be found tilling the depths of His Altar Throne, or one standing by The Wayside of unbelief?

What you're about to read throughout the pages thereof, has always been in the beginning of Scripture. Regarding this deep subject matter of The Altar Thrones in Genesis 1:1, I have not come across a similar work that I am aware of. So, what the reader holds in their hands is the original and one of a kind. The Hebrew language contains layer upon layer upon layer of revelation, so to exhaust this subject area would be impossible. Moreover, this revelation, which is impressed upon all creation itself, is at our very fingertips. This has come to us from the Mind of The Creator, which is at our fingertips.

Something to think about that I will mention throughout this revelation is this, there are 7 Hebrew words, which are 7 Altar Enigmas in their own respect. 7 Hebrew Words, which are 7 Mystical and tangible Altars, found in Genesis 1:1 expressed throughout the entirety of Scripture. These 7 Altar Thrones are also 7 Altar Songs, which I might have as the sequel to this Book. Each Altar contains revelation of a vibrational frequency, which is emanating throughout all of Creation the Scriptures have recorded! Yes, you heard me correctly, each contains a Song of its own discovery. These Altar revelations are intertwined with each Day of Creation's Week along with everything created on those days. These 7 Hebrew words, which begin our Bibles, are more than the words on paper. These 7 Hebrew words are Altar Thrones containing all the mysteries and secrets within the scrolls that were scribed.

The first Word or, Altar revelation, we will engage in is the Crown of all the others - **In the Beginning** - בראשית.

Genesis 1:1 is a musical symphony of Creation, which constantly vibrates, sustaining all that comes from that Place of the Eternal Past. This is why the rabbis believe When Elohim Spoke, (ויאמר – **Vayomer - And He said**…) He actually Sang Creation into existence. There is a numerical connection to this Hebrew phrase, I will address further. The numerical connection is: סוּמְפּוֹנְיָה – Soom'po'neyah, which means, a musical instrument air passes through. By the Breath/Ruach/Spirit of His Mouth all things were created! This would make sense because the Hebrew phrase Vayomer originates from Amar, which means: vibrational utterances like musical notes. This same numerical value gives us another revelation now revealed, נֵזֶר – Nezer, or Crown! From The Crown of all Creation these came forth! This word Nezer is where Nazerene comes from, but this will be addressed in more detail later as well.

This word is used in conjunction with the Hebrew word Dabar, which means the Word, in Psalm 19:14, when the Psalmist expresses from his heart, the CONNECTION to The Words manifesting from the depths of intimacy with The Creator! So, Amar when used in Creation, is the intimate love language the Creator has for all He Created and Made! Zephaniah 3:14-17 says 'YHWH Elohim spreads Joy over us in singing'! There is a Musical Garment spread over His people through the Song of The Creator! We are covered in the Songs each Altar Throne of Genesis 1:1 emanates. This is a powerful thought, which our Savior and King Yahshua manifested all of them! He Crowns us with Song! His Song is our Garment and Royal Authority Seal.

This is probably an unorthodox approach to what is written here, but nevertheless it is ever present and recorded. No one that I know of has wrote a book on or even taught on such an insight we are about to explore in this written interchange. Think about this, in Genesis 2:7, YHWH Elohim <u>fashioned</u> The Adam from the '**DUST**' of The Ground. In Hebrew the phrase for 'the Ground' is, HaAdamah, which can be read another way. This phrase HaAdamah, when read the opposite way, is HaAdomeh, which means: The **Likeness** and **Resemblance**. This 'HaAdamah' is an Altar in His own respect, who is not mentioned, verbatim in Genesis 1:1, but stands concealed within a Hebrew letter – Vav, who is connected to the 6th Altar:

(Diagram 1)

Genesis 1:1 in Hebrew read right to left

בראשית ברא אלהים את השמים **ו**את הארץ

The Adamah Altar concealed in one Hebrew letter. Adamah or Adomeh, 'I will be like – all these Altar Kings'

This one Hebrew letter is the secret, who contains ability and authority to manifest in the Likeness and Resemblance of all 7 Altar Thrones as we will see later in this Book. Having said that,

He was be able to put on and manifest each of the 7 Altar Powers of Genesis 1:1, when He entered through the womb of a woman. When He was born, all these Altar Powers and Kings of Genesis 1:1, were given the legal right to manifest here on Earth through The Word, our Adamah Altar. This is why The Kingdom of Heaven is said to be <u>demonstrated</u> through Yahshua HaMashiach, who is the manifested Word, our Altar King. The Word made flesh was revealed in each Altar that was unveiled. The Word manifests Each Altar King of Genesis 1:1 through demonstration and power.

This book is not written for the sake of knowledge and revelation alone, but to reveal the majesty and power of our Creator. This has been hidden throughout the Scriptures regarding, Himself and His manifested Altar King-Priest Yahshua HaMashiach our Melchitzedeq. All of this will unfold as we focus on this first verse of our Bibles – Genesis 1:1.

Please get a Hebrew copy of the Scriptures, and begin your archaeological journey through the first verse of Genesis 1:1, the Gene pool of Beginnings and the Genesis of Genesis. Make sure you have your lap top or pen and paper ready as well, because you will need to connect some dots with what you will read. In Genesis 1:1 there are Seven Hebrew words, which stand as the foundation of all Scripture, that will be mentioned many times throughout this writing. To attempt to exhaust this revelation is never tedious. It's like eating fresh Manna from Heaven every time.

These are the 7 Hebrew words, which are read as:

(Diagram 2)

<u>Genesis 1:1 in Hebrew read right to left</u>

בראשית ברא אלהים את השמים ואת הארץ

HaAretz	Va'et	HaShamayim	ET	Elohim	Bara	B'resheet
The Earth	and	The Heavens	'Word'	G-d	Created	In the Beginning

This first verse of Scripture reveals a truth found throughout

Scripture, when read from two directions: "In the beginning Elohim Created '**Alef-Tav**' the Heavens and the Earth." When this verse is read the opposite way – "The Earth and the Heavens **the Word** Elohim Created in the Beginning." There are 7 powerful Altar revelations, who sustain everything that was, is and ever will be. When we think of the number 7, there are many areas of 7 in Scripture. There are the 7 days of Creation. The 7 celestial bodies of the Luminaries with the Sun or Shemesh/Shamash being in the center, the 7 layers of Light in the rainbow, 7 layers of dreams with Joseph; these 7's just go on and on.

This information is a pattern to this Altar study. As the Center Hebrew word in **Purple**, who is the Shamesh or Servant Branch to this mystical looking Menorah, connects the Altar Words inscribed in Genesis 1:1. This Center Branch to these Hebrew Words/Altars, is the 4th Altar. I call Him the High Priest-King of Genesis 1:1. This Hebrew word (את) is never translated, but a few times, because He is one who must be revealed and not translated by men! It's as if it/He is intentionally placed in the text pointing to the direct objects of discussion. This untranslated Hebrew revelation never brings attention to Himself and yet the concealed things emanating from Him express His Presence. Isn't it interesting that The Word or, Yahshua, manifested in flesh on the 4th Day since Adams fall?

Psalm 90:4 says that a Day is like a thousand years and a thousand years as a Day to Elohim. From Adam to Yahshua was 4000 years or, can I say 4 days?

Another interesting thought on the number 7 is, the blood, which was sprinkled 7 times upon the Ark and Mercy Seat as well as before the Ark and Veil during the Tabernacle and Temple times –

- **Lev 4:6** And the priest will dip his finger in the blood, and **sprinkle** the **blood seven times** before YHWH and before the Veil of the Sanctuary.

This lets us know, where the Blood is, there is a conversation taking place on behalf of the one it represents. It took Solomon 7 years to build the Temple, there are 7 Feasts of YHWH, 7 pieces of the Armour of Elohim in Ephesians 6 – the Belt of Truth, the Breastplate of Righteousness, both Feet bound in the Kingdom Good News of Shalom/Peace, The Shield of Faith/Belief, Helmet of Salvation and the Sword of the Ruach/Spirit, which is The Word of Elohim – 7 pieces; the 7 Kingdom Parables Yahshua spoke, which were keys to unlocking the Kingdom of Heaven, which will unfold later in this book. There are 7's everywhere throughout Scripture; I would encourage you to spend some time digging those out.

The King of all Altars is The Word known as the Adamah Altar, we will see in this book. It is from this place YHWH Elohim stimulated the embers of Holy Fire called Aphar in Hebrew – Dust, from this Platform Altar of Genesis 2:7, forming The Masterpiece of Creation, The Adam! It isn't a coincidence that science has connected the universe at the molecular level, known as ATOMS, which is a related word to ADAM, hmmm.

The Word, who is the Adamah Altar, is He, who Created all things! **(Hebrews 1:1-3; John 1:1-3)** Yes, the very place the first Adam was formed from is the Threshold, if I may interject, who was the Door and Bridge between Paradise and The Everlasting place. The Dust from this Altar was stimulated from the Bosom of the Adamah Altar - The Mashiach Adam. The Scripture will later reveal, for the Salvation of many, the Last Adam in the form of Yahshua HaMashiach. From the Word all things came into being, carrying within it, the seed and spark of Creation's light. From the Altar Word of all things came the lesser altars, which represented the lower kingdoms, which is what I call, 'Altar Levels' and 'Altar Dimensions'.

When we speak about Altars there are so many intricate details that come with this revelation. Altars have been around for thousands of years as history attests to. As we remain with our scriptural account, I will focus solely on the Altars where The Creator Himself meets with man. This should give anyone something to consider because altars are actual bridges and platforms, which execute transactional activity, contracting the performance redemption or the rejection of a thing. Altars can be a Mercy Seat or a Seat of Judgment! Something to ponder as each Altar Throne is unveiled.

What is an Altar?

First, let us look at this word for Altar from its Hebrew origin –

~ **Altar** – Strong's #4196 – Miz'be'ach/מִזְבֵּחַ defined as the place of sacrifice. This Hebrew word is seen about 402 times in the Tanakh. Now, I must mention, that numbers and mathematics are pivotal when engaging into the Hebrew language. Having said this, the number 402 links two other Hebrew words, which reflect The Altar itself and what it does –

- בָּקַשׁ – Ba'qash which means: to seek out, to request, desire.

- בָּרַר – Ba'rar which means: to purify, to cleanse, choose, polish.

The power of the Altar holds the authority to seek out the one who comes close, purifying their life as it crushes all opposition and defilement that stands against its purpose!

The Tanakh is commonly known as The Old Testament. This would have been the Scriptures all the writers of The New Testament would have preached from. Now, back to Altar insight. The place of Sacrifice or, the place where animals would be brought to, was where a transfer and exchange took place. The Altar was and still is the location Elohim does personal business with His people. Now, what I mean by 'still does' is not fastened to actual animal sacrifice, as we will discover in this writing, but fully bound to One Altar that is higher than any altar on Earth, which is the Altar of our Melchizedek Himself – Yahshua HaMashiach.

This word for Altar comes from its root origin Zabach/זָבַח

meaning: to sacrifice. It is the action of doing and alludes to activation. The action in Hebrew is always preceded by or, clothed in this interesting Hebrew letter 'mem/מ,' which means: **out of** or **from**, when used as a prefix, making the action an actual place. Place in Hebrew – Maqom is the prophetic part in this entire revelation because the wrong Place/Maqom, produces an annulment, while **The** Place strengthens The Altar itself. In addition to this, the sacrifice turns that which is offered, into an actual Place itself! The sacrifice that is offered on the Altar, which is stationed on The Place, has now become the point of release. When we make this personal according to what is written in Romans 12:1, we essentially create an actual Place of sanctification, where, we are met by The Presence of The King!

In Hebrew, 'The Place', would be called HaMaqom/המקום, which is defined as: **The Place**, not just any place, but **The Place**. When Yahshua was offered up on the Adamah Altar Throne known as Golgotha/Golgolet in Hebrew, that sacrifice created **The** Place for all to come to through, which was The Door – Mashiach Yahshua. This Sacrifice created the stationed point of entry to Abba the Source of all things. If you study Hebrew for some time, you will discover, that the powerful connection of this numeric system is intertwined with the Hebrew language. A few examples are as follows:

HaMaqom/המקום has the numerical value of 191, which is the same for: המלכי כהונה המזבח - **Ha'Malkhi Kehunah HaMizbe'ach** – '**The Priesthood Altar of The King**!' The basis of this study is to proclaim our King's Majesty and Priesthood! The Place has always been The Priesthood Altar of our King! The Priesthood Altar is The Place where all things became new through Yahshua HaMashiach, and that Place was on Golgotha! The Seat of Royal Power and Redemption is The Altar Enthronement of The King of all The Earth – Yahshua HaMashiach!! The Altar of Earth has always been the Place He walks and spreads the Kingdom Influence! The Son of Elohim is the extension of Heaven on Earth.

Miz'be'ach has a numerical value related to a few other riveting Hebrew words such as:

הַבֵּן – HaBen = **The Son**; בֹּנֶה – Bo'neh = **To Build up**; בָּךְ יהוה– YHWH Bakh = **YHWH in you**. The Power of The Altar of Elohim is seen through "The Son, who has come to Build up The Name of His Abba in you!" No wonder in John 17:3&6 The Son, who is The Builder, revealed the Eternal Life of The Father. The Son, also manifested the Name of His Father to His people, who came to The Place of The King of Israel, who is Enthroned – The Altar Throne!! The Altar walked the streets of Jerusalem, manifesting wholeness through The Father's Name by what He did! This is called: demonstration of The Kingdom, which was what He preached as well!! Mark 16:17 "These signs will follow them that believe on My Name, they will cast out demons and they will speak with new tongues." We must believe in His Name and then the miraculous will follow.

1. The Altar is the place where the realm of the spirit meets and the realm of flesh, making contact with man. Ponder this thought, we are **spirit** beings inside of a **flesh and blood bodies**, which have a governing seat of authority called a **soul**. We are spirit with a driver's seat called the soul inside a body made of flesh, blood and bones.

    a. **Gen 12:7** And YHWH appeared unto Abram, and said, Unto your seed will I give this land: and there he **built an altar** unto YHWH, who **appeared** unto him.

YHWH said, "…I will give this EARTH…" not LAND but, EARTH. Then Abram BUILT an altar. An altar is always lifted above the Earth, just something to consider as we open up this revelation. Throughout scripture, you will notice, before man wanted to commune with Elohim, he would build an altar. We read this in the lives of Noach, Abram and the other Patriarchs. The Altar becomes the place of communication. It's the legal place, which the Voice of Heaven's Throne speaks with man. The

Voice of Heaven is enveloped with the dimension of Earth in order for it to be Heard. The Voice is so pure and Set Apart that ears filled with impurity can't hear it unless the sound barrier is broken over them. Heavens Voice puts on a Garment of Earth. Earth is the platform for Heaven's Altar entrance, manifests by way of The Adamah Altar. The Altar discloses the Voice in the Blood, which was clothed in the Blood itself –

- b. **Heb 12:24** And to Yeshua the Mediator of the New Covenant, and to the **blood** of sprinkling, that **speaks** better things than Abel's blood. WAIT!! The Blood actual has a language? Yes! The Blood is ever speaking for us. The blood has one language and that is the language of forgiveness and redemption.

2. The Altar is the place of transaction and exchange –

    a. **1John 3:5** And you know that he was **manifested** to carry away our sins; and in him is no sin.

    b. **1Peter 2:24** Who by himself carried our sins in his own body **on the tree**, that we, being dead to sins, should live unto righteousness: by whose stripes you were healed. Man was removed from The Garden by a Tree length and man was restored back into fellowship by the Tree length of The Altar King!

3. The Altar is the place of new beginnings –

    a. **2Co 5:17** Therefore if any man be in The Messiah, he is a new creation: old things are passed away; now behold, **all things have become new**. 2Co 5:18 And all things are of Elohim, who has reconciled us to himself by Yeshua The Messiah, and has given to us the ministry of reconciliation; 2Co 5:19 In this manner, Elohim was in Messiah, reconciling the world unto himself, not **taking an inventory** of their trespasses; and has committed to us **the word of reconciliation**. We all have the same ministry with the same message, RECONCILIATION! This is altar language!

4. The Altar is the place where Covenant is established, recorded and certified with the Seal of Heavens' Altar Throne, by way of The Blood–

   a. **Gen 22:13** And Abraham lifted up his eyes, and looked, and behold behind him a mighty ram caught in a thicket by his horns: and Abraham went and took the ram, and offered him up for a burnt offering as a substitute for his son. Gen 22:14 And Abraham called the name of <u>the Place YahwehYireh</u>: as it is said to this day, In the mount of YHWH it shall be seen. Gen 22:15 And the Messenger Host of YHWH **called** to Abraham **out of The Heavens** the second time, Gen 22:16 And said, By myself have I sworn, says Yahweh, for because you have done this thing, and have not withheld your son, your chosen son: Gen 22:17 That in blessing I will bless you, and in multiplying I will multiply your seed as the stars of **The Heavens**, (Note Isaiah 14 regarding Lucifer) and as the sand which is upon the sea shore; and your seed shall possess the gate of his enemies; Gen 22:18 And through your seed will all the nations of **The Earth** be blessed; because you have obeyed my voice…**Gen 17:7** And I will **establish** my **covenant between** us and your seed after you in their generations for an everlasting covenant, to be Eloah for you, and to your seed after you.

Now, in Genesis 17:7, the English translation captures this principle, that the Hebrew holds revelation to, regarding HOW this is established and the strength it permeates from:

- And I will **establish** my **covenant between** – בֵּינִי וַהֲקִמֹתִי אֶת־בְּרִיתִי – Va'haqee'mo'tee et-B'riti Bei'nee. When we take these Hebrew words back to their origins or roots, we can read this phrase like this: '**I will resurrect my covenant Word Son between Me and you**…' The Son is the end goal of Covenant seen throughout the lives of all the Patriarchs and Matriarchs. Covenant is ultimately established by The Son of The Most-High, Yahshua our Messiah! This cannot be enforced without The Altar that releases The Voice of The Blood that confirms this. The Altar becomes the most important Place above The Earth in order for the most important Work to be completed while The Place becomes the most important position beneath The Altar.

Earth activates the Power within The Adamah Altar because of its invitation. Yahshua even speaks on this in Matthew 23:19. The Altar sanctifies the Gift of substitution because the Altar is the legal platform and actual spiritual bank account for the accused. Paid in full is what we are given at His Altar!

The Blood is the Voice between The Altar and the Flesh, whose location has no authority, without the prescribed Altar that sanctifies the Sacrifice. If Yahshua was killed in Herod's Halls it would have just been the death of an innocent man. But, because Yahshua was crucified at **The Place** prescribed, which prophesied His sinless life, that Blood, that Bread of Heaven, carried the complete dominion and authority executed the Covenant exchange. Having accomplished this brought about our Redemption and Acceptance into The Kingdom of The Heavens where Abba sits.

The Blood is silent UNTIL witnessed from **The Place of The Altar**! The Altar is the Throne of The Blood, which speaks. When the Blood speaks, it is because the Blood has made contact with The Altar Throne! Haleluyah! Now this revelation continues with another beautiful and powerful insight, regarding language emanating from The Place of the The Altar –

The Place & The Altar in Hebrew – הַמִּזְבֵּחַ הַמָּקוֹם – Ha'Maqom and **Ha'Mizbe'ach** have the numerical equivalency of 257 for: נֶזֶר – **Nezer** which means: **Crown**. There was a Crown with the Sacred Name of YHWH that Aaron the Levitical High-Priest was donned with. There was a Crown on The Ark, the Altar of Incense and the Table of Face Bread. Each was a representation of Kingship. This Hebrew word Nezer also means: Nazarene! Yahshua The Nazarene King is in this Parable construct called the Tabernacle or, Mishkan. There is another numerical connection: סוּמְפּוֹנְיָה – **Soom'po'neyah** which means: musical pipes, symphony, a united sound or voice.

When the Place and The Altar come in contact with one another, the sacrifice offered projects the Song of Salvation, which The Nazarene ascended through, on our behalf. His Blood released the Song of Redemption, which not even the Angels can sing, that we couldn't even hear in the natural, but was manifested from the Highest Heavens. One day, as it's written in the book of Revelation 15, we will all sing this song of the Lamb – Revelation 15.

    b. **Matthew 23:17** You fools and blind: for what is greater, the gold, or the temple that **sanctifies** the gold? Mat 23:18 And, Whosoever will swear by **The Altar**, it is nothing; (Why? Because the gift contains the container inside that captures the sound. The Blood records words. The Altar will release that voice from the Blood when the Body is offered up. The Blood speaks.) but whosoever swears by the **sacrifice** that is upon it, he is guilty. Mat 23:19 You fools and blind: for **which is greater, the sacrifice, or The Altar that sanctifieth the sacrifice**? Mat 23:20 Whoso therefore shall swear by **The Altar**, swears by Him, and by all things upon him. Mat 23:21 And whosoever will swear by the temple, swears by it, and by him that enthroned inside. Mat 23:22 And he that will swear by **The Heavens**, swears by **The Throne** of Elohim, and by him that is enthroned upon it.

The Altar is the Lawful Place of Covenant Seal and Agreement. The Altar activates The Sacrifice placed on it or, can I say, Him. The Place where the Altar sits is activated, unveiling the full power and authority, which the Sacrifice who placed upon, was demonstrated. The Blood is the language that unites The Heavens and The Earth Altars! (Heaven in Hebrew is always a plural word – HaShamayim)

For thousands of years, sages of old have excavated the scrolls and have discovered that, in order to exhaust the written word in a lifetime is beyond impossible. Man's life is but a vapor, when compared to the depths of what is written, and beyond complete discovery. The sages of old, who have studied the Hebrew text of our Bibles, invested their lives endeavoring to mine the hidden treasures beneath the surface of what is written. Only to find out that the endeavor was one which was addicting, contagious and never-ending.

In Proverbs 25:2 it is written, "It is the Glory of Elohim to conceal a Thing/**Dabar** and it is the honor of kings to search out this Matter/**Dabar**." In order for anyone to discover the concealed Word, the cultivation and tilling of the Word/Dabar, which Adam was instructed to do regarding The Ground or HaAdamah – The Altar that he came from! Tilling the Word is tilling The Altar Throne! It is The DNA of these 'Altar Thrones' message waiting to be heard! The Blood is the interpreter of what comes to The Altar, not Man, but the Blood who speaks from this Altar Seat. When we arrive to this place, there are no words needed to be heard from us, because, we have now entered the Chambers of Voices!

The English translation gives no distinction between, thing and matter, when in fact, the Hebrew rendering is one and the same - **Dabar** which means **Word**. Contemplating this Hebrew word

Dabar, which can be pronounced as: Deber which means a **'Carpet'**. When we 'till' the Word, it's as if Heaven itself rolls out the Red Carpet of the Word, giving us passage as a King would do by extending his Scepter in favor. Each Altar is a Scepter Throne as well, which contains a protocol for passage, creating acceptance and access over the threshold. The Threshold is the demarcation point for the Altar, which cannot be dishonored, disrespected, trampled underfoot or disqualified by any power known or unknown. Only a true King bears the Scepter of passage allowing man to enter where no other has before. Having been given this, Man can now extract the secrets, the mysteries and the revelations concealed. Did you know? One of the words for a King's Scepter is Shebet, the same for a Tribe.

Each Tribe of Israel is a type of Scepter - Shebet/שבט – Scepter and Tribe. One of the Greek words used, which translates this Hebrew word is: **Anthropos, which means: the face of a man**. So, when we read in the Scriptures regarding, The Face of Elohim, He has revealed the Scepter to His Throne, which is a Scepter with many Faces! In Genesis, we read that the rain was waiting until the first Adam would come. So that He, the FACE or Scepter of The Earth, would be seen from the Face of the Adamah Altar Himself. The Earth needed the Adamah Altar King then, and the Earth needs the Adamah Altar King now! The numerical value of this Scepter is 311, the same for Iysh/איש – man/husband! Men, especially fathers, are extensions for the Throne of The Heavens here on Earth. You will either give passage to the family, which will lead them to the Altar Throne or, you will not. The choice is in the hands of Men, especially fathers!

Yahshua (aka Jesus) said that the words He spoke were spirit and life. The Apostles responded to His question regarding, whether they were going to leave with the multitude of people, who left after the breath-taking insight Yahshua spoke regarding the eating and drinking His Flesh and Blood. "Where shall we go, for you have the words of everlasting life?" What a powerful response!

In my years of studying this amazing library of eternal truths, I have discovered that up until this present time, my research and excavation as a scriptural archaeologist, has only begun. Where can I go, I have been entrusted with The Word of Life!? I will stay tilling this sacred Ground of His Altar, it is the place, we will one day experience like never before.

In this book, to the best of my ability, I was determined to unpack, dig out, piece together the enigma of truth that has been hidden in the language to what is written. My premise will be on an Altar language and an Altar revelation, which hasn't been communicated in this fashion before from Genesis 1:1. Yet, this is where Biblical History discovers its prophetic and supercoiled Helix beginnings. The presupposition and goal to this work, will be the focus and introduction to the Mastery of all Creation – King Yahshua, our King of Righteousness and High Priest of Honor. My heart's desire is that your life will be challenged to excel beyond the veil of religion. My intent of this book is to provoke the reader to draw closer to The Voice, who speaks from the Altar Thrones.

In this first verse of our Bibles, from the language it was originally scribed, are, 7 distinct Hebrew words, which will set the precedent for the rest of what is written. I have my own views on the enigma of this Genesis 1:1 revelation, which is the expression from the mind of our Creator Elohim as some may call God. This verse, or Mother to the rest of what is written, will be examined from the aspect of 7 distinct, and yet unified Altars, each containing their own revelation and musical vibrations.

This verse contains 7 Hebrew words, which are compiled from 28 Hebrew letters or characters, mystically known as, the DNA Guardians of The Infinite Power! No, that does not mean I am saying the Creator was from some created origin, far be it from the truth! The Hebrew language, in my own opinion, is like the very DNA of our Creator in Word form. The original Scrolls had no spaces or Chapter breaks as we see today. The Eternal Word was clothed with the garment of a writing instrument, as well as, one of flesh. This would make sense as we read throughout the Scrolls or Scriptures the Infinite One Himself - YHWH - tends to manifest Himself, epitomizing John 1:1:

~ "In the beginning was The Word and The Word was with Elohim and The Word was Elohim. The same was In the Beginning with Elohim. All <u>THINGS</u> were made by Him and without Him was not <u>anyTHING</u> made that was made." John 1:1-3 (Emphasis mine)

What a radical statement astounding the minds of many today, as if sitting there listening to the one, who once laid his ear upon the very heartbeat of This Word made flesh! Notice my emphasis on the word THING, it is the same suggestion to what is in Proverbs 25:2. This same 'THING' is His Word Dabar or, the Word that was made flesh. His Word came speaking the secrets of Creation, as well as the Restoration of all things. The Word that created everything was talking to people and eating with people, who would have imagined that? Frankly, for those with no sense of humor, He was probably even laughing with the ones close to Him. Without altering the contextual intent to what was written, we can read this another way - 'In The Beginning was the **Altar** and the **Altar** was with Elohim and the **Altar** was Elohim. The same **Altar** was in the Beginning with Elohim.'

Continuing with this section of scripture, we have John saying that John The Baptist was a man sent from Elohim or, from The Highest **Altar** of the Heavens, who testified as witness to The Light or, that revelation of the **Altar** called the Word so, that many would believe! Faith outside of the Altar is not really faith at all. The Altar revelation must be received in order to obtain the manifestation of this Altar of The Light.

This Altar, which is mentioned in verse 10 says, "He was in the world but the world that was made by Him or, that had come forth from The Altar Word, did not know Him - The Altar King!" In verse 12 the revelation unfolds even further saying, "As many as <u>RECEIVED</u> Him, The Altar, to them this Altar gave The Power/exuosia to <u>BECOME</u> sons of Elohim or, sons of The Altar, who Created all things from the Beginning!" (emphasis mine) One MUST receive this Altar in order to BECOME the sons or, Kingdom heirs of Him! The heirs of The Highest Altar, what demon can compare or even challenge that?!

Everything seen and unseen is either an Altar or, connected to some kind of an Altar. Altars are places where the Spiritual can legally meet with the Natural realm. One prominent place, we read about, which a powerful Altar connection manifested is in Genesis 28:11-17, which says, 'Jacob had an encounter **IN** The Place', which would later be called, The Gateway of Heaven or Altar of the Heavens! Genesis 28:17.

Altars are access points, bridges and gateways. Continuing with this thought, The Hebrew language in Genesis 28:11 is scribed as such: **וַיִּפְגַּע בַּמָּקוֹם** – (Reading right to left) **Va'yeef'ga Ba'Ma'qom** = And he/Jacob had an **encounter** from **within/with** this specific **Place**. This was not any place, but **The Place**. It's as if He came into contact with something or, someone in **The Place**. Like the three Hebrew men in the fiery furnace, which the Prophet Daniel wrote about. They were not burned because The Adamah Altar, the 4th Man in the Furnace – The 4th Altar, was in there with them. The Altar High-Priest and King was walking around in the furnace with them. WOW!

Later as we read throughout the Scripture, this specific **Place** would be where Yahshua would offer up His life upon the Loftiest and most powerful Altar ever on Earth, The HaAdamah Altar Throne, who was '**The Place**' - **HaMaqom**. This is where the phrase 'After the order of MelkhiTzedeq' comes in. The Hebrew word for 'After' is Al/**עַל**, which means: to be above all other things. This becomes the Bridgepoint in Hebrew for those who come to this Altar are now lifted above the circumstance and challenges below!

Jacob had an **encounter** – **פגע** – Paga, with something or someone outside of merely, a physical place. From this 'Someone' or 'Something', he would gather a count of stones, unify them as one stone, which he would rest his head. The revelation given to Jacob was called a Sulam in Hebrew, which means a type of ascending and descending Altar system or Ladder. Jacob sees someone looking at Him from the top of this Ladder. Further, Paga, when read the opposite way, we proof to this statement – גַף – Gaf, which means: **a body of a man**. Add the Hebrew letter Ayin/ע and you have the revelation, manifest and to this.

Jacob **saw** the **body figure of a man**, not any man, but a specific man or, can I say The Altar Mashiach! Jacob had an encounter with the Altar Man!! Jacob would hold on to this Altar Man that would manifest in the future! Jacob was holding onto the Altar of our Redemption some thousands of years before His manifestation. When we hold fast to the Altar of transformation, He will transform our former altar, which is connected to the generational iniquities which were before us! From inside this Place of The Altar Master Himself, are the Altar Ambassadors of The Kingdom! Paga has the same numerical value as HaPesach/הפסח – The Passover Lamb and Altar Himself – Yahshua HaMashiach!

From this Altar known as The Word, all things would come forth from. What a deep and provoking thought to ponder for any Bible student. The One who Created the Earth, the Seed, the Crops, the Laws of Nature, which causes them to sprout, was sitting and eating these very things with those close to Him while He was on in Jerusalem 2000 years ago. Imagine leaving a meal with The Word, then arriving back home as your father asks you, "Hey son, how was the gathering?" And your response, "Oh hey dad, it was great! I was having a meal with the One who Created all things and He was sharing some deep things to us that we have never heard before." What a mind-blowing thing to even fathom!

My approach to this study was actually born back in 2001, I began to listen to the late Dr. Myles Munroe speaking on the Kingdom. At that time, my attention was drawn to the Hebrew language and a more rabbinical approach to these truths. I began to discover there was so much more than appeared on the surface of English translations of the Bible. So, I began to cross the Threshold of religious boundaries and into the ancient scrolls. Fast forwarding, I began to see the actions, language and work of Yahshua HaMashiach (aka as Jesus Christ) in a deeper light. I began to realize His Priesthood was one of Royal Power and Kingly Rule with Dominion. I began to connect the enigma of His arrival to that of our MelkiTzedek or, Righteous King's status. We have shared this over the years and therefore, I will not get into the details at this time.

Suffice it to say, I began to focus on the revelation of His Altar and the necessity of **'The Place'**, where He would be crucified, called in Hebrew **HaMaqom/המקום**, which is first mentioned in Genesis 1:9. To my amazement, I discovered that 'The Place' was just as important, if not more so, than the Sacrifice Himself. I would concur to the fact that both are intertwined equal in significance and importance, when it comes to The Redemptive work of Yahshua HaMashiach, the Son of Elohim. The Place gave legal access to The Altar, which then sanctified the assignment placed there. Then, the assignment, or gift on the Altar was released for active duty. Yahshua said, "For this purpose was I sent…" The place of arrival is always bridged by The Altar Himself.

As we begin, keep in mind that this book is focused solely upon the 7 Altars of Genesis 1:1, which all Creation originates from. We will investigate the Hebrew language, the numbering system embedded inside each Altar Throne for greater clarity and insight. We will also take a glimpse at the 7 Kingdom Parables Yahshua taught, regarding further interchange between Heaven and Earth. We will peak into the depths that sit between Genesis 1:1 & 2, commonly known as the Gap Theory, where Lucifer fell to as the now Satan and Prince of the Power of the Air. These 7 Altars of Genesis 1:1, Creation's 7 Pillars of Wisdom and Revelation, are the foundation everything written in The Scriptures. Let us enter the Eternal and Everlasting Chambers of the Altar Throne mysteries.

Chapter One

The Seven Altar Thrones of Genesis 1:1

בראשית ברא אלהים את השמים ואת ארץ

When we think about the Book of Genesis what comes to mind? Creation, the 7 Days, creation of the Animals, the Planetary Systems, Man and Woman, The Garden, Eden, The River of Life, Tree of Life and the Tree of the Knowledge of Good and Evil and so many other concepts. As we open the pages to this book, this will be an entirely different view than common perspective of Genesis 1:1. We will utilize the language and begin to extract from this Creative Tongue of our Scriptures, while discovering something magnificent and extraordinary! I am excited to present this revelation of The Altars, from an entirely different angle - The Altar Thrones of Genesis 1:1. Their Eternal and Everlasting Dimensions will be riveting and exciting as there is much wisdom to glean from regarding this revelation.

I have researched on this Altar revelation for some years now and it seems to me that the entirety of Scripture is based upon the power of the Altar. Altars are where transactions take place, where a Divine exchange takes place with the world of the natural. Where Immortality touches the world of mortals!! Altars are where the Natural is touched and accepted by the Spiritual. It's where the Natural is engulfed into the Super giving us the

Supernatural experience in this World. I believe this is the season where the supernatural is being manifested upon the lives of every son and daughter of the Kingdom. It is the season of Altar power!

It is the season altars that have been built by the men and women of Elohim are beginning to speak! Every altar has a voice, that just needs to be unlocked by a sacrifice! It is the season where even though the powers that be in the natural have tried to cover the mouths of the Kingdom Heirs, yet, cannot cover the mouth of the Altar of our Righteous King: the altars you have built are speaking!!!

Altars have been known throughout millennia by all cultures. The power of altars has been embedded inside of man along with the connecting affect they have between the natural and the spiritual worlds. How much more the Altars of this first verse, which are all interconnected. As one Altar revelation, which is beyond our reasoning and explanation in natural tongues, is now manifested by The Spirit of The King Elohim.

Did you know there is an Altar of Beginnings, and Altar of Elohim, an Altar of Creation, an Altar of The Beginning and The End also known as the Altar Alef Tav or Aluf/Champion Tav/Redeemer? There is the Altar of Heaven/Shamayim and Altar of Earth, and Altar of Let there Be, an Altar of The 1st, 2nd, 3rd, 4th, 5th, 6th Days and an Altar of the 7th Day known as: The Creators Sabbath Crown. There is an Altar of Health, there is an Altar of Grace/Favor, an Altar of Belief/Faith, an Altar of Redemption, an Altar of Deliverance, an Altar of Salvation, an Altar of Unity, an Altar of Prosperity, an Altar of Abundance, an Altar of victory, an Altar of Multiplication and more than enough? There is an Altar of Power and Might, an Altar of Angels, and Altar of Prayer, an Altar of Marriage, an Altar of Worship, an Altar of Praise, an Altar of Giving, an Altar of unity, an Altar of Trust, an Altar of Inheritance, an Altar of Holiness/Qadusha. There is an Altar where the Voice of Blood speaks. There are many Altars in Scripture that we didn't realize were actual Altars. Altars give access and Altars reveal the Crowning season of a thing.

When we come near The Altar, we must approach with total trust and expectancy for what we have believed for! The revelation seen in the beginning is staggering to the mind. The Sages and Rabbis have said; because of the wisdom embedded here, that even after 70+years they have only begun to scratch the surface regarding what has been concealed in the Beginning.

Genesis 1 contains 28 Hebrew revelations also known as Letters compiling 7 Hebrew revelations or words forming the face of a Menorah. The end of each Altar revelation, or the last Hebrew letter of each of these 7 words, give us the Ordinal value of 111. **(Numeric Chart in the back of the book)** This number is the value of: **Aluph/אלף** which means Master in Hebrew and Wonder or Miracle when read the other way – **פלא** - Pela. The number 111 is also the revelation of another Hebrew phrase: **אבן חן** – Eben Chen which means: Precious Stone or Stone of Grace. It is by Grace you have been saved… it is by this Precious Stone we have been saved and redeemed! This Precious Corner Stone is the Foundation of The Altar system of Heaven!!

The final revelation of these Altars of Genesis 1:1 is to bring honor and majesty to The Master! Now, the numerical value of these final letters of the seven Altars or Hebrew words of Genesis 1:1 is: 1,370, a number which gives us a numerical value of the name of a pagan deity – **עשתרת** – Ashtaroth, which is the Fertility demon, who with all her altars, has been a huge problem for thousands of years. Ashtaroth is the problem in Church, we see this fertility ritual embraced every year on Easter Sunday. The **Master** (Aluph), The Altar of Righteousness, has come to destroy all other altar systems birthed out of **Ashtaroth**! Just a little insight to ponder.

There is a side note regarding these 7-words I will address another time, but which, reveals further revelation of The 7

Kingdom Parables and the secret of an Enigma, which stood between The Earth and what would be called Tohu V'Bohu.

If we can look at Scripture as a blueprint of Altar language, we can then discover the path to apprehending what we have been believing for. The first word carried the rest of the Scriptural revelation. It's like a mother who carries the seed and nurtures the seed until full term. When we begin to ponder the power and magnitude of The Creators revelation of Creation itself, we come to a standing halt because we find out that within the very first verse, we have the totality of all things that are about to be unveiled through the Altar of Beginnings.

Genesis One contains the entire revelation of creation and the plan of mankind from the beginning to the end of this very book we know as The Scriptures. I don't even have to pull on other extra Biblical writings which in my own small opinion were part of the compiled library of Scripture UNTIL men BEGAN to do away with what seemed too complicated or too challenging for their small minds. When we do what is called a word study, we MUST not limit ourselves to the English language as we will see this as a kindergarten approach to the Master Language of Crossing Over, the Hebrew Tongue, which was scribed before man was ever created.

Listen to these two areas of mind-blowing revelation:

> **Job 19:26 And even after**[H310] **my skin**[H5785] *worms* **destroy**[H5362] **this**[H2063] *body,* **yet in my flesh**[H4480 H1320] **shall I see**[H2372] **Eloah:**[H433]
>
> **...yet in my flesh shall I see Eloah."**

"**וּמִבְּשָׂרִי אֶחֱזֶה אֱלוֹהַּ** ..." And from my **flesh** I see Eloah. Job is saying that there would come a day when man would have the ability to look **inside** his DNA and discover there - The Fingerprint and Seal of The Creator!! Also, in this verse are two different Hebrew words for 'FLESH'. We have the Hebrew word Ore/**עוֹר** which was the Flesh or Skin covering given to Adam and Eve AFTER the fall. And no, this wasn't an animal sacrifice that we know of as that is absent from the text. It is something more telling that we see unfold throughout the Scriptures. Then we have the Hebrew word Basar/בשר which means Flesh, but more so Good News. The Kingdom Message is The Good News. It is the Garment of Light Adam once wore. He fell from The Message of Good News, which the Last Adam came preaching and demonstrating This Good News!

We can connect a part of this truth in the Laminin cell. The late great friend of mine Dr. Brad Scott whose voice still lives on gave an in-depth study on this revelation. Not only does the Hebrew convey this fact, but the Hebrew phrase we have as 'I see' can also be read as: 'I see **through** the prophetic realm Eloah'. Man is now holder of the revelation of The Creators handiwork. No wonder the enemy, since the fall, has been trying to corrupt the very DNA of Man! Though Science still can't figure it out, The Mysteries of Man's DNA contains the blueprint of Creation in code through a numbering and lettering sequence!

This Hebrew phrase Oo'mi'Besar'ee comes from the word Basar which means Flesh and also Good News!! The Good News in a sense, is the vibration and voice of the Creators DNA, the revelation of the Beginning, or can I say the first Altar!!

Remembering the Former Things of Old

- **Isaiah 46:9** Remember[H2142] the former things[H7223] of old:[H4480 H5769] for[H3588] I[H595] Elohim,[H410] and none[H369] else beside me;[H5750] I am Elohim,[H430] and there isn't any[H657] like me,[H3644] Isa 46:10 **Proclaiming**[H5046] **the end**[H319] **OUT OF the beginning,**[H4480 H7225] and from ancient times/ Qedem[H4480 H6924] signs that[H834] are **not**[H3808] **yet done,**[H6213] saying/singing,[H559] My established purpose[H6098] stands witness,[H6965] and I will do[H6213] all[H3605] my pleasure:[H2656]

First off, this word Proclaiming in Hebrew is – נָגַד = **Nagad** = to **foretell (Prophecy)**, to say something in order to bring forth through words, to be at the front, to pull something from behind to the forefront like a tugboat; to praise something until it manifests!! Example: Genesis 3:11 YHWH asks, "Who **TOLD** you that you were naked?" Our word **Nagad**. With this thought when we read Isaiah's words the very END is brought forth out of the Beginning by a voice. The thought is also that the very END is brought forth through singing and or Praise!! One of these eternal insights is hidden with the numerical values of the family of the Hebrew word, which follow, each having the value of 57.

Within these numerical values, we find intertwined like the DNA Helix, other Hebrew concepts such as – מִזְבֵּחַ = & הַבֵּן & בֹּנֶה = Bo'neh & Ha'Ben & Miz'be'ach– Build & The Son & Altar. '**It was through the Son Elohim Built all Creation and each creative act was revealed through The Altar of The Son who Built all things and upholds all things**!!' Hebrews attest to this fact:

> **Hebrews 1:1** Elohim,G2316 who at many timesG4181 andG2532 in multiple seasonsG4187 spokeG2980 in time pastG3819 to theG3588 fathersG3962 byG1722 theG3588 prophets,G4396 Heb 1:2 Has inG1909 theseG5130 lastG2078 daysG2250 spokenG2980 to usG2254 byG1722 **His Son**,G5207 whomG3739 he has appointedG5087 heirG2818 of all things,G3956 byG1223 whomG3739 alsoG2532 he madeG4160 theG3588 worlds;G165... POWERFUL thought!! That word for **made** is the Hebrew word **Bara**. This Hebrew word is ONLY ever used with The Creator and NEVER man!! Did you hear that? Bara is ONLY used with Elohim and NEVER man. Having said this that means The Son is not a man, but Elohim inside a flesh man's body!!! Elohim The Creator created all things through and by The Son who is The Creative acting eternal Word that upholds all things because He is Creator of all things and He is The

Altar which all things came forth from. Let's get back to the Isaiah revelation of the beginning.

Let's listen to the Hebrew rendering –

- מַגִּיד מֵרֵאשִׁית אַחֲרִית וּמִקֶּדֶם – Mageed M'resheet A'chareet Oo'mee'qedem = **"Out of The Beginning I foretell/ prophecy the End and ancient times…"**

The end of all things was INSIDE the very BEGINNING and just needed to be unlocked. This is similar to Genesis 2:5, which I will address later. Frankly, ANYTHING, you can name regarding, Doctrine, Prophecy, Revelation, Historical accounts, etc., can be found INSIDE the Beginning or, perhaps, In the Beginning! Each Altar is a reflection of the Beginning and can't be separated from it!

The Beginning is the literal womb, containing the End and, the entire process getting there - all inside of one Hebrew word - or might add, Miz'be'ach/Altar. With a Word? Yes! There is a difference between The Scriptures and The Word. The Word has always been, the Scriptures are the written account of the actions of The Word that has always been. I want to take a journey inside the beginning. I'm not sure how far I will be allowed to go. Or how much wisdom and revelation will be given to me that I can give to all the readers of this book, but I will be obedient with what is given to me.

Give Me the Rhema Word

I have mentioned before two Greek concepts used quite often in charismatic and Pentecostal churches, which are **Logos** and **Rhema**. A Logos word or a Rhema word, which are, the Manifested Word and the Revelation Word. Rhema is the word of Revelation made known. As a matter of fact, when we look at the scriptures using this Greek term we would be baffled at their connection, example:

- **Matthew 4:4** But[G1161] he[G3588] answered[G611] saying,[G2036] It is written,[G1125] Man[G444] shall not[G3756] live[G2198] by[G1909] **bread**[G740] alone,[G3441] but[G235] by[G1909] every[G3956] **word**[G4487] that comes forth[G1607] from[G1223] the mouth[G4750] of Elohim.[G2316]

- **Romans 10:17** So then[G686] **faith**[G4102] cometh by[G1537] hearing,[G189] and[G1161] hearing[G189] by[G1223] **the word**[G4487] of Elohim.[G2316]

Yes, our word here is the Greek word **Rhema**. Man is to live by **Rhema** or Revelation that proceeds out of The Creators mouth and NOT despising the Bread or natural substance for the body. Rhema is directly connected to The Adamah Altar! Also, Emunah/Faith comes by the hearing of The Quickening or Rhema word! Faith is born or manifested when The Quickening Word is heard! Rhema gives birth to Emunah/Faith! And this is the Word from The Beginning!

Paul/Shaul was caught up into the Heavens (Altar of Heaven) where voices are heard and Heard the Rhema or Quickening words that were unlawful to speak here on earth. Why? Because of this corrupt flesh, it is illegal to utilize this level of language on Earth, as it can be destructive to fallen and frail, fleshly bodies. Shaul/Paul entered the Heavens of B'resheet also known as, World of Altars Thrones, where the origin of life is constantly speaking! Side note, Scripture says, we are SEATED in Heavenly PLACES. These are Thrones. To be seated is Altar and Throne language. You and I are more than what we can see and touch!

Here is a powerful thought, when we read John 1:1, 14 The Word that was INSIDE the Beginning and that was manifested is the **Dabar** in Hebrew or Greek **Logos**. Logos is always manifested while Rhema is revealed! Follow me, the Logos ONLY communicated The Rhema Word that was missing. The Rhema word is The Kings Word!! The Rhema Word is the Covenant Word!! The Rhema Word is the sustaining Word!! The Rhema Word is the Word of Creation!! The Rhema Word is The Altar

John-James of the House of Flores.®

Word! When we read the account of Yahshua speaking, He is The WALKING Logos/Dabar speaking and what He said was ALL Rhema or Revelation!! Peter responds to Yahshua's question after speaking the hardest WORD and says,

🍇 **John 6:63** It is^{G2076} the^{G3588} spirit^{G4151} that quickens;^{G2227} the^{G3588} flesh^{G4561} (^{G3756}) profits^{G5623} nothing:^{G3762} the^{G3588} ==words^{G4487}== that^{G3739} I^{G1473} speak^{G2980} unto you,^{G5213} are^{G2076} spirit,^{G4151} and^{G2532} are^{G2076} living.^{G2222} **(The WORDS/Rhema are Spirit and are Life. Rhema is the food for the Ruach/Spirit of man!! The Logos is the written word holding no breath and the Rhema word is the written Word made alive!)** Joh 6:64 But^{G235} there are^{G1526} some^{G5100} of^{G1537} you^{G5216} that^{G3739} believe^{G4100} not.^{G3756} For^{G1063} Yeshua^{G2424} knew^{G1492} ==**from^{G1537} The Beginning^{G746}**== **(The Beginning is the First Altar Throne of Genesis 1:1) Yahshua knew because He was in this place of The Beginning!)** who^{G5101} they were^{G1526} that believed^{G4100} not,^{G3361} and^{G2532} who^{G5101} should^{G2076} betray^{G3860} him.^{G846} Joh 6:65 And^{G2532} he said,^{G3004} Therefore^{G1223 G5124} I said^{G2046} unto you,^{G5213} that^{G3754} no man^{G3762} can^{G1410} come^{G2064} to^{G4314} me,^{G3165} except^{G3362} it were^{G5600} given^{G1325} unto him^{G846} of^{G1537} my^{G3450} Father.^{G3962} Joh 6:66 From^{G1537} that^{G5127} time **many^{G4183} of his^{G846} disciples^{G3101}** went^{G565} back,^{G1519 G3694} and^{G2532} walked^{G4043} no longer^{G3765} with^{G3326} him.^{G846} Joh 6:67 Then^{G3767} Yeshua^{G2424} said^{G2036} to the^{G3588} twelve,^{G1427} "Will^{G2309} (^{G3361}) you^{G5210} also^{G2532} go **astray?"^{G5217}** Joh 6:68 Then^{G3767} Simon^{G4613} Peter^{G4074} answered^{G611} him,^{G846} Master,^{G2962} to^{G4314} whom^{G5101} will we go?^{G565} you have^{G2192} the ==**words^{G4487}**== of **eternal^{G166} life.^{G2222} (The Rhema of Eternal Life was a download into their spirit that Yahshua was manifesting all Seven Altar Thrones at this moment to them. Eternal Life is that of the Eternal Realms, the first three Altar Throne revelations that Genesis 1:1 begin with.)**

> Joh 6:69 And^{G2532} we^{G2249} believe^{G4100} and^{G2532} are sure^{G1097} that^{G3754} you^{G4771} are^{G1488} **The Mashiach**,^{G5547} the^{G3588} Son^{G5207} of the^{G3588} living^{G2198} **Elohim.**^{G2316}

Peter said that Mashiach had the very Rhema or Quickening words of Eternal life where the first three Altar Thrones are. They were given an Altar Throne download right then and there. The only word that can quicken your mind, your heart, your soul, your spirit is a Rhema Word! Haleluyah!

He Commanded Them Together

> **Colossians 1:11** being empowered with all power, according to the might of His esteem, for all endurance and patience with joy, **12** giving thanks to the Father who has made us as one to share in the inheritance of the set-apart ones in the light, **13** who has delivered us from the authority of darkness and transferred us into the reign of the Son of His love, **Col 1:14** in whom we have redemption **through His blood**, the forgiveness of sins, **15** who is the **resemblance** of the invisible Elohim, the first-born of all creation. **Col 1:16** Because in Him were created all that are in **The Heavens** and that are on **The Earth**, visible and invisible, whether thrones or rulerships or principalities or authorities – all have been created through Him and for Him. **17** And He is before all, and in Him all things are **held** together. (**held** together is the Hebrew idea of being **commanded together**, like an unbreakable bond and covenant.) **18** And He is the Head of the body, the assembly, who is the beginning, the first-born from the dead, that He might become the One who is first in all. **19** Because in Him all the completeness was well pleased to dwell, **20** and through Him to completely restore to favour all unto Himself, whether on earth or in the heavens, having made peace through the blood of His stake.

B'resheet begins with the Hebrew letter Bet/בּ and gives us the hint of a House, or that which is Higher than all the Heavens where YHWH Elohim lives. A house is where a family comes in to become a home. His Throne is something different. His Throne is above where Creation exists from and where He rules from. Yet, never absent from either place!!

The Letter Bet speaks of the House and is the picture of a House, His House. House in Hebrew means a Sanctuary or in Hebrew Beit Miqdash. From His House all things come into existence. Notice Genesis 1:1 doesn't have The Creator speaking it is as if the writer has captured a Place of the Mind of The Creator. The place before The Word communicated and Created. Language is not something in this place of revelation it is what comes after. We are dealing with something bigger than creation itself here. If we still make sounds with our mouths it's because we are in the world of Action and Creation that is reflected in the last Altar revelation called The Altar of Earth where The Kingdom Reign is settled.

Job has a download of some interesting things pertaining to this:

> 🟣 **Job 26:7 He stretches out**[H5186] **the north**[H6828] **over**[H5921] **the empty place,** [H8414] **hanging**[H8518] **The Earth**[H776] **upon**[H5921] **nothing.**[H1099]

'Stretches Out', comes from the Hebrew concept bending of Light, and conforming to an environment because of its influence. Bending of Light, comes from the scientific term: Refraction. This can happen with Sound, Water, Airwaves, and other types of Waves. This bending effect makes it possible for us to have magnifying glasses, lenses, prisms and the ancient covenant sign in the sky, the rainbow.

Did you know that influence is a powerful gift, which functions similar to this refraction of light? Here is revelation: **Refraction** in Hebrew is: שָׁבַר – Sha'bar – which also means to break into pieces or split into pieces, similar to the prism effect of light. Yahshua said He was The Light... His Body was a gift from The

Heavens. On Passover night He 'BROKE' Bread and said take eat for this was His Body BROKEN for man. The Light of the World demonstrated all Seven Altars on Passover night, I will only address one of these. The bread that was broken He said was His Body, His Body was a Rainbow in the meal of Passover night. The Light of The World demonstrated The Altar of Elohim, causing His Body to refract, prism, and then Covenanted to His Disciples. They ate the Light of The World that was refracted by the power of The Altar Throne of Elohim.

These same Hebrew letters for 'Refraction' form the word: Basar/בשר – Flesh, or, Good News! The Disciples ate the Rainbow Message of Good News, which is The Kingdom of Heaven Message Yahshua preached and demonstrated all along.

When Yahshua said in Matthew 13:33 that the Kingdom of Heaven was like Leaven... He was saying that there is a Kingdom from a higher place called Heaven. This is an Altar of mystical proportions. And then Yahshua says that this Kingdom that came from Heaven is like Leaven. There is a bending effect, also seen as an Influence effect, that must bend us in order for us to enter into its' dominion! Bending or stretching is the sign just before crowning through the stratosphere layer. To be 'stretched' precedes an unspeakable 'rest'. The numerical value of this Hebrew word for stretch/נטה is 64, the same for: נוח/ Nuach which means 'rest'.

He bends the North Place like the bending or refraction of Light.

He does this through the idea of 'Al/על in Hebrew which is the Hebrew word connected to all sacrifices, blood and even, the ORDER of Melkhitzedeq. It would be through this idea; the Expanse of Light would expose the Tohu or Empty Place. In Jeremiah it says Elohim does not create anything Tohu. This is beyond us to fully understand.

Looking at the very first letter that begins all Scripture, we have a House or a Sanctuary. From this single, House/Sanctuary/Letter, the entire revelation of Scripture would be born or revealed through this realm called the Rhema or the Quickening Revelation Word! The Creation of crowning would take place because of the seven Altar revelations in Genesis 1:1.

A book of its' own could be written from this simple insight: That man is to live by, more than natural substance, The Rhema Word! It is what shut Satan down in the wilderness. We can stay right here for days, but we must move on. Genesis 1:1, The Altars where all things originate from. Each one of them is layered upon another forming a picture of an Eternal House of Temple of sorts! What a concept that will make perfect sense as we move along each revelation!

B'resheet can be seen as 'The Altar of Beginnings'!!! So B'resheet becomes the first Altar revelation used to reveal the Creating of the Heavens and The Earth. Some might say, "Wait a minute, if this is the Altar of Beginnings that created The Heavens and The Earth then does that mean God is Created?" NO!!! Scripture says Elohim is HIGHER than the Heavens, BUT His Throne is <u>INSIDE</u> The Heavens as we will read! The Beginning stands as the Stairway to The Altar which is at the foot of The Throne of The Eternal One. The First Temple and Tabernacle had a Ramp, so the shame of the priesthood would not be seen. The Temple in Ezekiel has the Altar facing East or Qedem, and instead of a Ramp, this Altar has Stairs. The change is indicating that The Shame of Man has been removed!

A Greater Priesthood

Think about the Power and Majesty of The Melkhitzedeq Priesthood for a second. This Priesthood of Yahshua HaMashiach is HIGHER than The Heavens! So, we must realize that The Throne of Elohim is Higher than the Highest Heavens as it is written:

- **Hebrews 7:26** For it is fitting that we have such a **High Priest** – kind, innocent, undefiled, having been separated from sinners, and **exalted above The Heavens**, (HaShamayim/השמים, our fifth Altar revelation in Genesis 1:1)

- **Psalm 11:4** Yahweh in his holy temple, YHWH's Throne *is* **in The Heavens**: his eyes behold, his eyelids try, the children of men.

One verse says YHWH's Throne is IN or INSIDE the Heavens and YHWH Elohim Himself is far ABOVE the Heavens. His Throne is IN the Heavens. If possible, read the Book of Enoch and you will see Enoch went into more detail about the Heavens and the multidimensional layers of it. So, with this thought, Genesis 1 contains the Highest of the Heavens. Above this is The Place Yahshua would later say that He goes to prepare a Place for you and I, which in His Father's House are many Mansions. The Heavens below are the Place where Dimensions are.

The Highest of Heavens are what I would call Di-Mansions!! Or the Place where The Word of B'resheet goes to prepare a place for His Bride, this is where the New Jerusalem comes from as seen in Revelation 21.

Another verse says The High Priest which is Melkhitzedeq Yahshua Himself is HIGHER than the very place where The Throne of YHWH is. What a mind staggering concept to grasp! I want to share something that is emanated from Genesis 1, a concept seen throughout Scripture regarding what is known as, 'The Place of Worlds'.

There Is A World of Difference

1. **Asiyah = The World of Actions**. The Place of what we know as this reality of Time and Matter. The place the Place we know as Time and Matter.

The Place where we can activate The Kingdom or Malkhut Yahshua HaMashiach spoke about. There is a Place we should get to and walk in where Prayer stays at the Door BECAUSE we have <u>BECOME</u> Prayer. Regarding prayer, it's as if we time travel through the mystical Ladder Jacob saw in Genesis 28. When we pray, our prayer ascends to the Highest of Heavens where the Throne is. The Kingdom is where things are established. When Yahshua said, "I give you the KEYS of The Kingdom and whatsoever you **BIND** on Earth shall be **BOUND** in Heaven/Shamayim and whatsoever you **LOOSE** on Earth shall be **LOOSED** in The Heavens." This is Asiyah, another name for the Place of HaAretz where we move UP the Primordial Ladder of revelation.

Also, when looking at the Entrance of the Temple or Tabernacle we can see this Revelation beginning with HaAretz, the image of The Outercourt yard, also known as – חָצֵר – Chatzar, in Hebrew. It speaks of a sacred enclosed time place. With the same letters we have another word that reflects this place of the Outercourt yard – רחץ – Rachatz = Washed. We have another Hebrew word with the same numerical value that reflects something shown and given to the one accepted in this Outercourt Altar system – רחמים/Rachamim means Mercy and Loving-kindness.

The Outer courtyard area is the place where death occurs, life in exchange for death and the washing in order to ascend into the next level to those who didn't deserve it which this is called Mercy/Rachamim. The Outercourt area is where things are prepared for ascending or for Disposal!! The Outercourt prepares you and I for Inner Chamber areas of the most sacred space or for the Ash-heap of discard. This world we live in is parallel to this idea.

When Mashiach Yahshua said, "Broad is the way…and Narrow is the way…" That word for NARROW is Tzar/**Tzor** – the same word indicating the time of Tribulation, as well as, the birth canal where life would begin to make its way through the crowning stage. It is where the cervical wall thins out and this is connected to the Hebrew concept Teshuvah/Repentance.

When we come to the words spoken by Yahshua and stand upon what is written, from that time forward, we will not be deceived away from the path of Holiness and Ascension, leading to the Altar that is Higher than the Heavens - The Door to Abbas House – Yahshua HaMashiach. Elohim sits upon the Throne and when The Blood of Yahshua speaks, His Blood gives us passage beyond the Highest Heavens where Elohim's Throne is and INTO the House of Abba where **'The Place'** is prepared for us. The Place is in agreement with the Voice of His Blood. He is The Word, but His Blood contained a specific voice needed to be Heard. While Yahshua lived, He couldn't pronounce us redeemed until He shed His Blood. His Blood had a voice that was released at His Death, and as it was released from His Altar, which was above The Altar of Earth, this voice spoke – 'It is finished!' More of this revelation later.

The Place is Higher than the Heavens. This is only an introduction to B'resheet and the other Altar Thrones because I don't want to dishonor the process given to us through The Son, who is The Word, that made The Way for us to experience these Altar revelations inscribed in Scripture.

The next Altar Throne is the Va'Et, which **connects** the Earth to The Lowest of the Heavens above. This is like a Bridge connecting us as inheritors to what is beyond the Highest Heavens!! Note the diagram:

(Diagram 3)

John-James of the House of Flores.®

This Altar Throne reflects the first Veil formerly known as The Door in the Temple. The manifestation was so powerful, The Veil of Yahshua's Flesh that was Torn, an act so powerful that it caused the Veil of The Temple from the Outercourt into the Holy Place to be torn in half from top to bottom. Why Top to bottom? Because it was evidence that the Greater Priesthood had put to rest the corrupted priesthood system of that day. The Scriptures reiterate that the Garment Ephod of Aaron was forbidden to be torn – (Leviticus 21:10). By this symbolic act of the Temple Veil garment being torn from top to bottom, Caiaphas did as well, in tearing the sacred vestments of Aarons' Garments! (Matthew 26:65) Remember, the priesthood had been infiltrated by Antiochus 4th two centuries earlier?

This priesthood was only a 'Voice' crying in the wilderness while the Priesthood of Yahshua is The Voice that walks above the chaos! The transfer between a Crying Voice in the Wilderness with the Walking Voice of Heavens Throne took place, by The Last Adam – Yahshua HaMashiach!

The Next Level is HaShamayim – **The Heavens**. Not Heavens, but **The Heavens**. The Endless Dimensional planes where layers of Temple revelation reside!! Where endless revelations of Life reside!! Where endless revelations of Creation expand!! HaShamayim. Notice what The Prophet Isaiah says,

> 🔴 **Isaiah 66:1** Now says Yahweh, "**The Heavens** are My Throne, and The Earth is My **footstool**. Where is this house that you build for Me? And where is this place of My rest? The Actual Heavens ARE His Throne. What else does Scripture say regarding this thought?

Isaiah 66 gives a powerful revelation of YHWH sitting on HIS Throne while the Earth is his footstool. Quickly, The Heavens is His Throne where The Crown is or Head, The Earth is His Foot stool so that means there is a revelation of another Altar between the two which is The Adamah Altar of Yahshua HaMashiach who is at the right side of The Heavenly Throne. The Hebrew word footstool is: הדם – HaDom which is also HaDam or The Blood.

The Blood carries the weight and the Blood is the Path the Throne goes on. The Blood of Yahshua was the victory place of The Throne of The Heavens to stand, not trample, but stand. Read another way we have: Domeh/דמה – Resemblance and Likeness. One more Hebrew word is: המד/Ha'Mad: The Garment Measured for The Blood. This refers to the manifested Last Adam, The Altar King!

(**Diagram 4**, Right to left)

There is The Throne of Creator and His Creative Power and there is The Throne of YHWH or The Name. The name of YHWH is ALWAYS connected to the sacrificial system, NEVER Elohim. When Blood is involved, The Name is ALWAYS present!! The Name is manifested when The Blood speaks!! Yahshua said He revealed The Name or manifested His Father's Name. The Name is always in communion with The Word!!The Word is the walking Voice manifested that demonstrates The Authority and Dominion of The Father's Name Yahuwah.

Revelation 4:2 we have John seeing ONE sitting on The Throne.

Revelation 3:21 which is the remedy revelation of Genesis 3:21, the one who overcomes what is coming will SIT with The Word/Yahshua on His Throne just as He sat with Abba on His Throne. This is Higher than The Heavens!!! Before The Heavens is the one who is First and Last, Higher than The Heavens. (Note the diagram below.)

John-James of the House of Flores.®

(Diagram 5)

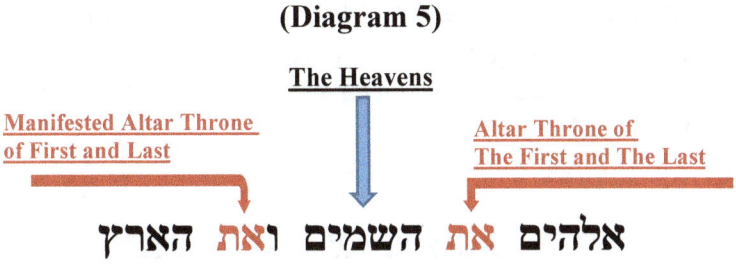

Next Altar Throne is the **Alef** and The **Tav**, or He, who is The First and The Last, The Beginning and The Ending. The Word which holds all things together. The Word that STANDS between Elohim and The Heavens and The Earth, connected them all. Revelation 1 records His words as He is The Alef and The Tav, The First and The Last, The Beginning and The End. Right here, all this time, was the revelation that was scribed in Genesis 1:1.

What do we do? Let's keep digging –

- **Matthew 5:33** "Again, you heard that it was said to those of old, 'You cannot swear falsely, but will perform your oaths to Yahweh.' **Mat 5:34** "But I say to you, do not swear at all, neither by **The Heavens**, because it **is** Elohim's **Throne**; Mat 5:35 neither by **The Earth**, for it is His **footstool**; neither by Yerushalayim, for it is the city of the great King;

WOW!! The words of Yahshua confirm that the Heavens or HaShamayim IS the actual Throne of Elohim. Not the Heavens we can see, not the Heavens or world of Angels, but The Shamayim Altar Throne of Genesis 1:1 which the Angelic Powers surround. This is a hint from the revelation of PaRDeS. **(Peshat, Remez, D'rash and Sod)**

Yahshua was using the wisdom of Creation to point back to Genesis 1 where Thrones and Altars are first seen on the highest of spiritual levels!!! HaShamayim IS The Throne of Elohim, why? Because from this Throne came forth all Creation!!! Genesis 1:1-4 confirms the secret to this. The High Priest who over sees the Creative Work of Elohim stands Guard over The Altar Throne of Elohim!! Just like the earthly priests STOOD over The Altar sacrifices, we have the same revelation given. What a thought!!

The Majesty of the Beginning

Let us open with Genesis 1 along with Psalm 119:89 which says:

- **Genesis 1:1** In the beginning[H7225] Elohim[H430] created[H1254] (H853) The Heavens[H8064] and The Earth.[H776]

בראשית ברא אלהים את השמים ואת הארץ

- *****Psalm 119:89** Forever,[H5769] Yahweh,[H3068] your word[H1697] is appointed over[H5324] **in Heavens**.[H8064]

לְעוֹלָם יהוה דְּבָרְךָ נִצָּב בַּשָּׁמָיִם

Meditate on these verses as they are saying so much. Each word is a revelation of an Altar. The first word is the Altar to the rest of the verse. The first verse is the Altar to the rest of the Chapter and chapter one of Genesis is the Altar for the rest of Scripture. Never ending power and revelation at the Altar. Take note of Psalm 119:89 says the WORD/Dabar stands as the Chief Officer/Natzav in the Heavens/Ba'Shamayim. When we research this Hebrew word, we discover that the word Dabar/Word is translated into the Greek as Logos. This makes so much sense as the Logos/Dabar was the manifested Rhema/Amar of Elohim in the flesh – John 1:1-3, 14. The only concept used in all the Creation account is the Rhema or Amar Word. All of Creation was total Rhema/Amar or Quickening Power manifested!

So, the Dabar Word is what is Standing as Chief Commander in and over The Heavens. This is why the verse in John 1 cannot be comprehended solely from an English translation, we must dig deep into the origins of the word. We can preach good sounding sermons and miss the bigger plan of our Creator, why limit ourselves.

Let's look at another section of text that contains the most mystical thought with no end –

- **Hebrews 1:1** Elohim,[G2316] who at many times[G4181] and[G2532] in multiple ways[G4187] spoke[G2980] in time past[G3819] unto the[G3588] fathers[G3962] by[G1722] the[G3588] prophets,[G4396] Heb 1:2 Has in[G1909] these[G5130] last[G2078] days[G2250] spoken[G2980] unto us[G2254] by[G1722] The Son,[G5207] whom[G3739] he has appointed[G5087] heir[G2818] of all things,[G3956] by[G1223] whom[G3739] also[G2532] **he made**[G4160] **the**[G3588] **worlds;**[G165] Heb 11:3 Through faith[G4102] we understand[G3539] that the[G3588] **worlds**[G165] **were framed**[G2675] **by the word**[G4487] **of Elohim,**[G2316] so that things which are seen[G991] were not[G3361] **made**[G1096] of[G1537] things which do appear.[G5316]

This word for **'worlds'** is our Hebrew word **Olam** which speaks of all ages. Every level of existence. The worlds came through the Gateway of an Altar. We will dive into in this Altar, known as Bara, at a later time, the Altar of Creative Powers, the Hebrew word Bara, which no flesh man could operate in, only Elohim - because it speaks of the One who can pull Matter out of Eternity and manifest it in the World.

The very word of Elohim is Spirit and Life. Mashiach said, "The words I speak unto are spirit and they are life." **(John 6:63)** As we consider these words, we understand that we are dealing with the source of all that exists. I want to reiterate a powerful thought and concept the sages of old have mentioned – "Every single word, every single character or letter and even the very spaces between these are sacred." Also, the very fact of this revelation was scribed in a language like no other, Hebrew, the Qadosh tongue, which is from the origin of the Highest Heavens. The rejection of this Divine Language The Creator used, is to reject His deepest revelation the Spirit desires to reveal.

Raqia, The Expanse of Distinction

There is another Altar concept I believe is vital to the comprehension of The Creators Word and what is expressed in Genesis 1 –

> 🟥 **Genesis 1:6** And Elohim[H430] said,[H559] Let there be[H1961] a **firmament**[H7549] in the midst[H8432] of the waters,[H4325] and let[H1961] it divide[H914 H996] the waters[H4325] from the waters.[H4325] **Gen 1:7** And Elohim[H430] made[H6213] (H853) **the firmament,**[H7549] and divided[H914 H996] the waters[H4325] which[H834] were under[H4480 H8478] **the firmament**[H7549] from[H996] the waters[H4325] which[H834] were above[H4480 H5921] the firmament:[H7549] and it came to be[H1961] so.[H3651] **Gen 1:8** And Elohim[H430] called[H7121] **the firmament**[H7549] **Heaven.**[H8064] And the evening[H6153] and the morning[H1242] were[H1961] the second[H8145] day.[H3117]

(Diagram 6)

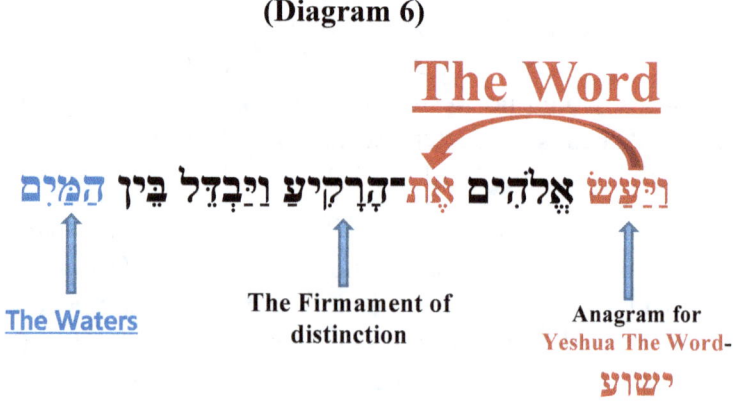

The Firmament – Note the specific language in here, we go from a Firmament to **The** Firmament. Elohim **Made** the firmament/expanse through the revelation of the Anagram above – Yeshua! His Son is who brings distinction. Many would read past this and miss a greater revelation and message. In Hebrew we have what is called the definite Article 'THE'. This tells us it's not just any Firmament but it is a specific one and the text connects this Firmament to The Heavens. What is a Firmament? It is an expanse of some sort between two worlds, between a higher place from a lower place. This firmament was placed BETWEEN the waters beneath the firmament and the waters above the firmament. Listen to the Hebrew in **Genesis 1:7** –

וַיַּעַשׂ אֱלֹהִים אֶת־הָרָקִיעַ – Va'ya'as Elohim Et HaRaqia – "And Elohim MADE The Alef Tav Firmament/Space/Expanse…"

וַיַּבְדֵּל בֵּין הַמַּיִם אֲשֶׁר מִתַּחַת לָרָקִיעַ – Va'yav'deil Bein HaMayim Asher Mi'tachat LaRaqia – "…and He separated/brought distinction a difference between the waters which were beneath The Seat of a Throne and the waters which were above/Mei'al – מֵעַל - the Firmament…"

This Altar language conveys there is a distinction BETWEEN the Firmaments that exists ABOVE the Firmament below. From above is: Ma'al in Hebrew. Ma'al is also the same word for an unfaithful act toward a Covenant acceptance and agreement! The Text could have just used the Hebrew word 'Al/עַל' without the Mem prefix. This Mem prefix makes this an actual thing that had taken place as well as an actual Place where things happen – Ma'al.

I don't find it a coincidence that the numerical connection to Ma'al in Scripture has ALWAYS referred to Israel's unfaithfulness toward the Covenant Keeping Elohim and the unfaithfulness of kings. The numerical value of this word is 140 - the same as other Hebrew words, which follow: מְלָכִים – Melakhim = Kings, סָף – Saf meaning a Threshold Covenant & הַקָּהָל – HaQahal = The Congregation/The Called-Out ones/aka The Church! The Church/The Congregation is to be one of Kings and Priests after the Order of Melkhitzedeq who have crossed the Threshold and into Covenant!

The Seven Altar Thrones of Genesis 1:1

It is The Called-out People of YHWH who are ONLY invited to The Altar where an exchange takes place. To come to the Altar by invitation is to SIT at the Altar which is also known as Enthronement!! Yashev or Sit/Settle in Hebrew also refers to one who is enthroned upon a throne as a king!!! This is Altar language. This firmament is mysterious! I have lost so much sleep over the revelation of this Firmament and its revelation. Let us see if we can connect this concept to the actual Altar –

Examine the Numbers 16 and 17 where we have the sons of Levi, specifically, Korach's rebellion and The Earth swallowing them up. The Earth is another Altar who opens its mouth! This is powerful revelation for later when we get to the Earth Altar. Notice afterwards that Eliazer is instructed to do something very powerful –

> **Numbers 16:37** Speak[H559] to[H413] Eleazar[H499] the son[H1121] of Aaron[H175] the priest,[H3548] that he take[H7311] (H853) the censers[H4289] out of[H4480 H996] **the burning,**[H8316] and scatter[H2219] the fire[H784] abroad;[H1973] for[H3588] they are sanctified.[H6942] **(Scatter the fire is seed language, scatter is the word for seed. The fire was to be turned into seed form as when Adam was once first created from – embers of fire!!)** Num 16:38 (H853) The censers[H4289] of these[H428] sinners[H2400] against their own souls,[H5315] let them make[H6213] (H853) **broad**[H7555] **plates**[H6341] for a covering[H6826] of **The Altar:**[H4196] for[H3588] they offered[H7126] them before[H6440] Yahweh,[H3068] therefore they are sacred:[H6942] and they shall be[H1961] a sign[H226] for the children[H1121] of Israel.[H3478] **Num 16:39** And Eleazar[H499] the priest[H3548] took[H3947] (H853) the copper[H5178] censers,[H4289] which[H834] they were **burnt**[H8313] **(This is where we get the word Seraphim from. The flames of the Altar, unlike any Altar, reveals in Heaven the image of the fiery ones before the Throne crying "Qadosh, Qadosh, Qadosh YHWH Tzevaot" day and night! This becomes the Decree that whatever TOUCHES the Altar,**

> whatever ascends from The Altar is Qadosh, Qadosh, Qadosh unto The Master of Heaven's Hosts!!!) had offered;^H7126 and they were made **broad**^H7554 plates for a covering^H6826 of **The Altar:**^H4196

First let me highlight that the language moves from Dabar to Amar or from Logos to Rhema again. Rhema – **(Greek)**/Amar – **(Hebrew)** gives the revelation regarding the Raqia because it is at the Altar all things are transformed from Logos to Rhema or from death to life! Also, Eliezer picks up two distinct things, Seraph and Eish – Burning Ones and Fire. Powerful!! Seraph is ALWAYS connected to the Altar of Heaven or the Altar revelation that is above and Fire is always connected to the Altar of Earth or the Altar revelation from below. Logos/Dabar is ALWAYS connected to The Earth Altar below and the Rhema/Amar is ALWAYS connected to the Altar above. Example, Levitical system ALWAYS connected to the Altar below and the Melkhitzedeq ALWAYS connected to the Altar above. This is why Mashiach Yahshua says we MUST be born from above. This is the Altar language referring to our Melkhitzedeq – The Adamah Altar Throne, who is above The Earth!!

Continuing with Numbers 17:1-3 (English Trans. 16:37-39):

- רִקֻּעֵי פַחִים צִפּוּי לַמִּזְבֵּחַ – "...**beaten** out sheets as a covering to the Altar..."

Notice our word Raqia/**Ree'qoo'ei**. The Raqia is for the Altar, like the opening of its mouth. Every Altar has a mouth and this one received the Nefesh of the sacrificial animals where they first originated from. The Altar gives passage to the origins of life. The mouth of The Altar speaks when the blood touches it. The whole time an animal would be burning on the Altar, its voice would be conversating with The Heavens above, on behalf of the one who brought it. Can we even imagine such a concept?

At that time, the animals that were sacrificed unlocked a concealed voice in their Blood. Notice, animals don't communicate with language as people do, but they are aware of the language we use. Inside their blood was the response to the confession of the priest, who officiated the ceremony. The sins of the one who brought it were confessed over the flesh body of this animal. Then, this animal which was offered up on the Altar, would be sanctified. Then the blood of that sacrifice became an edict released from The Altar's mouth on behalf of the guilty – "Acceptance and Forgiveness."

Notice what is happening in 2020 as I write this book, the systems that be, are trying to enforce MASKS over the mouth of your Altar, your mouth! You can't MUZZLE an Ox while it treads the grain! This is Altar language no matter which way anyone looks at it. I have to say this because it is heartbreaking to see some of the most well-known Expositors, Preachers, Prophets, Apostles, Evangelists, Pastors and Teachers today complying with a mandate that contradicts the mandate of Heaven!!

Korach tried to cover the ordained Altar of Elohim and the result of his rebellion, the Altar of Earth swallowed he and all with him. I want to encourage EVERY single man and woman of Elohim to OPEN the Mouth of your Altar and do not consent to Pharaoh's mandate of a Korach Kovering of that which is a Bridge between Heaven and Earth - your Mouth and Firmament! The Firmament/Expanse in the Beginning was the Mouth of the Altars!! Our words are Spirit: Death and Life are in the Power of the tongue. Don't accelerate death and hinder the life that is screaming to come forth from the mouth of your Altar Firmament!

Here is revelation: When we preach the Good News of the Kingdom, we create a type of Raqia for many to ascend to where repentance and the forgiveness of sins is granted. The Raqia of the Altar is the Expanse of the Altar that is created by The Word. As far as the east is from the west so He has removed our sin from us! I say all the time, The Kingdom is made up of **Expansive** people not **Expensive** people, so, become **Expansive**.

I proclaim that this season YHWH Elohim is Expanding your territory. The more Expansive we become the more power is unleashed from The Altar of Power, Deliverance, Freedom and Victory!!! Elohim hammers out and flattens the flesh nature in order to invoke the Altar in your life!!! The Altars fire is never quenched, always thirsty for the weakness of the flesh. Bring your struggles to the Altar, bring all your setbacks and transfer them into your **NOW** come back!!! I will close this section which will Segway into the revelation and majesty of our Altar Thrones.

The Keys OF This Kingdom, Concealed in the Blood

In Matthew 16:19 it is written:

- **Matthew 16:16** And^{G1161} Simon^{G4613} Peter^{G4074} answered^{G611} saying,^{G2036} You^{G4771} are^{G1488} the^{G3588} Messiah,^{G5547} the^{G3588} Son^{G5207} of the Living^{G2198} Elohim.^{G2316} Mat 16:17 And^{G2532} Yeshua^{G2424} answered^{G611} saying^{G2036} to him,^{G846} Blessed^{G3107} are^{G1488} you, Simon^{G4613} Bar Yonah:^{G920} for^{G3754} **flesh**^{G4561} and^{G2532} **blood**^{G129} has not^{G3756} revealed^{G601} this to you,^{G4671} but^{G235} my^{G3450} Father^{G3962} who^{G3588} is on^{G1722} **The Heavens**.^{G3772} Mat 16:18 And^{G1161} I also say$^{G2504\ G3004}$ to you,^{G4671} That^{G3754} you^{G4771} are^{G1488} Peter,^{G4074} and^{G2532} upon^{G1909} The^{G5026} **Rock**^{G4073} I will build^{G3618} my^{G3450} church;^{G1577} and^{G2532} the gates^{G4439} of hell^{G86} will not^{G3756} overcome^{G2729} it.^{G846}

- Mat 16:19 And^{G2532} I will give^{G1325} unto thee^{G4671} **the**^{G3588} **keys**^{G2807} **of** The^{G3588} **Kingdom**^{G932} **of The Heavens:**^{G3772} and^{G2532} whatsoever$^{G3739\ G1437}$ you will bind^{G1210} on^{G1909} Earth^{G1093} will^{G2071} be bound^{G1210} in^{G1722} **The Heavens**:^{G3772} and^{G2532} whatsoever$^{G3739\ G1437}$ you will lose^{G3089} on^{G1909} Earth^{G1093} will be^{G2071} released^{G3089} in^{G1722} **The Heavens.**^{G3772}

Flesh and Blood has not revealed this to you. The words for Flesh and Blood in Hebrew would have been: עוּר דָם – **Ore** and **Dam**. The numerical value of these is 320. This numerical connection reveals what is blinded to The Kingdom of Heaven and that is the nakedness of the fall. The things of Elohim are foolishness to those who are perishing or can I say, Naked? 320 is the value of the Hebrew word: עֵירֹם – Ei'rom which means nakedness. This is found in Genesis 3:20.

The emphasis on words in these verses is mine. Notice, Yahshua didn't say He gave the Keys TO the Kingdom, but the Keys OF the Kingdom. The Keys **TO** the Kingdom is ACCESS while the Keys **OF** the Kingdom is RELEASE. He came here to release the Power of the Kingdom hidden in the soul of man. Yahshua gave Access because **of** His manifestation and by doing so, He gave the Body the Keys **OF** the Kingdom! It is because of The Adamah Altar, who is Yahshua HaMashiach – The Word made flesh, which was able to manifest all Seven Altar Thrones in the flesh, by what He said and did. He demonstrated this Altar sequence everywhere He went.

Through the Adamah Altar, the Keys of The Kingdom RELEASE the Dominion and Authority of the Genesis 1:1 Altar Thrones here on The Earth. The Leaven of the Kingdom Yahshua brought is the Influence of all Altar Thrones. He is the starter Agent, who begins the Leavening Process. Prayer is one of the secrets to this release upon the Earth. Prayer is what Yahshua insisted and did more than anything else. Prayer is Altar activation and the walking Authority man is to become.

Inside the first Adam was the reality to this truth. A quote from John Wesley, "It seems that Without God man cannot and without Man God will not." When Man returns to the place of Divine Altar access, where Elohim communes with him, the results are limitless. The first Adam didn't fall from the Garden or Heaven, but from his place of Dominion and Authority. When Authority and Dominion are lost, man's naked condition becomes his new place. You can be in a place where the Kingdom and Dominion is present and yet still absent from it. It wasn't until after the fall from DOMINION and AUTHORITY, which YHWH Elohim expelled them. Adam and Eve were still in the Garden after falling from Dominion!

The Last Adam arrived, ushering in the Dominion and Authority of The Altar Thrones. His message of The Kingdom of Heaven was the declaration of what He came to do. By doing so, we now have access to manifest this Place of Dominion and Authority here on Earth. Therefore, because of this fall, all Creation has been crying out for the manifestation of the Sons of Elohim or - The Sons and heirs of the Altar Throne of Elohim. It is time to ascend through The Altar revelations and unlock the – 'Greater is He who is in you than the he that is in the world!'

Chapter Two

First Altar: The Altar of Beginnings

בראשית

It was with a single vibration, a single Word that all things were Manifested, Created, Formed, Fashioned and Stabilized by and through this very Altar/Word that has expressed them and filled them with meaning and purpose. Just to encourage someone here, your life is hidden in The Beginning. Therefore, it is filled with purpose and meaning. It was through The Beginning, not 'A' Beginning that all things came into being. This Hebrew word dealing with Beginning is a fascinating word. It has several defining factors, with over 79 Hebrew words composed from six Hebrew letters that make up this Altar word.

This Hebrew word **B'resheet** comes from the word **Rei'sheet**. The Hebrew letter '**Bet**' is a prefix pointing to an action, which speaks of a House or something complete and fulfilled. Before Creation itself, our Most High and Almighty Elohim was already showing us a completed House, therefore a completed you. Before you were in your mother's womb you were already known. You were already complete. You were already intended to be a part of something that has no vacated spaces or incomplete chambers. This revelation is fitting because 911 is also the numerical value of the Hebrew word Teshurah/תשורה –

meaning a Gift from Eternity. Scripture says the 'Gift' of Elohim IS Eternal Life. Eternal life is found within the Altar of Beginnings!

Rei'sheet is known as 'Firstfruits' and 'Beginning(s)' as we will discover later in the Book of Leviticus 2:12; *Deuteronomy 26:10–

> 🌺 **Deuteronomy 26:10** 'And now, see, I have brought the **first-fruits/ראשית** of **the land** which You, O Yahweh, have given me.' Then you shall place him before Yahweh your Elohim, and bow down before Yahweh your Elohim. Let us look at this phrase in Hebrew –

וְעַתָּה הִנֵּה הֵבֵאתִי אֶת־רֵאשִׁית פְּרִי הָאֲדָמָה

HaAdamah P'ree   Rei'sheet   ET   Hei'veitee   Hee'neh   Ve'atah

What a mind-blowing revelation that you can't get from an English translation. Hidden in the Hebrew language of our verse is the revelation and power of what The HaAdamah Altar holds in conjunction with The B'resheet Altar! That is Resurrection of Life. This verse is saying that the fruit is The First Born from The Adamah Altar! The resurrected Last Adam is King of all and He who conquered Death, Hell and the Grave! This is another subject, but fitting when looking at verses like this. You can see our fourth Altar here in the **purple**. Now look at this UNBREAKABLE connection –

Why Purple? This is a Royal color. Kings wore purple robes. In John 19, Yahshua was given a purple robe that the soldiers cast lots for and did not tear. The Royal Priesthood of our Mashiach Yahshua cannot be broken or torn asunder. His position and Royal Priesthood are matchless in strength and power. The created cannot destroy the Creator! Purple in Hebrew is Argaman/ארגמן and is seen 38 times in the Tanakh or Old Testament. Argaman just happens to have the same numerical value as the phrase found in Psalm 110 and in the Priestly Epistle to the Hebrews, which speaks of The Son of Elohim – Yahshua HaMashiach. This phrase is: מלכי־צדק – Melkhitzedeq or King of Righteousness!! Back to the Rei'sheet of this chapter.

Our word here for Firstfruits is Rei'sheet/ראשית, which is also the word for our first Altar revelation. Notice what this Altar revelation is attached to when it comes to bringing the first of the fruits, the HaAdamah Altar. We will touch on this when we get to the 6th Altar which is the manifested Royal High-Priest and Adamah Altar revelation of Genesis 1:1!

Let us enter The Beginning, the First Altar given in Scripture:

> In *the* Beginning – בראשית – From this Altar, we have a firsthand revelation of the Covenant of Fire!! A Melkhitzedeq Connection!! Let us see what comes forth out of The Beginning, as I have discovered just with this first word there are 76 Hebrew words made up from these same Hebrew letters without adding to these 6 letters:

We know that our Elohim is a Consuming fire and that He is the covenant keeping Elohim. In the Scripture we have this:

> **Deu 33:2** And he said,H559 YahwehH3068 cameH935 from Sinai,H4480 H5514 and rose upH2224 from SeirH4480 H8165 to them; his Light to shine forthH3313 from mountH4480 H2022 Paran,H6290 and he cameH857 with ten thousandsH4480 H7233 of set apart one:H6944 from his right handH4480 H3225 went **a fiery law**H799 for them.

> **Hebrews 12:18** ForG1063 you have notG3756 arrivedG4334 to the mountainG3735 that might be touched,G5584 andG2532 that burnedG2545 with fire,G4442 norG2532 to darkness,G1105 andG2532 thick darkness,G4655 G2532 tempest,G2366
> **Heb 12:19** AndG2532 the soundG2279 of trumpets,G4536 andG2532 **the voice**G5456 of **words;**G4487 whichG3739 voice they that heardG191 prayedG3868 that the wordG3056 should notG3361 be spoken to them any more:G4369 G846 **Heb 12:20**

For^{G1063} they could not^{G3756} endure^{G5342} that which was commanded,^{G1291} And if so much as^{G2579} a beast^{G2342} touch^{G2345} the^{G3588} mountain,^{G3735} it would be stoned,^{G3036} or pierced through^{G2700} with a javelin:^{G1002} **Heb 12:21** And^{G2532} so^{G3779} terrible^{G5398} was^{G2258} the^{G3588} sight,^{G5324} Moses^{G3475} said,^{G2036} I exceedingly fear^{(G1510) G1630} and^{G2532} quake:)^{G1790} **Heb 12:22** But^{G235} you arrived at^{G4334} mount^{G3735} Tzion,^{G4622} and^{G2532} unto the city^{G4172} of the living^{G2198} Eloah,^{G2316} the heavenly^{G2032} Jerusalem,^{G2419} and^{G2532} to an innumerable company^{G3461} of angelic beings,^{G32} Heb 12:23 To the general assembly^{G3831} and^{G2532} Assembly^{G1577} of the firstborn,^{G4416} which are written^{G583} in^{G1722} heaven,^{G3772} and^{G2532} to Eloah^{G2316} the Judge^{G2923} of all,^{G3956} and^{G2532} to the spirits^{G4151} of just men^{G1342} made perfect,^{G5048}

Heb 12:24 And^{G2532} to Yeshua^{G2424} the mediator^{G3316} of the new^{G3501} covenant,^{G1242} and^{G2532} to the blood^{G129} of speaking,^{G4473} that speaks^{G2980} better things^{G2909} than^{G3844} that of Abel.^{G6} Heb 12:25 See^{G991} that you refuse^{G3868} not^{G3361} him that speaks.^{G2980} For^{G1063} if^{G1487} they^{G1565} escaped^{G5343} not^{G3756} who refused^{G3868} him that spoke^{G5537} on^{G1909} **earth**,^{G1093} much^{G4183} more^{G3123} shall not we^{G2249} escape, if we turn away from^{G654} him^{G3588} that speaks from^{G575} **heaven:**^{G3772} Heb 12:26 Whose^{G3739} **voice**^{G5456} then^{G5119} shook^{G4531} the^{G3588} **earth:**^{G1093} but^{G1161} now^{G3568} he has promised,^{G1861} saying,^{G3004} Now^{G2089} once more^{G530} I^{G1473} shake^{G4579} not^{G3756} **the**^{G3588} **earth**^{G1093} only,^{G3440} but^{G235} also^{G2532} **Heaven.**^{G3772}

Heb 12:27 And^{G1161} this^{G3588} word, Now^{G2089} once more,^{G530} signifies^{G1213} the^{G3588} removing^{G3331} of those things that are shaken,^{G4531} as^{G5613} of things that are made,^{G4160} that^{G2443} those which cannot be shaken^{G4531} ^{G3361} may remain.^{G3306} Heb 12:28 Wherefore^{G1352} we receiving^{G3880} a Kingdom^{G932} which cannot be moved,^{G761} let us have^{G2192} grace,^{G5485} whereby^{G1223 G3739} we may serve^{G3000} Elohim^{G2316} acceptably^{G2102} with^{G3326} reverence^{G127} and^{G2532} reverencing fear:^{G2124} Heb 12:29 For^{G1063} (^{G2532}) our^{G2257} Eloah^{G2316} is a **consuming**^{G2654} **fire.**^{G4442}

In the Book of Revelation, we read something so powerful –

- **Revelation 13:8** And^{G2532} all^{G3956} that dwell^{G2730} upon^{G1909} The^{G3588} Earth^{G1093} shall worship^{G4352} him,^{G846} whose^{G3739} names^{G3686} are not^{G3756} written^{G1125} in^{G1722} the^{G3588} book^{G976} of life^{G2222} and of **the**^{G3588} **Lamb**^{G721} **slain**^{G4969} **from**^{G575} **the foundation**^{G2602} of the world.^{G2889}

Hidden in the womb of B'resheet is the revelation of The Lamb slain BEFORE or from the **foundation** of the worlds. This Greek term for foundation is *Katabole* which means the time of '**Conception**'. The time when the worlds, ages, cosmos were conceived inside the idea of Elohim. Before there was even a spoken word!! Your life and my life are hidden inside the Beginning. The Beginning is The Crown of the Altar revelation just like Sabbath is the Crown of the six days of Creation.

Covenant Power

Covenant of Fire – Brit Eish/בְּרִית אֵשׁ – The Greatest Covenant ever made was the one sealed in and by the Blood of Yahshua. This first revelation, remember is the Altar of Beginnings. Where all other things were first originated, inside B'resheet.

- **Hebrews 12:24** And^{G2532} to Yeshua^{G2424} the mediator^{G3316} of the new^{G3501} **covenant,**^{G1242} and^{G2532} to the blood^{G129} of speaking,^{G4473} that speaks^{G2980} better things^{G2909} than^{G3844} that of Abel.^{G6} Heb 13:20 Now^{G1161} the^{G3588} Eloah^{G2316} of shalom,^{G1515} that brought again^{G321} from^{G1537} the dead^{G3498} our^{G2257} Master^{G2962} Yeshua,^{G2424} that great^{G3173} shepherd^{G4166} of the^{G3588} sheep,^{G4263} through^{G1722} the blood^{G129} of the everlasting^{G166} **covenant,**^{G1242}

Everlasting is to the right of The High Priest-King of Genesis 1:1. This is where Covenant is executed and established! Within this Covenant of Fire would come forth Bara Shayeet/בְּרֵאשִׁית which means: Created to Appoint or Create the Place, Create the Foundation, Create The Side of The Altar (Libation). Sages of old would agree that the first thing that would come forth from the Place of Bara/Creation would be The Foundation Stone. This Stone we already would find its revelation in the Word made Flesh. Foundation Stone in Hebrew is:

אֶבֶן הַשְׁתִיָה – Eben HaShe'tiyah – The Foundation Stone. We can go all over the place here. If you notice this word contains the concept, we are discussing in B'resheet – Sha'yeet. At the right side of our first Word or can I say Altar called In the Beginning is the Foundation Stone revelation. Yahshua IS the Foundation Stone, He is The Stone of Drinking –

Luke 6 Yahshua gives the parable of the house built upon The Rock or The Foundation Stone. Also, we have this:

- **Matthew 13:34** All^{G3956} these things^{G5023} Yeshua^{G2424} spoke^{G2980} to the^{G3588} multitude^{G3793} in^{G1722} parables;^{G3850} and^{G2532} without^{G5565} a parable^{G3850} he did not^{G3756} speak^{G2980} unto them:^{G846}

- **Matthew 13:35** That^{G3704} it might be fulfilled^{G4137} which was spoken^{G4483} by^{G1223} the^{G3588} prophet,^{G4396} saying,^{G3004} I will open^{G455} my^{G3450} mouth^{G4750} in^{G1722} parables;^{G3850} I will speak^{G2044} things which have been kept as mystery^{G2928} from^{G575} **the foundation**^{G2602} of the world.^{G2889} **Our word – Shetiyah or Foundation!!!**

B'resheet – Bara Sha'yeet - The Creation of the Foundation Stone. The secrets of the Parables are locked up in the Foundation Stone. The out pouring from this Stone of drinking is hidden in the parables He spoke. Furthermore, Sha'yeet also means to put or set a Garment over someone or something. It is like when a King puts on a Royal Robe. Sha'yeet is the Royal

Robe to the Foundation of The Beginning. Every other Hebrew word in Genesis 1:1 after B'resheeth is part of this Royal Robe that rests over the shoulders of the King Priest of this Verse, the Center Altar! He is draped with three Altar powers on one side and three Altar powers on the other!

(Diagram 7)

Now, Bara doesn't mean to create something that has never been revealed per se. It contains the ability of The Creator alone to reveal something that has never been seen before. Bara is The Altar that releases that which is from the B'reshith Altar. Bara also has the idea of inflating or expanding something into formation. Sitting at The Right Hand of Bara is the Foundation or Chief Corner Stone!!! He is the Stone and The Rock we drink from. Sha'yeet also means to Drink!! Furthermore, Sha'yeet also means a special type of Garment or disguise. The B'resheet Altar gives us the revelation of The Foundation Stone who would come as the Sustainer of all Creation.

Yahshua is the fountain of Living Waters. The words of the Prophet –

> **Isaiah 28:16** Therefore[H3651] now[H3541] says[H559] Yahweh[H136] Elohim,[H3069] Behold,[H2009] I establish[H3245] in Tzion[H6726] for **a foundation**[H3245] **a stone**,[H68] a tested[H976] stone,[H68] a precious[H3368] corner[H6438] stone, a sure[H3245] foundation:[H4143] he that believeth[H539] shall not[H3808] make haste.[H2363]

This foundation Stone is the Source of Gichon or the Belly of

The Promise. Doesn't it say that out of our bellies would come forth Living waters?!! Examine these words:

- **Hebrews 1:10** And,^G2532 You,^G4771 Master,^G2962 **in^G2596 The Beginning^G746** have laid the **foundation^G2311** of The^G3588 Earth;^G1093 and^G2532 The^G3588 Heavens^G3772 are^G1526 the works^G2041 of YOUR^G4675 hands:^G5495

Inside of B'resheet a foundation was laid for the Altars. In The Altar of Beginnings the Stone of Drinking has always been. The Earth represents the footstool of this mystical Ladder of Altars. There are these Seven Altars in the form of a body. This foundation would be the Chief Corner Stone of all Creation. The Rock, The Word, The Son, The Builder, The Mashiach is your Chief Corner Stone in your life. He is the author and finisher of your Faith! He who has begun a good work inside of you will see it through to its completion UNTIL the coming of Mashiach!!

The Concealed Body of the Altar Thrones

(Diagram 8)

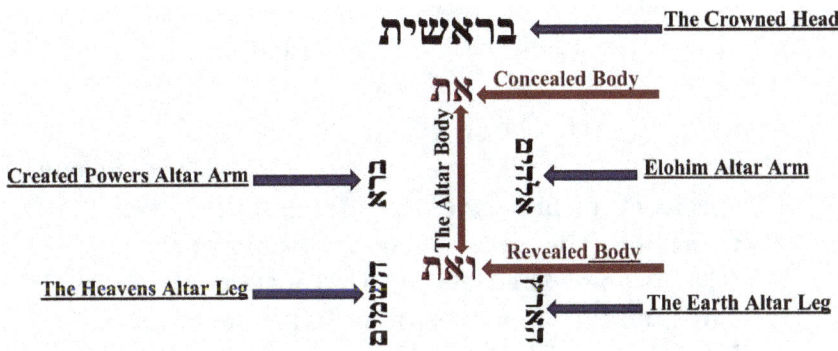

This diagram above also pictures the Tabernacle vessel set up from the Mercy Seat to the Altar of sacrifice in the Outer Courtyard. We have a form of a Body, something seen by Jacob in Genesis 28. The sages have agreed, that the Tabernacle was laid out like Adam was before his formation from the Dust/Embers of fire, who The Creation from the Adamah Altar. These are powerful revelations to excavate. 7 Vessels and 7 Altar revelations of Genesis 1:1.

This is why the words of John in Revelation 13:8 concur, "Behold the Lamb slain from the FOUNDATION of the world." Inside this revelation the whole plan of redemption was brought forth!! Within the Altar called B'resheet, we have The Covenant of Fire, and from this Covenant of Fire was the Foundation Stone. This Stone of Drinking would be summoned to execute the very Will of Abba.

Eternal life was hidden inside B'resheet. Eternal life is for all to come to know YHWH Elohim –

> **John 17:1** These words[G5023] Yeshua[G2424] spoke[G2980] and[G2532] lifted up[G1869] his[G848] eyes[G3788] to[G1519] **The Heavens,**[G3772] **(The Heavens of Altar Throne)** and[G2532] said,[G2036] Father,[G3962] the[G3588] hour[G5610] is come;[G2064] glorify[G1392] Your[G4675] Son,[G5207] that[G2443] Your[G4675] Son[G5207] also[G2532] may glorify[G1392] You:[G4571] **John 17:2** As[G2531] You have given[G1325] him[G846] power[G1849] over all[G3956] **flesh,**[G4561] that[G2443] he should give[G1325] **eternal**[G166] **life**[G2222] to as many as[G3956 G3739] You have given[G1325] him.[G846] **(The hour speaks of the process of sacrifice and the Laver transition. The Laver speaks of the Stargate Dimension of The Heavens we translate into. Eternal Life is on the other side of the Judgement Seat of Mashiach, our 4th Altar Throne in Genesis 1:1)**

> **John 17:3** And[G1161] this[G3778] is[G2076] **eternal,**[G166] **life**[G2222] that[G2443] they might know[G1097] You[G4571] the[G3588] only[G3441] true[G228] Elohim,[G2316] and[G2532] Yeshua[G2424] Messiah,[G5547] whom[G3739] You have sent.[G649]

John-James of the House of Flores.®

(Diagram 9)

(Eternal Life once again is on the other side of The Altar High-Priest King of Genesis 1:1. Here is another diagram of Genesis 1:1 in Hebrew below:)

- **John 17:5** And^G2532 now,^G3568 Father,^G3962 glorify^G1392 You^G4771 me^G3165 with^G3844 your own self^G4572 with the glory^G1391 which^G3739 I had^G2192 with^G3844 you^G4671 **before**^G4253 the^G3588 **world**^G2889 **was.**^G1511

- **John 17:24** Father,^G3962 I will^G2309 that^G2443 these,^G2548 whom^G3739 gifted to^G1325 me,^G3427 be^G5600 with^G3326 me^G1700 where^G3699 I^G1473 am;^G1510 that^G2443 they may behold^G2334 my^G1699 glory,^G1391 which^G3739 You have given^G1325 me^G3427 for^G3754 You love^G25 me^G3165 before^G4253 **the foundation**^G2602 of **the world**.^G2889

- **1Corinthians 3:10** According^G2596 to the^G3588 grace^G5485 of Elohim^G2316 which is given^G1325 to me,^G3427 as^G5613 a wise^G4680 master builder,^G753 I have laid^G5087 **the foundation,**^G2310 and^G1161 another^G243 builds upon it.^G2026 But^G1161 let every man^G1538 take heed^G991 how^G4459 he builds upon Him.^G2026

- **1Cor. 3:11** For^G1063 no other^G243 **foundation**^G2310 can^G1410 no man^{G3762} lay^{G5087} than^{G3844} that is laid,^{G2749} which^{G3739} is^{G2076} Yeshua^{G2424} Messiah.^{G5547}

🌹 **Ephesians 2:16** And^{G2532} that he might reconcile^{G604} both^{G297} to Elohim^{G2316} in^{G1722} one^{G1520} body^{G4983} by^{G1223} the^{G3588} Tree,^{G4716} having **slain**^{G615} **the**^{G3588} **enmity**^{G2189} thereof:^{G1722 G846} **Eph 2:17** And^{G2532} came^{G2064} and preached^{G2097} peace^{G1515} to you^{G5213} which were afar off,^{G3112} and^{G2532} to them that were near.^{G1451} **Eph 2:18** For^{G3754} through^{G1223} him^{G846} we both^{G297} have^{G2192} access^{G4318} by^{G1722} one^{G1520} Spirit^{G4151} before^{G4314} the^{G3588} Father.^{G3962} **Eph 2:19** Now^{G686} therefore^{G3767} you are^{G2075} no more^{G3765} strangers^{G3581} and^{G2532} foreigners,^{G3941} but^{G235} fellow citizens^{G4847} with the^{G3588} sanctified ones,^{G40} and^{G2532} of the household^{G3609} of Elohim;^{G2316} **Eph 2:20** And are built^{G2026} upon^{G1909} **the**^{G3588} **foundation**^{G2310} of the^{G3588} apostles^{G652} and^{G2532} prophets,^{G4396} Yeshua^{G2424} Messiah^{G5547} himself^{G846} being^{G5607} **the chief corner**^{G204} **stone**; **Eph 2:21** In^{G1722} whom^{G3739} all^{G3956} **the**^{G3588} **building**^{G3619} **fitly framed together**^{G4883} grows^{G837} unto^{G1519} an set apart^{G40} temple^{G3485} in^{G1722} the Master:^{G2962} **Eph 2:22** In^{G1722} whom^{G3739} you^{G5210} also^{G2532} are **built together**^{G4925} for^{G1519} a habitation^{G2732} of Eloah^{G2316} through^{G1722} the Spirit.^{G4151}

Even more profound, we can read tons of verses regarding the Foundation of All Creation, even pulling on some extra Biblical writings that concur with this ever-abiding truth. In Genesis 1:1 we can stay here for lifetimes to come. Think about this scribed revelation in our opening verse –

Bara Shiyt Bara… -

ברא שית ברא – **Bara Sha'yeet Bara**. Shayeet means to Appoint as well as put a Garment upon the King. Bara can be pronounced *Bei'ra meaning Son. **(*Hebrew Etymological**

Dictionary page 82 bottom of 2ⁿᵈ column). This Hebrew concept Shayeet is also the founding word for a Messianic term known as **Sheti'Yah** or Foundation Stone, in Hebrew the word for the Stone of Drinking. Drink offerings were poured out on the Altar of sacrifice. There is a place on the Altar where Blood was poured which is the Appointed place of Redemption, Salvation, Restoration, Sanctification, Justification, Empowerment, Sonship, Kingship and Priesthood. There is an Appointed place for you and I and that is found outside the gate of religion and temple hierchy. This place is first hinted at in Genesis 1:9 where the seas are gathered into one PLACE – Maqom/מקום.

This blood was then drained out from the PLACE known as Shayeet. In Genesis, we see from The Altar Throne of Beginnings, that this was the Appointed Place where this Blood would be poured out from. Side note, this word בראשית – B'resheet is found in another form when Israel is instructed specifics pertaining to the tithe of the land or first fruits –

- **Devarim/Deuteronomy 26:2** That you shall take^H3947 of the **first**^H4480 H7225 of all^H3605 the fruit^H6529 of **The Earth,**^H127 which^H834 you will bring^H935 from your **land**^H4480 H776 that^H834 Yahweh^H3068 your Elohim^H430 gives^H5414 you, and shall put^H7760 it in a **basket,**^H2935 and will go^H1980 to^H413 **The Place**^H4725 which^H834 Yahweh^H3068 your Elohim^H430 chooses^H977 to place^H7931 His Name^H8034 there.^H8033

- **26:3** And you shall go^H935 unto^H413 **the priest**^H3548 that^H834 shall be^H1961 **in those**^H1992 **days,**^H3117 and say^H559 unto^H413 him, I profess^H5046 this day^H3117 unto Yahweh^H3068 your Elohim,^H430 that^H3588 I am come^H935 unto^H413 the country^H776 which^H834 Yahweh^H3068 swore^H7650 to our fathers^H1 to gift^H5414 us with.

- **26:4** And **the priest**^H3548 will receive^H3947 **the basket**^H2935 out of your hand,^H4480 H3027 and set it down^H5117 before^H6440 **The Altar**^H4196 of Yahweh^H3068 your Elohim.^H430

The Hebrew word for <u>**of the first**</u> is: מראשית – **M'resheet** - Meaning **out of** or **from** the first fruits. This is received from **The Land/HaAdamah**!! The same word used where The Adam was first created from. This is The Altar of Priesthood and Kingship. Then it goes to speak of The Priest in those days. This is prophetic of the Days Mashiach Yahshua will be on The Land of Inheritance. We are to bring the first fruits of The Altar of Beginnings or the Redemptive work of Yahshua as The Lamb slain BEFORE there was an Earth. This is why we see the revelation of Adamah, the Land of Adamah, before the Earth was. This is what is hidden inside The First Altar of Genesis 1:1. There is a Place, and there is a Land, and that is The Kingdom of The Heavens!

Looking at the Hebrew word between the two words Bara, Shayeet. The first time this word is seen is in Genesis 3:15 with The first Prophecy uttered from The Throne –

> **Genesis 3:15** And I will put[H7896] enmity[H342] between[H996] you and the woman,[H802] between[H996] your seed[H2233] and her seed;[H2233] He[H1931] shall crush[H7779] your head[H7218] and you[H859] shall bruise[H7779] His heel.[H6119]

Put – שית – **Sheet** = To place, appoint, to establish someone in an official position, to place the hand upon another as to assist or become as they are in order to carry the weight. The Robed King who comes crushes the Altar of the Kingdom of Darkness! What was appointed was the ENMITY! This is powerful because several words we will look at are words of strength and action PLACED between the two seeds. Redemption is placed BETWEEN the seeds! Salvation, Deliverance, Inheritance, Substitution, Healing, Kingdom Dominion, Authority, Power, Might, Beauty, Splendor, Mercy, Lovingkindness, Forgiveness, Reconciliation, Acceptance, Victory, Strength, etc. are all placed between the two opposing seeds. The ONE placed between them to carry out the Order from The Throne in order for us to return to our Heavenly Seats of Holiness and Grace is The Son.

Let us read Genesis 3:15, the Scriptures first actual Peshat Prophecy:

וְאֵיבָה אָשִׁית בֵּינְךָ וּבֵין הָאִשָּׁה וּבֵין זַרְעֲךָ וּבֵין
זַרְעָהּ הוּא יְשׁוּפְךָ רֹאשׁ וְאַתָּה תְּשׁוּפֶנּוּ עָקֵב׃

Ve'eyvah A'shiyt Bein'khah oo'bein Ha'Ishah oo'bein Zar'a'cha oo'bein Zar'ah Hoo Ye'shoof'khah Ve'atah Te'shoo'fe'noo A'qeiv.

Enmity – וְאֵיבָה - Ve'eyvah is reminding us of the prior verse about the Nachash on its Belly and its function would be directed AT the womb area. We see this more than ever today. The true IDENTITY of The Son will and Should become ENMITY with the lie's religion has portrayed through names, observances, traditions that all stand in hostility with the true identity of The Son of Elohim who has now brought the season in for introspection and distinction. YHWH Elohim hints that the One who would stand as the Enemy BETWEEN the two is The Son! He stands as The Life source for us all. He would come through the womb or Belly. The enemy's focus has always been toward the womb. Jeremiah is given the word that BEFORE he was in the Womb, YHWH Elohim was known to his very spirit. You are hated by the enemy because you have been known BEFORE you were in your mother's womb.

You can hear the Hebrew sound of The Son who stands BETWEEN the seed – **oo'Bein** or can we say **Ve'Be'nee** – **And My Son**! Pictographically this Hebrew word says: "**Behold I Create the Power to Save My House through My Son**" Even the LXX reveals the function of this word. The Priesthood recognition of Yahshua HaMashiach will even UNITE the enemies of Elohim –

- 🔴 **Luke 23:11** And[G1161] Herod[G2264] with[G4862] his[G848] men of war[G4753] set him at nought,[G1848] [G846] and[G2532] mocked[G1702] *him,* and **arrayed**[G4016] **him**[G846] **in a gorgeous**[G2986] **robe,**[G2066] and sent him again[G375] [G846] to Pilate.[G4091]

- **Luke 23:12** And^{G1161} the same^{G846} day^{G2250} Pilate^{G4091} and^{G2532} Herod^{G2264} were made^{G1096} friends^{G5384} together:^{G3326 G240} for^{G1063} before^{G4391} they were^{G5607} at^{G1722} **enmity**^{G2189} between^{G4314} themselves.^{G1438}

- **Ephesians 2:15** Having **abolished**^{G2673} in^{G1722} his^{G848} flesh^{G4561} the^{G3588} **enmity**,^{G2189} the^{G3588} **law**^{G3551} **of commandments**^{G1785} contained in^{G1722} **ordinances**;^{G1378} to^{G2443} make^{G2936} in^{G1722} himself^{G1438} of the two^{G1417} (^{G1519}) **one**^{G1520} **new**^{G2537} **man**,^{G444} making^{G4160} peace;^{G1515}

- **Ephesians 2:16** And^{G2532} that he might **reconcile**^{G604} both^{G297} unto Elohim^{G2316} in^{G1722} **one**^{G1520} **body**^{G4983} by^{G1223} the^{G3588} Tree,^{G4716} having slain^{G615} the^{G3588} **enmity**^{G2189} thereby:^{G1722 G846}

It was abolished in the FLESH of Yahshua, The Son, who CARRIED the enmity which Elohim KILLED that Enmity or that Hostility born through the woman and Adam, on The Tree of Crucifixion! The Law of Commandments and Ordinances are known even by the song of Moses, not the song Miriam sang at the Red Sea crossing, but the Song Moses sang in Deuteronomy about the rebellion that would take place. This part of The Law would be set into the side of The Ark as a witness against Israel. Side note, Yahshua had His side pierced and Blood and Water came forth. Forgiveness and Cleansing were appropriated. Let me clear up something really quick that religion says the opposite of and doesn't realize they are at ENMITY with the Creator because of –

Law of Commandments – The instituted Sacrificial System which was NEVER the desire of YHWH Elohim:

- **Hebrews 10:4** For it is **impossible** for blood of bulls and goats to take away sins. **10:5** Therefore, coming into the world, He says, "Slaughtering and meal offering You did **not desire**, but a **body** You have prepared for Me. **10:6** "In burnt offerings and offerings for sin You **did not** delight.

- **Isaiah 1:9** Unless Yahweh of hosts had left to us a **small remnant**, we would have become like **Sodom**, we would have been made like **Gomorrah**. **1:10** Hear the word of Yahweh, you rulers of Sodom; give ear to the Torah of our Elohim, you people of Gomorrah! **1:11** "Of what use to Me are **your** many slaughtering's?" declares Yahweh. "I have had enough of burnt offerings of rams and the fat of fed beasts. I do not delight in the blood of bulls, or of lambs or goats. **1:12** "When you come to appear before Me, who has required this from your hand, to trample My **courtyards**? **1:13** "**Stop** bringing **futile** offerings, incense, **it is an abomination to Me**. New Moons, Sabbaths, the calling of meetings – I am unable to bear unrighteousness and assembly. **1:14** "My being hates **your** New Moons and **your** appointed times, they are a trouble to Me, I am weary of bearing them. **1:15** "And when you spread out your hands, I hide My eyes from you; even though you make many prayers, I do not hear. Your hands have become filled with blood. **1:16** "Wash yourselves, make yourselves clean; **put away** the evil of your doings from before My eyes. Stop doing evil! **1:17** "Learn to do good! Seek right-ruling, reprove the oppressor, defend the fatherless, plead for the widow. **1:18** "Come now, and let us reason together," says Yahweh. "Though your sins are like scarlet, they shall be as white as snow; though they are red like crimson, they shall be as wool.

Your Sacrifices and YOUR appointed days, not His. Big difference. Follow me as we continue with this thread –

- **Ezekiel 20:10** Wherefore I caused them to go forth out of the land of Mitzrayim/Egypt, and brought them into the wilderness. **20:11** And I gave them **My** statutes, and shewed them **My** judgments, which if **The Adam does, he shall even live in them**. (This is powerful and I must communicate this truth. The Hebrew is saying that as we live according to His Covenant Laws it's as if The Adam, not the first Adam, but The Adam which is His Son lives through us! **הָאָדָם וָחַי בָּהֶם:** – HaAdam Va'chai Ba'heim can be read as: The Adam that lives within them. Who? Those who keep these Laws we are to live by! It's our Mashiach being seen through us.) **20:12** Moreover also I gave them **My** sabbaths, to be a sign between me and them, that they might know that I am Yahweh that **sanctifies** them. (How are we Sanctified? Through HIS statutes, judgments and Sabbaths that reveal who really lives inside of us.) **20:13** But the house of Israel rebelled against me **in the wilderness** (How? Exodus 32, the Golden Calf system. Which would institute the animal sacrificial system School Master until the times of refreshing would come walking the streets of Jerusalem with His Kingdom Message and Salvation Gift of Eternal Life.) they **walked** not in **My** statutes, and they despised **My** judgments, which if a man do, he shall even live in them; and **My** sabbaths they greatly **polluted**: (Polluted in Hebrew is Chalal/חלל which means to make a hole through or empty something out of its substance. It also means to be deprived of Priesthood. Israel profaned His Sabbaths or Appointed Times and even though operating as a priesthood were still deprived of The MelkhiTzedeq INTENDED priesthood that was embedded in The Beginning!!) then I said, I would pour out my fury upon them in the wilderness, to consume them… **20:16** Because they despised **My** judgments, and walked not in **My** statutes, but polluted **My** sabbaths: for their heart went after their idols… **20:24** because they had **not done My** right-rulings, and they rejected **My** laws, and they profaned **My** Sabbaths, and their eyes were on their fathers' idols. **20:25** "And **I also gave them up to laws that were not good**, and right-rulings by which they would **not live by**…

🔴 **Psalm 81:11** "But **My** people did not listen to **My** voice,

And Yisra'ĕl would not submit to Me. **81:12** "So I gave them over to **their own** stubborn heart, to walk in their own counsels. **81:13** "If **My** people had listened to Me, Yisra'el would walk in **My** ways, **81:14** "I would subdue their enemies at once, and turn **My** hand against their adversaries! Also read: Isa. 30:28, Acts 7:42, Rom. 1:24-28, 2 Thess. 2:11.

The Phrases such as: My People, My Son, My Laws, My Ways, My Sabbaths, My Statutes, My Kingdom, My Name, My Word ALL go hand and Hand, we MUST not separate them. There was a difference between what the people chose and what was INTENDED by Elohim at that time! We can't claim one and reject any of the others, then we risk being at ENMITY with The Creator for the sake of respecting another man and his gifts or fivefold office he or she might be operating in. We MUST be like the Bereans and TEST all things so we can be found WORTHY when The King comes. This might be a hard statement for some, but it has been this way ever since the Beginning or can I say B'resheet!

So, we see from one word – ENMITY – we can unpack so much. We don't want to be at enmity with our Creator. There is no such thing as a Dispensational Break. I have taught this and many believe this till this day. This is something that has been on my heart and spirit for years. Dispensational deception will keep you out of the Kingdom. We are not in the dispensation of Grace. Noach found Grace in the eyes of Elohim. Grace has always been the tool of strength in the lives who have chosen to follow Elohim.

Abraham found Grace, Moses found Grace, Joshua found Grace, the 12 Tribes of Israel found Grace. Grace has been since The Beginning. Grace means more than Unmerited favor; it is the Hebrew Concept that blesses us with the ability to continue on in the WAYS of Abba because of His unwavering power in us.

Grace is concealed in Genesis 1:1. Grace or Chen/חן in Hebrew means one who pitches a tent with another. Amos 3:3 says, "How can two walk together unless they are in agreement." Grace is the power of agreement. Not the Almighty agreeing with us, but us agreeing with Him. Mercy is extended to those who are in disobedience whether knowing or unknowing. There are several Pastors and Leaders I know who teach Dispensationalism and we are still friends. But the truth of the matter is this is truly a distorted teaching that is about to be exposed in the coming months and years like never before. Dispensational teaching will always be tied into escapism. Just like the Pretrib Rapture doctrine, in my opinion, which I'm not addressing at this time, which comes from the same bag of tricks. Let us read what Isaiah says –

- **Isaiah 26:20** Go, **My** people, enter your rooms, and shut your doors behind you; hide yourself, as it were, for a little while, until the **Displeasure** has past. 26:21 Look, Yahweh is coming out of His place to punish the inhabitants of the earth for their crookedness. And the earth shall disclose her blood, and no longer cover her slain.

- **Displeasure** is the same for The **Wrath** of Elohim. We will be in what I call Goshen's and taken out of the way before the wrath hits. The Altar of Earth will bring forth the evidence of those who have slain innocent blood. One of the ways a man or woman can do commit this act is by **not** leading those who cross their path to the truth of salvation for their souls –

- **Ezekiel 3:16** And it came to pass at the end of **seven days**, that the word of Yahweh came unto me, saying, Eze 3:17 Son of man, I have made you a watchman for the House of Israel. Therefore, hear the word at my mouth and give them warning from me. Eze 3:18 When I say unto the wicked, You shalt surely die; and you give him not warning, nor speak to warn the wicked from his wicked way, to save his life; the same wicked man shall die in his iniquity; **BUT** his blood will I require at thine hand. Eze 3:19 Yet if you warn the wicked, and he turn not from his wickedness, nor from his wicked way, he shall die in his iniquity; **BUT** <u>you have delivered your soul/life</u>.

So, the Grace we have been given is tied to the One New Man spoken of in Ephesians which we just read. The Grace to remain the One New Man in Mashiach. Paul/Shaul said in Romans 6 –

- **Romans 6:1** What shall we say then? Shall we continue in **sin**, that **grace** may abound? **6:2** Elohim **forbid**. How shall we, that are dead to sin, live any longer by it?

Sin has several categories which religion once again lumps all together and yet Elohim distinguishes between them. There is a sin that LEADS to death which we are not to pray for (1 John 5:16). There is a sin that leads to death, and others that do not. Study on your own time, pretty interesting!!

So, ending the Ephesians insight, the ENMITY was SLAIN on the Tree/Cross of Mashiach through His Flesh Body! This is the Good News! We are no longer at enmity with Elohim because that was SLAIN in the flesh of Yahshua HaMashiach. This could have only been done through our Melkhitzedeq High Priest! His Altar crushed the enmity!

Appointed Foundation

Why all this information from one word? Because the enmity between the two seeds contains many things, we would never have thought would be. The next word I want to look at connected to the Hebrew word Sha'yeet, where we get the Appointed Stone from, is the action of PUTTING that Enmity between the two seeds, from the LXX Greek word –

- Genesis 3:15 "…I will put…" – A'shee'tah/**Shayeet**. **Appointed**. What does the LXX give us when keeping in mind the Altar concept of Genesis 1:1 and our Righteous King?

- **1Thessalonians 5:9** For Elohim hath not ==appointed== us to wrath, but to obtain salvation by our Master Yahshua HaMashiach,

- **Hebrews 1:1** Elohim, who at many times and in unique manners spoke in time past unto the fathers by the prophets, **1:2** Has in these last days spoken unto us by his Son, whom he has ==appointed== heir of all things, by whom also he made the worlds;

- **1Peter 2:8** And a stone of stumbling, and a rock of offence, even to them which stumble at the word, being disobedient: whereunto also they were ==appointed==. **2:9** But ye are a chosen generation, a Royal Priesthood (**Melchizedek**), a holy nation, a peculiar people; that you should show forth the praises of him who has called you out of darkness into his marvelous light: **2:10** Which in time past were not a people, but are now the people of Elohim: which had not obtained mercy, but now have obtained mercy.

How many come along side those chosen to lead and help carry the weight of a vision and goal? How many have **PUT** their hands to the plow (our word Shayeet) and continued on the narrow path? In this section of verses, we have the ENTIRE plan SET or APPOINTED by YHWH Elohim that will unfold from this point on. Eve and Adam even name their first son after the fall of Cain and Abel Seth, our word Shayeet/Seth, as a Prophetic promise of returning to Eden one day. From DUST/Embers of Fire you came and to DUST/Embers of fire you shall return. Also, side note there is something called the Power of APPOINTMENT ACT. Check it out.

From the very Beginning was Created the Plan of Appointment!!! The substitute for us! The Redeemer for a fallen people separated by The Qadosh Elohim only able to come as close to Him as the Garments of another man during Tabernacle and Temple days. It was Appointed INSIDE the Beginning to bring forth The One who would take our place at a specific place and pour out His

Blood onto and into that Place. This One is The Son of Elohim, the Champion of The Kingdom!! The One seated upon The Altar far above The Heavens!! Yahshua HaMashiach our Melkhitzedeq High Priest of Righteousness!!!

In The Beginning Concepts

Some more words within B'resheet from the 76 I have found:

ברית אש – Brit Eish = Covenant of Fire. We serve the Covenant Keeping Elohim. Religion has dispensationalized away the Covenant Power of our Creator by naming things that are unbiblical such as the Adamic Covenant, Noah Covenant, Abrahamic Covenant, and so on. Untrue! He keeps COVENANT with thousands. Yes, we read about the Covenants of Promise, but what are these? These are expansions of The Covenant keeping Elohim with His People!! The Covenant of Fire is that which comes from the Altar of Mashiach. All other covenants made that had fire involved are pointers to Yahshua on the Tree. Covenant has to do with a cutting. Adam had his side opened up. Noach had His Ark opened up. Abraham had his seed opened up, etc. How do we know a Covenant is in place? There are four aspects to a Covenant we must mention briefly –

1. **Proposal** – When Elohim Presents the relationship to another. Adam was given the **Proposal** of Dominion over the earth with the choice to accept.

2. **Acceptance/Agreement** - Adam **accepted** this as soon as he began to name the animals.

3. **Blood Ratification** - When their very SOUL was infused inside them that is when a Blood **ratification** took place. Later after the fall, we see that from light bodies we would go to flesh and blood which CANNOT Inherit The Kingdom. The Kingdom is for those born out of the Covenant of Fire Altar of our MelkhiTzedeq.

4. **Covenant confirming Meal** – When Adam and the woman ATE from the tree of the knowledge of Good and Evil, they came into a Pledge with the Serpent and forfeited their Inheritance and Right. If Adam and the Woman would have sealed the Covenant of Light/Fire by eating from the Tree of Life we would all be in a different place.

Four things that are revealed when a Covenant is made in Scripture – **Proposal**, **Acceptance**, Blood **Ratification** and the **Covenant Confirming** Meal. Abraham did this and all the Patriarchs. Fast forward to Yahshua HaMashiach. We are only in the first Revelation of B'resheet – Covenant of Fire/Light. The Creator YHWH Elohim gives the Proposal to the woman – Mary, who Accepts this Proposal by asking, "How could this be?" The language grammar suggests an Acceptance of this Truth. The Acceptance causes The Word to enter into Her Womb and 9 months later The Word comes forth out of the Womb through the river of Virgin Blood. A covenant confirming meal is instituted as Mary offers her breasts to The Word/Yahshuah/Immanuel!!!

1. The Jordan River Priesthood Transfer = **Proposal**.
2. The Leading into the Wilderness **Acceptance**.
3. The Blood Shed of Mashiach at the completion of His Ministry was the **Ratification**.
4. The Marriage Supper of The Lamb is the **Covenant Confirming** Meal. We are waiting and anticipating this. Between the Blood Ratification and The Covenant Confirming Meal is the Birth Canal or the Narrow Place. Yahshua said Narrow is the Way that leads to Righteousness.

🔴 **Matthew 7:14** Because^{G3754} strait^{G4728} is the^{G3588} Gate, ^{G4439} and^{G2532} narrow^{G2346} the^{G3588} Way, ^{G3598} which^{G3588} leads^{G520} into^{G1519} life, ^{G2222} and^{G2532} few^{G3641} there are^{G1526} who desire^{G2147} it. ^{G846}

שִׁיר תָּאב – Shir Ta'av = "Longing for the Song of Creation." When Creation was brought forth, it is believed that The Creator Sang Creation into existence. Psalm 19 says the Heavens Declare His Glory. Glory is never talked about in Scripture, it is either manifested or it is revealed when Heaven sings along with all the Angelic creatures. Really quick, the numerical value of these words also gives us a reflection of the Covenant of Fire –

- 510 = תּוֹקַד – To'qad = a continual burning, passion, vibration. Found in Leviticus 6:2 the Parashat Tzav (My Nativity Parashat) and the phrase says this: תוקד בו – Toqad Bo = a Continual burning in him. There is a constant burning, a constant vibration from Creation's song that should be burning inside the Body of Mashiach. Music is powerful so we can imagine the power of Creations Song!! Mashiach released the Song of Creation when He said it is finished. That song cracked the Earth Platform and Altar cover!!

- 403 = הַמְשִׁחִים – HaMeshichim – The Anointed. The Longing for the Song of Creation is the revealing of the Continual Vibration of the Anointed ones.

Creation cries out for the sons of this Creative Song. Rom 8:19 For the **intense longing** of the creation eagerly waits for the revealing of the sons of Elohim. Intense Longing is Ta'av!!! In Revelation 15 we have something powerful as well:

Revelation 15:3 the Song of Moses and The Song of The Lamb.

יְרֻשׁ תָּאב – Ye'roosh Ta'av means: **Longing for Inheritance**. When we think of Inheritance so many things should come to mind. Embedded inside the first word of our Scriptures is the Power of Inheritance. This is Legacy. What are we leaving to the Generations beyond us? What have we accomplished for The Kingdom while on Earth? Notice the same letters for Sing is the same letters for Inheritance. Embedded inside the Altar of B'resheet is the song of your inheritance. Sometimes you have to just Sing your way out of the darkness! Sometimes you just have to press into the Inheritance that is there for you! Those who worship the Most High Yah are those who know their Inheritance. Those who Long for their Inheritance are those who worship FROM that place of The Inheritance. True worshippers are tillers of The Altar of Yahshua, and it is these The Father seeks for. **(John-4:23-24)**

The first time this Hebrew word Yarash is seen is Genesis 15-

- **Genesis 15:3** And Abram[H87] said,[H559] Behold,[H2005] to me you have given[H5414] no[H3808] seed:[H2233] and, look,[H2009] one born[H1121] in my house[H1004] is my ==heir.[H3423]== 15:4 And, behold,[H2009] the word[H1697] of Yahweh[H3068] came unto[H413] him, saying,[H559] This[H2088] shall not[H3808] be your heir;[H3423] but[H3588 H518] he that[H834] shall come forth[H3318] out of your own bowels[H4480 H4578] shall be your ==heir.[H3423]==

- **...15:7** And he said[H559] to[H413] him, I[H589] am Yahweh[H3068] that[H834] brought[H3318] you out of Ur[H4480 H218] of the Chaldees[H3778] to give[H5414] you(H853) this[H2063] Land[H776] to ==inherit[H3423]== it.

This last verse is in the Feminine and speaks of Inheriting Her, the New Jerusalem that will be set up on The Earth!

- **Galatians 4:4** But when the fulness of the time was come, Elohim sent forth his Son, made of a woman, made under the law, 4:5 To redeem them that were **under the law**, that we might receive the adoption of sons. Gal 4:6 And because you are sons, Elohim has sent forth the Spirit of his Son into your hearts, crying, Abba, Abba. 4:7 Wherefore you are no more a servant, but a son; and if a son, then an **heir** of Elohim through Messiah.
(Servanthood should always lead to sonship.)

- **Romans 8:14** For as many as are led by the Spirit of Elohim, they are the sons of Elohim. **15** For you have not received the spirit of bondage again to fear; but you have received the Spirit of **adoption**, whereby we cry, Abba, Abba. **16** The Spirit itself bears witness with our spirit, that we are the children of Elohim: *__Rom 8:17__ And if children, then **heirs**; **heirs** of Elohim, and **joint-heirs** with Mashiach; if so be that we suffer with him, that we may be also glorified together.

Once again, the word Ye'roosh/Inheritance happens to be the family word for Yerushalem or Yerush Shaleim/The Complete Inheritance! The Prince of Peace gives us the Complete Inheritance which is The Kingdom reign on Earth, not in Heaven but on Earth where those who till the ground of The Adamah Altar have their feet standing on Earth because of sonship.

יָשַׁב תאַר – Ya'shav To'ar– To be seated, To be Enthroned in The Image. The Royal Priesthood and empowerment of His Spirit is the Altar place. We are Diplomats of His Kingdom!! We are enthroned in the very Image of Mashiach. We put on Mashiach!! If we put Him on then who He is becomes what we are to reflect, especially here on Earth.

- **Ephesians 2:6** And has raised us up together, and made us **sit** together in heavenly places in Messiah Yeshua.

This word for **SIT** is seen in Genesis 15:11 when Abram is confronted by fowls of the Air that come to the Covenant Pieces. The LXX reveals something more than what we see here. The word translated in the LXX from the Hebrew is SIT. This word was translated meaning to blow or drive something away. Since we are seated in Heavenly Places in Mashiach, In His Priesthood then as we are journeying through this Earth, our seated position will drive away that which tries to come and disrupt the process.

Abram was a MelkhiTzedeq and as he returned to the ways of Abba, He was given an Authority while on Earth. He was given a Diplomatic Anointing to establish The Kingdom Dominion at this

The Seven Altar Thrones of Genesis 1:1

moment of the Covenant Pieces Agreement!!

יֵשׁ ברא – Yeish Bara = There is the New Creation. Embedded inside The Beginning is the New Creation. I am speaking on the very first Altar of Genesis 1:1 still. This is deep revelation to grasp. Way before The Heavens and The Earth, the idea of a New Creation was already in place! The plan for you and I was hidden inside The House of the first Altar! Inside the Firstborn of all Creations is your life and mine - Colossians 3:3 says our lives are HID inside Yahshua!!!

שׁבי תאר – To'ar Shoo'vi = I return to the Image and formation *of YHWH Elohim.* This speaks of being Born from Above. From dust you came Adam and to Dust you shall return!!! The image we are to return to is the Image of Light!!! Aphar/עפר in Hebrew finds its root meaning in 'embers of fire'.

- **Colossians 3:10** And have put on the new *man,* which is renewed in knowledge after the **image** of him that created him:

- Rom 8:28 And we know that all things work together for good to them that love Elohim, to them who are the called according to *his* purpose. Rom 8:29 For whom he did foreknow, he also did predestinate *to be* **conformed** to the **image** of his Son, that he might be the firstborn among many brethren.

The Image we are to return to will bring us back INTO the Beginning before the Earth ever was. This is what the Love of Elohim is. This is what Yahshua prayed for and mentioned concerning The Glory He had with His Abba BEFORE there was even a world.

ברי אשת – Bar'ee Ee'shoot = I desire the purity of Matrimony. The Bride of Mashiach. Embedded inside the First Altar of Genesis 1:1 is the Wedding Chamber revelation. The reason the New Jerusalem can come down as a Bride adorned is because this Garment was hidden inside the realm of B'resheet.

Remember the Hebrew word Sha'yeet also means to be robed in Royalty! Your bridal chamber, your wedding garment was already waiting for you BEFORE there was even an Earth or a Heaven! This Mansion called Beit, or House contains the many houses or the Garment of The Bride.

את שביר – Et Sha'biyr = The Word that Breaks and has become broken for you and I. He was Bruised and Broken down in the flesh for our healing and Deliverance. Mashiach said Healing is the Bread of the children. The Word that is broken brings Healing. Revelation says Yahshua is The Lamb slain BEFORE the Foundation of the world. The Word or Dabar or Logos is the Word that came and broke the world!! The breaking forth speaks of the greatest revelation ever known to man!!

The Word that breaks the stronghold of ownership off Satan's hands – The Altar of Redemption. For this purpose, was the Son of Elohim Manifested that He would DESTROY the works of Satan. The manifestation of this crushing power took place on the Adamah Altar at the place called Golgotha. Remember Yahshua IS The Adamah Altar that unites Heaven and Earth as we will see later.

The Word that breaks the laws of shattered vessels or misplacement. The Altar of Restoration. The Word or the Logos Dabar Word restores the misplaced vessels that have been shattered!!!

- **Isaiah 42:22** But this is a people robbed and spoiled; they are all of them snared in holes, and they are hid in the prison houses: they are for a prey, and none delivers; for a spoil, and none proclaims, **Restore**.
- **Psalm 51:12** Restore unto me the joy of your salvation; and uphold me with your willing spirit.

Final nugget inside this B'resheet Altar revelation. Restore is seen in two dominant Hebrew words – Shuv and Shalam. Shuv is the word Repentance comes from. Restoration begins, when we approach The Altar. True repentance is not something we say, but something we actually do. If someone asked you how do you make repentance what would you say to them? It should be a simple answer. Repentance means to RETURN to the ways of Elohim that connect us to a Covenant Relationship which guarantees our Seat in Heavenly places.

Many preachers today say a lot of good sounding things, but how many are really returning to The Ways of our King Yahshua? When we have RETURNED to The Altar of Beginnings it is then we move onto the next concept which is Shalom.

Shalom is the root for Shalom, Peace or Wholeness. More than this, Shalam means to be At Peace with The One you were once an enemy of. Shalom is when all Chaos that led you away in the first place is no longer your guide and Staff of stumbling. Shalom gives the picture of when Chaos, that leads away, is reduced and we are now connected to The Restoration found inside The Beginning, known as Born again!

The Altar of Beginnings has now given way to the door of revelation to Creative Power and meaning. We make our transition from the beginning of all things to the Creative acts of this truth now crowning from the seat of the Altar Throne of Bara, King of Creative Powers. Shalom.

Chapter Three

Second Altar:
The Altar of Creating Origins, Bara

ברא

Let us recap on some of the revelations inside The Altar of The Beginning, **B'resheet**:

The Altar of B'resheet, or The Altar of Beginnings, contains our secrets of The Blood, giving us many concepts, we will get into. We now move to the next word in sequence, our next Altar Throne called Bara?! But, before this, here are the unexhausted categories found INSIDE the first Altar Throne, B'resheet – The Altar of Beginnings:

Altar Extensions

- The Altar of Redemption – Ephesians 1:7 with Romans 5: 9-10
- The Altar of Restoration
- The Altar of Deliverance
- The Altar of Substitution
- The Altar of Identity

- The Altar of Justification – Romans 5:9
- The Altar of Salvation
- The Altar of Purpose
- The Altar of Empowerment
- The Altar of Royal Ambassadorship Position in Mashiach Yahshua
- The Altar of Divine Nature – Galatians – 3:27 – We have been immersed INTO Mashiach and now have put on Mashiach!! The Walking and Breathing Altar extensions, or can I say Dust/Embers of Fire particles from this Adamah Altar!
- The Altar of Eternal Life – John 17:3 - And this is Eternal Life, that we would come to know Abba again.
- The Altar of Sanctification – Hebrews 13:12
- The Altar of Peace through His Blood – Colossians 1:20
- The Altars of Creation – Genesis 1

Bara – ברא – <u>The Altar of Creation</u>!

Let's begin with the insight of Scripture, this very word Bara which is seen 53 times in the entire TaNaKH. Bara can be pronounced as Bei'ra which is another Hebrew word for Son. This goes in line with what several verses say regarding all Creation coming into existence by and through The Word which is The Son manifested! **(John 1:1-3, 14; Hebrews 1:1-3)** In Genesis Bara is used ONLY with the Sea Creatures, Man and the three levels of his makeup, and the Luminaries. There were certain WORKS that Elohim Created and Made, two different operations from The Creator. CREATE is ALWAYS used with the Creator and no one else! Bara is seen 53 times in Scripture which happens to be the numerical value of the word HaYobel/היובל – The Jubilee or The Freedom.

At the Altar of Creation there is true freedom. Not only freedom from sin and death on a beginning level, but from this Genesis 1:1 level as Freedom or Jubilee is RELEASED from a higher dimension into a lower one. Jubilee or Yobel in Hebrew is the SOUND that is made when a Trumpet or Shofar is sounded. So, in essence, The Bara Altar is the origin of the Sound that all creation comes into existence by. The Power of this Bara Altar is the glue holding all things together indefinitely.

By the Altar of Mashiach, which is Yahshua, there is true freedom, or the releasing revelation of what was concealed. There was no freedom at any other Altar before until this moment in time! True freedom is when we have become new in Him –

- **2Corinthians 5:17** Therefore^{G5620} if any man^{G1536} be in^{G1722} Messiah,^{G5547} he is a new^{G2537} creature^{G2937} old things^{G744} are passed away;^{G3928} behold,^{G2400} all things^{G3956} are become^{G1096} new.^{G2537}

- **Ephesians 2:15** Having abolished^{G2673} in^{G1722} his^{G848} **flesh**^{G4561} **(Flesh here is the Hebrew term Basar or Good News. In and by His Flesh, The Good News of The Kingdom He demonstrated, the hostility was abolished!)** the^{G3588} **enmity,**^{G2189} *even* the^{G3588} law^{G3551} of commandments^{G1785} contained in^{G1722} ordinances;^{G1378} for to^{G2443} make^{G2936} in^{G1722} himself^{G1438} of two^{G1417} (G1519) **one**^{G1520} **new**^{G2537} **man,**^{G444} *so* making^{G4160} peace;^{G1515} (Before I address this **enmity** again let me give you an insight into the commandments and ordinances of Covenant. When we keep the Covenant code of Torah, this becomes the unlocking process that reveals who you really are in Mashiach Yahshua. The word, commands and ordinances are a protected garment, which in the process of time manifests the forming and fashioning power of The Word Himself in the lives of those who live by them.

  He abolished in His Flesh the enmity, why? Because the enmity would only have access to the flesh of man not his

> spirit. WITHIN Himself, not us, he made One New man. What a POWERFUL thought! In Him we are One New Man! He made one New Adam! From the Altar of Bara, we are a New Creation! You can hear this in the words themselves. From this Altar His Peace is manifested. The Shalom that removes the Chaos. There is Shalom at the Altar of Bara! Shalom comes from the Bara Altar!**)**

Bara describes the function of Elohim alone!! In Isaiah we have something so powerful:

> 🩸 **Isaiah 43:1** But now[H6258] so[H3541] says[H559] Yahweh[H3068] that **created**[H1254] you, **Jacob,**[H3290] and he that **formed**[H3335] you, **Israel,**[H3478] Fear[H3372] not[H408] for[H3588] I have redeemed[H1350] you, I have called[H7121] you by your name;[H8034] you[H859] are mine.

Jacob originated from Bara/**Created** and Israel from Yatzar/**Formed**!!! Another interesting verse:

> 🩸 **Isaiah 45:7** I **form**[H3335] **the light,**[H216] and **create**[H1254] **darkness:**[H2822] I make[H6213] peace,[H7965] and **create**[H1254] **evil:**[H7451] I[H589] Yahweh[H3068] do[H6213] all[H3605] these[H428] things. **(Evil is His Hammer to shatter clay vessels in order to retrieve the sparks of light within them.)**

When we keep in mind this revelation while visualizing the Hebrew word Bara, we can reflect on what John the Apostle said in 1 John –

> 🩸 **1John 5:7** For there are three that **bear record** in **The Heavens** (Altar Throne of The Heavens – Genesis 1:1.), the **Father**, the **Word**, and the **Holy Spirit**: and these three are one.

> 🩸 **1John 5:8** And there are three that **bear witness in The Earth**, the **Spirit**, and the **water**, and **the blood**: and these three agree in one.

The Heavens hold the Court system recordings and The Earth is where the witness stand takes place. The Hebrew word Bara could stand as an acronym: **Bet** for Ben The Son, **Resh** for Ruach or Spirit and **Alef** for Abba or Father. The Father, Son and Spirit all working together to reveal The Kingdom System within the World beyond Creation. On a simple note, this fits the verses we just read.

B'reshith, The Altar of Beginnings is Creation Clothed, which is the combination of the two Hebrew ideas: Clothe/Shayeet and Create/Bara. Within B'reshith we have The Covenant of Fire. Within The Beginning we have The Head of The House – Beit Rosh. The Head of all Creation came as The Ambassador of The Father here on Earth.

Bara not only means to Create something that had not been seen before but it is more than that. Bara speaks of bringing forth something and inflating it. Bara can also be pronounced as: Bei'ra which means SON as I mentioned! The Son/Word is the one that Elohim Created THROUGH:

Let's tackle a few verses –

> **Psalm 119:89** Forever[H5769] Yahweh[H3068] **Your Word**[H1697] **stands firm**[H5324] in **The Heavens.**[H8064]

Your Word – Dabar is the Appointed One over and in The Heavens or Altar of Heavens. Heavens means many. This Altar is the Governing seat over all The Heavens. What a mind-blowing thought! The Dabar Word is what holds the Heavens together. Dabar when translated into the Greek is Logos. Logos is used in John 1 pertaining to Yahshua HaMashiach, who is the Garment of The Word. So, when we read in John 1 - 'IN The Beginning was The Word...' we can connect this to the Word Bara, which is another form for the word Son! The Son was the Agent of Creation because He is The Word that is Natzav/Settled, Enthroned and Appointed **in** The Heavens, or Commander in Chief Holding all things together!

In these next set of verses, we can stay right here because of the knowledge embedded in them:

The Seven Altar Thrones of Genesis 1:1

🌹 **Colossians 1:12** Giving thanks^{G2168} unto the^{G3588} Father,^{G3962} which has made us^{G2427 G2248} to be partakers^{G1519 G3310} of the^{G3588} **inheritance**^{G2819} of the^{G3588} set apart ones^{G40} in^{G1722} light:^{G5457}

🌹 **1:13** Who^{G3739} has **delivered**^{G4506} us^{G2248} from^{G1537} the^{G3588} power^{G1849} of darkness,^{G4655} and^{G2532} has **translated**^{G3179} us into^{G1519} **the**^{G3588} **kingdom**^{G932} **of his**^{G848} **dear**^{G26} **Son:**^{G5207} (This Kingdom is the Kingdom of The Beginning. The place where Bara initiated the revealing of Creation! This Greek word for translated is found in the LXX Deuteronomy 17:17 as: סור – Sur. It means to depart, to cause to exit a place because of outgrowing that place. This word also means leaven. Yahshua said The Kingdom of Heaven was like Leaven, Sur, meaning it expands and breaks out. The Kingdom of Bara is working in you and me and one day this revelation will outgrow our physical bodies and crown us into the next world with Mashiach! This numerical value is also equal to TzimTzum/צמצום which means contraction. Contracting something into a Narrow place in order to crown that very thing!)

🌹 **Colossians 1:14** In^{G1722} whom^{G3739} we have^{G2192} **redemption**^{G629} (One of the concepts inside The Altar Bara that expands. Remember, this Bara Altar is the Dominion of expanding all that is seen and unseen. That is why it's used with Elohim in Creation. He expanded what was unseen so it could be seen.) through^{G1223} his^{G846} blood,^{G129} the^{G3588} forgiveness^{G859} of sins:^{G266} (Forgiveness was in The Bara Altar of Genesis 1:1)

🌹 **Colossians 1:15** Who^{G3739} **is**^{G2076} **the image**^{G1504} **of the**^{G3588} **invisible**^{G517} **Eloah,**^{G2316} **the firstborn**^{G4416} of every^{G3956} original formation:^{G2937} (The Firstborn of every original formation doesn't mean He was created, but rather that He is the SOURCE of Creation – Bara = Son and that every original formation has The imprint of The Word who is The Son!!)

- ***Col 1:16** For^{G3754} by^{G1722} **him**^{G846} **were all things**^{G3956} **created,**^{G2936} that^{G3588} are in^{G1722} **The Heavens**^{G3772} and^{G2532} that^{G3588} are in^{G1909} **The Earth**^{G1093} visible^{G3707} and^{G2532} invisible,^{G517} whether^{G1535} thrones,^{G2362} or^{G1535} dominions,^{G2963} or^{G1535} principalities,^{G746} or^{G1535} powers:^{G1849} all things^{G3956} were **Created**^{G2936} by^{G1223} him,^{G846} and^{G2532} for^{G1519} him:^{G846} **(Notice the Three Altars referenced in Bold here.** This is our key verse, He-The Son, The Source, The Word and all things visible, invisible, in Heaven or on and in the earth were Created by Him – Altar of Bara. At the Altar Things are Created and Transformed and Reformed! By the Power of The Altar of Bara all things would come forth. Genesis 1 is the revelation to Creation's process of RETURNING, or can I say Repentance. It was Order out of Chaos that was taking place. Things BECAME Tohu V'Bohu and would take the actions of The Son – The Bara Altar to RESTORE all things back to Order!! We see this being counterfeited today, imposed and manmade chaos in order to bring about a controlled Elite Order upon the People who originate from Genesis 1:1!)

- **Colossians 1:17** And^{G2532} he^{G846} is^{G2076} **before**^{G4253} **all things,**^{G3956} and^{G2532} by^{G1722} him^{G846} all things^{G3956} **consist.**^{G4921} (This word **Consist** is the Greek word **suni'stemi** which means to 'Hold together like glue'. The Son is the Bara Agent that holds all things together like a glue. He IS the Bara Altar as well where all things are held together and then restored from being a shattered result of man's fall. The Last Adam will hold any shattered life together, if that shattered life will just come to Him through the Power of Shoov/Repentance! **Suni'stemi** comes from Tzavah in Hebrew and means to command together in unity. The Bara Altar unites what was shattered vessels of a chaotic order and commands the chaos to retreat and restores through His healing touch.)

🔴 **Col 1:18** And^G2532 he^G846 is^G2076 the^G3588 head^G2776 of the^G3588 body,^G4983 the^G3588 called out ones:^G1577 who^G3739 **is^G2076 the beginning**,^G746 the firstborn^G4416 from^G1537 the^G3588 dead;^G3498 that^G2443 in^G1722 all^G3956 he^G846 might have^G1096 the sovereignty.^G4409

🔴 **Col 1:19** For^G3754 it pleased^G2106 the Father that in^G1722 him^G846 should all^G3956 fulness^G4138 dwell;^G2730

🔴 **Col 1:20** And,^G2532 having made peace^G1517 through^G1223 the^G3588 blood^G129 of his^G846 Tree,^G4716 by^G1223 him^G846 to reconcile^G604 all things^G3956 unto^G1519 himself;^G848 by^G1223 him,^G846 whether^G1535 things^G3588 in^G1909 **The Earth,**^G1093 or^G1535 things^G3588 in^G1722 **The Heavens.**^G3772 (The Bara Altar of Creation is The Word of The Beginning that ushered in the first revelation out of The Beginning which is the Son who is the FIRSTBORN/Beginning of all Creation/Bara!!! The Altar of Bara is The Altar of The Son. When Yahshua ascended Golgolet/Golgotha, which means to Reveal what was concealed, He opened the Door to the power of Bara for the first time since Genesis 1:1! Golgotha was the demarcation of Dominion restored between The Earth Altar and The Heavens Altar, amazing thought.)

🔴 **Hebrews 1:1** Elohim,^G2316 who at many times^G4181 and^G2532 in divers manners^G4187 spoke^G2980 in time past^G3819 unto the^G3588 fathers^G3962 **by^G1722 the^G3588 prophets,**^G4396

🔴 **Heb 1:2** Has in^G1909 these^G5130 **last^G2078 days^G2250** spoken^G2980 unto us^G2254 **by^G1722 his Son,**^G5207 whom^G3739 he has **appointed**^G5087 heir^G2818 of all things,^G3956 by^G1223 whom^G3739 also^G2532 **he made**^G4160 **the**^G3588 **worlds;**^G165 (Appointed is the word between Bara and Bara of Genesis

1:1 – ברא שית ברא – **Bara Shayeet Bara** – In The Beginning He Created a Place and Garment which is The **Appointed**/Shayeet **One**. The numerical value of the Bara double is 406 which gives us the words: הָאֹת תָּאָה – Ha'ote Ta'ah which means: The Sign of Covenant! The Covenant sign between the people of Elohim is clothed/Sha'yeet back in Genesis 1:1.)

Hebrews 1:3 Who[G3739] being[G5607] the brightness[G541] of glory,[G1391] and[G2532] the express image[G5481] of his[G848] person,[G5287] and[G5037] **upholding**[G5342] **all things**[G3956] **by the**[G3588] **word**[G4487] **of his**[G846] **power,**[G1411] (The Word, The Son, The Bara Altar of Genesis 1:1 upholds ALL things by The Word of His Power. This is powerful now!! The Bara Altar Throne that was manifested through The Word, He upholds ALL things by Himself, but the 'ALL' things are held up by what is called the Amar or Rhema WORD! The revelation of The Bara Altar is what causes ALL things to Ascend up to a whole new level.

Yahshua said man shall not live by bread alone but by every WORD/Rhema that proceeds out of the mouth of Elohim!! The Mouth of Elohim is seen at the Top of the Altar!!

The revelation of Life is the Life source of all Creation that is born from the Bara Altar!!! There is not only a Dunamis Explosive power but an actual level of Rhema revelation of that Dunamis Power that is the Expansive Explosive Altar which we find our One New Man in Mashiach!

In Yahshua, whose flesh was Created and Formed in the womb of Mary, we experience the death of the flesh, but in Mashiach which is The Word, The Rhema, The Bara Altar; we are The Kingdom Leaven carriers of Heaven! **(Matthew 13:33)** This truth teaches us that the manifestation of His Flesh is from the place of Bara which came down through the Heavens – John 6 – and that was the Legal Scepter used to establish The Kingdom of The Heavens on The Earth! Hebrews speaks of the Rhema of This Dunamis that upholds all things!! Dunamis is explosive and demonstrative Power in Greek. The Explosive Revelation of this truth is what is being communicated. The upholding of All things is an Altar revelation!) when he had by[G1223] himself[G1438] purged[G4160 G2512] our[G2257] sins,[G266] sat down[G2523] on[G1722] the right hand[G1188] of the[G3588] Majesty[G3172] on[G1722] high;[G5308]

- **Heb 1:4** Being **made**[G1096] so much[G5118] better[G2909] than the[G3588] angels,[G32] as[G3745] he has by inheritance obtained[G2816] a more excellent[G1313] name[G3686] than[G3844] they.[G846] (Yes and No the Son has always been! Meaning, when we speak of the Flesh, that part was Born which made Him legal to be here in order to carry out the Redemptive Orders of Abba if I may say. When it comes to Mashiach, which isn't his last name, that part speaks of the Eternal Word that has always been, the very Spirit of Elohim living in and through Him and yet completely Echad as One, the eternal Source of all Creation. The revelation of The Son is to reveal the heart of Abba with the desire for Sonship to all who come.)

- **Micah 5:2** But you,[H859] Bethlehem[H1035] Ephrathah,[H672] though you be[H1961] little[H6810] among the thousands[H505] of Judah,[H3063] yet out of[H4480] you will He **come forth**[H3318] unto me to be[H1961] ruler[H4910] in Israel;[H3478] whose goings forth[H4163] are from of old,[H4480 H6924] from everlasting.[H4480 H3117 H5769] — (The going forth was the root of parashat Ki Teitzeh. The word here is Yatza a Bursting forth into the battle. The Word, The Bara Altar Bursted forth the nativity and crowning of The Promise Son.)

- **John 1:1** In/Through[G1722] **The Beginning**[G746] was[G2258] the[G3588] Word,[G3056] and[G2532] the[G3588] Word[G3056] was[G2258] with^(G4314) Elohim,^(G2316) and^(G2532) the^(G3588) Word^(G3056) was^(G2258) Elohim.^(G2316)

🌹 **John 1:2** The same^(G3778) was^(G2258) in^(G1722) the beginning^(G746) with^(G4314) Elohim.^(G2316)

🌹 **John 1:3** ==All things^(G3956) were made^(G1096)== by^(G1223) him;^(G846) **(Through, With The** Beginning has let us know this Word is in all seven Altar Thrones, originating out of The Altar of Beginnings. Each Altar Throne is revealed out of The First One. MADE is from the word Hayah in Hebrew which means to cause something to BE. The idea of made in English tells us that all things were created out of a tangible substance. But the Hebrew meaning excavates the depths for more clarity and true balance of what is being communicated, and ultimately what has taken place then.) and^(G2532) without^(G5565) him^(G846) was not^(G3761) anything^(G1520) made^(G1096) **(Hayah, Came into being)** that^(G3739) was made.^(G1096) ...**John 1:12** But^(G1161) as many as^(G3745) received^(G2983) him,^(G846) to them^(G846) gave^(G1325) the ==power^(G1849)== (Exuosia in Greek means magistrate function, an authority, but in Hebrew we have something more powerful – Mem'Shalah/ממשלה = Dominion and Ruling Presence!! From the Bara Altar we have been given the Dominion Authority to Rule here on Earth! It is a Heavenly Decree to those of the Kingdom of Heaven – Luke 10:19.) to **become**^(G1096) the sons^(G5043) of Elohim,^(G2316) (It's all about sonship!! Sonship brings in the inherent right to operate as royalty because you are royalty. This sonship is first found in Bara, the Altar of Creation, where the Creative Acts manifest from! I have to bring this up as my spirit is driven toward the Altar revelation, the numerical value of this Hebrew concept Mem'Shalah is 435 the same for what comes through the HaRaqia/הרקיע means: **The Firmament**, the place or threshold where all things cross with permission, this is

The Seven Altar Thrones of Genesis 1:1

called Ghabar or Hebrew - עבר. The Raqia is a powerful concept that was made in Genesis 1:7 and in verse 6 it was something that just came into existence. Let us examine this revelation connected to Bara –

The Firmament of Distinction

(Diagram 10)

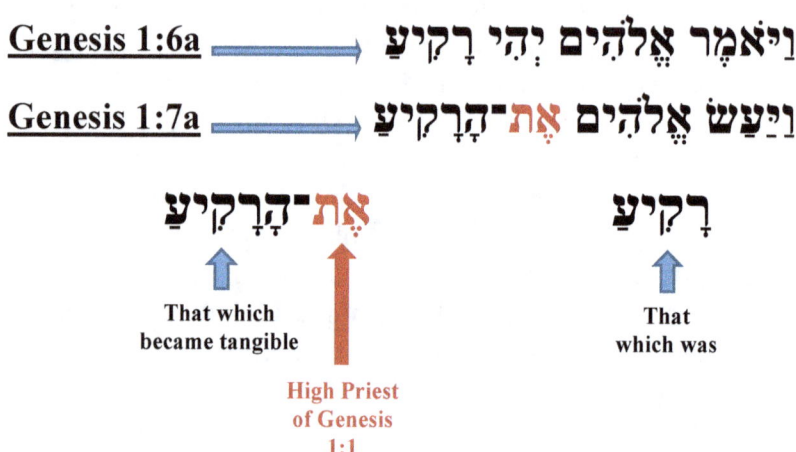

The first phrase is taken from Genesis 1:6a – "And Elohim said Let there be Firmament..." This doesn't do justice in English, but the Hebrew would say something more like: And Elohim said, **"Firmament, Become/Happen..."** This Raqia was one that could not be touched but was and is set in place as a protective layer. Here is an example: The Raqia stood between The Altar of The Earth and The Void Chaotic and Empty place. This was intended to keep the impurities of Tohu V'Bohu from overtaking The Earth Altar. Let me give an example:

In the physical body of man is something called the Mucus Membrane. This system was put in our physical bodies to protect from all external harmful AGENTS. Two functions of this Mucus Membrane are used as a protective barrier, or can I say threshold:

Because of its dense structure, the epithiel tissue in this membrane forms a barrier which prevents pathogens from entering. You can google this on your own time, I just want to make a down to Earth, no pun intended; connection. The Hebrew word for MUCUS is: ריר – Riyr, which also means saliva or spittle. The Strong's Number is H7388 and is seen only twice in Scripture. Moving forward, Yahshua used 'Riyr-ריר' and Dust to restore a man's eyes – John 9:1-7. Yahshua restored a protective layer over this man's eyes. Yahshua demonstrated this Altar Throne of Power. To lose sight or hearing of the Word of Elohim is a breach in the protective HaRaqia/The Firmament. The numerical value for the Hebrew word Riyr/Mucus is: 410, the same for – Le'Raqia/לְרָקִיעַ of Genesis 1!

There are four more Hebrew words I must address with this same numerical value, with one Historic event –

410 is the value of: קָדוֹשׁ שָׁמַע מִשְׁכָּן – (Right to left) – **Qadosh** means Set Apart/Holy; **Shema** means: Hear; **Mishkan** means: Tabernacle, Dwelling place for The Presence. Each is a protective Membrane for the soul. When either of these are removed, the touch of sickness and even Death comes in. When Holiness is breached, the pathogens of unholiness takeover the body. When the hearing and obeying The Voice, then the Pathogens of Rebellion come in. when our bodies which are the Temple of Ruach HaQodesh are given over to idolatry and lust, then there is no more abiding Presence.

Last numerical connection to this insight is with Solomon's Temple. The first Temple stood for 410 years, the same numerical number to what I just mentioned. So, in a sense, anything manmade is like crossing the protective layer. This temple was aloud and once Solomon brought idolatry and witchcraft into what was sacred, that protective layer was breached. In the physical body we have a mucus membrane that protects a sacred place some might call the third eye or where the Soul and Spirit connect. This portrays the Holy of Holies or Qadosh

HaQadoshim which has a numerical value of 875, the same for: מִשְׁפְּתַיִם – Mish'pe'tayim means: Two Sheepfolds or Fire Heaps – Genesis 49:14. Issachar whose name means: To lift a Contract off of, is a prophecy that the Contracts between two sheepfolds (The Whole House of Israel scattered abroad) would take place by Yahshua HaMashiach! 875 also means: הכתנת – HaKatnot or, The Garments covering Adam and Eve after the Fall – Genesis 3:21. These flesh bodies are like a Mucus because of the fall and all manner of sickness and disease of death is always trying to come against it. Thank you for the Power of the Resurrected Body and Blood of Yahshua! One day we will put on our bodies of light when this Raqia, this flesh body like a mucus is removed.

Back to The Firmament insight. What I'm about to say is very deep and connects to Yahshua and the condition He would take on in our place. The numerical value of the Hebrew phrase – יְהִי רָקִיעַ – Ye'hee Raqia has the numerical value of: הַמְצֹרָע – HaMetzorah – The Leper. There is a concept called The Leper Messiah referring to Mashiach who would take on the Leprous condition of Israel. Leprosy was an untouchable disease and yet highly contagious. This firmament stood as an untouchable place that was stationed between the waters/people, which would bring distinction between those on one side of the Firmament/Leprous One and those on the other side of this Threshold.

This is a thought to capture the depths of this place of separation that stood 'between' the waters. The only thing in Scripture containing a secret to its origin and purpose is found in the mystery of The Leper Scholar we know to be Yahshua HaMashiach our Altar King.

In verse seven the wording switches from an untouchable place to one that is specific – "And Elohim MADE the Alef Tav Firmament…" Va'ya'as Elohim **Et HaRaqia. HaRaqia** means '**The Firmament** or the contracted layer. Et HaRaqia can be read as: Atah Raqia which means: You are the Raqia or manifested

One! He became, or chose, to take on our leprous condition of sin in order to legally redeem us. This message is deeper than we know because we are dealing with Lawful and Legal things from a loftier dimension!

The Word has always been, but the body was prepared and had to be Born! One was made and the other came to be. One would be manifested while the other always was. This Altar would manifest through the Bara system of Elohim and walk among the waters/people bringing distinction and taking on their leprous condition. Prophecy is embedded inside the beginning with these Altar revelations.

Follow me for a second here, the Hebrew word **HaRaqia** has the value of 385. When we add the one word with its numerical value, we have 386 which is the value of Yeshua/יֵשׁוּעַ, who is the manifested Word. Now, Yeshua is also a town in southern Judah that was repopulated by some of the exiles of Judah. Yeshua is the name of a priest of the Sanctuary; also, he was a Levitical priest in charge of various offerings in the Temple; the name of the priest who returned with Zerubbabel; the father of Jozabad the Levite; one whose descendants returned from exile; father of one who helped repair the wall of Jerusalem; another Levite who decoded the Torah and communicated it to the people; one who sealed The New Covenant with Elohim after the redemption of exiled souls!!

So, **Et HaRaqia** can be said to be: **Et HaYeshua**! The manifested Firmament is The Yahshua who redeems the exiled souls that pass through Him! Yahshua was the Flesh Firmament of His own Altar, we have now been redeemed and healed by. We must ascend the Ladder of Philippians 2:5-9. His flesh was torn the same time the Temple veil of the second Temple era was. His flesh was the virgin Hymen the Word broke through for us all. I know this sounds too personal and private, but we must grasp that Yahshua came through an untouched womb and would be broken and pierced through as the sinless – untouched flesh womb of The Word, for us all. The Word needed an empty womb

The Seven Altar Thrones of Genesis 1:1

coming here, and a sinless one leaving here – 1 Peter 1:18-19; 1Peter 2:22; 2 Corinthians 5:21; Hebrews 4:15; Luke 1:35; 1 John 3:5; John 19:4.

The manifested Altar would put on the firmament type Garment in order to be tangible as He would walk among and in the midst of the waters/people. Water in Scripture also refers to people just read Revelation. So, this firmament in Genesis 1:7 is a revelation of the Altar King Yahshua who would be contracted in seed form in order to manifest here on Earth, executing The Redemption. All must come through Him in order to get to The Father.

The Souls of all living things must passthrough this Raqia that was made, not the one that came into being as shown above. HaNefesh is defined as The Soul!! I have mentioned before that this Firmament is the Threshold between the Heavens and the Earth. It is also seen in Numbers 17 with the fire pans of Korach that were **flattened** out and placed as the Altar's **NET** covering!! The NET is a revelation in and of itself as it is used when Mashiach Yahshua told Peter to cast the NET on the Tzadiq/Right side and get a catch. The manifested Raqia instructed His NET to divide the waters above from the waters below in order to get a prophetic catch.

The Bara Altar was right there with Peter instructing him to pull out from the Mayim while the Fire was on the Land the 153 or Bnei HaElohim – The Sons of Elohim of the Kingdom! Fire and Water give us Shamayim!!! The Bara Altar was on the sands of revelation connecting The Waters to The Shin or Fire of Creation!! He holds the Power of The Fire on the Bara Altar!) even to them that believe[G4100] on[G1519] his[G846] name:[G3686] ...Joh 1:14 And[G2532] the[G3588] Word[G3056] was made[G1096] flesh,[G4561] and[G2532] tabernacled[G4637] among[G1722] us,[G2254] and[G2532] we beheld[G2300] his[G846] glory,[G1391] the glory[G1391] as[G5613] of the only begotten[G3439] of[G3844] the Father,[G3962] full[G4134] of grace[G5485] and[G2532] truth.[G225]

This revelation of the second word of our Genesis of Genesis study, The Altars of Genesis 1:1, is very powerful. This second

John-James of the House of Flores.®

Hebrew word Bara begins the revelation of the Creative revelation of all we know we have seen so far!! Inside this Altar are the origins of the Altar Corner stone which is the Even Shetiyah or the Stone of Drinking – The Chief Corner Stone which is Yahshua HaMashiach. From here we have the connection to Kingdom Power and Redemption and the restoration of all things. At the Altar in the Tabernacle and Temple whatever came there was restored back to its original standing. The Bara Altar contains the origin of perfection. All Angels, come out from this place.

> 🌀 **Psalm 148:1** Praise^{H1984} Yahweh.^{H3050} Praise^{H1984} (H853) Yahweh^{H3068} from^{H4480} **The Heavens**:^{H8064} praise^{H1984} him in the heights.^{H4791} **148:2** Praise^{H1984} him, all^{H3605} his angels:^{H4397} praise^{H1984} him, all^{H3605} his hosts.^{H6635} **148:3** Praise^{H1984} him, sun^{H8121} and moon:^{H3394} praise^{H1984} him, all^{H3605} you stars^{H3556} of light.^{H216} **148:4** Praise^{H1984} him, you heavens^{H8064} of **The Heavens**^{H8064} and you waters^{H4325} that^{H834} are **above**^{H4480 H5921} **The Heavens**.^{H8064} **148:5** Let them praise^{H1984} (H853) the name^{H8034} of Yahweh:^{H3068} for^{H3588} he^{H1931} commanded,^{H6680} and they were **created.**^{H1254}

> 🌀 **Colossians 1:16** For^{G3754} by^{G1722} him^{G846} all things^{G3956} **came into being,**^{G2936} that^{G3588} are **in**^{G1722} **The Heavens,**^{G3772} and^{G2532} that^{G3588} are **on**^{G1909} **The Earth,**^{G1093} visible^{G3707} and^{G2532} invisible,^{G517} whether^{G1535} thrones,^{G2362} or^{G1535} dominions,^{G2963} or^{G1535} principalities,^{G746} or^{G1535} powers:^{G1849} all things^{G3956} were **created**^{G2936} by^{G1223} him,^{G846} and^{G2532} for^{G1519} him:^{G846}

Even Lucifer himself was from this very Altar of Bara and yet rebelled –

> 🌀 **Ezekiel 28:13** You have been^{H1961} in Eden^{H5731} the garden^{H1588} of Elohim;^{H430} every^{H3605} precious^{H3368} stone^{H68} was your intertwined covering,^{H4540} **the**

Adam/Sardius,^{H124} topaz,^{H6357} and the diamond,^{H3095} the beryl,^{H8658} the onyx,^{H7718} and the jasper,^{H3471} the sapphire,^{H5601} the emerald,^{H5306} and the carbuncle,^{H1304} and gold:^{H2091} the workmanship^{H4399} of thy drum^{H8596} and of your **pipes**^{H5345} was prepared^{H3559} in thee in the day^{H3117} that thou wast **created.**^{H1254}

He was from a place called Bara. Now this is very telling because one of Lucifer's descriptions is one of 'pipes' which in Hebrew is called: נקב – Neqev which means pipes, passage, an empty place where wind can pass through. This is also one of the character revelations that Adam was made up of which most translate as 'female'. Genesis 1:26-27 says that Adam was made up of male and female character descriptions, but this is deeper than that, but for the sake of space I will connect something regarding this insight.

The woman that was pulled out of Adam is called: נקבה – Na'qebah. The root of this Hebrew word is Ne'qev, pipes or a place of passage. The woman was the place of passage where those with breath would legally come through. Her womb was the passage place that the breathing man would come through because it is the legal way of walking on this Earth Altar. You have to be born in order to come here. Satan came at the woman first because she contained the fufillment to the Neqev or place of passage. Every child born is entwined with a song, a melody that is heard as soon as they are born. Lucifer, the now fallen one known as Satan wanted the breath of life passage in order to take over this lower dominion called Earth.

The Bara Altar represents the Heavenly Court system and Chamber record library of where all things, whether seen or unseen, are recorded as to their designated kingdoms. Satan was out of bounds and rejected the Bara Altar which created him and now he became the first vagabond entity and cherub. The naked and uncircumcised one who was stripped of his beauty, splendor and majesty. Because of the fall of man, all men became sick and infected with sin. Therefore, the remedy requirement was Sent in the form of a promise, in the form of a baby, who is The Word made flesh. Let us look at some connections to this Word that was sent to touch the ones He loved the most.

The Altar manifestations, The Word

In this section we will connect the works done through The Word. All Healing, Wholeness is found from the Altar. Let us look at some aspects of The Bara which is The Word which is The Son:

~The WORD (Altar) is Strong Meat: Strong Meat was Created in The Beginning!!

- Heb 5:14 But^{G1161} **strong meat**^{G4731} ^{G5160} belongs^{G2076} to them that are of full age,^{G5046} those who by reason of^{G1223} use^{G1838} have^{G2192} their senses^{G145} exercised^{G1128} to^{G4314} discern^{G1253} both^{G5037} good^{G2570} and^{G2532} evil.^{G2556} (The **strong meat** comes from a Hebrew concept the Greek uses, found in Numbers 8:4, speaking of The Menorah as it is BEATEN into formation. The Strong Meat is like the Hammer of the Word, fashioning the soul of man into that vessel which is to project the Light of The Kingdom and all its strength, which is metaphor of the King's Dominion here on Earth! The Hebrew word is: Mi'Qeshah/מקשה meaning: too hard, difficult, stiff-necked, stubborn. The Strong meat is for those who have come to full age and are now ready to have the difficulties of stubbornness, stiff-necked and prideful ways hammered out of them if I may say in order for them to be the vessel trustworthy to project the Light of Truth and of His Kingdom Authority. A side note, the man named Betzalel whose name means in The Image of God/El did not hammer the work of the Menorah into the gold per se, but he hammered away the layers of gold that hid the Menorah. The Eternal Light was in need of the Body of the Menorah. The Incense was in need of the Body called The Incense Altar. The Bread of multi-dimensional Faces was in need of a Body called The Table. Each waited for the touch from Betzalel, The Image of El! He was not Creating/Bara, but he was reflecting this strength of what The Bara Altar does. Bara means to reveal that which is concealed and then expand it into a three-dimensional form. He removed all the layers of excess in order to bring forth what was there all along. He revealed the hidden Platform beneath the gold. Each Body/Vessel was the Altar to its function.

The numerical value of Qeshah is 405 the same for: 'I will make Holy' – אֲקַדֵּשׁ – A'qadeish!! So, Holiness is something Created from The Altar of Bara which is a gift from the Son. True Holiness gives access beyond the veil and into the Qadosh Place or that Sacred Space outside of time called The Place.)

~The WORD (Altar) is Fire and like a Hammer: The smashing power of The Word like a Hammer was Created in the Beginning!!

- **Jeremiah 23:29** Is not[H3808] My Word[H1697] like[H3541] **fire**?[H784] says[H5002] Yahweh[H3068] and like a **hammer**[H6360] that breaks[H6327] the rock[H5553] in pieces? (Fire and Hammer. In this section of Scripture, The Word is like a Fire and Hammer against false prophets and their evil deeds. The Word demolishes all evil. The Word crushes all altars that oppose the Altar of Bara. Bara meaning Create, speaks of perfection. No need to add to or take away from what is born from The Bara Altar. The Word destroys what tries to alter what comes from the Bara Altar.

  This word for Word is once again Dabar in Hebrew which is the Logos in the Greek – The Word made Flesh!! The Word is The Bara Altar who was manifested in flesh. All His miracles from opening blind eyes, raising the dead, healing the diseased, new limbs appearing, lepers cleansed without a trace of leprosy, lame deaf and dumb bodies restored to health were all acts from this Bara Altar power and dominion! All I'm sharing is directly connected to the revelation of Bara, the Altar Throne of Creation.)

~The WORD (Altar) is like a Mirror: The Mirror of The Word was Created in the beginning. What you and I were supposed to bear the image of was Created in the beginning!!!

- **James 1:23** For^{G3754} if any^{G1536} be^{G2076} a hearer^{G202} of **The Word,**^{G3056} and^{G2532} not^{G3756} a doer,^{G4163} he^{G3778} is like^{G1503} a man^{G435} discovering^{G2657} his^{G846} natural^{G1078} face^{G4383} in^{G1722} a mirror^{G2072} (Hearing and Doing is the evidence you have come to the Altar of Bara, the Altar of Creative Power. To hear and not do is not hearing at all. The word mirror comes from the Hebrew word Kasaph/כסף – Silversmith. One who deals with precious metals. When you spend time in the fire of The Bara Altar we come out as fine gold and silver. All impurities are removed. Kasaph also means to long for something. The Word is the Mirror we are to reflect the image of!! Where do we find this Word reflection first? On the Tree. We are to take up our cross/tree DAILY and crucify the flesh nature. The Value of this Hebrew word Kasaph is 160, the same for Eitz/עץ – Tree/Cross.)

~The WORD (Altar) is like a Sword: The cutting effect of The Word as a Sword was Created in the Beginning and comes from the Altar of Creative Powers – Bara, able to discern all and mold all!!

- **Hebrews 4:12** For^{G1063} the^{G3588} Word^{G3056} of Elohim^{G2316} is quick,^{G2198} and^{G2532} powerful,^{G1756} and^{G2532} sharper^{G5114} than^{G5228} any^{G3956} two-edged^{G1366} sword,^{G3162} piercing^{G1338} even^{G2532} to^{G891} untangle the soul tie^{G3311} of$^{(G5037)}$ soul^{G5590} and^{G2532} spirit,^{G4151} and^{G5037} of the joints^{G719} and^{G2532} marrow,^{G3452} and^{G2532} is a discerner^{G2924} of the thoughts^{G1761} and^{G2532} intents^{G1771} of the heart.^{G2588} (The

Word is Dabar once again. So, this Dabar word goes back to our study of The Bara Altar. Bara is also Bei'ra which means Son. Bara IS the Son. This is why He can be The Beginning as I have mentioned. The Bara is sharper than ANY TWO-EDGED Sword because it is The Creative Path of all existence and is the true discerner between the THOUGHTS & INTENTS of the heart. Thoughts comes from a Hebrew word that is interesting and that is Domeh or 'I will resemble'.

Thoughts can mold and shape false images or the Image of The Word that get intertwined in the DNA! This Hebrew word Domeh can also be HaDam which means: The Blood or DNA. WOW! What are your thoughts like because they are recorded on your DNA? INTENTS is Kavanah in Hebrew. What are you connected to? Thoughts mold and shape the Connection or brings shape to what you have been meditating upon. Meditation upon the Word will manifest that Word in our lives. Domeh is the related word to Adamah or Adomeh means: I will Resemble. Our Inheritance is Adamah/Adomeh The Resemblance of The NEW ADAM!!! Bara will lead you to the Adamah Altar where Heaven and Earth are connected. The Bara Altar reveals the Sword aspect of The Word which is The Son. We are Carved out as a mirror image of The Son!!)

~The WORD (Altar) is Bread: Bread was Created in the Beginning. From the Bara Altar the Bread of Heaven was revealed. The revelation of each one of these was inside the Bara Altar. The Bread came forth from the Bara Altar. The Bread of Heaven or The Kingdom was inside the Bara Altar of Genesis 1:1!!

> **Matthew 4:4** But^{G1161} he^{G3588} answered^{G611} and said,^{G2036} It is written,^{G1125} Man^{G444} shall not^{G3756} live^{G2198} by^{G1909} **bread**^{G740} alone,^{G3441} but^{G235} by^{G1909} every^{G3956} **Word**^{G4487} that proceeds^{G1607} out of^{G1223} the mouth^{G4750} of

Elohim.^G2316 (From the Bara Altar the Bread of Heaven came forth!! This word Bread used here in Greek is **Artos** and speaks of the Bread that rises. The Rising Bread!! The Resurrected and Expanding Bread of The Kingdom. The expanding influence of Resurrection Power came forth from the Bara Altar or The Creation Altar of Genesis 1:1! Now this gets more powerful as we think upon the concept of this Bread and Genesis 1:1 Bara Altar - **Gen 3:19 In the sweat**^H2188 **of your face**^H639 **you will eat**^H398 **bread,**^H3899 **untill**^H5704 **you return**^H7725 **upon**^H413 **the ground;**^H127 **for**^H3588 **out of**^H4480 **it were you taken:**^H3947 **for**^H3588 **dust**^H6083 **you**^H859 **are and to**^H413 **dust**^H6083 **you will return.**^H7725

Bread here is Lechem, first found in Genesis 3:19. Lechem would be the Kingdom Bread that would bring life to the Aph/אף in Hebrew and can mean a PERSON or a Strawman type figure. The fictional flesh of man. The Bread is to strengthen this flesh in a way that it becomes overwhelmed with the Leavening Agent of the Bread, breaking it and reshaping it into a New Lump!! This Hebrew word also means to cause something to stand!! Raising up that which had fallen down!! So, by the sweat of persistence the fallen man is raised up to Stand!!! The elements of The Kingdom bring about the power to stand in the midst when all is weakened!! This is The Kingdom's Influence found in the Bara Altar!)

🌹 **Deuteronomy 8:3** And he humbled^H6031 you, and suffered you to hunger,^H7456 and fed^H398 you with^H854 **manna,**^H4478 which^H834 you knew^H3045 not,^H3808 neither^H3808 did your fathers^H1 know;^H3045 that^H4616 he might make you know^H3045 that^H3588 Adam^H120 does not^H3808 live^H2421 by^H5921 **bread**^H3899 only,^H905 but^H3588 by^H5921 every^H3605 **word** that proceeds out^H4161 of the mouth^H6310 of Yahweh^H3068 does Adam^H120 live.^H2421 (In the LXX we have words the Masoretic Texts had removed. The Greek words Artos and Logos are in the LXX, but missing in our translations today. The Artos is the Bread Yahshua gave His disciples in order for them to become Apostles of The Melkhitzedeq Order. This Artos is expanding Bread. The Bread of the Priesthood of Mashiach!! The Bread is The Kingdom and the Leaven of that Kingdom Bread is the Melkhitzedeq Priestly Order of Yahshua HaMashiach! So, man isn't to stop at the Artos/Lechem, but to move into the EXPANDING of this very Bread that rises!! The Bara Altar reveals the Expanding Order of The Kingdom and Priesthood!! The Priesthood that cast out demons, raises the dead, heals the sick, opens blind eyes, opens deaf ears, cleanses the lepers, multiplies the fish and bread, defies the law of Nature and reigns in Authority here on Earth!!

The word for 'Word' is removed from the Masoretic text in the verses above, but in the LXX, that word is what we see Yahshua bringing back when He spoke – the Rhema Word!! The Amar or Revelatory, Revolutionary Word that comes forth from the Mouth of YHWH Elohim!! This is our life source! This is the expanding agent of the Bread of the Kingdom of priests! This is what makes us Qadosh/Holy before The Throne!! Because it is connected to the Blood that speaks from The Altar!)

- **John 6:26** Yeshua[G2424] answered[G611] them[G846] and[G2532] said,[G2036] Truly,[G281] Truly,[G281] I say[G3004] unto you,[G5213] you seek[G2212] Me,[G3165] not[G3756] because[G3754] you saw[G1492] the miracles,[G4592] **but**[G235] because[G3754] you did eat[G5315] of[G1537] the[G3588] **loaves/bread,**[G740] and[G2532] were filled.[G5526]

(There are layers upon layers of The Bread of Heaven revelations! This word used here for loaves is Artos in Greek. There multiple dimensions of revelation and Dominion found in this leavening effect of The Bread! It's wasn't the miracles that captivate the true followers of Mashiach, but it was the Expanding Kingdom of Righteousness! This is also known as His Priesthood order that has no beginning and no ending, neither natural father nor genealogical limitations!!! It's an ever-expanding Power that comes forth and was hidden INSIDE the Bara Altar. The Bara Altar holds the revelation that John 1:1-3; Hebrews 1:1-3; Colossians, Revelation teaches us about the Son being the Agent of Creation/Bara! I am still speaking on the subject of The Word like Bread from this Altar of Creation.**)**

🔴 **John 6:27** Labor[G2038] not[G3361] for the[G3588] **meat**[G1035] which perishes,[G622] but[G235] for that meat[G1035] which endures[G3306] unto[G1519] everlasting[G166] life,[G2222] which[G3739] the[G3588] Son[G5207] of man[G444] shall give[G1325] unto you:[G5213] for[G1063] him[G5126] has Elohim[G2316] the[G3588] Father[G3962] sealed.[G4972] ...

🔴 **John 6:31** Our[G2257] fathers[G3962] did eat[G5315] manna[G3131] in[G1722] the[G3588] desert;[G2048] as[G2531] it is[G2076] written,[G1125] He gave[G1325] them[G846] **bread**[G740] from[G1537] **The Heavens**[G3772] to eat.[G5315] **6:32** Then[G3767] Yeshua[G2424] said[G2036] unto them,[G846] Truly,[G281] truly,[G281] I say[G3004] unto you,[G5213] Moses[G3475] gave[G1325] you[G5213] **not**[G3756] **that bread**[G740] from[G1537] **The Heavens**;[G3772] but[G235] my[G3450] Father[G3962] **gives**[G1325] you[G5213] the[G3588] true[G228] **bread**[G740] from[G1537] **The Heavens.**[G3772]

🔴 **John 6:33** For[G1063] the[G3588] **bread**[G740] of Elohim[G2316] is[G2076] **He** which comes down[G2597] from[G1537] **The Heavens,**[G3772] and[G2532] gives[G1325] life[G2222] unto the[G3588] world.[G2889] ...**6:35** And[G1161] Yeshua[G2424] said[G2036] unto them,[G846] **I**[G1473] **am**[G1510] **the**[G3588] **bread**[G740] **of life:**[G2222] he that comes[G2064] to[G4314] me[G3165] shall never[G3364] hunger;[G3983] and[G2532] he that believeth[G4100] on[G1519] me[G1691] shall never[G3364] [G4455] thirst.[G1372] (There is a counterfeit Artos and a Genuine Artos if I may. There is an antichrist and there is The Mashiach Himself!! There is a genuine Altar and a counterfeit one. There is the kingdom of Darkness and there is the Kingdom of Heaven!! Mashiach is saying He is that Artos/Lechem or Expanding Leavening Agent that starts the process of expansion!! From His Altar the Kingdom expands!! He is The Bread of Life!! Life comes forth from the Bara Altar!!! His Life in exchange for our Death penalty!! Substitution comes from the Bara Altar of Genesis 1:1!!)

🔴 **Luke 22:19** And^{G2532} he took^{G2983} **bread,**^{G740} and gave thanks,^{G2168} and **broke**^{G2806} it, and^{G2532} gave^{G1325} unto them,^{G846} saying,^{G3004} This^{G5124} **is**^{G2076} my^{G3450} **body**^{G4983} which is given^{G1325} for^{G5228} you:^{G5216} this^{G5124} do^{G4160} in^{G1519} **remembrance**^{G364} **of me.**^{G1699} (First off we have our word study for Bread – Artos. It is the Bread that rises. He holds this very Bread that speaks of the Risen Kingdom as well as prophetically His own body. He was demonstrating that He holds the power in His hands to brake and lift up, to lay His life down and raise it up again in His own Power!! The Greek word for Body here comes from the Hebrew word Pagar/פגר and means: a corpse, to be totally exhausted from labor and toil. First seen in Genesis 15:11 with Abram sitting or Ya'Sheiv – Enthroned IN the Melkhitzedeq Order. His presence repels fowls of the air that are after the dead corpse/Pagar, which is there to seal the Covenant. Yahshua is making a statement as if to say that His resurrection BREAKS the power of the exhaustion of animal sacrifice by the power of Substitution! Substitution found in this Kingdom Bread of expansion. Eating in a sense is a transfer of Divine revelation and information. Here, Yahshua was saying that when we eat of or internalize the truth of His Sealed Covenant by His death, burial, and resurrection that's when we partake of the Kingdom that has risen. His Flesh body was the Tabernacle to The Voice of His Father's Throne, who was manifested through the Son. The Son revealed the Power of The Altar Throne of The Heavens by the Bara Altar Throne that expanded His flesh body. The Kingdom was inside of Him and it burst forth created

pieces of this Kingdom Bread for all of us to eat. Now, when we eat from His Table, that Bread cannot be taken by any only rejected by the one who received it.)
Luke 22:20 Likewise G5615 also G2532 the G3588 cup G4221 after supper, G1172 saying, G3004 This G5124 cup *is* G4221 the G3588 new G2537 covenant G1242 in G1722 my G3450 blood, G129 which is applied G1632 for G5228 you. G5216

~The WORD (Altar) is like Water:

- 🌹 **John 15:3** Now G2235 you G5210 are G2075 clean G2513 through G1223 the G3588 Word G3056 which G3739 I have spoken G2980 unto you. G5213

- 🌹 **Ephesians 5:25** Husbands, G435 love G25 your G1438 wives, G1135 even as G2531 Messiah G5547 also G2532 loved G25 the G3588 Assembly, G1577 and G2532 gave G3860 himself G1438 for G5228 it; G846 **5:26** That G2443 he might sanctify G37 and cleanse G2511 it G846 with the G3588 washing G3067 of water G5204 by G1722 the word, G4487 **5:27** That G2443 he might present G3936 it G846 to himself G1438 a glorious G1741 Assembly, G1577 not G3361 having G2192 spot, G4695 or G2228 wrinkle, G4512 or G2228 any G5100 such thing; G5108 but G235 that G2443 it should be G5600 set apart G40 and G2532 without blemish. G299

What is so powerful here is water symbolizes the effect of The Word. The effect of the Word makes one Qadash or Sanctified/Holy!! The Greek word Sanctify comes from the Hebrew word Qadash, going from being a Harlot to being The Sabbath Bride!! The word Qadash is first found in Genesis 2:3 – He sanctified The Sabbath Day to make the man Qadash/Holy. Sabbath is more than a Day; it is the Garment of The Bride. Shabbat is the adorning Crown of Beauty of the other Six Days. Holiness and Shabbat cannot be separated. The religious mind will stop at the place of location of a day when The Creator expanded this idea of Holiness as a Garment called Shabbat!! You can gather on the

The Seven Altar Thrones of Genesis 1:1

weekly Shabbat and not be clothed with the beauty of The Sabbath.

I believe the days are all scattered along with their Calendars because The Body has lost the deeper meaning of the gathering INTO this Shabbat enclothement that comes out from the Altar of Bara as this verse ends with Bara. Elohim BLESSED the 7th Day and He Sanctified/Qadash Him, The Mashiach revelation. When we come to Mashiach we find the sanctification of true rest and this is the Sabbath Day we are to enter and without disregarding the weekly gathering, we express this finish work of Mashiach on this earthly plain of observance. No wonder from the priestly Epistle to The Hebrews (aka Book of Hebrews), those who have crossed over from death to life, or from sin to righteousness, or from animal blood to the Blood of Yahshua HaMashiach says this:

> **Hebrews 4:9** There **remains**G620 thereforeG686 **the restG4520** to theG3588 peopleG2992 of Elohim.G2316 **4:10** ForG1063 he that is enteredG1525 intoG1519 **hisG846 rest,G2663** heG846 alsoG2532 has **ceasedG2664 fromG575 his ownG848 works,G2041** asG5618 ElohimG2316 did fromG575 his.G2398 **4:11** Let us laborG4704 thereforeG3767 to enterG1525 intoG1519 thatG1565 **rest,G2663** unlessG3363 any manG5100 fallG4098 afterG1722 theG3588 sameG846 exampleG5262 of unbelief.G543

(The Greek word for REST is sabbatismos from the Hebrew word Shabbat which when we really grasp this concept its outside religious arguments. Shabbat speaks of the abiding Heavenly Kingdom. Yahshua HaMashiach brought that rest to those sick, possessed, leprous, blind, deaf, lame, dead, rejected, forgotten, prostituted out, and placed upon them The Shabbat or Tangible substance of The Kingdom!!

The early Christians or Christeins called this Heaven on Earth or The Kingdom of Heaven, the very thing Mashiach Yahshua was preaching and demonstrating!! We are to DEMONSTRATE Shabbat every day of the week and not forget to assemble on the weekly Shabbat which is only a small reflection of The Substance known as The Rest of Yahshua HaMashiach!! The Bara Altar reveals this revelation that needs to be brought back as The Tangible Day that touches all seven days of the week!

The Melkhitzedeq Order in Yahshua HaMashiach already showed us this truth!! It was the Ruach of This Kingdom that raised Him from the dead and it is this same Ruach that lives in us today!!! The washing of the Word is the removal of the mud off the eyes of His Kingdom people!! The Bara Altar reveals the Water of the Word that brings the revelation of this truth of His Shabbat. Then the scripture continues on with HIS REST, it's from the word Me'noach which comes from Nu'ach or Noach!!

The generation of Noach is that generation that walks in this revelation. It is this revelation that will unite the Body of Mashiach and crush the religious walls of separation bringing unity once again just before the great appearing of our Melkhitzedeq or our Righteous King Yahshua HaMashiach!! The washing of the Water of the Word is that Rhema or Amar Word that reveals the Order of Melkhitzedeq!! The Word that washes is from the Bara Altar which clothes our minds with the truth of The Priesthood and Kingdom!!)

~The WORD (Altar) is like an Anchor:

- **Hebrews 6:18** That^{G2443} by^{G1223} two^{G1417} unchanging^{G276} things,^{G4229} in^{G1722} which^{G3739} it was impossible^{G102} for Eloah^{G2316} to lie,^{G5574} we might have^{G2192} a strong^{G2478} consolation,^{G3874} who have fled for refuge^{G2703} to lay hold upon^{G2902} **the hope**^{G1680} set before^{G4295} us: **6:19** Which^{G3739} hope we have^{G2192} as^{G5613} an **anchor**^{G45} **of the**^{G3588} **soul,**^{G5590} both^{G5037} sure^{G804} and^{G2532} steadfast,^{G949} and^{G2532} which enters^{G1525} into^{G1519} that within^{G2082} **the**^{G3588} **veil;**^{G2665} **6:20** Whether^{G3699} the forerunner^{G4274} is for^{G5228} us^{G2257} entered,^{G1525} Yeshua,^{G2424} made^{G1096} an High-Priest^{G749} forever^{G1519} ^{G165}

after^{G2596} the^{G3588} order^{G5010} of <u>Melchizedek</u>.^{G3198}

(From the Bara Altar of Creation, we have the revelation of The Word as our Anchor. We have an Anchor of Hope. Mashiach is our Hope, the Hope of the Higher Calling. The calling from the highest Altar where our very souls are recreated after the DNA image of YHWH Elohim. It becomes the place of enthronement!

This word for anchor is related to a Hebrew word found in the coupling of the Tabernacle Curtains and Veils. The Tabernacle revelation conceals the revelation of the Hope that holds us together. We are the carriers of this revelation now!! We can unveil the Hope to a hopeless generation! We can reveal the Anchor that Holds us all together even when the storms come. The Bara Altar of Creation reveals the Hope of all Creation and that Hope as the writer of Hebrews reveals is found in the Melkhitzedeq Order! The soul that has set its own sail and has rejected The Word that has come is one that will drown.

The Word now comes walking upon The Waters with Hope, to Anchor us back to Himself!! The Hebrew word for the Soul that is anchored is Nefesh. The numerical value of Nefesh is the same for a word found in Acts 2 with the **CLOVEN tongues of Fire –** שֶׁפַע – She'sagh. Now at Mount Sinai the nation of Israel heard 'The' Voice that sat upon the top of this mountain. Then, they 'SAW' voices/Qolot descending the mountain. In Acts 2 the Voice was heard and described as a rushing mighty wind and tongues of fire sat upon each of them. That means the writer is saying that The Voice of Heaven's Altar was Heard and they lived. Then they SAW Tongues of Fire/Voices sitting upon each that were there. Each of these in the upper room BECAME the voice of the Bara Altar, the Altar of creative power! From here the biggest miraculous things would be seen through men.

This word cloven means to cleave, to split. Man had his surgery done by the finger of Elohim and his Soul and Spirit were now split apart, making room for the Recreation infusion of the Ruach HaQodesh. And for this creative power of the Bara Altar to be in full operation through willing voices of the Altar of Heaven!)

🔸 **1Peter 1:3** Blessed[G2128] the[G3588] Elohim[G2316] and[G2532] Father[G3962] of our[G2257] Master[G2962] Yeshua[G2424] Messiah,[G5547] which according[G2596] to his[G848] abundant[G4183] mercy[G1656] has begotten us again[G313 G2248] unto[G1519] a living[G2198] hope[G1680] by[G1223] the resurrection[G386] of Yeshua[G2424] The Messiah[G5547] from[G1537] the dead,[G3498] **1:4** To[G1519] an inheritance[G2817] incorruptible,[G862] and[G2532] undefiled,[G283] and[G2532] that fades not away,[G263] reserved[G5083] **in**[G1722] **heaven**[G3772] for[G1519] you,[G2248] **1:5** Who are kept[G5432] by[G1722] the power[G1411] of Elohim[G2316] through[G1223] faith[G4102] unto[G1519] Salvation[G4991] ready[G2092] to be revealed[G601] in[G1722] the last[G2078] appointed time.[G2540]

~The WORD (Altar) is like a Seed: (The Bara Altar reveals the Seed of The Word. The origin of all substance and Creation. One of the Greatest parables ever spoken by Yahshua was that of the Word as a Seed. It germinates, produces the blueprint of life, holding the very potential to give Eternal life! The Bara Altar revealed the revelation of the Seed which is the beginnings of all things. Bara also means to split open the Head of Grain!! It contains the depths of Harvest seasons. Each Altar is opened up by Bara in their season on Earth.

The Seed Parable that The Altar of Creation conceals is all about The Kingdom. The Altar of Bara reveals all the aspects of this very Kingdom through the seven days of Creation. The Altar of Bara holds the Seed of all creative power!! Even as Scripture speaks of the seed of Abraham which was the seed of Promise through Covenant. The Seed of Abraham is the revelation of Covenant. So, the Scripture says:

- **Galatians 3:16** Now^{G1161} to Abraham^{G11} and^{G2532} his^{G846} seed^{G4690} were the^{G3588} promises^{G1860} made.^{G4483} He says^{G3004} not,^{G3756} And^{G2532} to seeds,^{G4690} as^{G5613} of^{G1909} many;^{G4183} but^{G235} as^{G5613} of^{G1909} one,^{G1520} And^{G2532} to your^{G4675} seed^{G4690} which^{G3739} is^{G2076} Messiah.^{G5547}

- **Galatian 3:29** And^{G1161} if^{G1487} you^{G5210} be Messiah's,^{G5547} then^{G686} are^{G2075} you Abraham's^{G11} seed^{G4690} and^{G2532} heirs^{G2818} according^{G2596} to the promise.^{G1860}

- **Hebrews 2:16** For^{G1063} truly^{G1222} he did not put on^{G1949} ^{G3756} garments of angels;^{G32} but^{G235} he put on^{G1949} the seed^{G4690} of Abraham.^{G11}

- **1Peter 1:23** Being born again,^{G313} not^{G3756} of^{G1537} corruptible^{G5349} seed^{G4701} but^{G235} of incorruptible,^{G862} by^{G1223} the Word^{G3056} of Elohim,^{G2316} which lives^{G2198} and^{G2532} remains^{G3306} forever.^{G1519 G165}

- **Revelation 12:17** And^{G2532} the^{G3588} dragon^{G1404} was angry^{G3710} with^{G1909} the^{G3588} woman,^{G1135} and^{G2532} went^{G565} to make^{G4160} war^{G4171} with^{G3326} the^{G3588} remnant^{G3062} of her^{G848} seed^{G4690} which keep^{G5083} the^{G3588} commandments^{G1785} of Elohim,^{G2316} **and**^{G2532} have^{G2192} the^{G3588} testimony^{G3141} of Yeshua^{G2424} Messiah.^{G5547}

The Seed holds the Testimony. The Testimony is not ours but Yahshua HaMashiach's Testimony. What is that Testimony? It is that The Bara Altar revealed the Redemptive plan and His Kingdom now bursting forth from within all who come to This Altar revelation. His Testimony is that He finished what Abba sent Him to do. He is the Seed of that Bara Altar!!

So, the Bara Altar is like Meat to strengthen the weak and mature the immature. The Bara Altar is Like a smashing Hammer that smashes all limitations of generational restrictions and limitations. The Bara Altar is like a Mirror which reveals who we truly are and can be in The Word who is the Altar of Creation. The Bara Altar is like Bread we can eat that will leaven our lives with its Kingdom influence. This isn't just any bread but the Kingdom Bread that holds new life and expands that influence into every area of my life. The Bara Altar is like Water we are cleansed by and renewed by.

Our promise of renewal was embedded inside the second word of all Scripture which is the second Altar of Genesis 1:1 – The Bara Altar of Creative Power. The Bara Altar is like a Sword that discerns the thoughts of the heart, an Anchor of Hope for the Hopeless, and like the very Seed of Eternal life springing up out of my Soul regenerating my being and placing my life in the promise before the world ever was!! I have come to the Altar of Bara where all these things are mine, the things Created from The Altar of Bara before there was even a Heaven and an Earth:

Repentance, Restoration, Redemption, Reconciliation and Salvation to name a few:

- **Repentance** –

Repentance IS NOT a New Testament thing. In fact, it is seen clearly in Genesis 1-3 where all Doctrinal subjects originate from. Going even further, Repentance is not even something you SAY it is something that is DONE. Let's look at this first concept that was inside the second Altar of Genesis 1, The Bara Altar:

Repentance is the actual pre-requisite to a few things in sequential order –

To True Revival, then the next thing in line would be The Regathering of The People and then the actual Return to The Land of Inheritance which is the place where New Jerusalem will descend upon.

There is the promise of Return given to the first Adam – From DUST you are and to DUST you shall RETURN/REPENTANCE.

Repentance in Hebrew:

One word is Nacham which means to exile with sorrow. This is not the Repentance of our subject matter that was embedded in

The Seven Altar Thrones of Genesis 1:1

The Altar of Bara. The Hebrew word we are engaging in that is a direct threat to the Kingdom of Darkness and sin is:

שׁוּב – Shoov. The actual decision to RETURN to the place we first came from. Inside the Altar of Bara is the revelation of returning back to the place we first came from.

If we stick with the English language to do a word study on Repentance, we can miss the original intent of the concept from which it first came. Hebrew is verb oriented. Where is Repentance first seen? Back in Genesis 3 where Repentance, Restoration, Reconciliation, Substitution, Justification, Acceptance and Salvation are all first established –

- **Genesis 3:19** In the sweat[H2188] of your face[H639] you will eat[H398] bread,[H3899] until[H5704] you return[H7725] unto[H413] the ground;[H127] for[H3588] from[H4480] it were you received:[H3947] for[H3588] dust[H6083] thou[H859] are, and unto[H413] dust[H6083] you will return.[H7725] (Repentance is first seen right here. The concept and intent are to bring us back to Adamah, the place where I will resemble YHWH. Adamah is also pronounced A'domeh/אֲדוֹמֶה/אֲדָמָה = I will Resemble; I will silence. The Accuser of the brethren is silenced BECAUSE of this Altar revelation found in Adamah/Adomeh. Yes, you heard me correctly, the revelation of this Altar of Creative Power is in Yahshua and was also demonstrated. There were never miracles done like the level demonstrated by Yahshua until He arrived on the scene.)

- **Genesis 3:20** And Adam[H121] called[H7121] his wife's[H802] name[H8034] Chavah/Eve;[H2332] because[H3588] she[H1931] was[H1961] the mother[H517] of all[H3605] lives.[H2416] (Did you hear that? Adam now clothes his wife in a Tent Garment named Chavah or Eve, and now she is the hidden place of The Resemblance, or the A'domeh!! The Alef prefix speaks of first-person action future tense, I WILL… Alef also means Power, Strength, ability to bring forth a thing or a people. Speaks of the power to lead. The inference here is attached to The Altar of power – Elohim, the third Altar Word of Genesis 1:1 which we will get into next.

Eve or Chavah means a Tent; to declare something without actual speech – to show or reveal by impression or pressing forward; to experience deeply. Adam SPEAKS her name which becomes her Garment. Adams last act as the sovereign, on Earth before his dethronement, was over his wife Ishah. He covered her, he blessed her, he stood for the generations to come as he now realized he had fallen from The Power of being The Altar on Earth, The Dominion and Authority, to the one in need of Approaching the Altar himself. Adam, the once Tiller of the ground, now naked and stripped of Dominion and Authority, would now be the man of sweat, blood and tears.)

Genesis 3:21 Unto Adam[H121] also and to his wife[H802] did Yahweh[H3068] Elohim[H430] make[H6213] **coats**[H3801] **of skins,**[H5785] and **clothed**[H3847] them. ("By the sweat of your brow you shall eat bread until you return to the ground that you were received from…" in Hebrew: בְּזֵעַת אַפֶּיךָ תֹּאכַל לֶחֶם עַד שׁוּבְךָ אֶל־הָאֲדָמָה כִּי־מִמֶּנָּה לֻקָּחְתָּ – "Through the sweat/tremble (Daniel 6:26&5:19) in worship of your brow/breathing in and exhaling Adam and Eve would experience the worship of YHWH Elohim through the function in flesh bodies you shall eat bread UNTIL/as a witness to the RETURNING/Repentance to the Adamah/A'domeh – Resemblance that from HIM you were once received by…"

We go from Adam being given an instruction – To Adam covering the Power of Resemblance that would now take place inside the womb of Eve. HaDomeh/הַדּוֹמָה. We go from the Priestly covering of a fallen state now called the garments of shame, to walking in the power of Royal

Priesthood Ambassadorship, where there is no more shame. To offer up animal blood is proof that man is covered in shame, trying to RETURN to his once Royal position. In Yahshua HaMashiach we have this Dominion restored back and the Power of The New Covenant, containing the depths of truth. This has gotten the attention of Abba, who sent His Word that would not return void.

We transition from the source of Creative Power itself to the Altar King that manifests the very power of it**, The Altar of Powers - Elohim!)**

Chapter Four

Third Altar:
The Altar of Powers, Elohim

אלהים

The Altar Throne, Elohim – **אלהים הכסא מזבח**

We now come to the third Altar of Genesis 1:1, the activated Altar for revealing the unseen things –**Elohim HaKese Miz'be'ach, The Altar Throne of Powers**. This is the third Altar in Sequence when you read this from the Hebrew text. (Hebrew is read from right to left) Isn't it amazing the Hebrew word for The Throne and Elohim have the same numerical equivalency?

~ **הכסא** = 86; **אלהים** = 86.
(Refer to Alef Bet Numerical and Ordinal value chart)

In John 14:6 Yahshua makes claim that He is: The Way, The Truth and The Life. All of these are a study of their own. I want to address a n insight to The Way –

~ The Way in Hebrew is: **הדרך** – HaDerekh. There is only one way back to The Tree of Life and that is through The Power of The Altar Throne known as The Word. Our Altar, Elohim HaKese Miz'be'ach has the numerical value of this phrase HaDerekh, The

Way. There is only One Way and that is through The Altar Throne!

I find it very interesting this Third Altar Throne Elohim is reflected in the Temple NOT made from the hands of men, but created out of the Resemblance of The Son, who is the Word made flesh, the Chief Corner Stone of The Living Tabernacle! Each of the Seven Words of Genesis 1:1 stand as Altar Thrones in their own dimension. The Altar Throne of Beginnings is The Altar of Origins and Creation of all that is. We begin to move into the Altar Throne of Powers.

Elohim in Hebrew means Powers, the plural form of God/El. It is translated as God, Angels, Judges at times, but means Powers. It is a Plural Hebrew concept used throughout Scripture some 2,605 times.

The Elohim Altar is that of Demonstration and Action. This Altar Throne is the Cause of all things. When John the Baptist was preaching REPENTANCE and prepared the Way in the wilderness, he was actually activating, by way of invitation, the revealing of an Altar greater than the Levitical Altar. He was making way for the Greater Altar of those of the past! Greater than any altar of the prophets and patriarchs of old! John, the rightful High Priest after the Order of Aaron was ushering in the Altar of Power and Demonstration! John would be the last voice after the order of a Levitical Priesthood who was 'crying' in the wilderness, ushering in The Voice of the loftiest Altar on Earth. The crying voice finds its rest in The Walking Voice, The Altar Throne of The Word made Flesh. The Voice that once spoke from Sinai now came walking toward the last School Master High Priest of Aarons bloodline, Yochanan HaMatbil – John The Baptist.

Just as the Priesthood prepared animal sacrifices and temporary reprieve for the people of Israel, so John as High Priest after Aaron, the 8th Order according to 1 Chronicles 24, by authority offered up the people to Elohim through the Ramp of Repentance I call the Levitical Priesthood. The Altar of Elohim is what metamorphosizes all that come close to this footstool!

The ramp was given so that the SHAME of the Priesthood would not be seen. Having said that, even the priestly path to the Altar had to experience a demonstrative shifting to one much greater! John represented the voice to the Ramp of Repentance where the shame is present. John was now about to be Overshadowed by The Mercy of The Altar of Power!! The Mercy Seat of The Ark promised the coming of the Greater Ark!

Forgiveness, Restoration, Acceptance, Substitution, Regeneration, Justification and Salvation are all present gifts at this Altar Throne of Powers, can I say the Altar of Elohim our Third Altar Word of Genesis 1:1?

Repentance is the Father of Forgiveness, the Father of Acceptance, the Father Justification, Sanctification, Restoration, Reconciliation, and Revival! Repentance or Teshuvah in Hebrew ultimately leads us back to the Adomeh/Adamah – 'I will Resemble', to The Resemblance which is found only at one place, The Adamah Altar of Royalty! It is written that Elohim/Powers – The Third Altar of Genesis 1:1, was INSIDE Yahshua who is The Word, The Son, The Redeemer, The King, The High Priest after the Order of Melkhitzedeq, that RECONCILED The Whole world unto Himself!! Yahshua was the Garment for The Altar Throne of Powers. This Altar was covered in the flesh of man. This Altar Throne holds the secret to The Power of His Resurrection as Shaul/Paul said -

- **2Corinthians 5:17** Therefore[G5620] if any man[G1536] be in[G1722] Messiah,[G5547] he is a new[G2537] creature:[G2937] (To be IN Mashiach is to be in the finished work of His Altar. Since Elohim was INSIDE Yahshua then we can say that the Altar of Elohim/Powers, was INSIDE the Adamah Altar called Yahshua. The Heavens Powers was inside of The Son reconciling us unto Himself! He who sits upon this Throne wants us to ascend through Yahshua, The Door to The Altar Throne of Abba our Father and Source of Life!

The Seven Altar Thrones of Genesis 1:1

Remember, Yahshua was Born (Flesh) and Mashiach (Spirit) has always been. The flesh of Yahshua was Heavens gift to mankind, especially Israel!! To be in Mashiach is to be a part of The Altar Throne of Power because Abba was in The Son reconciling all things to Himself.) old things^{G744} are passed away^{G3928} behold^{G2400} all things^{G3956} are become^{G1096} new.^{G2537}

🌹 **2Corinthians 5:18** And^{G1161} all things^{G3956} are of^{G1537} ==Elohim,^{G2316} who hath reconciled^{G2644} us^{G2248} to himself^{G1438} by^{G1223} Yeshua^{G2424} The Messiah,^{G5547}== (Elohim/God means The Elohim Altar of Genesis 1:1. Yahshua was the Garment to This Altar of Reconciliation. He was the Skin Garment that concealed this ultimate Power! The Altar of Powers brings the power of reconciliation, by way of the Power of Repentance. Repentance is the voice that Witnesses that sound in the Heavens. The writer of Luke 15:10 says it invokes rejoicing in the heavenlies over one sinner who repents! That one sinner becomes a song that Heaven has never heard before. We enter through the Door which is Yahshua and by Mashiach, The Finished result of the mission.) and^{G2532} has given^{G1325} to us^{G2254} the^{G3588} ministry^{G1248} of ==reconciliation;^{G2643}==

We all have the same Altar ministry called Reconciliation. Reconciliation begins when Repentance takes place. Substitution initiates Justification and Acceptance. Reconciliation brings Restoration and Deliverance. Reconciliation brings Acceptance and Salvation. The ministry of Reconciliation has been misconstrued by religion. We thought it meant becoming a part of Christianity, Judaism or some Hebrew Roots when all along it was meant to connect us back to the Adomeh, the Resemblance of Elohim YHWH, who through the Son Yahshua is the Carrier of this Altar of Powers/Elohim. (2 Corinthians 5:19)

Remember, Yahshua is The Flesh Cover that gives **mobility**

to the Altar of Powers, while Mashiach is The Power Elohim moves **by**. As a matter of fact, the Scripture says in the priestly book to the Hebrews, Chapter 1:1-3, says Yahshua is the Son of Elohim, the extension of the Altar of Powers - All Powerful One, and Elohim is the express IMAGE or Resemblance of His Person.

The Greek word *hupostasis* used here for **person** comes from the Hebrew word משׂא — Ma'sa, which means: utterance, singing; also related to the idea of a Banner. So, Yahshua is the very Image or Resemblance on Earth of Elohim's Utterance, Song and Banner. The laws of Flags/Banners speak of Territory and Jurisdiction. The Word made Flesh executed this Jurisdiction of the Altar of Powers here on The Earth!! **Ma'sa** in Hebrew read the other way is **Asham** which means Guilt. The Son carried our Guilt and Shame because He was that very Altar of Power our Melkhitzedeq High Priest!

We have heard that God/Elohim is Immutable, He changes Not; God/Elohim is Omnipotent, He is All Powerful and Matchless; God/Elohim is Omniscient, He is All Knowing; God/Elohim is Omnipresent, He is everywhere at the same time. As we continue this revelation to this teaching, Elohim is Powers, not God perse. This concept is more of a Plurality meaning Powers! Connecting to this third Altar revelation lets insert the revelation as such:

1. The Altar Throne of Powers is **Immutable**, it never changes. The Altar demands the same process for all and shows no respect of persons. This Altar demands the same protocol for all and will give to all the same result. Repentance has not and will not change because religion changes with the times, the Word is unchanging. We must render our heart and soul, not our garments, along with all the different ideals fading away including the biases we might have.

2. The Altar Throne of Powers is all powerful - **Omnipotent**. This Altar holds Creation together and therefore has the Authority to recreate any and all who come to the mouth of its matchless Power. This is why Elohim in Hebrew means Powers, which is plural because there are many revelations of its power! This third Altar holds the key to your breakthrough and New season! This Altar of Power contains the Authority to break – Sin, Sickness, Dis-ease, demonic attack, poverty, lack, rejection, satanic holds, demonic influence, strife, other voices, religious manipulation, pride, arrogance, altars of evil, death, hell and the grave.

   The Altar of Powers is All Powerful and reveals the secret to The Priesthood of Yahshua HaMashiach which carries Dominion to lay to rest the deception of any Levitical Hierchy insurrection that is on the rise. The Altar of Powers destroys all manner of disease or plagues, including this flu virus rampant in 2020, regardless how small or big it may be. The Altar of Power can break all generational Curses and Iniquity squatting in the DNA line of your family!

3. The Altar Throne of Genesis 1:1 is All Knowing - **Omniscient**. We cannot hide anything from this Altar Throne of Powers, He knows all things. This Altar was In Yahshua HaMashiach and knew the lives of all He came acrossed – **Psalm 139:2** You know when I sit and when I rise; you perceive my **thoughts** from afar. **Luke 11:17 Yeshua** knew their **thoughts** and said to them: "Any kingdom divided against itself will be ruined, and a house divided against itself will fall. **Matthew 12:25 Yeshua** knew their **thoughts** and said to them, "Every kingdom divided against itself will be ruined, and every city or household divided against itself will not stand. **John 2:24** But Yeshua did not

commit himself unto them, because he knew all, **2:25** And needed not that any should testify of man: for he knew what was **in** man. **4:28** The woman then left her waterpot, and went her way into the city, and said to the men, **4:29** Come, see a man, which told me all things that ever I did: is not this <u>the Messiah</u>?

Notice the language she uses regarding The Messiah/HaMashiach. This was her Altar encounter! The Altar of Powers spoke through The Adamah Altar of Redemption. Many stood **before** Yahshua but never came **through** Him to Mashiach for their Reconciliation. Many have **come** to Yahshua/Jesus but haven't gone **through** Him/The Door to Mashiach The Altar! Yahshua is the Lamb that still gives Access to The Altar. He is The Anointed One who breaks shackles and bondages!! The Altar of Powers is Omnipresent/All knowing!!

4. The Altar Throne of Powers is **Omnipresent**, He is Everywhere at the same time. You can be on your dying breath and cry out to Abba and the Altar of Powers is right there to hear your cry and cause your cry to turn into a shout of praise with Him! There is no place that Elohim is not! Put this revelation of The Altar right where you see God/Elohim in your Bibles! The Altar Throne of Powers awaits you and I wherever we might be. There are no limitations to the Altar of Powers except the rejection of Him - The Altar King!)

- **2Corinthians 5:19** To wit,^{G5613} that^{G3754} <mark>Elohim^{G2316}</mark> was^{G2258} in^{G1722} <mark>Messiah,^{G5547}</mark> <mark>reconciling^{G2644}</mark> the world^{G2889} unto himself,^{G1438} not^{G3361} placing^{G3049} their^{G846} trespasses^{G3900} onto them;^{G846} and^{G2532} has committed^{G5087} unto^{G1722} us^{G2254} the^{G3588} word^{G3056} of <mark>reconciliation.^{G2643}</mark> (Reconciliation in Greek thought means to place one back in a favored position, WOW!

The Altar of Powers holds the key to bringing the Grace, Favor of Abba back upon your life. What is Grace/Favor? If I asked you to draw me a picture of Grace, what would that look like? I can describe it right now to you.

Grace/Favor – Chen/חן in Hebrew thought, where our Scriptures come from, is when generations continually dwell together in the inner chambers of the **Tent or House**. It is the place where we develop as friends and family. This is Grace, where one is strengthened by the other to Continue on.

Grace is given to those who have Repented/Returned to The Covenant ways of Elohim, our Altar Throne of Powers. Actually, the Hebrew word Chen numerically is 58. This is the number that connects us to Mashiach or the Altar of Throne of Powers, who was INSIDE Yahshua HaMashiach reconciling the world unto Himself.

The Land Mark of The Name

When we look at the Hebrew letter Shin it is made up of four yoods and 3 vavs – ייי ווו = ש. The three Vavs and four yoods give us the value 58. Now, when we add 58 to the Hebrew Letter Shin, we have a total of 300 in value. Giving us the numerical total of: 358, the same for Mashiach/משיח – Messiah/aka Christ. The Altar of Throne gives us the revelation of oneness in Mashiach!!!

358 is also the value pf Nachash or Serpent in Hebrew which means divination. The Altar of Power breaks the Divination spell off the Repentant man or woman comes to The Altar. Look up all the verses on repentance, this is astonishing when we keep this in mind. All four of these ideas pertaining to God/Elohim, who is our third Altar of Genesis 1:1, Immutability, Omnipotence, Omniscience and Omnipresence now take on a much deeper revelation when it comes to the sacrifice of Mashiach Yahshua. The

Altar of Powers reveals that which was concealed in The Begininning of our Scriptures!

- **2Corinthians 5:20** Now then^{G3767} we are ambassadors^{G4243} for^{G5228} Messiah,^{G5547} as though^{G5613} Elohim^{G2316} did call you close^{G3870} by^{G1223} us:^{G2257} we pray^{G1189} in Messiah's stead,^{G5228} ^{G5547} be you reconciled^{G2644} to Elohim.^{G2316}

- **2Corinthians 5:21** For^{G1063} he has appointed^{G4160} him to put on sin^{G266} for^{G5228} us,^{G2257} who knew^{G1097} no^{G3361} sin;^{G266} that^{G2443} we^{G2249} might be made^{G1096} the righteousness^{G1343} of Eloah^{G2316} in^{G1722} him.^{G846}

I mentioned earlier how the Altar Throne of Powers holds the secrets to the Power of Resurrection which Paul/Shaul expresses in these words:

- **Philippians 3:7** But what things were gain to me, those I counted loss for Messiah. (All things are counted as a loss when we measure them up to the Altar Throne who is inside Mashiach Yahshua, The Door of access.) **3:8** Yes doubtless, and I count all things loss for the excellency of the knowledge of Messiah Yeshua my Master: for whom I have suffered the loss of all things, and do count them dung, that I may win Messiah, (Paul was expressing his desire to be intimate with his final step into Glory, the revelation of the Altar of Powers in Resurrection! This life does not compare to the Power of resurrection from the dead! The Altar of Powers makes this an unchanging reality and truth!)

- **3:9** And be found in him, not having mine own righteousness, which is of the law, (Not having my own righteousness which is of The Law, what Law? All the Old Testament? NO! The binding Law between the Husband and the Bride in marriage that only Death can undo. As well as the Animal sacrificial system instituted is part of the EVIDENCE to the unfaithfulness that has occurred between Israel and Elohim. Mashiach The Altar King, Yahshua HaMashiach, destroys the death penalty position that is witness against His Bride! The Altar of Elohim/Powers has an answer to any attack from the enemy!) but that which is through the faith **of** Messiah, the righteousness which is of God by faith: (Emunah/Faith of Mashiach is The Emunah and Amein of Heavens Courts on our behalf. This brings us to the enclothement of Righteousness, the Garment of Beauty in Yahshua HaMashiach, who, by His Blood has purchased for us. Insert the word Altar of Powers for God and read it that way, He is the Power of Reconciliation standing before us!!)

- **3:10** That I may know him intimately, and the explosive power of his resurrection, and the fellowship of his sufferings, being made conformable unto his death; **3:11** If by any means I might attain to the resurrection of the dead. (The End Goal of the A'domeh, the returning to the Ground as promised back in Genesis 3:19, is seen in Mashiach as the Ambassador of This Altar Throne of Powers! Adomeh, once again, means: to be like or resemble. He holds the Authority to be like and resemble any of the seven Altar Thrones of Genesis 1:1. He is our Altar King.)

The Ordained Place

The Altar of Powers prepares us to meet the author and finisher of our Faith! The Altar of Powers contains the Power to Heal every area of Creation that has been TOUCHED. The Hebrew word for Altar is seen a total of 402 times in Scripture. 350 times as Altar, in the singular. The grammatical Hebrew, every noun is assigned a gender, masculine or feminine. The Hebrew word for Altar, Miz'be'ach, is in the feminine. This would be addressed to Adams wife Eve, the first mother of man. 350 is the numerical value for a place we first came from. It was a place where the

Creator YHWH Elohim blew a piece of Himself INTO the nostrils of Adam. 350 is Aphar/עפר – The DUST of The Adamah, where man was formed from. What is revealed when the DUST is pulled out of the ADAMAH?

- אדמה – אלף דלת מם הי – These remaining letters give us a word and a number – Mit'palel & 590. When Aphar/350 is pulled OUT OF the 590 we have 240 that remains. 240 gives us another revelation connected to the redemptive work of Yahshua HaMashiach as our Kohein HaGadol Melkhitzedeq –

- 240 = לְעֵצִים – La'eitzim which means: To the Tree/Wood.

There is an Altar believed to be that Adam was first created from and it is from this place the Foundation Stone of all Creation would bring Tikkun or Repair to the breach of Genesis 1. This is the place known where the souls of men, after the fall, continued to incarnate from cell to cell, from DNA to DNA and from Generation to Generation. This idea is called: **גלגלים הנשמות** – **Gilgulim HaNeshamot** – **The Incarnation of Souls**. I don't agree with the English idea or western view of this idea, but the Hebrew concept is very powerful. We don't reincarnate as another man or woman or some animal or rock. It is appointed ONCE for man to die and after this the judgement Scripture says (Hebrews 9:27).

We can read about things happening at a place called Gilgal, the same family word. The word Gilgulim means to reveal cycles or rotations from inner things!! There is another place where the full power of The Altar of Powers was demonstrated and that is the place called Golgolet/**גלגלת** – Golgotha, the crucifixion site of The Word made flesh – Yahshua HaMashiach, who is the Loftiest Altar on Earth! Having said this, every man MUST have this truth within his own head. When the mind is connected to the reality of this truth, that is when The Altar of Mashiach has manifested to those who have received Him. Golgotha is the word for a man's Head or Tabernacle of his mind. The Tabernacle of your mind must have the Death, Burial and Resurrection Truth seated there.

It was from Golgotha the cry of Restoration was proclaimed! It was from here the Power of The Altar King Yahshua HaMashiach crushed the hold that Death claimed to man's soul! It was from this place; The Heavens Decreed our Atonement as The Kingdom Power shattered the Bread of Heavens Body, the Passover Lamb who slain BEFORE the foundation of the World. Therefore, This Bread was distributed to all who make Teshuvah/Repentance. Remember this statement: The Adamah Altar can Resemble ANY of the Seven Altar Thrones of Genesis 1:1 because of a few facts:

- HaAdamah can be pronounced as: HaAdomeh meaning: The Resemblance and or The Likeness. The Son is the Image and Likeness of all The Altar Thrones. HaAdomeh or I will Resemble the Likeness and Image of... You fill in the blank here when it comes to the seven Altars of Genesis 1:1.

Just as Yahshua BROKE the Bread, which He said take eat (Connection to Genesis 3:19 where Adam was to: Tokhal Lechem – Eat Bread...) for this is My Body broken for you. The shattered Lamb is now given to all who come from the north south east and west!! The broken Kingdom Bread, not the broken Kingdom, contains the Leaven of The Heavens Power and Altar Authority. When you eat Him, you eat these Altar revelations and the broken Bread are the revelations of His Altar Dominion!

Conclusion:

Let's look at a few places where the Altar of Powers was demonstrated –

- **Luke 7:21** And^{G1161} in^{G1722} that same^{G846} hour^{G5610} he healed^{G2323} many^{G4183} with^{G575} infirmities^{G3554} and^{G2532} plagues,^{G3148} and^{G2532} of evil^{G4190} spirits;^{G4151} and^{G2532} unto many^{G4183} blind^{G5185} he gave^{G5483} sight.^{G991} **7:22** Then^{G2532}

Yeshua^{G2424} answering^{G611} said^{G2036} unto them,^{G846} Go your way,^{G4198} and tell^{G518} John^{G2491} what things^{G3739} you have seen^{G1492} and^{G2532} heard;^{G191} how that^{G3754} the blind^{G5185} see,^{G308} the lame^{G5560} walk,^{G4043} the lepers^{G3015} are cleansed,^{G2511} the deaf^{G2974} hear,^{G191} the dead^{G3498} are raised,^{G1453} to the poor^{G4434} the Kingdom Good News is preached.^{G2097}

🟣 **John 2:7** Yeshua^{G2424} saith^{G3004} unto them,^{G846} Fill^{G1072} the^{G3588} **waterpots**^{G5201} with water.^{G5204} (The Waterpots here find their origin in a Hebrew word – כד – Kad. Meaning, some type of an earthen vessel. I found this prophetic that the numerical value of this Hebrew word is 24. This is how many priestly courses were after Aaron's order – Chronicles 24. So, Yahshua was saying many things regarding this Bread and one of those was that the 24 priestly courses gave out their wine and have now been emptied out the school master system old wine. The High Priest of Israel, King Yahshua our Melchizedek, has come to fill up the earthen vessels with the revelation of who He is, so one day that which is drawn out of them will only be the New Wine of His Kingdom Reign.) And^{G2532} they filled^{G1072} them^{G846} up to^{G2193} the brim.^{G507} **2:8** And^{G2532} he saith^{G3004} unto them,^{G846} Draw out^{G501} now,^{G3568} and^{G2532} bring^{G5342} unto the^{G3588} governor of the feast.^{G755} And^{G2532} they carried^{G5342} it. **2:9** ^(G1161) When^{G5613} the^{G3588} ruler of the feast^{G755} had tasted^{G1089} the^{G3588} water^{G5204} that became^{G1096} wine,^{G3631} and^{G2532} knew^{G1492} not^{G3756} which^{G4159} it was^{G2076} but^{G1161} the^{G3588} servants^{G1249} which drew^{G501} the^{G3588} water^{G5204} knew;^{G1492} the^{G3588} governor of the feast^{G755} called^{G5455} the^{G3588} bridegroom,^{G3566} (The Altar of Powers alters the laws of nature and Time element. Yahshua removed the component of 'Time' out of the equation, therefore showing the power of The Altar of Bara that was in Him. The water '**BECAME**' wine, not the wine, but actual wine. There were no grapes mentioned and yet, Mayim BECAME Yayin. Now please follow with me: Water is Mayim, Grapes is Ei'nav and Wine is Yayin. Remember, Yahshua fills the **empty** earthen vessels with the revelation of Himself – New Wine. Look at the diagram below. The revelation here is Yahshua operated as all seven Altars of Power from Genesis 1:1. He demonstrated this truth by what He did. When we do the math pertaining to the elements of making wine, we are left with the 32 times Scripture says, "And Elohim said…" in the Creation account of Genesis 1:1! Yahshua demonstrated The Altar Throne of Elohim.)

(Diagram 11)

Wine – יין = 70   Grape – עֲנָב = 122   Water – מים = 90

70 + 90 = 160 – 122 = 32

Numerical difference when the Grape are removed give us 32, the amount of times Scripture records, "And God…" in Genesis 1:1. The Word manifested The Elohim Altar Throne!

בראשית ברא **אלהים** את השמים ואת הארץ

There 28 Hebrew letters here, each like a body with a soul. The numerical value of 28 is: אַהֲבְךָ – A'heiv'khah = He/I love you. Abba's love is intertwined with The Seven Altar Thrones and this love shown through The Son.

- **Luke 4:31** And[G2532] came down[G2718] to[G1519] Capernahum,[G2584] a city[G4172] of **Galilee,**[G1056] and[G2532] taught[G2258 G1321] them[G846] on[G1722] the[G3588] Sabbaton.[G4521] (One of the seven weeks leading up to Shavuot/Pentecost) **4:32** And[G2532] they were astonished[G1605] at[G1909] his[G846] teaching revelation:[G1322] for[G3754] his[G846] word[G3056] was[G2258] with[G1722] **dominion authority.**[G1849] **4:33** And[G2532] **in**[G1722] **the**[G3588] **synagogue**[G4864] (The Altar of Power exposes and dismantles the religious deception. The Altar of Power commands the Atmosphere for the sake of the people to be infused with tangible revelation. The Altar of Power crushes the demonic hold that has masked itself as a believing leader for the people. The Altar of Powers breaks the strongholds of every satanic altar and pulpit in its vicinity!**)** there was[G2258] a man,[G444] which had[G2192] a spirit[G4151] of an unclean[G169] demon,[G1140] and[G2532] **cried out**[G349] with a loud[G3173] voice,[G5456] **4:34** Saying,[G3004] leave us alone;[G1436] what have we to do with you,[G5101] [G2254] [G2532] [G4671] Yeshua[G2424] of Nazareth?[G3479] are you come[G2064] to destroy[G622] us?[G2248] I know[G1492] you[G4571] who[G5101] you are;[G1488] the[G3588] Holy One[G40] of Elohim.[G2316] **4:35** And[G2532] Yeshua[G2424] rebuked[G2008] him,[G846] saying,[G3004] **Peace arrest you,**[G5392] and[G2532] come[G1831] out of[G1537] him.[G846] And[G2532] when the[G3588] devil[G1140] had thrown[G4496] him[G846] in[G1519] the[G3588] midst,[G3319] he came[G1831] out of[G575] him,[G846] and[G2532] hurt[G984] him[G846] not.[G3367] **4:36** And[G2532] they were[(G1909)] all[G3956] amazed,[G2285] [G1096] and[G2532] spoke[G4814] among[G4314] themselves,[G240] saying,[G3004] What[G5101] a word[G3056] this is![G3778] for[G3754] with[G1722] **authority**[G1849] and[G2532] **power**[G1411] he commands[G2004] the[G3588] unclean[G169] spirits,[G4151] and[G2532] they come out.[G1831] (This seems to be one of the many recorded instances you see the Authority of The Kingdom Altars and their explosive, expansive influence and power touching at the same time. All this from the Adamah Altar named Yahshua HaMashiach!)

- **Luke 4:38-39**. (The Altar of Powers heals family lines and heritages. The Altar of Powers restores the interpretation of the wombs! The mother here is the interpreter of the Seed planted in the womb; she unlocks the blueprint. The Altar of Power changed the script of Peter's life!!!)

- **John 5:1-11** – (The Altar of Power INSIDE Yahshua HaMashiach stirs up the pool of Repentance and Healing. The Altar of Power restores the years the famine has eaten up. The Altar of Powers can reverse a 38-year death sentence. The Altar of Power provokes the hunger inside which causes the lame to leap for their liberation and freedom!! 38 is the numerical value of the Hebrew word Ko'chi/כֹּחִי = **My Power, My Life**. The Altar of Power restores your power to live again. Someone reading might have lost hope for living or you might know someone who has; I have news for you, The Altar of Power which is everywhere at once, is all powerful and present with you now and forever. Be free!)

- **Luke 6:6-11** – (The Altar of Powers restores the withered hands of life and ministry. The Altar of Power restores your work in ministry and the Kingdom in you. Come to the Altar all who are heavy laden and He, The Altar, will give you rest and comfort from all your troubles!!)

- **Luke 8:22-25** – (The Altar of Powers calms the storms of life. The Altar of Powers is what gets you and I to the other side of any storm or challenge. The Altar of Powers holds the victory for you, before the Earth ever was. The Altar of Power rebukes the breath of Leviathan and muzzles the waves of chaos it causes! The Power of The Miz'be'ach Elohim, The Altar of Powers, commands the winds and waves of life!)

- **Luke 6:6-11** – The Altar of Powers reveals the manifested Sabbath in any given situation of the week. The Altar of Power reveals and demonstrates the true Sabbath Rest!! The Altar of Powers causes the Shabbat to visit your life on a daily basis not just once a week. The Altar of Power ushers in the rest of His Kingdom!)

- **Luke 8:36-39** – The Legion enter the swine – The Altar of Power teaches us about dietary laws, what I mean is, the Altar of Power frees up a man from legion and the pigs jump into the sea. The Altar of Power takes Dominion over the spiritual beasts no matter what ranking they are!!)

- ***Luke 8:42-48** – (The Altar of Powers dries up the blood flow of your life and all that is connected to it. The Altar of Power can heal the bleeding out relationship in marriage, heal the children from torment and death and unite that same family. The Altar of Power cancels the contracts of chaos over your life in exchange for Peace and wholeness!!)

- **Matthew 9:32-34** – (The Altar of Powers cause the mute to speak and sing the highest praises. The Altar of Power will cause the Tongue of power to be heard. The Altar of Power releases The Teruah of freedom to be known and the breakthroughs of life to be contagious to everyone and everything around you and connected to you.)

- **John 6:16-21** – (The Altar of Powers can over power the laws of nature just to pay you a visit. The Altar of Powers will cause you to walk where no man has gone before. The Altars of Powers will make the path straight for you to come close as the chaotic storms of life are expelled.)

- **1 Kings 18** – The Altar of Powers mocks at all evil, witches and warlocks. The Altar of Powers accelerates the Prophetic power of song with its prophetic Altar Voice. The Altar of Power consumes the false prophets of Baal and the seed beds of Jezebel!!)

- The Altar of Powers has a voice of redemption that says, "It is finished!!!"

- **Romans 12 & Hebrews 7-9** – The Altar of Powers laid to rest the animal sacrifice in exchange for living sacrifices! The Altar of Power exchanged a cry in the wilderness for a standing Voice of Redemption!

- The Altar of Power will call us all one day and say, "Come up here my Bride!!"

Remember when Paul gets bit in the Book of Acts 28? In 28:3 the Greek word for LAID the wood upon the fire is the Greek word *epitithemi* which means to IMPOSE something upon someone. Embedded in here is a hint to why this is recorded. Paul, who was a Pharisee, lived supporting the religious community where sacrifice was IMPOSED on them. Paul was called to lay the IMPOSED system against the fire of Holiness to expose the Serpentine system engaged in it!!! The Altar of Powers can reverse the venom of serpents that have bitten the generations that have passed by just one man or woman decides to stop looking at the fire and FUEL the fire of The Altar! I can go on and on and on, but you get the picture.

The Altar of Power has now made the Lamb available to as many as come!! This is why Yahshua was pronounced as 'The Lamb of God/Elohim…" or The Lamb of The Altar Throne of Powers who takes away the sin of the world! The Atonement of man Bursted forth from the Flesh Body of the Lamb slain from the foundation of the World and made this all possible! The Word just came to pronounce and reveal the finished work before there was this Garment called The World! La'Etzem – The Tree or To the Tree, that The Altar was secured by, has now become the Power to Heal the cry of Creation –

> ⬢ **Romans 8:19** For^{G1063} the^{G3588} exceeding expectation^{G603} of the^{G3588} creature^{G2937} waits for^{G553} the^{G3588} manifestation^{G602} of the^{G3588} sons^{G5207} of Elohim **(Altar of Powers, emphasis mine)**.^{G2316} **8:20** For^{G1063} the^{G3588} creature^{G2937} was made subject^{G5293} to the fading away,^{G3153} not^{G3756} willingly,^{G1635} but^{G235} by reason of^{G1223} him who has subjected^{G5293} in^{G1909} hope,^{G1680} **8:21** Because^{G3754} the^{G3588} creature^{G2937} itself^{G848} also^{G2532} will be delivered^{G1659} from^{G575} the^{G3588} bondage^{G1397} of **corruption**^{G5356} into^{G1519} the^{G3588} glorious^{G1391} freedom^{G1657} of the^{G3588} children^{G5043} of Elohim.^{G2316}

It is time for the manifestation of the sons of The Altar of Powers/Elohim to come forth!! The Power of sonship and the

Power to **BECOME** as John 1:12 says is now. As many as believed in Him, who? The Altar of Elohim, The Word made flesh, the Redeemer of all Creation – Yahshua HaMashiach!! As many as believed on Him to them He gave the POWER to **BECOME** the sons of Elohim! The power to **BECOME** is born from the Altar of Powers, the third Altar of Genesis 1:1. This revelation brings us into the great mystery of our High Priest Himself, who orchestrates this entire truth, the High Priest of Genesis 1:1. It is He who made this All Possible for those whom He loves.

He stood concealed in the Beginning as the One who would manifest these Altar Throne truths. Let me introduce to our High-Priest King of Creation, The Alef Tav – The First and The Last!

Chapter Five

Fourth Altar:
The Altar Throne of The Word,
The Royal High Priest of Genesis 1:1

את

~Et HaKese Miz'be'ach – **את הכסא מזבח**.

We now come to the 4th Altar of Genesis 1:1. This is the one that stands at the center like the Shamesh Branch of the Menorah. There are 7 Altars in Genesis 1:1. Yes, seven literal Hebrew words, but we have discovered by now that these are Altar Thrones in written form. The amount of 7's in Scripture, which we have seen a few at the beginning of this book, is riveting as we take a journey through the corridors of Scripture. One I want to share is this, The Tree of Life is mentioned 7 times in the Tanakh. Not only does Genesis 1:1 have 7 Hebrew words, our 7 Altar Thrones, but it is also the picture of the Tree of Life in a different form. The leaves of this Tree are Healing to the Nations!

The Alef Tav, the First and Last Letters of the Hebrew Language, are the next Hebrew word given, the 4th Altar of Genesis 1:1. This Alef Tav concept is found everywhere in the Tanakh. It is usually attached to a Hebrew word and stands as the pointer to the direct object of scriptural conversation in grammatical

Hebrew. You won't see it unless you open the Hebrew text of Scripture. Now, when this Hebrew concept is standing alone, we must ask questions regarding this important PLACEment. This Alef-Tav revelation is seen inside Hebrew words as well which hold their own revelation, we can't divest at this time due to its lengthy discussion. The Alef-Tav is seen 611 times not connected to any specific Hebrew word and 111 times with the Patriarchs and prophecy.

Now this is significant because 111 and 611 are important Numerical values that expand the revelation. The first numerical value 111 is connecting us to the Hebrew letter Alef **(אלף – א)** which contains the Sacred Name – YHWH, also connecting to the creation of Adam or mankind! The word **Alef** is also **Pela** - **פלא** which means: a wonder or time of Awe. The number 611 is the numerical value of: **תורה** – Torah, The Covenant Word spoken from Mount Sinai for the children of Israel. Also, 611 is the value of: **בני ישראל** – B'nei Yisrael – Children of Israel. No coincidence whatsoever!

So, we can safely say this 4th Altar contains the essence of the sacred Name of the One who created Adam and who is the Chief Leader of all Creation. I am speaking about the 4th Altar of Genesis 1:1, The Altar High-Priest.

When looking at the verse, we have this mystical structure of The Menorah presented to us. We have dealt with the three extensions or branches of Genesis 1:1, our Altar Thrones at the Right side when looking at the text. Scripture says, "Righteousness and Justice have kissed…"

(Diagram 12)

Everlasting Altars	High Priest Altar of Genesis	Eternal Altars
⬇	⬇	⬇
השמים ואת הארץ ⟶	את ⟵	בראשית ברא אלהים
Justice ⟶	**Kissed** ⟵	**Righteousness**

The Right side is the Tzadiq side. When Yahshua HaMashiach told Peter to cast the Net on the RIGHT side, (John 21), this was a statement regarding the Restoration of all things. The Menorah speaks of The Light. When the Light is cast into the Darkness of Chaos, this produces Order and Restoration, which produces The Healing of all things. Many today will hear the revelation I speak of and make the personal connections to The Light of His Truth being cast into the Darkness of uncertainty, which Restores the Truth where there was none.

Also, the Shaft of the Menorah is essential to its purpose. The central Shaft is the source of the Oil to this Menorah for the illumination produced by spontaneous combustion of Oil and Fire. As a matter of fact, Lucifer who was the son of the dawn or the breaking of light, was after the Shaft of the congregation in the North because the Shaft speaks of 'The Leg of Covenant'! The Shaft is the source of the seed! The sides of the North speak of the one who keeps Covenant!

The Shaft or central Altar of the Beginning stands as the Covenant Leg of Fathering the Altar, Fathering the prophecy and Fathering the Seed. We have a responsibility to father the fatherless as they willingly come to this Altar. Many today as leaders, who are to be representatives of this Altar of Power and Fathering, have misguided many with the manipulation of The Word. This is all changing though as this season has created a SHIFT for the sake of the SHAFT!!

The phrase: 'SIDES of the North', is the Covenant Keeping Oath revelation to the Enigma. The Tzaphon/North, from Tzaphan, hints toward an Enigma, a Parable, Paradox or Riddle. The Enigma unlocked reveals the Oath of The Covenant from this 4th Altar. This 4th Altar is He who came speaking in parables and unlocking the Mysteries of The Kingdom. We see Yahshua is our Altar King-Priest, who repairs the foundation hinted to in the parable language used by Him. Elohim hid the secrets of the Covenant in 7 Altar Thrones and Lucifer desired these Master Keys of Rulership!!!

- **Isaiah 14:12** How^{H349} you have fallen^{H5307} from Heavens,^{H4480} ^{H8064} (Lucifer was once a covering Cherub of The Heavens Altar Throne who was cast down from that place. Lucifer, the Light bearer or Armour Bearer of The Light, had multiple weapons and titles. Lucifer was the Covering Guardian Cherub of the Light at one time. He was close to The Shamayim Altar of Genesis 1:1 and was cast down to The Earth Altar. I mentioned earlier that Lucifer had, what I call a reverse immersion/baptism, through the Waters that separated the Waters. When he fell, the void took place which caused the separation between the Waters, hence, The Firmament. Elohim steps in and brings a distinction by use of the Firmament, or can I say, the hidden language of Tzaphan – Parables?! Yes, The Firmament stood as a Parable, an Enigma Threshold forbidden to be crossed. **(Contact me at the Ministry with any questions on this subject matter – remnantoftruth.net)**

    Lucifer's rebellion breached the Threshold that The Last Adam would come and repair, The Repairer of The Breach. The first Adam was to bring the restoration to the Earth Altar but failed, so now The Last Adam, who is the manifested Word Altar and Altar King-High Priest of Genesis 1:1 has begun to do some 2000 years ago.) Lucifer,^{H1966} son^{H1121} of the morning!^{H7837} you are cast down^{H1438} to the ground,^{H776} which didst weaken^{H2522} ^{H5921} the nations!^{H1471} (The phrase: 'cast down' in

Hebrew is: **גדע** – Ga'da which means: cut off or separated and detached without remedy. This word can be pronounced as: **גִדְע** – Gi'de'ah which means to dehorn an animal. The horns of an animal are its battle strength and character trait. Lucifer was dehorned, dethroned and cut off. This is serious business here because when Lucifer fell, this disrupted the Celestial bodies as well. The numerical value of this Hebrew word is: 77, the same for: **מזל** – Mazal which means a flow from above. This is the word used for the function of all Galaxies.)

- **14:13** For you,H859 have said,H559 in your heart,H3824 I will **ascend**H5927 **into The Heavens,**H8064 (**הַשָּׁמַיִם אֶעֱלֶה** – HaShamayim E'eleh – **The Heavens**, speaks of The Altar Throne of The Heavens/HaShamayim. Lucifer's statement in his heart, 'I will ascend' is what he coveted for, The power of Ascension. The Hebrew word Alah or Aleh consists of the entire sacrificial system as a whole burnt offering. Hidden in the sacrificial system was the everlasting record of this Luciferian rebellion and the remedy to it. Lucifer wanted the Throne of The Heavens, in order to present himself as The Olah Offering which sanctifies The Altar! He was committing high Treason against The Prophecy, the Courts of Heaven and the Throne that Governs them.) I will exaltH7311 my throneH3678 aboveH4480 H4605 the starsH3556 of Elohim:H410 **I will sit**H3427 **also upon the mount**H2022 **of the congregation,**H4150 **in the sides**H3411 **of the north:**H6828 Isa 14:14 I will ascendH5927 aboveH5921 the heightsH1116 of the clouds;H5645 **I will resemble myself**H1819 **to The Most High.**H5945

I want to address the last phrase here first because it is the ultimate intent of satan still to this day –

~ **I will resemble myself**H1819 **to The Most High.**H5945 – In Hebrew this reads: **אֲדַמֶּה לְעֶלְיוֹן** – **E'dameh Le'El'yon** which can mean: 'I will reflect the Resemblance to The Most High'. Can you see the language here as it hints to the Altar we speak of? The Adamah Altar is the manifested High Priest Altar. Lucifer desired to resemble the Highest Altar revelation, which the only way of Ascension, through the Adamah/אדמה – The Altar that can manifest all Seven at any time. This Hebrew phrase reveals what Lucifer desired to do as the Light Gaurdian and Bearer - אֲדָמֶה לְעֶלְיוֹן. The value of this Hebrew phrase is 246, which is the same for: לְהָאִיר – **Le'Ha'iyr** which means: **To project Light**! Didn't Yahshua say that we are the Light of the world? **(Matthew 5:14)**

The next phrase I want to address is:

~ **in the sides**H3411 **of the north:**H6828

בְּיַרְכְּתֵי – Be'yar'khetei – from: יָרֵךְ – Ya'reikh = side, thigh, flank, shaft of the Menorah, leg of the Shulkan Table, Table of Shewbread. The Menorah and Table were placed on the SIDES of the Tabernacle, which were two unseen legs that held up the Tent. Why couldn't they break the LEGS of the Word made flesh in John 19:33? Because, The Legs/Ya'reikh/Shaft, hold the Covenant Oath from Genesis 1:1 that cannot be broken by mere men! Also, this word for LEG/Ya'reikh, when read the opposite way, reveals another Hebrew word: כָּרִי – **Kh'aree** = **Royal Bodyguard**, one who stands close to The King!! One who watches over the Temple Vessels!!

The Word, The Son could not have His legs broken because you can't break the Source of all Creation with manmade weapons, or manmade manipulation or any angelic powers! The Word is the Royal Guardian to The Oath of Covenant Promise! This Hebrew word also speaks of a Royal Decree as found in Daniel 5:29 as The Prophet was introduced by Royal Decree. We are in the days when the true Prophetic voices will be ushered in by Royal Heavenly Decree for this last day and end times events! Get ready, things are getting prepared and the curtain of this world is about to be pulled back.

The whole burnt offering, which allowed the entire sacrificial structure to ascend as an aroma, was sacrificed on the NORTH SIDE of the Altar. Hmmm!! Why the North Side of The Altar? It's because of what the verse says in Isaiah 14:13. It was a direct accusation against the Accuser of the brethren! It was an indictment against Satan himself! It was a promise from the One who would come and undo the curse of sin and death that was born out of the rebellion of Lucifer, the Shaft Hunter!!! He is after the Shaft! He wants the Thigh of The Tabernacle Adam!! He was after the Shaft of the Altar system of Genesis 1:1. He wants the Covenant keepers!! He wants the Guardians of The Mysteries! He wants the Fathering authority over the pathway of the seed!! Lucifer is thirsty for New Wine in New Wine Skins that are anointed with The Oil of The Kingdom!

Satan wants those who hold the secrets to the Parable!!! We are the Guardians of the Light. We are His Shaft/Body filled with Ruach HaQodesh! The Shaft is the Body and Source to all other 6 branches. We have the revelation of the secret of the 7 days of Creation given to us from just seven Hebrew words of Genesis 1:1! The Shamesh Branch, the Ya'reikh Branch is the continual source of all Creation!

Another amazing revelation is when the 2nd Temple era during the days after the death of Yahshua HaMashiach this Ya'reikh or Shaft of the Menorah did not stay lit anymore. Why? Because the Head of The Ya'reikh had departed in His resurrection!! The Light of the world was not here anymore!! The Guardian of the Covenant Oath of Promise was exalted to the Highest seat of Power!!

So, this Shaft or this 4th Altar of Genesis 1:1 is the Source, the Thigh and the Covenant keeping Altar of Genesis 1:1 which becomes the very source of Covenant that will be revealed throughout the whole of Scripture!

There are three Hebrew words/Altars on either side of this 4th Altar Throne as the diagram above shows. On one side we have the beginning of all things created and on the other side the place where all things are revealed. Right in the middle is this very interesting Hebrew word/Altar that seems to say something by standing as the Servant Branch of this Mystical Menorah seen in Genesis 1:1, the Source of what would be created.

In John 1:1 we are given a very powerful statement. As a matter of truth and fact, to what is written, there are several areas where the Mystery of The Word is expressed as being the concept found in Genesis 1:1:

🌹 **John 1:1** In^{G1722} the beginning^{G746} was^{G2258} the^{G3588} **Word,**^{G3056} and^{G2532} the^{G3588} **Word**^{G3056} was^{G2258} with^{G4314} Elohim,^{G2316} and^{G2532} the^{G3588} **Word**^{G3056} was^{G2258} Elohim.^{G2316} **John 1:2** The **same**^{G3778} was^{G2258} in^{G1722} the beginning^{G746} with^{G4314} Elohim.^{G2316} **John 1:3** **All things**^{G3956} came to be^{G1096} by^{G1223} him;^{G846} and^{G2532} without^{G5565} him^{G846} was not^{G3761} **any thing**^{G1520} created^{G1096} that^{G3739} was made.^{G1096} **John 1:4** In^{G1722} him^{G846} was^{G2258} life;^{G2222} and^{G2532} the^{G3588} life^{G2222} was^{G2258} the^{G3588} **light**^{G5457} of men.^{G444} **John 1:5** And^{G2532} the^{G3588} **light**^{G5457} shines^{G5316} in^{G1722} the darkness;^{G4653} and^{G2532} the^{G3588} darkness^{G4653} perceived^{G2638} it^{G846} not.^{G3756} **John 1:6** There was^{G1096} a man^{G444} sent^{G649} from^{G3844} Elohim,^{G2316} whose^{G846} name^{G3686} was John.^{G2491} **John 1:7** The same^{G3778} came^{G2064} as^{G1519} the witness,^{G3141} to^{G2443} **bear witness**^{G3140} **of**^{G4012} **the**^{G3588} **Light,**^{G5457} **(Lucifer was to be Heavens Witnessing Cherub of The Light.)** that^{G2443} all^{G3956} *men* through^{G1223} him^{G846} might believe.^{G4100} **John 1:8** He^{G1565} was^{G2258} not^{G3756} that Light,^{G5457} but^{G235} was sent to^{G2443} **bear witness**^{G3140} of^{G4012} **The Light.**^{G5457} **John 1:9** That was^{G2258} the^{G3588} true^{G228} Light,^{G5457} which^{G3739} illuminates^{G5461} every^{G3956} man^{G444} that enters^{G2064} into^{G1519} the^{G3588} world.^{G2889}

- **Colossians 1:15** Who^{G3739} is^{G2076} the **image**^{G1504} of the^{G3588} invisible^{G517} ELohim,^{G2316} the firstborn^{G4416} of every^{G3956} creature:^{G2937} **1:16** For^{G3754} by^{G1722} him^{G846} were all things^{G3956} created,^{G2936} that^{G3588} are in^{G1722} **The Heavens,**^{G3772} and^{G2532} that^{G3588} are on^{G1909} **The Earth,**^{G1093} visible^{G3707} and^{G2532} invisible,^{G517} whether^{G1535} thrones,^{G2362} or^{G1535} dominions,^{G2963} or^{G1535} principalities,^{G746} or^{G1535} powers,^{G1849} all things^{G3956} were created^{G2936} by^{G1223} him,^{G846} and^{G2532} for^{G1519} him:^{G846} **1:17** And^{G2532} he^{G846} is^{G2076} before^{G4253} all things,^{G3956} and^{G2532} by^{G1722} him^{G846} all things^{G3956} are commanded together.^{G4921}

- **Hebrews 1:1** Elohim,^{G2316} who at appointed times^{G4181} and^{G2532} in many ways^{G4187} spoke^{G2980} in time past^{G3819} unto the^{G3588} fathers^{G3962} by^{G1722} the^{G3588} prophets,^{G4396} **1:2** Has in^{G1909} these^{G5130} last^{G2078} days^{G2250} spoken^{G2980} unto us^{G2254} by^{G1722} his Son,^{G5207} whom^{G3739} he has appointed^{G5087} heir^{G2818} of all things,^{G3956} by^{G1223} whom^{G3739} also^{G2532} **he made**^{G4160} **the**^{G3588} **worlds;**^{G165} **1:3** Who^{G3739} being^{G5607} the brightness^{G541} of his glory,^{G1391} and^{G2532} the manifested image^{G5481} of his^{G848} being,^{G5287} and^{G5037} upholding^{G5342} all things^{G3956} by the^{G3588} **word**^{G4487} **(Rhema, Revelation Word)** of his^{G846} power,^{G1411} when he had by^{G1223} himself^{G1438} purged^{G4160} ^{G2512} our^{G2257} sins,^{G266} was enthroned^{G2523} on^{G1722} the right hand^{G1188} of the^{G3588} Majesty^{G3172} on^{G1722} The Highest;^{G5308}

- **1Corinthians 15:45** And^{G2532} so^{G3779} it is written,^{G1125} The^{G3588} first^{G4413} man^{G444} Adam^{G76} was made^{G1096} a^(G1519) living speaking^{G2198} soul;^{G5590} the^{G3588} last^{G2078} Adam^{G76} a quickening^{G2227} spirit.^{G4151}

- **Revelation 1:8** I^{G1473} am^{G1510} (^{G3588}) Alef^{G1} and^{G2532} (^{G3588}) Tav,^{G5598} **The Beginning**^{G746} and^{G2532} the Ending,^{G5056} proclaims^{G3004} the^{G3588} Master,^{G2962} which is, and which was, and which is to come,^G3801 the^G3588 Almighty.^G3841 (which is, was and will be, The Almighty is Yahshua The 4th Altar, Alef and Tav who IS The Name and El Shaddai – The Almighty. Who was, is and will be is a Hebrew idiom or figurative speech of The YHWH Name!)

🔴 **Revelation 1:11** Saying,^G3004 I^G1473 am^G1510 (G3588) **Alef**^G1 **and**^G2532 **(G3588) Tav,**^G5598 the^G3588 **first**^G4413 **and**^G2532 **the**^G3588 **last:**^G2078 and,^G2532 What^G3739 you see,^G991 write^G1125 in^G1519 a scroll,^G975 and^G2532 send^G3992 it unto the^G3588 seven^G2033 assemblies^G1577 which^G3588 are in^G1722 Asia;^G773 unto^G1519 Ephesus,^G2181 and^G2532 unto^G1519 Smyrna,^G4667 and^G2532 unto^G1519 Pergamos,^G4010 and^G2532 unto^G1519 Thyatira,^G2363 and^G2532 unto^G1519 Sardis,^G4554 and^G2532 unto^G1519 Philadelphia,^G5359 and^G2532 unto^G1519 Laodicea.^G2993 Rev 1:12 And^G2532 I turned^G1994 to see^G991 **the**^G3588 **voice**^G5456 that^G3748 spoke^G2980 with^G3326 me.^G1700 And^G2532 being turned,^G1994 I saw^G1492 seven^G2033 golden^G5552 menorot/lampstands;^G3087 Rev 1:13 And^G2532 in^G1722 the midst^G3319 of the^G3588 seven^G2033 menorot/lampstands^G3087 One **resembling**^G3664 the Son^G5207 of Adam,^G444

🔴 **Revelation 1:17** And^G2532 when^G3753 I saw^G1492 him,^G846 I fell^G4098 at^G4314 his^G848 feet^G4228 as^G5613 one dead.^G3498 And^G2532 he laid^G2007 his^G848 **right**^G1188 hand^G5495 (All angelic powers are Ambassadors of the Right Arm which is the Right side of The Altar Throne.) upon^G1909 me,^G1691 saying^G3004 to me,^G3427 Fear^G5399 not;^G3361 I^G1473 **am**^G1510 **the**^G3588 **First**^G4413 **and**^G2532 **the**^G3588 **Last:**^G2078

🔴 **Revelation 2:8** And^G2532 unto the^G3588 messenger^G32 of the^G3588 Assembly^G1577 in Smyrna^G4668 write;^G1125 These things^G3592 proclaims^G3004 **the**^G3588 **First**^G4413 **and**^G2532 **the**^G3588 **Last,**^G2078 which^G3739 was^G1096 **dead,**^G3498 and^G2532 **is alive;**^G2198

This 4th Altar is The Place of The Voice, The First and The Last, The Alef and The Tav, the Word that was WITH or Beside

Elohim as seen in Genesis 1:1. This 4th Altar is Creations Altar King-Priest! In Revelation 2, we have 7 Assemblies or Congregations who all bear a piece of the Enigma, a piece of the Riddle or Parable that Restores Earth back to its original Order. I can't get away from the depths of this idea that Elohim hid inside the seven days of Creation the pieces to the Parable. Each Day still stands as a King of this Creative week. Each Day holds a secret and a key of the restoration of all things. Each Day is a vessel for each of the Altars of Genesis 1:1 with the Seventh Day Sabbath as the Mother Crown of each Day.

Seven Hebrew words, Seven Altars, Seven Days, Seven Colors when Light refracts, Seven Colors in the rainbow that reverberate the vibrational frequencies to the concealed Songs of each Altar Throne.

When Adam was Created and formed, YHWH Elohim hid inside him the secrets and key to put the Parable back together. Man chose the knowledge of Good and Evil instead of eating from the Tree of Life first, which reflected the Genesis 1:1 Tree of Life and Throne of Altars! I mentioned that Satan would be the hunter after the Keys to the Parables. Satan desires the Parable Keys, but cannot have them, he is not omnipresent nor is he one of the Altar Powers. Knowing this, he tries to cause those drawing close to this Altar truth, to stumble and fall along the way. Come to The Altar Throne all who are thirsty and hungry. Come and stand upon The Rock of your Salvation where no room for the accuser of the brethren resides.

When This 4th Altar was manifested, The Word was clothed in flesh, revealed Himself and Tabernacled among us. He would hold the Keys to restoring the Earth back to its Paradise Place before it BECAME Tohu V'Bohu. The Son holds the keys of the restoration of all things. On a personal level, He holds the keys to putting your life back together. Someone might be reading these words and this hits you personally. The Son has the keys to remove the void and chaos from your life!! There is a Parable that perfects your place. You are the Pearl of Great price He came to Redeem!! You are His Treasured People, we are His Segullah!!**)**

- **Revelation 21:6** And^{G2532} he said^{G2036} unto me,^{G3427} It is accomplished.^{G1096} ==I^{G1473} am^{G1510} (^{G3588}) Alef^{G1} and^{G2532} (^{G3588}) Tav,^{G5598} the^{G3588} Beginning^{G746} and^{G2532} the^{G3588} End.^{G5056}== I^{G1473} will give^{G1325} to him that is thirsty^{G1372} of^{G1537} the^{G3588} fountain^{G4077} of the^{G3588} waters^{G5204} of life^{G2222} freely.^{G1432}

- **Revelation 22:12** And,^{G2532} behold,^{G2400} I come^{G2064} quickly;^{G5035} and^{G2532} my^{G3450} reward^{G3408} is with^{G3326} me,^{G1700} to give^{G591} to every man^{G1538} according as^{G5613} his^{G848} work^{G2041} shall be.^{G2071} **22:13** ==I^{G1473} am^{G1510} Alef^{G1} and^{G2532} Tav, ^{G5598} the Beginning^{G746} and^{G2532} the End, ^{G5056} the^{G3588} First^{G4413} and^{G2532} the^{G3588} Last.^{G2078}== **22:14** Blessed^{G3107} are they that do^{G4160} his^{G848} commandments,^{G1785} that^{G2443} they^{G846} may have^{G2071} right^{G1849} to^{G1909} ==the^{G3588} tree^{G3586} of life==,^{G2222} and^{G2532} may enter in^{G1525} through the^{G3588} Gates^{G4440} into^{G1519} the^{G3588} city.^{G4172}

The Right to partake of the Tree of Life is the revelation of our Inheritance. One Leaf from this Tree seals the Restoration the Kingdom people. Adam and the Woman never ate one leaf from The Tree of Life back in the Beginning before or after the fall. At this 4th Altar, we have the Restoration of all things, the Source of The Oil or the Anointing that brings us to this Place! Note:

- **Isaiah 41:4** Who^{H4310} has ordained it^{H6466} and fashioned it,^{H6213} calling^{H7121} the generations^{H1755} from the beginning?^{H4480 H7218} I^{H589} Yahweh,^{H3068} the first,^{H7223} and ==with==^{H854} the last;^{H314} I^{H589} am he.^{H1931}

Bringing forth the generations out from Bre'sheeth is the work of The Alef and The Tav who is YHWH Mashiach! The 4th Altar of Genesis 1:1 is the One who points to The Creator, YHWH Mashiach/משיח יהוה. This phrase contains the numerical revelation to this – Et HaKese Miz'be'ach/את הכסא מזבח has the numerical value of 544.

יהוה – when each number to the letter is squared we have 186.

משיח – Mashiach has the value of 358.

The numbers 186+358 = YHWH *The* Mashiach, the same numerical value of this Altar Throne.

The Alef-Tav are the DNA Book Ends of all Creation. Alef to Tav contain all the building blocks of this Hebrew language where our Scriptures come from. Having said this, the Ordinal value of all 22 Hebrew Letters is: 253. This is the numerical value of:

הרחם – HaRacham meaning: The Womb or, רַחְמָה – Rach'mah meaning Her Womb. The Hebrew language are not only the building blocks of all Creation, but collectively are The Womb of Creation. The Letters are also The Seed of Elohim that was received into The Womb of Creation, Her Womb. This is the revelation to the DNA of all Creation, from Alef to Tav. When we read Alef to Tav the opposite way we have the Hebrew idea of a chamber, a cell, a DNA Cell. Inside this DNA cell contains the very Soul or lifeforce of what would come right after – The Heavens and The Earth. We know according to The Prophet Isaiah –

> **Isaiah 45:18** For[H3588] now[H3541] proclaims[H559] Yahweh[H3068] that Created[H1254] (Created is: Bara, the Altar of Creation.) The Heavens;[H8064] (The Heavens is the HaShamayim Altar.) Elohim[H430] (Elohim is the Altar of Powers I addressed in this book.) himself[H1931] that formed[H3335] The Earth[H776] (The Earth is the HaAretz Altar or Genesis 1:1. The final Platform of all things.) and made[H6213] it; he[H1931] has established[H3559] it, (To establish was because of The 6th Altar – Va'Et. He Established The Kingdom here on Earth.) he created[H1254] it not[H3808] in Tohu/Empty,[H8414] he formed[H3335] it to be **enthroned**:[H3427] I[H589] am Yahweh;[H3068] and there is none[H369] else.[H5750]

Elohim is the cause and source of Creation and it is through The Alef Tav, who is The Agent of Creation Himself which all things are established and sustained!! When we read this Word ET/את, the Source of the Creative Language, the opposite way, we have 'Te/תא', the Chamber of Creation. This 4th Altar stood at the SIDE of Elohim as a message, who would come forth from the RIGHT Side of Elohim. Who comes forth is The Heavens and The Earth, The Garment and the Feet of The Bride! The Bride is The Kingdom of Heaven Yahshua came seeking. From the first Adam, the layers continued INSIDE this revelation of the Bride. YHWH Elohim would get the very Tzela, the Essence of Adam, which contained the Keys to all 7 Altars – the Keys to Healing the Earth from the Chaos.

The very Source and Key to unlocking the Parable layer, a spiritual type Hymen which was stretch out **between** the Earth and the Empty Chaotic place called Tohu v'Bohu, is found at the Foot of Genesis 1:1! YHWH Elohim says in Genesis 2:22 that the woman would contain the Essence of The Garden, the Essence of Paradise, and the Essence of this concealed enigma Parable inside her womb.

Scripture says, Vayiven YHWH Elohim Alef Tav HaTzela/ וַיִּבֶן יהוה אֱלֹהִים אֶת־הַצֵּלָע – "And YHWH Elohim **Built up** inside The Woman the Essence of the **Alef Tav Altar**…" This Woman of Genesis contained the prophecy of the Word who would come, the Altar of Restoration and the Power to Build. This Genesis Woman was Built, not Created! She was built to protect The Keys of the Parable mysteries. The Son would be The Key and The Alef Tav she carried inside of her – Alef Tav HaTzela – את־הצלע, The Essence of The Word!! The Essence of The Altar!! This is never ending revelation.

The Bride, a prophetic message of The Kingdom, who needed to be circumcised, now prepares to Crown the Mystery hid since the Beginning. The numerical value of this Hebrew phrase is 596 is the same for the Mother of us all – ירושלים – Yerushalayim! (Galatians 4:26)

Now, we read a revelation in the Book of John -

> 🔴 John 18:10 Then^{G3767} Simon^{G4613} Peter^{G4074} having^{G2192} a sword^{G3162} drew^{G1670} it,^{G846} and^{G2532} struck^{G3817} the^{G3588} high priest's^{G749} servant,^{G1401} and^{G2532} cut off^{G609} his^{G846} Right^{G1188} ear.^{G5621} ^(G1161) The^{G3588} servant's^{G1401} name^{G3686} was^{G2258} Malchus.^{G3124}

Malchus comes from Malkhut or Kingdom. The numerical value of Alef Tav HaTzela is 596 the same for the Hebrew phrase that reflects Psalm 96:10 – **במלכי־צדק עצם** – **Be'Melkhitzedeq Etzem = 'Through the Tree of our Righteous King'**. It was through the Tree of our Righteous King, who was Crucified upon it, which He Ruled and Reigned from. Therefore, restoring the Mother Kingdom of us all, The New Jerusalem that will one day descend out of The Heavens. The New Jerusalem is adorned AS a Bride and comes OUT OF **The Heavens** or **HaShamayim Altar**! It is through Tree/Altar, we hear The Blood speak Forgiveness, Acceptance, Healing, Restoration, Adoption, Justification, Sanctification, Regeneration, Newness and the Power to make the bastard children into the Sons of the Inheritance!! All that is come to the Altar Tree, the Alef Tav Altar of our Source, have now Inherited the Blessing of Sonship!!

The Altar is sitting and establishing the Kingdom people –

We have all gone astray, we find our iniquity removed and laid upon the back of this this 4th Altar Throne. What we didn't learn in Church was, there is a big difference between sin, guilt, trespass and iniquity. There are different categories of sin, Iniquity being one of the worse of the sins. There are some leading to death, which, we are not to pray for, then, there others that just miss the Mark.

There is a verse, Isaiah 53:6, which we have Avone/Iniquity mentioned. Iniquity is perversity, high treason against the King and willful rebellion – punishable by DEATH. The Alef Tav, our 4th Altar, is the power source to absorb the Death penalty position that was against us! Let's look at a few more places where this 4th Altar is seen:

- Exodus 39:22 And he made^{H6213} **(H853) the robe^{H4598} of the Ephod^{H646}** of woven^{H707} work^{H4639} all^{H3632} of blue.^{H8504}

This Robe of the Ephod emulates the Power and Majesty of this 4th Altar called Et/Alef Tav. The verse says, "He made the Alef Tav Robe of the Ephod." The Alef Tav Altar stands as The Robed High Priest! Aaron, The High Priest, was given an Earthly symbol of The Heavens and The Earth Altars, The Ephod of Genesis 1:1 – the Ephod of Creation.

The 12 stones of Aaron's Ephod and Shoulder pieces emanated the Hebrew phrase – את השמים ואת הארץ, the three Altar Thrones I have begun to address in this chapter. These Next 3 Altars, in their respected order, are the 12 Stones of the Ephod to The Alef Tav Altar and High Priest of Genesis 1:1. The Alef Tav is like the two Shoulder Stones containing the revelation of the 12 Letters/Stones to these 3 Altars, reflecting the 12 Tribes of Israel!! It is believed that each of the 22 Hebrew Letters of the Language of Creation, where our Scriptures come, have a Soul of their own. Creation itself, who is the Physical Body to the Soul of these Hebrew Letters, is result of the DNA Code to what was spoken.

The Phrase: Made of a WOVEN work – Arag/ארג means to weave together like a Crown of thorns! The Alef Tav would stand as The High Priest of Genesis 1:1 who would be Robed and Crowned with Thorns at His Manifested completion! Arag has the value of 204 which is the same for continued revelation to this Altar – צדיק – Tzadiq = The Righteous One Who Restores the Generations/דר – Dor which also equals 204!!!

Can you see this revelation? Alef Tav, The Heavens and The Earth, in Hebrew, are the 12 Stones of this Ephod of Genesis 1:1.

The Seven Altar Thrones of Genesis 1:1

There are 12 Hebrew DNA Letters and the Alef Tav is the Robed High Priest of Genesis 1:1 who wears them all. The 2 Shoulder Stones that hold up the Ephod itself are an interwoven mystical work, seen in the last three Altars of our verse! The entire nation is held up by this Altar of pure and complete Power!! All of Creation is the result of these Three Altars.

Let me speak on this area of the Alef Tav in more detail pertaining to The High Priest of Genesis 1:1. When the Tabernacle system was instituted and the priesthood after the order of Aaron was established as the plan 'B', we are given many areas of revelation regarding Yahshua HaMashiach. One specific one I want to address is the Urim and Thummim, which begin with Alef and Tav. Think about this, the Urim and Thummim are a symbol of promise The High Priest of the Aaronic priesthood was upholding during its temporary season. This revelation contained the Everlasting details of The Ephod of Genesis 1:1.

> • **Leviticus 8:8** And he put^H7760 (^H853) the breastplate^H2833 upon^H5921 him also he put^H5414 in^H413 **the breastplate**^H2833 **(H853) the Urim**^H224 **and the Thummim.**^H8550

Urim and Thummim were placed inside the breastplate –

(Diagram 13)

Ha'**T**umim   Va'Et   Ha'**U**rim   ET   Ha'Choshen

At the inauguration of Aaron, we have the priestly garments given to him. (Leviticus 6-8) Inside the breastplate were two special and prophetic stones. These stones are believed to have lit up when The Voice behind the veil manifested on Yom Kippur.

Yes, I said 'manifested' because The Voice of YHWH Elohim is so pure, He needs a Garment to be clothed in so His Holiness wouldn't demand immediate judgement upon the unholy. The Urim begins with The Hebrew letter Alef and Thummim begins with the Tav.

The Hebrew phrase Ha'Choshen or The Breastplate, has the numerical value without the definite article Hei/ה of **358**, the same for Mashiach/משיח or Mashiach/Messiah!! This can be read from Ha'Choshen to HaMashiach because of the Prophetic number system built into the language. The Breastplate was the Garment to Mashiach!

So, the Urim and Thummim can be read another way, "**The Mashiach IS the Urim and The Thummim of the Ephod Breastplate!**" Concealed inside the Breastplate of the Ephod, which had the 12 Stones of the Names of Israel, was the revelation of our Altar I speak of, The High Priest or Alef Tav Altar Throne – The Word before the manifestation in the flesh!! The Alef Tav of Genesis 1:1 is the adorned High Priest that would later be echoed from Aarons Ephod that was lit up by the Alef and the Tav – The Urim/Lights and Thummim/Perfections!

These 7 Altars represent the 7 major Garments Aaron, the High Priest would have worn! This High Priest is adorned with 7 Altars of the Eternal and the Everlasting Spiritual Realms!

The entire world is sustained by this Altar Throne as it is written in Hebrews 1:1-3 and Colossians 1:17! The entire Genesis 1:1 verse is sustained by this 4th Altar who stands as the Shaft, the Leg and Seed source to the revelation. He is the Enigma and Parable Key Master who unlocks the Restoration and Tikkun. He is the Repairer of the Breach, what Breach? The Breach that took place between Genesis 1:1&2!!

When it came to the Covenant words in Exodus 20:1, Elohim spoke THROUGH the Alef Tav, which was an emanation of The Alef Tav Altar Throne of Genesis 1:1 here at the Mount Sinai. Sinai means: Thorny Place. Mount Sinai was a part of this revelation as we will see next.

Here is a verse that parallels this revelation of the piercing through of The Word made flesh, the Son of Elohim!!

> 🔴 **Zechariyah 12:10** And I will pour^H8210 upon^H5921 the house^H1004 of David^H1732 and upon^H5921 the inhabitants^H3427 of Jerusalem^H3389 the spirit^H7307 of grace^H2580 and of supplications:^H8469 and they will gaze^H5027 **upon**^H413 **Me**^(H853) **whom**^H834 **they pierced,**^H1856 and they shall mourn^H5594 for^H5921 him as one mourns^H4553 for^H5921 his only^H3173 son and shall be grieved^H4843 for^H5921 him as one that is grieved^H4843 for^H5921 his firstborn.^H1060

וְהִבִּיטוּ אֵלַי אֵת אֲשֶׁר דָּקָרוּ

(Right to left) – **Ve'hee'bee'tu Ei'lai ET Asher Da'qaroo** – "**...and they shall burst forth toward The Word whom they pierced**..." This is a better meaning to the Hebrew words used.

Between: '**upon Me**' and '**whom they have pierced**' is our 4th Altar Throne, the **Word** made Flesh - **אֵת**. How can you pierce the **Alef Tav** without the grammatical connection of the text that is present?! The only connection we have to this statement is, the Alef Tav **was** the One who was pierced!!!

There are also 12 locations of this Alef Tav Altar when Joseph reveals Himself to his brothers. When all of Israel comes to the 4th Altar of the Redemption, it is only then that the Tohu V'Bohu is undone! By the power of this 4th Altar are the Heavens and the Earth created and established. All things consist because of this Alef Tav Altar who is our High Priest, Our King Priest, our Priest of War and Victory, Our Kinsman Redeemer. He is The Royal High Priest of Genesis 1:1 The Light of The World!!!

Our 4th Altar of Genesis 1:1 is the pivotal point where The Heavens and The Earth are influenced and Alef Tav Mashiach reveled! John 1:29 records the words, "Behold the Lamb who removes the sin of this the World." The Lamb Slain before the foundation of the world can be expressed from within these two Hebrew Letters, Alef and Tav, also known as the building blocks of all Creation!!

This revelation would ultimately find Himself concealed inside the woman, containing the full revelation of all 7 Altars of Genesis 1:1. The 7 Days of Creation are each an Altar Crown of their own as well as the emanations of a Song each echo. From this Altar, Elohim would bring forth His Tabernacle Adam who would contain the enigma within himself to all 7 Days of Creation. Just like the Tabernacle had the 7 Vessels of revelation – Altar of sacrifice, Laver of immersion, Table of Bread, Menorah, Altar of Incense, Ark and Mercy Seat, we now can see the enigma of Creation hidden in these Vessels on Earth.

Back to the Woman of Eden. The woman would-be built-in order to contain the revelation of this Parable inside her, the Essence of Adam. Some thousands of years later the Parable Key Master would be manifested as the 4th Altar revelation of The Beginning and walk the streets of Jerusalem. He would teach the Parables that held the key to unlock the revelation and piece back together the Breach now infecting mankind. There are seven main Kingdom Parables, each of them points to one specific Altar, while at the same time all illuminating from the Adamah Altar Yahshua HaMashiach. The Word contained the key and upon this Rock, this Revelational and Truth would His House, the Bet of Genesis, be built and the Gates of Hell would not prevail against.

The Mystery to unlocking the Parable Rock of His House, who is His Bride, is forever given to those who draw near to Him! Yahshua said to His Disciples, "To them I speak in parables, but to you it has been given to know the secrets of the Kingdom." He is the Enthroned King-Priest of Genesis 1:1 that has the entire Heavens and the Earth as His Supernal Ephod. The Ephod is about to speak, the Urim and Thummim are transmitting The Message from above the Heavens. The Womb is about to break open and The Crown of The Heavens Throne to be manifested.

Let me end this chapter with one section of Scripture that the rabbis all know is the mystery to the coming Mashiach. In Isaiah 9:6 we have a prophecy:

לְםַרְבֵּה הַמִּשְׂרָה וּלְשָׁלוֹם אֵין־קֵץ עַל־כִּסֵא

Le'mar'beh Ha'meesh'rah Ool'Shalom Aiyn Qeitz Al Ki'se – which translates: 'To the concealed Greatness of The Dominion and for the sake of Peace there will be no end that comes upon the Throne...' Notice the Hebrew grammatical error with the closed 'Mem'. The closed mem is placed at the end of a word, not at its beginning. This is a Messiah Mystery the rabbis know about. The closed mem speaks of the closed womb. Le'**m**ar'beh is speaking of the Greatness of The Throne. The Greatness of the Throne is the One who is clothed in Shalom, The Prince of Peace or Sar Shalom in Hebrew.

The Prince of Peace, mentioned in Isaiah 9:5-6 (6-7 E), comes through the closed 'Mem' or 'Womb' of the woman. He comes with the Kingdom mandate of His Father. Yahshua began His ministry preaching The Kingdom of Heaven has arrived. This Kingdom of Heaven Message is the emanation from the Altar Throne – HaShamayim/The Altar Throne of The Heavens, that empowers the 12 Stones of the Ephod. The Alef Tav foundation Voice to this Ephod, has spoken through The Ephod of Creation, so let us hear what is being said.

We now come to the Breastplate and Ephod of Creation's Altars. Let us hear what The Ruach HaQodesh is speaking through this Power Breastplate which Dominion is established through.

CHAPTER א׳ו

Fifth Altar:
The Altar Throne of The Heavens – Shamayim
The Kingdom of Righteousness
The Ephod Throne of Creation!

השמים

The Ephod, is more than what was given to the Levitical High Priest Aaron in the Scripture. The entire Heavens and Earth is an Ephod of supranatural proportions beyond our minds. Each Altar Throne emanates from The Ephod Priest Himself, which mirrors the 7th Day Sabbath, the Crown of the 6 days of Creation, and all these Days consist of.

The numerical value of this Altar Throne, HaShamayim/השמים, is 395. This is the same for השמן – HaShemen – The Oil. Shemen in Hebrew means: fatness, fulness, robust, to become oil, *evaluate and expansive. This Altar contains the fatness and power of The Kingdom, which evaluates all it comes into contact with. 395 also has the value of the Hebrew word Neshamah/נשמה, which means: to breathe, the sacred soul and spirit of man, to breathe. Neshamah is the power to combine spirit and soul in one single breath. Nishamah is another form of this word and it means to Breathe. The Kingdom of Heaven is a Breathing Kingdom, from whom The Altar Throne of HaShamayim emanates this truth. Our breath comes from above in which no man holds the authority to constrict or make a claim to. Neshamah is also the sign of our weakness, meaning: if we had no breath, we would cease to be alive.

HaShemen and Neshamah parallel each other, on the one hand we have the activating Oil, while on the other, we have the activating Breath. Without the Oil of the Anointing, we could not demonstrate The Kingdom of Heaven. Without the Breath, we could not communicate The Kingdom of Heaven.

We now transcend from the Eternal into the Everlasting realm, which is beyond the Veil. Stationed between these two-Dimensional Realities, STANDS two specific Altar revelations – The Concealed Alef Tav and the Revealed Alef Tav – את ואת. The first of these is the 4th Altar Thrones is known as The High Priest of Genesis 1:1, who is behind the veil of the Heavens. The following Altar Throne, the 6th one, is the manifested Altar King of Genesis 1 - ואת.

There is one Hebrew letter that speaks of man, the Hebrew letter Vav. This Vav is the connector and manifester to that which is unseen. Did you know that there is a name given to the Holy of Holies called הַדְּבִיר – Ha'Dvir which means The Word or the manifested **Voice**? Behind the Veil the High Priest Aaron, once a year, would SEE The manifested Word! He could not speak of what He saw, otherwise, risk dying before the words would even come out of his mouth.

On one side of the Alef Tav Altar King and High Priest is the <u>Eternal</u> and endless Realms. On the other side of Him are the <u>Everlasting</u> and Spiritual realms.

(Diagram 14)

The Crowned Altar High-Priest and King

12 Stone Everlasting Ephod	↓	14 Layer Eternal High Priest-King Garment
השמים ואת הארץ	את	בראשית ברא אלהים
Everlasting Realms		Eternal Realms

Once again, Altars are seen throughout Scripture. Even when the word Altar/Miz'be'ach is not mentioned in Scripture, there is still revelation of an Altar by the actions, permissions and words of the people. The Altar holds the source of connection between the Heavenly Dimensions. The Altar is the transaction point between The Creator and His Creation. No business can be done legally on Earth with The Creator and Creation without an Altar. I want to reiterate this: the greatest of all Altars on Earth is the Altar of Yahshua HaMashiach – The Adamah Altar. This is the Melkhitzedeq Altar! There in Genesis are multiple revelations of altars dealing with creation. From Day 1 through Day 6. When it comes to the everlasting dimension, the Heavens are the spear head of all other altars in this realm.

Between B'reshith Bara Elohim stands the Alef Tav Altar, the Governor, the Chief One, The High Priest and King of the Altars who connects one side of this verse to the other side. He is later seen standing between The Heavens and The Earth as the Ve'Et Altar we will get into next.

Coming soon we will deal with the 6th Altar which is the Scepter Throne of Creation. And finally, the 7th Altar which is the Altar of Dominion and Seal! I said Seal because we see that Seals are opened on the Altar of Earth while in the Altar of Heaven is where they are first Sealed. All three Altars we now engage in are made up of 12 Hebrew letters which parallel the 12 stones in the Ephod of the High Priest. These three Altars are the Ephod of Genesis 1:1.

One more thing as we enter in, from the Shamayim Altar to the Earth Altar revelation are parallels and revelations of The Outercourt, Inner Sanctum or Inner court and the Qadosh HaQadoshim or The Holy of Holies – Ha'Dvir. Think very deeply about this idea as you gaze into the Tabernacle, which contains the most revelation of all Tent and Temple structures. There were three major dimensions and Altars within this Tent Skin. When the Scripture connect the Flesh of Yahshua to the Veil, this becomes the key to what I am speaking about –

- **Hebrews 9:8** The^{G3588} Set Apart^{G40} Spirit^{G4151} now^{G5124} ministering^{G1213} that the^{G3588} way^{G3598} into the^{G3588} Most Sacred Space^{G39} was not^{G3380} made manifest,^{G5319} while as the^{G3588} first^{G4413} tabernacle^{G4633} was^{G2192} still^{G2089} standing:^{G4714}

- **10:19** Having^{G2192} therefore^{G3767} brothers,^{G80} boldness^{G3954} to enter into^{G1519} ^{G1529} the^{G3588} Most Sacred Space^{G39} by^{G1722} the^{G3588} blood^{G129} of Yeshua,^{G2424} **10:20** By a new^{G4372} and^{G2532} living^{G2198} way^{G3598} which^{G3739} he has consecrated^{G1457} for us,^{G2254} through^{G1223} the^{G3588} **veil,**^{G2665} that is to say,^{G5123} his^{G848} flesh;^{G4561} **10:21** And^{G2532} having an High^{G3173} Priest^{G2409} over^{G1909} the^{G3588} House^{G3624} of Eloah;^{G2316}

- **1Corinthians 4:20** For the kingdom of Elohim is not in word, but in **manifested in power**.

The Kingdom of Elohim is one of demonstration and power, because it is of a Heavenly Order. The Shamayim Altar Throne is where the Power is seen and actualized. There is another revelation the Shamyim Altar depicts, it has its own firmament. This firmament is seen in Genesis 1:14 having Lights and Luminaries that are INSIDE of it. In Numbers 17:3 the Firmament takes on another form called Ree'qoo'ei or the **beaten-out Net** for The Altar of sacrifice. When keeping the Altar of sacrifice in mind, the firmament is the threshold for all that has fallen to ascend to. The Shamayim Altar is the key to the

Ascension! It is no coincidence that we are called The Kingdom of Heaven by Yahshua The King Himself!! These Luminaries of revelation are to be the projecting power of The Shamayim Altar which Adam would have the authority to touch.

Shamayim comes from a word that contains several Altar connections:

~ Shamah/שמה which means the source of a thing, to be present. This Hebrew word is an anagram to other words such as: **Hashem/השם** - The Name or The Authority; **Mee'sheh/מִשֶּׁה** - From The Lamb; **Mosheh/מֹשֶׁה** to name a few. The Shamayim Altar reveals the Source of **The Name**, The Source of **The Lamb**, The Source of being **Drawn Out/Mosheh** from the water!! (John1:29; 17:6; James 4:8) This Power Altar speaks of being drawn out from the Source of The Lamb!! The Lamb is The King, The Lamb is The High Priest, The Lamb is The Name Manifested, The Lamb is The Altar of Redemption and Salvation!!

From this Altar comes the Parable of 7 Kingdom Days. Yahshua taught 7 main Kingdom Parables – The Parable of The Sower, which is the Crown of the Parables. The Parable of the Wheat and the Tares or The Man who sowed; The Parable of the Kingdom Leaven; The Parable of the Grain of mustard seed; The Parable of the Hidden Treasure; The Parable of the Kingdom Merchant Man seeking the Pearl of Great Price; The Kingdom of the NET. Might I add that this 5th Altar is The Kingdom Womb of the Parables where the hidden things begin to crown and then manifest, so, remember the closed Mem of Isaiah 9:6(7).

Yahshua HaMashiach was about to activate The Crowned Altar called 'The Kingdom of Heaven"! Note:

- **Matthew 13:10** AndG2532 theG3588 disciplesG3101 came,G4334 and saidG2036 unto him,G846 WhyG1302 do you speakG2980 to themG846 inG1722 parables?G3850

- **Matthew 13:11** (G1161) HeG3588 answeredG611 and saidG2036 unto them,G846 BecauseG3754 it is givenG1325 unto youG5213

The Seven Altar Thrones of Genesis 1:1

> to know^{G1097} the^{G3588} **mysteries^{G3466} of the^{G3588} kingdom^{G932} of heaven,^{G3772}** but^{G1161} to them^{G1565} it is not^{G3756} given.^{G1325}

The Mysteries of the Kingdom of Heaven are unlocked through Parables! The Hebrew word for Parable is Mashal/משל, which Adam was to walk in called 'to rule/Mashal' his wife. Having done this, Adam would become the Kingdom to her which she would cause to expand acrossed The Earth Platform. Adam was a Parable or, the Key to unlocking the Building ability that was Built into the Woman of Eden, his wife. The Kingdom is revealed from the Mashal, this Parable mystery and then manifested by The Precious Stone, our King Yahshua who then brings Complete Restoration. These Hebrew letters for Mashal, reveal to us another word: שלם – Shaleim, Shalam, which means: Complete Peace! The Kingdom manifested through the Parable Language, reveals the Power of our King Yahshua HaMashiach, who establishes complete peace!

Mashal read the other way is Le'shem/לשם which means: a precious stone! The Precious Stone is who The Altar of Yahshua HaMashiach was revealed through, the woman called The Bride! Satan sensed this threat, so, his attack was against the Womb of the woman, who conceived the Dominion Authority, which restores all things. Restoration is a major threat to Satan. Satan wanted the power over man in order to manifest his own kingdom.

> ● **Matthew 13:34** All^{G3956} these things^{G5023} spoke^{G2980} Yeshua^{G2424} to the^{G3588} multitude^{G3793} in^{G1722} parables;^{G3850} and^{G2532} without^{G5565} a parable^{G3850} spoke^{G2980} he not^{G3756} unto them:^{G846} **13:35** That^{G3704} it might be fulfilled^{G4137} which was spoken^{G4483} by^{G1223} the^{G3588} prophet,^{G4396} saying,^{G3004} I will open^{G455} my^{G3450} mouth^{G4750} in^{G1722} **parables;^{G3850}** I will utter^{G2044} things which have been kept secret^{G2928} **from^{G575} the foundation^{G2602} of the world.^{G2889}**

This word **foundation** is the word used in Hebrews 11:11 for - Sara **CONCEIVING** the promised son. Sara's Name comes from the word that means Dominion and Kingdom!! So, it would be OUT of or, FROM the Kingdom not of this world, who manifests the King Himself!! Our physical bodies are like a womb, we will all break out of one day, when the Trumpet sounds!

The first four Hebrew words of Genesis 1:1 stand as Pillars, Platforms and Altars throughout the remainder of Scripture. Also, the Altars of Genesis 1, are all revelations of the Kingdom Priesthood in Yahshua HaMashiach, who is The Alef Tav of Genesis 1:1. All Creation branch off from these first seven Hebrew words of Genesis 1:1, explicitly, the last six Hebrew words of this Genesis revelation.

The sages of old say, scratching the surface of Genesis 1, is to invest a lifetime of research, diligence, integrity and servitude. You and I must become Scriptural Archeologists in order to discover these hidden treasures. We must become one with The Word in order to hear the Voice of these Altars. Becoming one with The Word Himself, we then qualify to know the mysteries inside this eternal DNA Helix of Creation's Mysteries and Secrets the Universe conceals.

The first three Altar Thrones – B'reshith, Bara and Elohim, deal with the time before Creation itself, known as, the Eternal Dimensions. Each of them holding their own position, which Scripture records, having endless insights of truth unraveled over time.

This Alef Tav Altar is the Leg of Genesis 1:1, who is the very High Priesthood of Genesis 1:1. He is the one who oversees The Heavens and The Earth, which contain the secrets of both realms, ascending through this Ephod and into the realms of Eternity!! We must go from Everlasting Life to Eternal Life and there is a WORLD (no pun intended) of difference as Yahshua expressed in what He did. This Altar Throne stands between the Eternal Realms and the Everlasting Realms, which is the Everlasting Altar Throne - HaShamayim. Let's begin with this Altar Throne

HaShamayim – The Heavens, where we are seated - our Royal Dominion.

Our 5th Altar is the signature Seal of these Ephod Stones of Genesis 1:1. The truth of this is, the Heavens act as a type of Mikvah pool, which, those who descend must enter. Shamayim has the Hebrew word Mayim/Waters within its wording. As a matter of fact, this whole verse is a revelation of The Highest Royal Order and Highest Priesthood revelation that Mashiach Yahshua is after. Every High Priest needs an Ephod of Authority. The Ephod is the Breastplate of Judgement and Authority he would wear. (Exodus 28:15)

Every High Priest stands, as ambassador for The Voice, between both The Natural world and the Spiritual world bridging the gap. Just as it comes to your home, the man stands as the priest of that home holding the authority to build or to tear down. The priest of each home can change the course of a whole generation by the very words and decisions he makes! The words we speak, are the soul to what will manifest and take on form in the future. You are what you SPEAK.

This Altar of HaShamayim/The Heavens is the entirety of Spiritual worlds and Realms. The Break down could be as such – B'reshith Bara Elohim are the Eternal Realm. The Alef Tav is the Neshamah Realm connecting the Altars of the Soul and Spirit. HaShamayim Ve'Et Ha'Aretz are the Spiritual Realms, which becomes the branding of mankind. Let's examine a couple of concepts:

Eternal and Everlasting

1. **Eternal – קדם – Qedem**. These two ideas are interchangeable words, but I will focus on the ideas they convey. The Eternal speaks of no beginning and no ending, which always has been. Qedem speaks of Eternal things before there was a 'WAS'. Qedem comes from Qadam which means to project oneself in order to create

an image. Qedem also means The End or, where things connect to their origins, like the rising of the Sun. The Sun sets and rises which are Laws of Nature constantly cycling. The everlasting realm is the projection of the Eternal Realm also known as The Adomeh or Likeness and Resemblance mentioned earlier in this book. Here is an example to this idea Qedem:

a. Isaiah 46:10 - **Isa 46:10 Proclaiming**[H5046] **the End**[H319] **from the Beginning,**[H4480 H7225] **and from Ancient Times**[H4480 H6924] **the things which**[H834] **are not**[H3808] **made,**[H6213] **saying,**[H559] **My Counsel**[H6098] **shall stand,**[H6965] **and I will do**[H6213] **all**[H3605] **my Pleasure:**[H2656]

b. מַגִּיד מֵרֵאשִׁית אַחֲרִית וּמִקֶּדֶם –Ma'geed Mei'reishith A'charit Oo'mi'Qedem. A more literal translation of this Hebrew phrase is as such: "Manifesting from the Beginning, the End that is revealed from Ancient times of the past." The Hebrew language contains the prophetic ends from the Beginning of time and even before that. The one all Scripture points to is The Firstborn from Above, the One who holds the Birth right to all souls of men – Yahshua HaMashiach. He is called the Firstborn from the Dead because He is the Altar Throne of life, who came from above. The Ordinal value to this Hebrew phrase is 233, the same for: הַבְּכוֹר – HaBe'khor – The Firstborn; בְּכוֹרָה – Be'khorah – The Birthright.

An example is like the sound of the voice, the voice is what was projected from the mouth which is its source. The Hebrew word Qadam is seen 26 times in Scripture which connects us to the Sacred Name YHWH which has the numerical value of 26. **(See Hebrew chart in the back of the Book)**

2. **Everlasting – עוֹלָם – Olam.**

The Everlasting Realm is not what we would call: Forever and

Ever. This is for a time and a season. If you notice, there is numerical connection between these two ideas, which are: 144 and 146. The difference between them is the number 2. Two speaks of the Hebrew letter Bet. Bet is what begins the Scriptures. There were two realms all things would come from, the Eternal/Qedem and the Everlasting/Olam. When Moses was given the Tabernacle instructions, this would emanate this spiritual truth. The Holy of Holies would represent The Eternal Realm while the Holy Place would represent the Everlasting Realm. The numerical value of these two concepts is 290, which is the same for two important Hebrew words:

מרים – Miriam, the Mother of Yahshua who brought forth The Word from a closed womb (Isaiah 9:6 – Le'Marbeh/למרבה). She contained the Narrow place he had to come through which is the womb of a woman. To be here on Earth legally is to come through the womb of a woman. Passage through the waters of the womb is the only way a thing can be here lawfully and legally. Miriam's name means: waters of birthing. This concept Le'Marbeh is grammatically incorrect, but prophetically accurate. Le'Marbeh can be a statement in Hebrew, which says this: **"To the One who comes through the closed womb, He shall be greatly exalted!" – Le'Marbeh!"** The numerical evaluation of this truth brings to surface another Hebrew connection – בְּבִטְנָה הַצַּדִּיק – Ba'bit'nah Ha'tzadiq – "By way of The Womb, The Righteous One comes." The womb sometimes can be a place of tribulation as well as a place of peace. What is positioned between The World and The Womb is the birth canal.

צר – Tzar, Narrow Place, Birth Canal, Tribulation Time. The Tribulation is like the Birth Canal from the Eternal Realms, while the womb of a woman is the Narrow place leading into the Everlasting Realms. This Tzar is the umbilical cord between the two-dimensional realities. The Tribulation is the world we come <u>through</u> in order to legally be here on Earth. It is through Tribulation we all must go through in order to Lawfully enter the Worlds above.

The Heavens/HaShamayim Altar Throne is the origin of all breathing things. This Altar is the Altar of Kingship and Enthronement that was Born through The Word! The HaShamayim Altar would be the Belly of the Shemen or, The Oil. Yahshua spoke many Parables pertaining to the Kingdom of Heaven, in doing so, He was invoking the Shamayim Altar. Speaking what is written invokes the unseen power it is founded on. We must invoke the Altar He has established for us!! We are those who have RECEIVED Him and therefore, He has giving us the POWER to BECOME... from 'BECOMING' is the Platform of The Altar known as Sonship!!

Sonship is the building power of the Kingdom of Heaven Altar Throne!! The HaShamayim Altar is the unlocking key to the Parables! The HaShamayim Altar holds the key to the Throne that sits inside this dimension! The Power to activate to invoke, to release this Altar is what the legions of hell are afraid of! The power to unlock this Altar balances out all that happens on this Earth. The Shamayim Altar, I believe, is the Crown over the Earth that contain the ability to untangle the earthly chaos! This must be because of the Throne of The Name, The Authority, and Crown of This Place manifested in Flesh as YHWH!

In John 17 Yahshua prayed to Abba and said He REVEALED the Name to the ones given to Him. How did this happen? By what He did:

- **John 17:2** As^{G2531} you have given^{G1325} him^{G846} **power^{G1849}** over all^{G3956} flesh,^{G4561} that^{G2443} he should give^{G1325} **eternal^{G166} life^{G2222}** to as many as^{G3956 G3739} you have given^{G1325} him.^{G846}

- **John 17:3** And^{G1161} this^{G3778} is^{G2076} **life^{G2222} eternal,^{G166}** that^{G2443} they might **know^{G1097} you^{G4571}** the^{G3588} only^{G3441} true^{G228} Elohim,^{G2316} and^{G2532} Yeshua^{G2424} Messiah,^{G5547} who^{G3739} you have sent forth.^{G649}

Notice the language Mashiach uses, it's as if He is speaking OUTSIDE the place of Yahshua, The Flesh, and from the Place above, Mashiach. He is speaking from the place of The Word, who put on Yahshua as a Garment and demonstrated The Kingdom through HaMashiach, The Anointed One. Yahshua is the Tabernacle and Mashiach is the Anointed Altar King inside of this Flesh covering! Eternal Life is mentioned in this verse, which is the place of KNOWING the only true Elohim AND Yahshua HaMashiach who has been SENT!! He made the transaction of redemption here on the Altar of acceptance just before He sealed it in His Blood. The areas where His blood was spilled were the areas of ownership and Kingdom takeover. His Blood evicted the claim off of the land, off of the people, and off of His heritage and treasure!! Let's keep reading –

- **John 17:6** I have manifested G5319 your G4675 Name G3686 to the G3588 men G444 which G3739 you gave G1325 me G3427 out of G1537 the G3588 world: G2889 yours G4674 they were, G2258 and G2532 you gave G1325 them G846 me; G1698 and G2532 they have kept G5083 your G4675 word. G3056

- **John 17:11** And G2532 now I am G1510 no G3756 more G2089 in G1722 the G3588 world, G2889 (Wait, but He was still physically here.) but G2532 these G3778 are G1526 in G1722 the G3588 world, G2889 and G2532 I G1473 come G2064 to G4314 you. G4571 Set Apart G40 Father, G3962 keep G5083 through G1722 your own G4675 Name G3686 those G846 who G3739 you have given G1325 me, G3427 that G2443 they may be G5600 one, G1520 as G2531 we G2249 *are*...**John 17:12** While G3753 I was G2252 with G3326 them G846 in G1722 the G3588 world, G2889 I G1473 kept G5083 them G846 in G1722 thy G4675 name: G3686 those that G3739 you gave G1325 me G3427 I have kept, G5442 and G2532 none G3762 of G1537 them G846 is lost, G622 but G1508 the G3588 son G5207 of perdition; G684 that G2443 the G3588 scripture G1124 might be fulfilled. G4137

Yahshua was praying from a higher dimension. He was praying from a higher Throne and Altar, which was why Yahshua was able to say, "...**was in the world**..." while physically still here on

Earth. This gets even more staggering because He makes the distinction between Earth and the World. World here is a dimensional place. Yahshua manifested THE NAME while passing through this World. How? Through the Kingdom Altar called HaShamayim, which manifests that which is unseen. Yahshua makes an astounding statement here in verse 11, "I am no more **in** the world...", and yet, He was standing before everyone. His statement was the Language from another dimension beyond Earth. The World was the assigned place of passage in order for Him to make the transaction of redemption. What Yahshua claimed was, He completed the Influence by the Kingdom Message, and was now ready to seal this in His Blood.

As Yahshua continued to pray, He created the environment for the Name, which kept the ones given to Him in. As the Adamah Altar, Yahshua DEMONSTRATED the Altar of Heaven on Earth, who can resemble any of the Altar Authorities of Genesis 1:1 while in the flesh! WOW! The Heavenly Altar is manifested, when Earth emulates that Image.

Heaven is symbolic of The Throne which The Name YHWH sits!! Let us read from the prophet Isaiah -

> **Isaiah 66:1** Now[H3541] says[H559] **Yahweh,**[H3068] **The Heavens**[H8064] **My Throne,**[H3678] and the earth[H776] *is* my **footstool:**[H1916 H7272] where[H335] *is* the house[H1004] that[H834] you build[H1129] for me? and where[H335] *is* **the**[H2088] **place**[H4725] of my **rest?**[H4496]

As the Prophet spoke about the 5th Altar of the Heavens Throne, he conveys a message to the reader, regarding The manifested Name, who is seated on This Heavenly Altar Throne. This is the place of The Name, the place of Authority and Demonstration, just as the Ephod would be illuminated when the Urim and Thummim would enunciate The unseen Voice. This Altar is activated because of The Word MANIFESTED through The Name, who congealed from behind the veil! This Voice from behind the veil of the Tabernacle put on the vibrational garment of sound. This sound attached itself to the Urim and Thummim, causing illumination. At that point, the Ephod would disclose to Aaron Elohim's will. This unseen Voice had now taken on the form of Hebrew letters engraved in the Breastplate, and now Aaron was the walking Oracle on Earth once a year. This is where the Eternal One would descend and make His way to Man.

The Word for footstool here is: הדם – **HaDom** which means: dismembered or pieces. HaDom can also be: **HaDam** which means **The Blood**. As the blood touches the Altar, it releases the voice concealed within its chambers. The Earth is the place of sacrifice and legal grounds for the Spirit to walk IF it has a body matter and substance. When this word is read the other way we have: מדה – **Mo'deh,** which means: to fashion a thing, to piece together a puzzle or, restore a shattered vessel. Mi'dah is also defined as: to measure and balance the books. The Earth is the place where YHWH Himself pieces back together that which was shattered bringing balance again to His Creation. All of this comes by way of the HaDam, The Blood of His Son Yahshua HaMashiach!! We will address this idea when we address the last Altar.

Yahshua said in John 17 that He MANIFESTED The Name.

~ **Manifested** – G5319 *Phaneroo* which means to unveil, declare. From the Hebrew word Galah/גָּלָה which means: Exile or to reveal something hidden.

Yahshua came to the Exiles and Manifested the Power of His Altar through them. He activated the engine to this Shamayim Altar. He only came to the lost sheep of the House of Israel, Matthew 15:24. The Shamayim Altar is manifested when The Name is displayed! The Altar's power is activated when the Authority is present! When Elohim said, 'LET them have dominion', He was activating the Altar of Creative power upon Ish and Ishah back in Genesis 1! The Creative power is seen when a marriage takes place and the two become Basar Echad, One Kingdom Message. As the Creative power rests upon the man and woman, at that moment, Dominion is in operation!

In Ephesians 5, Shaul/Paul, conveys a revelation regarding marriage, connecting this to the Mashiach and His Bride. The Congregation of Mashiach IS the HaShamayim Altar here on Earth, who is the great mystery of marriage. The Priestly Power of this Altar is released through the womb of the Bride in order to birth the Kingdom Stones of the Ephod, which causes the message of The Kingdom, HaShamayim, The Kingdom Altar to be tangible. This is a term, regarding the believer, we must realize is manifested Kingdom according to Yahshua!! We are The Kingdom of the Heavens, who are to demonstrate the Kingdom, not just talk about it!

The Word summonsed the, "WHAT WE ARE SUPPOSE TO BE!" Yahshua said,

> ● **Matthew 6:10** Your^{G4675} Kingdom^{G932} come.^{G2064} **Your^{G4675} will^{G2307}** be done^{G1096} on^{G1909} **The Earth**,^{G1093} as^{G5613} it is in^{G1722} **The Heavens.**^{G3772}

This is a statement, 'Your Kingdom come Your will be done ON EARTH as it is in The Heavens', is a unifying message of The Word, who is The King!! Activation takes place when, we as His sons and daughters of the Kingdom, Mashiach is saying that we have the power, the authority, the dominion to remove the void! To Remove the Chaos is also Removing the confusion! The Uniting of the Kingdom on the Earth, is the Kingdom MANIFESTED! As Yahshua was teaching us how to pray here on Earth, He was also prophesying the coming of His Kingdom! Your Purpose and Will be done here on Earth as it already is in The Heavens!

"I want to prophesy to someone reading this, that the chaos, the void is being removed from your life as you **become** this Kingdom Prayer!!" As you move from the Enosh man or the sick, seemingly incurable place to the place of the Adam or the whole man, Wholeness and fullness in your life at this moment, Amein!

As we confirm this, when examining this Hebrew word Enosh, which is the picture of the lowest state of man, parallels an altar that cannot be satisfied due to its sickly condition! Seth, created an Altar, who, by naming his son Enosh, was prophesying what would take place. What Seth did, who would continue on the revelation given to Adam, named his son Enosh, causing the prophecy to resume. Whatever you name will become an Altar in your life!! What you constantly talk about becomes an altar in your life!! Cain and Abel were Adam and Eve's generational altars after the fall. Our children become the family altar we created, who continue with the Kingdom things!

By DOING what The Word says, we properly keep the fire of the Altar ignited. By mixing the holy with the profane is bringing strange fire to the Altar!! "My prayer at this time is that mixed generational altars will be broken down!! That all generational altar language born through oaths and covenants, opposite of The Altar of Elohim, be broken down! I pray that this day the HaShamayim Altar will be built up in all our lives because of the MANIFESTED Rhema Word! By the Power of the returning Exiles breaks the shackles off those, who have been scattered in the nations!!

The Hebrew word Enosh is also No'se/נשׁא which means: forgiveness, forgiving, the lifting of a burden. Enosh was the walking Altar of prophecy, his name communicated that man would be forgiven for: his profaning, his rebellion, his wickedness and his sin in one day. Just because a son is born and given a name that seems to make no sense to the Greek mindset, does not mean to change what Scripture says regarding its prophetic indication. Paul said we are to be Bereans and search out what is WRITTEN, not what some man's translation is!! To change the language of Scripture, is to accept the fallen place of man as an altar of defilement!!

Adam was The Altar that should have instituted restoration to a fallen world of chaos and emptiness. This is why Elohim said 'Whatsoever Adam CALLED/Qara THEM that's what they BECAME." The Last Adam was PROPOSED to Israel as Savior and King, and as many as ACCEPTED Him, to them, He gave the POWER to BECOME!! To become what? To Become a walking Altar Throne of demonstration and power!! Adam Proposed a Basar/Good News Body to the souls of the animals and as these souls ACCEPTED the PROPOSAL, the Shamayim Altar manifested them on the Earth, bringing balance. Genesis 1-2 says, that these LIVING beasts were INSIDE the Shamayim, might I add, the Shamayim Altar. Adam was conducting Heavenly Altar transactions here on the Earth from the Adamah Altar, who is the Advocate between the two! This is so deep, we will address these ideas throughout this book! We go from Adam to Cain and then with Abel, his murder takes place and stops the legs of the Altar Adam and Eve instituted. The Altar with legs is a penned idiom of mine, which conveys ACTIVATION of the Redemption plan.

We first see this Enosh revelation in our last couple of Torah portions in Genesis 4:

> **Genesis 4:26** And to Seth,^{H8352} to him^{H1931} also^{H1571} there was born^{H3205} a son;^{H1121} and he called^{H7121} (^{H853}) his name^{H8034} Enosh:^{H583} then^{H227} **began**^{H2490} men to call^{H7121} upon the name^{H8034} of Yahweh.^{H3068}

In this generation of Enosh, we have the revelation of man's lowest state of being, Enosh speaks of the frailty of the flesh and weakness of man's altar. Enosh comes from Anash which means to be weak, sickly, despised, polluted, profaned, etc. The verse reads as:

וּלְשֵׁת גַּם־הוּא יֻלַּד־בֵּן וַיִּקְרָא אֶת־שְׁמוֹ אֱנוֹשׁ

"And to Seth **NEVERTHELESS** was born also a son and he called his name Enosh…"

This can be the better translation because Seth, as the new stone of the family, was the foundation to those coming after him. Seth, the son of a new foundation, man's fall was unravelling into the generations because of sin, yet, YHWH Elohim would have a remedy **Graced** into the generations. The wording can confuse many because of the lack of knowing the Hebrew language. The context of scripture connects Enosh to the phrase, which the entire book of Leviticus is named after – **Vayiqra = And He Called**!! Enosh's name represented the frailty of man because his sinful fallen state, but Elohim would intertwine the Remedy of Mercy, man would find his way back to Eden!

Enosh is found in other verses, proving this fact, which is defined as a lower status compared to Adam. Enosh means Incurability, Sickly and even Wicked in some places. If we investigate this idea of the Enosh, whose name means: man's sinfulness and fallen state of being, which has been revealed throughout all generations, then, we risk saying Yahshua was of this blood line literally. This can be nothing further from the truth. Let us examine some scriptural demarcations pertaining to Enosh, who is revealed by definition:

- **Job 34:6** Should I lie^{H3576} against^{H5921} my right side?^{H4941} my wound^{H2671} is **incurable**^{H605} without^{H1097} transgression.^{H6588}

In this section of verse, Enosh is defines as an **incurable** disease by man's own power.

- **Isaiah 17:11** In the day^{H3117} you will make your plant^{H5194} to grow^{H7735} and in the morning^{H1242} you will make your seed^{H2233} to blossom:^{H6524} the harvest^{H7105} will be a pile^{H5067} in the day^{H3117} of grief^{H2470} and of **desperate**^{H605} sorrow.^{H3511}

In this section of verse, Enosh means to be **desperate**.

- **Job 4:17** Will **mortal man**^{H582} be more just than Eloah?$^{H6663\ H4480\ H433}$ shall a man^{H1397} be more pure^{H2891} than his maker?$^{H4480\ H6213}$

In this section of verse, **Mortal man** is our word Enosh. The term Mortal means the lowest state of being. The opposite of mortal is immortality!!!

- **2 Samuel 12:15** And Nathan^{H5416} departed^{H1980} into^{H413}

his house.^H1004 And Yahweh^H3068 touched^H5062 (^H853) the child^H3206 that^H834 Uriah's^H223 wife^H802 birthed^H3205 unto David,^H1732 and it **was very sick.**^H605

In this section of verse, Enosh is seen as **sickly**.

Jeremiah 15:18; 30:12, 15; Micah 1:9 also speak of a wound that is INCURABLE. Enosh, even though the son of Seth, who is after the Likeness and Image of Adam now, a fallen state, would bear a son whose named after man's condition. Seth picks up the Baton that was dropped by the first two sons in order to continue the redemptive story of man. Enosh, means frail man, but projects man's incurable state of being, sickly, wicked, fallen from Grace, which defines the CAUSE of man being in this status change.

Seth, who founded the message all over again regarding Adams children, which is the Message of The Kingdom, repentance and the return back to Eden's Paradise. These names of the sons conceal this revelation. Let us continuing reading the rest of this verse as it says one thing in English, but actually conveys deeper truth, when defined from its Hebrew origin. We can't go wrong as The Spirit of The Word concurs with the meaning behind this language which was used to scribe the original message.

The Spirit and The Word work in agreement and never detour away from the truth. The rest of this verse sounds like an exciting sermon to preach, but as we examine this section, we will connect the Power of our 5th Altar Throne – HaShamayim, or The Kingdom of Heaven Altar, as we investigate this from another perspective –

There are several titles given for mankind, for his body, which are – Ish, Adam, Enosh, Geber, Golem, Goof. The verse goes on to say something that sounds like a good thing when read from the English translation:

"…then **began** men to call upon the Name of YHWH."

אָז הוּחַל לִקְרֹא בְּשֵׁם יהוה:

"...then/SINCE man profaned himself (Enosh) For the sake of The Authority of The Name." What the Hebrew is conveying here is, that because man profaned Himself, the plan of Redemption would be instituted!!

The name of Enosh, as mentioned earlier, is defined as: uncurable, sickly, wicked, profane, wounded, defiled, etc. Having said that, it would be for the sake of The Name YHWH, man was first created after the image and likeness of, his Redemptive Advocate would come.

It's not that during the days of Enosh men **began** to defile the Name, which can't really be defiled, but that Seth who named his son, would emanate the position of Adam and Eve after the fall and where they fell to. The Scriptural evidence is, Adam, who named his son that was murdered Abel or HaBel which means a breath, vanity, the Redemption prophecy would begin to unfold. The names of children concealed the names of the redemptive plan by their definition. There is a revelation given from Adam to Yahshua, revealing the Redemptive plan for man, by defining their Hebrew names.

So, we can see just because a son's name is defined as bad, such as Abel, within this genealogical line, DOES NOT mean we change the prophetic message concealed in them! We must leave the oracles of His Word alone, otherwise we become like Moses, who changed the prophecy by striking the Rock twice instead of speaking to The Rock that second time!!

In addition, when we add the names Seth and Enosh and examine their Ordinal values we have 85. This is the same value as a **key** word found in Exodus 28:15 – אפד – **Ephod**. This Ephod of Aaron was the Earthly representation to the Breastplate of Righteousness containing the 12 Tribal Stones of a Royal and Holy Nation after the Order of Melkhitzedeq! These three Altars we have just entered into are a mirrored in the Ephod of Aaron's Levitical Priesthood!! Remember, within this Ephod of Genesis 1:1, are the Scepter, the Priesthood Dominion and Authority revelations, we will get into as this book unfolds.

Back to this verse where men **BEGAN**, we discover that the Hebrew word meant to defile, to pollute, to profane. This word also means to bore through a thing or even pierce through something. Cain murdered his brother and defiled the seedline which is reflected in the definitions to this word BEGAN.

The numerical value of the Hebrew word for BEGAN is 49, the same as the Remedy for Man – **HaDam** = **The Blood**!! It would be through The Blood that Redemption would manifest in the Flesh. We can see this revelation and prophecy unfolding from that time forward!! The Blood produces the Sons and Daughters of the Kingdom. The Blood speaks on behalf of those it purchased! This is where the Altar revelation was pivotal for mankind.

The Ephod and Altar Breastplate

The Ephod Throne of Creation and The Kingdom Parables mirror the HaShamayim Miz'be'ach/The Altar of Heaven, which are seen throughout Scripture. When Yahshua was here, He revealed them through speech and by what He did. Yahshua HaMashiach is the manifestation of The Adamah Altar as He walked this Earth. Adamah in Hebrew can be read as Adomeh, which means: **'I will be like and resemble'**. Yahshua, who is the Word, who is The manifested Altar King-Priest, who incarnates as any of the Altars of Genesis 1:1, manifested them as He walked on Earth.

He gave many a New Beginning and a New place to place their feet upon – **B'reshith**. He recreated the lives and hope of the people - **Bara**. He spoke with authority and not as the Pharisees and Sadducees - **Elohim**. He demonstrated His superior Priesthood as the Light shining in the dark World - **ET**. He connected The Heavens and The Earth by reunited all who believed in Him – **Va'Et**. He made distant man ever close to an Eternal Elohim! He became the canopy of Grace and Truth over The Earth – **Ha'Aretz**.

The Seven Altar Thrones of Genesis 1:1

As you will notice, I just mentioned the seven Altars with this statement. Let's look at this Altar Name:

מזבח השמים~ – **The Altar of Heavens**. Altars are bridges between the Mortal and Immortal dimensions. The Altar is the span between the Divine and the realm of Mortality. The Altar, we are speaking about, was unlocked when Yahshua came preaching the Kingdom and demonstrating The Kingdom here on Earth. Preaching The Kingdom will unlock the Kingdom revelation because preaching is a key. This Altar is that of Righteousness, Power, Kingship, Royal Priesthood and Dominion. The numerical value to this Altar says it all:

מלכי-צדק כס מלכים וכהנים – 452~ – '**Melkhitzedeq Keis Melakhim Ve'Ko'henim**', = "**The Melchizedek Throne of Kings and Priests!**" In Exodus 19, along with 1 Peter, we are given the goal for man –

> Exodus 19:6 And you[H859] will be[H1961] to me **a Kingdom**[H4467] **of priests,**[H3548] and an **Set Apart**[H6918] **Nation.**[H1471] These[H428] are the words[H1697] which[H834] you will speak[H1696] to[H413] the children[H1121] of Israel.[H3478]

> 1Peter 2:9 But[G1161] you[G5210] are a **chosen**[G1588] **generation,**[G1085] a **Royal**[G934] **Priesthood,**[G2406] an **Holy**[G40] **Nation,**[G1484] a **peculiar**[G1519 G4047] **people;**[G2992] that[G3704] you should show forth[G1804] the[G3588] praises[G703] of him[G3588] who has called[G2564] you[G5209] out of[G1537] darkness[G4655] into[G1519] his[G846] marvelous[G2298] light:[G5457]

I want to reiterate something, test everything you read in this book. Don't take my word for anything, but test what you read against what is written in Scripture especially with anyone who preaches the Word. You will read some ideas and concepts in this book, if you haven't already, that will challenge your religious position. This has and will happen because when engaging in the subject of the Altar Throne of the Heavens, we are dealing with complete Kingdom reality beyond our natural minds! This is pure and total Royal Power, which cannot be challenged by mere natural forces! This is total Sovereign influence from the Highest of the highest dimensions!

The Altar Throne of the Heavens, reveals our Garment of Beauty! Continuing, Yahshua came clothing the naked people with His Message, which is called Basar/Good News in Hebrew! Basar is defined by many concepts such as: Resurrected Flesh and the Good News. Man was first made of this Basar or Garment of Beauty and Light!! The Kingdom Message is what we should be preaching! This was the only message Yahshua preached when He began His ministry. This world is the fitting room for the Kingdom Garment measurements! We are measured, weighed in the balance to see who will be fit for the Altar Throne of the Heavens Garment!! Will you be dressed for the Marriage Supper of the Lamb?

> 🌹 **Matthew 5:20** For^{G1063} I say^{G3004} to you,^{G5213} That^{G3754} except^{G3362} your^{G5216} righteousness^{G1343} will surpass^{G4052} ^{G4119} the righteousness of the^{G3588} scribes^{G1122} and^{G2532} Pharisees,^{G5330} you will in no case^{G3364} enter^{G1525} **into**^{G1519} **The**^{G3588} **Kingdom**^{G932} **of Heaven.**^{G3772}

Listen to His words, "UNLESS your RIGHTEOUSNESS **exceeds** that of the Scribes and Pharisees you can't even **enter** The Kingdom of Heaven." What is between The Adamah Altar Yahshua and The Altar Throne of The Earth? Tohu V'Bohu!! We must ascend beyond that which is Earthly and Carnal, Void and Empty!! We must surpass that which is of the Pharisees and Scribes, who were the watchman of that Temple era that was fading away at that time. That part of The Law was never foundational, it only placed as a temporary reprieve because of the infiltration of the second Temple era, also known as The Harlot on The Hill!

The Righteousness that surpasses that religious system was is that of a Kingly Order!! It was That of a Royal Power and Dominion! I was that which was foundational from the very Beginning as our foundation platform! This is only executed by The King, who

The Seven Altar Thrones of Genesis 1:1

through His Altar, unlocked the Kingdom Dominion and built this revelation upon the Chief Corner Stone, who is The Rock of our Salvation!!

You cannot keep playing around in religion and man's altars expecting a breakthrough!! You can't fool around in animal blood and the bloodthirst of men!! It is time to walk as the Altar of Heaven on Earth and invade the territory and take back The Kingdom Reign from the kingdom of Darkness that haunts many pulpits around the planet today!!

The Altar of Heaven, or the 5th Altar Throne– HaShamayim Altar, is the Robed Kingdom with the Ephod Authority. When Yahshua was about to be crucified, the soldiers of the Roman Empire could not tear His Purple Robe –

- **John 19:2** And^{G2532} the^{G3588} soldiers^{G4757} pressed^{G4120} a **crown**^{G4735} of^{G1537} thorns,^{G173} and put it on^{G2007} his^{G846} head,^{G2776} and^{G2532} they put on^{G4016} him^{G846} a **purple**^{G4210} **robe,**^{G2440}

- **John 19:3** And^{G2532} said,^{G3004} Hail,^{G5463} King^{G935} of the^{G3588} Jews!^{G2453} and^{G2532} they struck him with their hands.^{G1325} ^{G846} ^{G4475}

- **John 19:4** Pilate^{G4091} therefore^{G3767} went^{G1831} forth^{G1854} again,^{G3825} and^{G2532} said^{G3004} to them,^{G846} Behold,^{G2396} I bring^{G71} him^{G846} forth^{G1854} to you,^{G5213} that^{G2443} you may know^{G1097} that^{G3754} I find^{G2147} no^{G3762} fraud^{G156} in^{G1722} him.^{G846}

- **John 19:5** Then^{G3767} came^{G1831} Yeshua^{G2424} forward,^{G1854} wearing^{G5409} the^{G3588} **crown**^{G4735} of **thorns,**^{G174} and^{G2532} the^{G3588} **purple**^{G4210} **robe.**^{G2440} And^{G2532} Pilate said^{G3004} unto them,^{G846} Behold^{G2396} the^{G3588} Adam!^{G444}

~**Purple Robe** – וּלְבוּשׁ הָאַרְגָּמָן

Our Bible is all about a Kingdom and The King of a special people. Here is another revelation to ponder, when Yahshua came and laid His life down on that crucifixion site, that was not the ultimate goal. The ultimate goal was, Yahshua redeeming The Kingdom that had become swallowed up into the Chaos and Emptiness of the fall. Remember, when Adam fell, a thick darkness covered the known world and infiltrated acrossed his DNA seed line. The **Purple Robe** is the Banner of The Altar Throne of the Heavens! The Banner is the Matchless Garment of Priestly Royal Dominion!

> **Luke 17:20** And when he was demanded of the Pharisees, when the **kingdom of Elohim** should manifest, he answered them and said, The **kingdom of Elohim** doesn't manifest with observation:

> **Luke 17:21** Neither shall they say, Look here! or, look there! for, behold, **the kingdom of Elohim is within you**.

> **1Corinthians 4:20** For^{G1063} **the**^{G3588} **kingdom**^{G932} **of ELOHIM**^{G2316} is not^{G3756} in^{G1722} word,^{G3056} but^{G235} in^{G1722} **power.**^{G1411}

The Kingdom of Elohim concealed inside and is manifested by demonstration! The Kingdom of Elohim is the expanding Authority to the Altar Throne of Heaven!! Notice this word for power, it's the same word used for the power of the enemy we are to trample under foot as well the authority of the kingdom of darkness!! In Luke 4:1-13 we have the temptation toward Yahshua and His response was, "**it is written**..." Yahshua, who is The Word, used the written word against the enemy. He was using the Constitution of The Kingdom of Heaven, if I may say, against Satan Himself. Satan knows about this Kingdom and Power of the Altar Throne of this Heavens, which he desired as Isaiah 14 described.

My premise is solely on Kingdom, Priesthood and Altar of Yahshua HaMashiach, which reflects of the will of Abba on the Earth. We should be preaching what The King came preaching and nothing else. Remember, in a religion your destiny is death, but in The Kingdom it's the Resurrection and Eternal Life, which death cannot touch. In religion there is only the hope that the sick, lame, blind, dead, leprous, backslidden get healed, raised and delivered. As for The Kingdom, these known altars are all crushed!!! You will read in this book many times this statement, 'Yahshua came demonstrating all Seven Altar Thrones by what He did'. The Kingdom of Heaven Altar Throne holds the Remedy to the frailty of fallen Man!!

Yahshua was sent for one reason and it wasn't to just die on the Cross/Tree. Golgotha, or The Place of The Adamah Altar, was the Altar of Highest Order on Earth, which gave Him the Lawful and Legal Right to Redeem the fallen Kingdom and prepare Her the Kingdom, for empowerment!! His Altar unlocked the access to all Seven Altars, which activated the Release from each of these Thrones. This is why Scripture says Yahshua gave us the Keys OF the Kingdom, not the Keys TO the Kingdom.

In Luke 4:14 it is written that Yahshua returned in the POWER of the Ruach/Spirit. The Altar of Yahshua was infused with the Power of all Seven Altars! The Spirit/Ruach is the Breath to all Seven Altar Thrones. This same Breath/Spirit is in every believer, we just need to release this concealed Power and that happens through Belief/Emunah! In Hebrews it is written, those who come to The father MUST BELIEVE that He is... Belief RELEASES Power from The Altar Throne and then that Power is manifested on Earth.

Yahshua was the walking Adamah Altar on Earth. Adamah is Adomeh, which means: I will Resemble or I will be Similar to. This Altar of Yahshua can take on the Form of any of the Seven Altar Thrones and because He came through the womb of a woman, He can manifest all Seven here on the Earth, which He did! Continuing with Luke, in 4:18 Yahshua ceased the prophetic word that unlocked His ministry!! We need the Prophetic Word of Yah in our lives, according to what is written, which will UNLOCK the ministry of The Kingdom we are to walk in! We are a voice to His Altar and a manifestation of His Altar here on Earth.

> **Luke 4:43** And^{G1161} he^{G3588} said^{G2036} to^{G4314} them,^{G846} <mark>I^{G3165} must^{G1163} proclaim^{G2097} the^{G3588} Kingdom^{G932} of Elohim^{G2316}</mark> to other^{G2087} cities^{G4172} also:^{G2532} for^{G3754} therefore^{G1519 G5124} <mark>am I sent.^{G649}</mark> (The Kingdom of Elohim is The Good News Message. The Message becomes the Scepter of The King extended here on The Earth Altar! This permits what is in The Heavens to be so on The Earth.)

> **Luke 4:44** And^{G2532} he preached^{G2258 G2784} in^{G1722} the^{G3588} synagogues^{G4864} of Galilee.^{G1056}

Let's read some Kingdom verses:

● **Psalm 145:13** Your **Kingdom**^{H4438} is an everlasting^{H3605 H5769} **kingdom,**^{H4438} and your **dominion**^{H4475} overcomes throughout all^{H3605} generations.^{H1755 H1755}

The word Dominion comes from: Mashal in Hebrew which means: Parable! The Kingdom holds the key to the protective layer between the Heavens and the Earth. This Shamayim Altar Throne is the governing power, which is activated on Earth through The Kings Scepter, which is Man himself. This will be expounded on in the next Altar Throne revelation, the 6th Altar Throne of Genesis 1:1. Yahshua is the extended Scepter, also known as The King of kings, who was manifested in a flesh body.

Once again, this powerful Hebrew word Mashal is also Le'shem when read the other way (משל לשמ) , which means Precious Stone. This was also one of the names of the stones on Aaron's Ephod Breastplate. The precious Stone that Lucifer could not walk among was the Kingdom Stone, which was Le'shem!! It is the Kings Jewel to the Priesthood, which is also the Authority Stone to The Name – Le'Shem – Le meaning: To and Shem meaning: Name/Authority!!

Every kingdom MUST have dominion and rule! In Genesis 1:26-27, YHWH Elohim GIVES the man and woman dominion and they are given the Name Adam! This was the historical account, which The Kingdom was given Authority to colonize, or, populate this Earth with the mastery of the Heavenly Kingdom!! Adam and the woman were to colonize this Earth from the Place called, the Altar of HaAdamah. The HaAdamah Altar revealed the Altar Throne of Heaven's Banner of rulership here on The Earth Altar! YHWH Elohim delegated His Authority to Adam from The Altar Throne of the Heavens, our Altar revelation in this section!

> **Psa 103:19** Yahweh ^H3068 has erected^H3559 **His Throne**^H3678 **in the Heavens**;^H8064 and His **Kingdom**^H4438 rules^H4910 over all.^H3605

His Throne is **IN The Heavens**. Having read this, since YHWH's Throne is **in** The Heavens or the Shamayim Altar Throne, this means, we speak of this Altar Throne. When we proclaim His Word, we are actually emanating that power from The Creator Himself, which manifests through His Name YHWH regarding the Kingdom sons of this Dominion and Authority!!

> **Daniel 4:3** How^H4101 great^H7260 are his signs^H852 and how^H4101 mighty^H8624 are his wonders^H8540 his **kingdom**^H4437 is an everlasting^H5957 **Kingdom**^H4437 and his **Dominion**^H7985 is from^H5974 generation^H1859 to generation.^H1859

Not only did Yahshua manifest The Fathers Name, which is The Voice behind the veil of this world, He manifested Abba/The Father to all who was given to Him. The Father/Abba is **IN** the Kingdom of the Heavens! The Altar of Heaven contains the favor of Abba, which is why our message MUST echo what Yahshua said regarding the words of Life and Power!! Notice:

> **Matthew 5:45** That^G3704 you may be^G1096 the children^G5207 of your^G5216 Father^G3962 which^G3588 is **in**^G1722 **The Heavens**^G3772 for^G3754 he makes his^G848 sun^G2246 to rise^G393 on^G1909 the evil^G4190 and^G2532 on the good,^G18 and^G2532 sends rain^G1026 on^G1909 the just^G1342 and^G2532 on the unjust.^G94

> **Matthew 5:48** You[G5210] will be[G2071] therefore[G3767] **perfect,**[G5046] even as[G5618] your[G5216] Father[G3962] which[G3588] is **in**[G1722] **The Heavens**[G3772] is[G2076] perfect.[G5046] (This Altar of Heavens is an unmixed Altar Kingdom!! The word **'perfect'** in Hebrew is defined as: Tamim or unmixed. We are commanded to be perfect or unmixed!! Noah was perfect in his generation, he was unmixed from the Nephilim seedline and races.)

> **Matthew 6:9** After this manner[G3779] therefore[G3767] you[G5210] pray:[G4336] Our[G2257] Father[G3962] which[G3588] is **in**[G1722] **The Heavens,**[G3772] Set Apart[G37] Your[G4675] Name be.[G3686] (The Father is in The Heavens or Altar Throne of Heavens and His Name is Qadosh/Set Apart. When we walk in this revelation, we are sanctified by His Name. The Voice is His Name manifested through language. We don't set His Name apart by pronunciation, we set His Name Apart when we walk in the Dominion and Authority this Name represents. He built His Name YHWH and His Power INTO the Tzela/Bone of Adam. His Kingdom Altar is substantiated from the Place of Demonstration and Power!)

> **Mat 6:10** Your[G4675] **Kingdom**[G932] **manifest.**[G2064] Your[G4675] will[G2307] be accomplished[G1096] in[G1909] **The Earth**[G1093] as[G5613] it is in[G1722] **The Heavens.**[G3772] **Mat 6:11** Give[G1325] us[G2254] this day[G4594] our[G2257] **daily**[G1967] **Bread.**[G740]

Here is another way of praying this:

"Your Altar of Heaven, Your Kingdom Throne manifest, may Your Power and Authority be demonstrated here on the Earth Altar as it always was from the Heavenly Altar Throne! Give us this day our daily Bread of Heaven - our Kingdom Authority and Kingdom Dominion!! Our Kingdom Altar Throne, which is always expanding and transcending in victory!! Give us this day our Altar of Heavens, Your influence here on this Altar of Earth."

The Earth Altar is the Outer Courtyard area of decision making.

This is The Place of sacrifice, substitution and where accusations are filed. You can have victory right now over ALL your situations if you ascend the Heavenly order of the Courts!

> **Matthew 6:20** ButG1161 lay-upG2343 for yourselvesG5213 **treasuresG2344 inG1722 The Heavens,G3772** whereG3699 neitherG3777 mothG4597 norG3777 rustG1035 does corrupt,G853 andG2532 whereG3699 thievesG2812 do notG3756 break throughG1358 norG3761 steal:G2813 **6:21** ForG1063 whereG3699 yourG5216 **treasureG2344** is,G2076 thereG1563 will yourG5216 **heartG2588** beG2071 also.G2532

The heart of man is the seat of the soul which should reflect the Voice of Heavens Altar Throne!! Out of the abundance of the heart, the mouth speaks. When the soul is arrested by the Power, Love and Acceptance of The King, His Scepter is extended from the Altar Throne of Heaven and to the Earth, where the HaAdamah Altar of Sacrifice is stationed. From this Place the soul becomes the treasure possession of the Heavenly Altar Throne!! The Hebrew word for treasure here means: storehouse, the place where treasures are stored!! Now here is where this gets very challenging –

> **Matthew 7:21** NotG3756 everyoneG3956 that **confessesG3004** to meG3427 AdonaiG2962 Adonai,G2962 shall enterG1525 intoG1519 **TheG3588 KingdomG932 of The Heavens;G3772** butG235 he that bearsG4160 theG3588 willG2307 of myG3450 FatherG3962 whichG3588 is inG1722 **The Heavens**.G3772 **7:22** ManyG4183 will sayG2046 to meG3427 inG1722 thatG1565 day,G2250 Master,G2962 Master,G2962 have we notG3756 **prophesiedG4395** by yourG4674 name?G3686 andG2532 by yourG4674 nameG3686 have **cast outG1544 demons?G1140** andG2532 through yourG4674 nameG3686 **doneG4160 manyG4183 wonderful works?G1411** **7:23** AndG2532 thenG5119 will I proclaimG3670 to them,G846 I neverG3763 knewG1097 you:G5209 departG672 fromG575 me,G1700 you that **workG2038 iniquity/Torahlessness.G458**

What we see in our time is a lawless, prostituting false miracle and false prophesying kingdom of the Harlot that Revelation chapter 18:4 speaks about. We are to come out this corrupt system. The Kingdom, which our 5th Altar represents, is one of true Power, Holiness and Demonstration of these pillars to The Altar Throne of the Heavens! The miraculous deeds mentioned in this section of scripture, are not the favored place of acceptance. Yahshua says, "Depart from me you workers of Iniquity, I never knew you!" Lawlessness is the sure way of being rejected no matter if miracles are made claim to. WOW!

The Greek word for Iniquity is: **Anomos**, which means: one who rejects The Law of Elohim, to be Torahlessness. This is the Law, which is our foundation to The Kingdom, we are to live by! This is Covenant Law not animal sacrifice, but Kingdom Covenant Law that remains for the Redeemed. You can do all the miraculous things like this and if you reject this Kingdom Law, which is the foundation platform of the Chief Corner Stone Himself, then you risk being rejected! We MUST live by Covenant and Demonstrate His Word; we must have both!! We commanded to Demonstrate and Live by What is written. Blessed are those who **DO** and **TEACH**. The doing is the initiator of the teaching!

> **Matthew 10:5** These^{G5128} twelve^{G1427} Yeshua^{G2424} sent forth,^{G649} and commanded^{G3853} them,^{G846} saying,^{G3004} Go^{G565} not^{G3361} into^{G1519} the way^{G3598} of the Gentiles,^{G1484} and^{G2532} into^{G1519} any city^{G4172} of the Samaritans^{G4541} enter^{G1525} not there:^{G3361} **10:6** But^{G1161} go^{G4198} rather^{G3123} to^{G4314} ==the lost^{G622} sheep^{G4263} of the house^{G3624} of Israel.^{G2474}==

(Why the lost sheep? Because they are The Altar Carriers whose fire went out! The Fire of the Altar is ignited by the preaching from the Altar Platform! Speak to the Altar the truth and ignite a wayward nation of sons and daughters again!!)

> **Matthew 10:7** And^{G1161} as you go,^{G4198} preach,^{G2784}

> saying,G3004 TheG3588 **KingdomG932 of The HeavensG3772 is at hand.G1448** **10:8** HealG2323 the sick,G770 cleanseG2511 the lepers,G3015 raiseG1453 the dead,G3498 cast outG1544 demons,G1140 freelyG1432 you have received,G2983 freelyG1432 give back.G1325

We are called to Preach the Kingdom of Heaven message and Demonstrate the Altar of The Heavens by what was proclaimed! We must crush all other altars of the kingdom of darkness by **becoming** Heavens Altar Ambassadors on Earth!! Yahshua commissioned us to walk as The Kingdom of Priests and Kings, not a Kingdom WITH... When this is done, we now become those royal altars on The Earth.

> ➤ **Matthew 12:48** ButG1161 heG3588 answeredG611 sayingG2036 to him that spokeG2036 to him,G846 "WhoG5101 isG2076 myG3450 mother?G3384 andG2532 whoG5101 areG1526 myG3450 brethren?"G80 **12:49** AndG2532 he stretched forthG1614 hisG848 handG5495 towardG1909 hisG848 disciples,G3101 and said,G2036 BeholdG2400 myG3450 motherG3384 andG2532 myG3450 brethren!G80 **12:50** ForG1063 whosoeverG3748 shall doG4160 theG3588 willG2307 of myG3450 FatherG3962 whichG3588 is inG1722 **The Heavens (Altar Throne),** G3772 the sameG846 isG2076 myG3450 brother,G80 andG2532 sister,G79 andG2532 mother.G3384

Just because they are relatives doesn't mean they are Kingdom people!! Blood is not thicker than water in this case. The Altar Throne of Heaven is just that, The Kingdom Altar of the Word! The Hebrew word HaShamayim comes from Mayim which means Water. In Ephesians chapter 5 the Bride is said to be washed in the water of the Word! Washing the Bride in the water of the Word is clothing the Bride in the Garment of The Altar of The Heavens. Water baptism, or Tevillah in Hebrew, is the change of status. The immersion into the Water of the Word changes the status of anyone who enters this place.

Malkhut HaShamayim

- **Matthew 3:2** And^{G2532} proclaiming,^{G3004} Repent^{G3340} for^{G1063} the^{G3588} **Kingdom**^{G932} **of The Heavens**^{G3772} has arrived.^{G1448}

- **Matthew 4:17** From^{G575} that time^{G5119} Yeshua^{G2424} began^{G756} to preach^{G2784} and^{G2532} to say,^{G3004} "Repent:^{G3340} for^{G1063} the^{G3588} **Kingdom**^{G932} **of The Heavens**^{G3772} has been activated."^{G1448}

- **Matthew 10:7** And^{G1161} as you jouney,^{G4198} preach,^{G2784} saying,^{G3004} The^{G3588} **Kingdom**^{G932} **of The Heavens**^{G3772} has been activated.^{G1448}

- **Matthew 11:12** And^{G1161} from^{G575} the^{G3588} days^{G2250} of John^{G2491} the^{G3588} Immerser^{G910} until^{G2193} now^{G737} the^{G3588} **Kingdom**^{G932} **of The Heavens**^{G3772} suffers violence,^{G971} and^{G2532} the violent^{G973} take it by force.^{G726 G846}

In Matthew 11:12 the word for 'VIOLENCE' is translated from the Hebrew idea of Pressing, Pushing, Squeezing when passing through a birth canal. The Kingdom of Heaven is Pressing and Squeezing THROUGH the canal of Belief/Faith!! (Hebrews 11:1,6 – Now faith is the substance of things hoped for and the evidence of things not seen...without faith it is impossible to please Elohim because he who comes to Elohim MUST believe that he is and that He is a rewarder of them who diligently seek Him.) The Kingdom is pressing, bursting through the veil of religion! Elohim NEVER desired to have a religion! The Patriarchs were never building a religion! They knew about the Kingdom that was expanding through the vessels of faith and hope!

This Hebrew idea in is: **פצר** – Patzar – to press through, squeeze through. This precious stone I just mentioned is the Kingdom that is pressing through, breaking out of the barriers of limitations. The Altar Throne of the Heavens is the King's Bench of Authority, which bursts out of the limitations of the natural. The numerical value of this Hebrew word is: 370, the same as: לשם – Le'shem = Precious Stone. The Jacinth Stone, we have seen the connection to!

This goes in line with our Altar thought since Le'shem is Mashal read the opposite way. This speaks of the Authority and Kingdom Rule through the language of the Kingdom, Parables!

The Kingdom of Heaven Altar is the Crown for the Bride of Mashiach! The Crown can never be Toho V'Bohu! The Crown contains the Authority and Seal of The King! This Crown represents The Shamayim Altar Throne, which is the Crown the Bride is adorned with! According to this thought, the Crown is the Governor of the Kings Scepter! The Scepter is the extension of the Crown and the Crown is the Authority of The Altar! The functioning Altar is the continual extension of the Kings Scepter, which delegates Power and Favor! Let's examine the Hebrew word for Scepter:

Scepter – שבט = Shevet: rod, staff, *tribe. There is a Messianic verse that is filled with Kingdom Revelation regarding this idea. Yahshua said over and over, "The Kingdom of Heaven, The Kingdom of Heaven..." He also used The Kingdom of Elohim/God in conjunction with The Kingdom of Heaven, which is The Robe of Bride. The Kingdom of Elohim is the Law that sustains this Dominion the Bride stands upon. The Kingdom of Heaven is the Grace of Elohim seen and administered to its subjects. The Law of Elohim is the Foundation of what He has Created and Made. Religion will say, The Law is done away with and we are no longer under it. This is a misinterpretation of Paul's writings for the lack of Kingdom knowledge and ancient near East custom language, which our Bibles were first communicated.

Yahshua didn't come to abolish The Law as Matthew 5:17 records. He came to communicate the Torah and fill it up with Kingdom meaning and balance. Religious men used The Law to crush the people at that time by inserting their own restricted guidelines into it while never truly abiding by what was written. The Law of Elohim was supposed to be The Kingdoms foundation to stand upon and still is!

Every kingdom and country have laws that establishes its foundation. Even nature itself is governed by laws of its own! Religion removes law foundation for the sake of escaping responsibility or to over protect what is sacred.

Back to this Scepter connection.

> **Genesis 49:10** The sceptre[H7626] shall not[H3808] depart[H5493] from Judah[H4480 H3063] nor a lawgiver[H2710] from between[H4480 H996] his feet[H7272] until[H5704 H3588] Shiloh[H7886] arrives[H935] and for him will be the gathering[H3349] of the people[H5971].

This can be better translated as: "The Kingdom Rule will not be plucked off from Judah nor a lawgiver from between his feet until the return of obedience of the gathered people arrives!" This Hebrew word Shiloh has the numerical value of 345. This is the same value for HaShem/The Name, in Hebrew. The Name is the Authority and Seat of the Kingdom. All the people will call upon The Name with one language and with one voice.

When the **SCEPTER PEOPLE** return from Religion, Islam, Christianity, Judaism and enthrone Yahshua HaMashiach as King in the midst of their minds and land, it is then the Scepter of rule will usher in Shiloh – The Kingdom Reign! Notice the connection between Scepter and Tribe(s) –

> **Genesis 49:16** Dan[H1835] shall judge[H1777] his people,[H5971] as one[H259] of the tribes[H7626] of Israel.[H3478]

The Hebrew words for Tribes and Scepter are the same word – Mateh/מטה. The tribes are the Scepter of The King. The Tribes are The Kingdom of Heaven Ambassadors! The Kingdom of Heaven has her King who sits upon the Altar Throne in the midst of His people. The Throne is His Altar called HaShamayim – The Heavens!!

The Hebrew words numerical value for Scepter and Tribes is 311, the same for three Hebrew phrases that reveal the extended Scepter of The King:

הָאִשָּׁה – Ha'ishah = **The Bride**; יִשָׂא – Yisa = **To Accept**, To Lift up, **to Bear up, to Pardon**; שָׁוֵה – Shaveh = found in Genesis 14:17 known as **The King's Valley**. This Hebrew word Shaveh is defined as: being like or resembling another in rank or position. The King's valley was The Dominion of Melkhitzedeq himself. This is where the Melchizedek Royal Priesthood transfer took place, bringing Shalom to a family feud, and extinguishing the Chaos. When the kingdoms were fighting and killing each other, the Royal Priesthood brought the Bread of Heaven and The Blood of the Covenant to Abraham! This Bread and Wine was the Covenant interchange of acceleration of a new seedline.

It's when the Scepter is extended that the chaos is removed and the Bride is pardoned, accepted, lifted up to the side of The King, who now expands His Kingdom! It's when the Kingdom finds Her final destination beside the Parable Key Master, The King, The Redeemer, The Creator and Covenant Keeping Husbandman! This Scepter of the Kingdom will unfold even more so the next Altar Throne revelation, which is He who stands between The Heavens and The Earth, activates!

Listen to the words of Mashiach –

- **Matthew 4:17** From^{G575} that time^{G5119} Yeshua^{G2424} began^{G756} to preach^{G2784} and^{G2532} to say,^{G3004} Repent:^{G3340} for^{G1063} the^{G3588} Kingdom^{G932} of **The Heavens**^{G3772} is now.^{G1448}

- **Luke 7:21** And^{G1161} in^{G1722} that same^{G846} hour^{G5610} he cured^{G2323} many^{G4183} of^{G575} infirmities^{G3554} and^{G2532} plagues,^{G3148} and^{G2532} of evil^{G4190} spirits;^{G4151} and^{G2532} for many^{G4183} that were **blind**^{G5185} he gave^{G5483} sight.^{G991} **Luke 7:22** Then^{G2532} Yeshua^{G2424} answering^{G611} said^{G2036} unto them,^{G846} Go your way^{G4198} and tell^{G518} John^{G2491} what things^{G3739} you have witnessed^{G1492} and^{G2532} heard;^{G191}

John-James of the House of Flores.®

> how that^{G3754} the **blind**^{G5185} see,^{G308} the **lame**^{G5560} **walk,**^{G4043} the **lepers**^{G3015} **are cleansed,**^{G2511} the **deaf**^{G2974} **hear,**^{G191} the **dead**^{G3498} **are raised,**^{G1453} to the **poor**^{G4434} the **gospel is preached.**

His Altar interrupted the altars of blindness! His Altar interrupted the altars of lameness and stagnancy! His Altar interrupted the altars of leprosy! His Altar interrupted the altars of the deaf! His Altar interrupted the altars of death! His Altar interrupted the altars of poverty! His Altar Throne of The Heavens - His Kingdom – interrupted all generational iniquity altars! His Altar is the Loftiest and Highest Altar on Earth, who holds the Keys of Restoration of all things! The Highest Altar in the Heavens is now unleashing creative power in these verses! The Light stepped into the darkness and illuminated all hopeless situations. Yahshua, The Light of the world in a flesh body, was like The Father's '**FLESH LIGHT**' in the darkness, not Flash Light!

The Altar of The Heavens is the Kings extension of The Throne! The Altar is The Kings Scepter extended to this Earth! The Altar of the Heavens is the Scepter extending favor from all the Altars, through the One Appointed by them all! When the King extends His Scepter, passage is granted to ascend the Throne! We have been given passage to ascend to the Throne of the Heaven by a more perfect way in Yahshua HaMashiach! I will pick this up in the next section. Imagine this my fellow believer, your name is written within this Everlasting Ephod of The King.

Authority and Jurisdiction of The Shamayim Altar Miz'be'ach HaShamayim – <u>The Ephod of Creation</u>

We have seen how the Kingdom of Heaven Altar Throne was interrupting the altars of sickness, blindness, lameness, death, leprosy, etc. Now we continue with this unfolding revelation. We are making our way through this Genesis 1:1 Seven Altar Candelabrum or, Menorah, of Holy Eternal Fire! Each Altar a Flame equal to the next Altar Throne in our Genesis revelation!

The Kingdom of Heaven Altar is the extension of The Heavenly Throne YHWH Elohim sits upon as we have seen in several verses. May I reiterate an important principle seen throughout Scripture? Man is the lawful Ambassador on Earth in order for Heaven to intervene as many expositors have communicated this fact for hundreds of years. The Altar of Heaven, we have been engaging in, requires a specific system of authorization from the Soul, which communicates intelligently. The Altar is one of the most mysterious subject matters in the Scriptures. There are so many unanswered 'WHY's' that come with concrete responses! The Mystery of the Altar is so powerful. Yahshua said in:

Matthew 23:16 Woe^G3759 to you^G5213 blind^G5185 leaders^G3595 who say,^G3004 "Whoever^G3739 G302 will swear^G3660 by^G1722 the^G3588 temple,^G3485 it is^G2076 nothing;^G3762 but^G1161 whoever^G3739 G302 will swear^G3660 by^G1722 the^G3588 **gold**^G5557 of the^G3588 temple,^G3485 he is a debtor!^G3784 **23:17** Fools^G3474 and^G2532 blind:^G5185 for^G1063 which^G5101 is^G2076 greater,^G3187 the^G3588 gold,^G5557 or^G2228 the^G3588 **temple**^G3485 that sanctifies^G37 the^G3588 gold?^G5557 **23:18** And,^G2532 Whosoever^G3739 G1437 will swear^G3660 by^G1722 **The**^G3588 **Altar,**^G2379 it is^G2076 nothing;^G3762 but^G1161 whoever^G3739 G302 swears^G3660 by^G1722 the^G3588 **gift**^G1435 that^G3588 is upon^G1883 it,^G846 he is guilty.^G3784 **23:19** Fools^G3474 and^G2532 blind:^G5185 for^G1063 which^G5101 is greater,^G3187 the^G3588 gift,^G1435 or^G2228 **The**^G3588 **Altar**^G2379 **that sanctifies**^G37 **the**^G3588 **gift?**^G1435 **23:20 Whoever therefore will swear**^G3660 G3767 **by**^G1722 **the**^G3588 **Altar,**^G2379 **swears**^G3660 **by**^G1722 **him,**^G846 **and**^G2532 **by**^G1722 **all things**^G3956 **thereon.**^G1883 G846 **23:21** And whoever will swear^G3660 by^G1722 the^G3588 **temple,**^G3485 swears^G3660 by^G1722 it,^G846 and^G2532 by^G1722 him that **dwelleth therein.**^G2730 G846 **23:22** And^G2532 he that will swear^G3660 by^G1722 **The Heavens,**^G3772 swears^G3660 by^G1722 **the**^G3588 **Throne**^G2362 **of Elohim,**^G2316 **and**^G2532 **by**^G1722 **him that's enthroned**^G2521 **upon it.**^G1883 G846

We keep going from one level to the next level as Yahshua rebukes the religious groups. We go from what religion depends upon to what the people need! We go from the Temple then to the Gift on the Altar and then to The Altar itself. Yahshua makes an interesting connection between The Altar and Heavens Throne! The Shamayim Altar is reflected through and by the believer! Yahshua says The Heavens Altar Throne, we are currently discussing, IS the Throne of Elohim or, might I add, Powers! Let us ponder this thought, The Shamayim Altar is the Throne **TO** the Elohim Altar Throne. Our 4th Altar King, who connects these two, responds to the Genesis 1:2a account, which The Earth became void and empty, by activating and functioning through The Shamayim Altar Throne, which cannot be affected by this!

This is why Yahshua Governs the Keys '**TO**' the Kingdom while overseeing the Keys '**OF**' the Kingdom delegated to His Apostles! As mentioned earlier in this book, the '**OF**' communicates the **RELEASE** from The Place of the Heavens, while '**TO**' is the **ACCESS** to the Place of the Heavens. You are The Kingdom of Heaven people enthroned upon Dominion; therefore, you are that Altar manifested on the planes of matter and substance!!

The Power of Enthronement

He sits and inhabits the Praises of His People Israel!!

- **Psalm 22:3** Yet You are set-apart, **Enthroned** on the praises of Yisra'ĕl. The word **Enthroned** communicates Altar and Throne language. The Holy One is Enthroned upon the Praises of Israel – His People! The Hebrew word Enthroned is – יָשַׁב – Yashav. Proof that YHWH is enthroned among His people is seen when we Remain in Him – Yashav is also Shoo'vee, which means: that which Remains! Those whom the King of The Altar Throne extends His Scepter of Power and Favor to, are those with the authority to remain standing!

This is Altar language and its Scepter Power!! We will end with the focus on one of the parables Yahshua spoke of, but first let me share a little insight to what we have been speaking on!

The Altar that Provides

~**The Altar** extends delegated power to those in its unbreakable binding covenant.

~**The Altar** contains the keys of release and loosing.

~**The Altar** is the sanctified system of authorization between the natural and spiritual worlds. It is the only legal and lawful system for spiritual busines to be completed!

~**The Altar** gives access into the Court systems of the Heavens which is seen in the outer courtyards of the Tabernacle and Temples of Israel.

~**The Altar** extends and grants passage into the Chambers of His Presence where accusations cease to exist.

~**The Altar** is the lawful and legal Platform where the realm of immortality establishes interface on neutral legal grounds with mortality. Altars are powerful. As the Creator sent the Bread of Heaven to Earth, He knew this fact so, He was received by the lawful access point, the womb of a woman. Therefore, His Body was the Legal and Lawful Altar of contact in order for Elohim to conduct Heavenly affairs on Earth. His manifestation gave legal passage here on Earth to all Seven Altar Thrones of Genesis 1:1. This expressed and demonstrated clearly by what He did on Earth. Every spirit is at the mercy of an actual body in order to function and communicate on the Altar of Earth.

~**The Altar** is the bridge between two voices and it is where actual Covenant is activated, Instituted and maintained. It is where a generation is reborn and reestablished. Without an Altar there can be no Covenant relationship of promise.

~**The Altar** is what gives legs to a Covenant agreement.

~**The Altar** is where kings are born and inaugurated for service.

This is the place, which stands as the generational reminder that two powers, who have an unbreakable bond together, which any breach results in a death penalty!

~**The Altar** is the life source to The Covenant.

~**The Altar** is the energy source for The Temple body. When that Altar is extinguished, the power source of it retires! It is written, "As long as the Heavens and Earth remain, Seed time and Harvest will remain". What is communicated here is, The Altars of The Heavens and The Earth are the ever-present sustaining powers, whom all matter and substance originate!!

~**The Altar** gives existence to all you can see and what you cannot see. As is written in the Epistle of Hebrews11:1, 3, "Faith or, The Altar, is the substance of things hoped for and the evidence of things not seen." Also, through this Altar called Faith, The Word brought forth the Heavens and the Earth and all that is in them. This Altar of Faith, which was the Place of The Word, who, through the birthing stool, brought all things into existence! No wonder the Scriptures emphasizes, to EVERY MAN, not angel or spirit, but to every **man** who spirit in a flesh body, was given a MEASURE of faith, which is concealed in this standard. The MEASURE of faith, or a measure of The Altar – is the place where this faith works from. The measure of the Altar was in cubits called אַמָּה – Amah. This Hebrew word is also pronounced as: אִמָּה – Emmah, which means mother. We all came from a mother, a womb which conceals our measure of faith. Your faith must be born, in a similar fashion, in order for it's lawful and legal operation to function on this Earth! Emmah gave birth to the measure of Creation. You don't need more faith; you just need to activate your Altar!! In the Scriptures, we have a word of measure identified as – the cubit. This cubit is the Hebrew word for mother, or, Emmah. The Scriptures convey to us, the Tabernacle structure and Temple structures, which had units of weight and measure, their details were symbolically born through Emmah – The Cubit Mother.

The Seven Altar Thrones of Genesis 1:1

~**Altars** contain the ability to unlock the voice of the soul, which was sacrificed. Your sacrifice, your offering, your gift speaks when placed on the Altar, whose message is unlocked! This is why the Scripture say in Psalms, our 'Tears' are in a bottle, most likely it's because what we could not articulate with language, was spoken through water – tears. The Altar unlocked the voice reserved inside the soul of that sacrifice. Tears in a bottle will speak volumes and many of you reading this book have shed many, which are recorded in Heavens Library!

There are different branches from The Altar of your life. One of the most powerful of these are the Altar of Prayer! The most effective and accurate measure of a man, as well as the health of his spiritual walk, is not how well he teaches, not how much kindness he might show, but his standard is found from the Altar of Prayer. Your spiritual health is measured accurately by the prayer life you have or don't have. The Altar of Prayer was concealed in of the first Adam, which we will discover later in the book. When he was laid down inside the dimension of stillness, his side was opened up and the very essence of this truth was pulled out of him. This essence was then BUILT up into a House of Prayer, which would be brought to him at that initial! Man's greatest place of intimacy is becoming a House of Prayer! Actually, Jacob saw this revelation in Genesis 28 with the Sulam/Ladder, whose head reached from the Altar of Earth to The Altar of the Heavens. Prayer is the language of humble Kings. When everything and everyone in this place are intertwined and interconnected as one voice – the voice of prayer, becomes the powerhouse of the manifested Altars!!

Prayer Concealed in the Inner Man

Here is the example of the concealment of prayer in the first man – ADAM. This was the first Lawful Altar from the place of **Adamah** – אדם = מם דלת אלף – When Adam is <u>expanded</u> out from his Hebrew bodies/letters, we have Kingdom revelation that remain from His called identity – The Adam. There are specific

Hebrew Letters, which are actual Pictures of the entire sacrificial system, which reflect how we are to present ourselves as living sacrifices, but this for a later discussion. The Hebrew letters remaining give us a powerful word – מִתְפַּלֵל – **Meet'pa'leil** which is defined as: one who prays or one who worships, a worshipper!! **Worship** becomes an undefeated **Warship** against all interference, which comes from the prince of the power of the AIRWAVES!! Our Prayer is an Altar that moves against the spiritual currents in the spirit realms! Our prayers are like the Seraph which move in all directions before the Throne of Elohim, His Altar Throne of The Heavens. Our prayers have the ability to unlock Heavens Fire, enclothing us like a garment. Yahshua directed us to address The Heavenly Altar Throne of Abba, "Our Father who is IN THE HEAVENS..."! We become the Altar of Prayer as Psalm 109:4b says – **Ve'Ani Tefillah** – **And I am Prayer**! The numerical value of Meet'pa'leil, whose value is 580, is the same as two other Hebrew words:

- שָׂרָף – **Seraph** = Fiery Ones before the Throne!; רֶשֶׁף – **Re'shef** = Demons. We have the Guardian of Prayer and Resisters of Prayer all in one word. The Seraph purifies the words of prayer that come from the Mouth of Men. Their faces and feet are covered, their hearing remains because they receive our ascended prayers. The Reshef are the enemies of to our prayers. Both words end with the Hebrew letter Peh, which means the Mouth. These dimension Guardians, work with words because they are assignments. Both are assigned to execute the lower realms with what is spoken. The Seraph are the Rosh/Chiefs or, Authority over other ranks while the Reshef are Sar/Prince over powers, principalities, thrones, altars, dominions, etc.

As a walking Altar of Prayer, your presence will be like a burning Seraph that expels the demonic interference! Altars interfere with the affairs of Earth and the Heavens!! Each tribe of Israel was symbolic to a walking Altar. The very name of each tribe revealed the Power of that altar. Each tribe became the Scepter of The King in their own rankings. The Tribe and The Altar are both reflections of the extension of The Kings Scepter!

- **Numbers 24:17** I will see^{H7200} him, but not^{H3808} now^{H6258} I shall see^{H7789} him, but not^{H3808} near^{H7138} there comes^{H1869} a <u>Star</u>^{H3556} out of Jacob,^{H4480 H3290} and a Sceptre^{H7626} will resurrect^{H6965} out of Israel,^{H4480 H3478} and will strike^{H4272} the corners^{H6285} of Moab,^{H4124} and destroy^{H4272} all^{H3605} the children^{H1121} of Shet.^{H8352}

The Scepter that comes forth within Israel is The resurrected Savior, The Right Hand of Power, the Altar that crushes all other kingdoms, the Altar made flesh, who alone has the Authority to be like and resemble all Seven Altar Thrones at any given moment! The Word had to put on flesh first in order to reveal the power of Elohim inside, who revealed this Authority from His Altar, which was concealed.

- **Psalm 45:6** Your throne,^{H3678} Elohim,^{H430} is forever^{H5769} and ever:^{H5703} **the sceptre**^{H7626} of your **kingdom**^{H4438} is a **right**^{H4334} **sceptre.**^{H7626}

The Throne of Elohim is the Altar of Creative Power, the foundation of all Creation and Righteousness, This was the very Dominion Yahshua told John had to be fulfilled in Him and then executed. Here we have the Scepter of The Kingdom called the Tzadiq, who is the Righteous and Royal One! The Altar Throne of the Heavens is the Seat of our Royal High-Priest and King!

Yahshua preached This Altar of The Heavens Kingdom as we read in a few places in scripture, where His Altar crushed all other altars. He delegated His Power, His Authority to Crush all the power of the enemy to us –

- **Luke 10:18** And^{G1161} he said^{G2036} to them,^{G846} I witnessed^{G2334} Satan^{G4567} as^{G5613} lightning^{G796} fall^{G4098} from^{G1537} **The Heavens.**^{G3772}

Lucifer fell from The HEAVENS, which was the place of The

Altar Throne. He was one of the covering Cherub's as Isaiah 14 defines. Remember, when we read from Isaiah 14, Lucifer, Son of the Morning Star, coveted to ascend this Shamayim Altar/Kingdom Throne? As he was cast down, Yahshua said He saw this event happen! Where was Yahshua when this happened? Let's see –

> **Isaiah 14:12 How**[H349] **are you fallen**[H5307] **from The Heavens,** [H4480] [H8064] **Lucifer/Heleil,** [H1966] son[H1121] of the morning![H7837] how are you dethroned[H1438] to **The Earth**[H776] who did decay[H2522] [H5921] the nations![H1471] (He was cast down from before The Altar of the Heavens down to the Altar of Earth. Notice he passed **by** the 6th Altar of our revelation. Look at this diagram below:)

Hidden in Plain Sight

(Diagram 15)

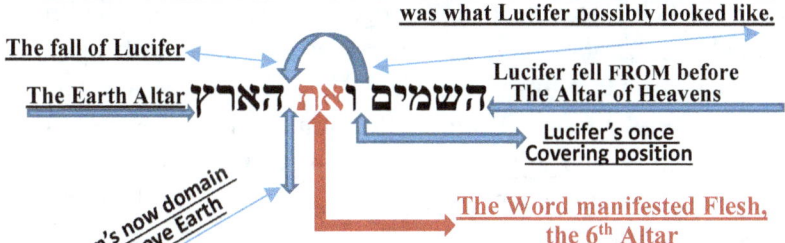

(The Prince of The Power of the Air's domain now. I would like to submit to you, Lucifer went from a Rainbow type spectrum of light body into a reverse type Mikvah, hence Shamayim is fire and Water, now to the accuser of the brethren, Satan the prince of the Power of the Air. The Power of the Air is greater than he. He is the Prince of this Power of The Air.)

Lucifer was probably right where the arrow points to with the other covering Cherub BEFORE his rebellion.
(to the right side of this diagram)

> **Isaiah 14:13** For you^{H859} said^{H559} in your heart,^{H3824} I will ascend^{H5927} into **The Heaven**,^{H8064} I will exalt^{H7311} my throne^{H3678} above^{H4480 H4605} the stars^{H3556} of Elohim:^{H410} I will sit^{H3427} also upon the mount^{H2022} of the **congregation**,^{H4150} in the sides^{H3411} of the north:^{H6828}
>
> (**Congregation** here is Mo'ed/מוֹעֵד which means Appointed times and place. The people who meet with YHWH Elohim at His appointed times are His appointed people and place.) **14:19** But you^{H859} are now cast^{H7993} out of your grave^{H4480 H6913} like an **abominable**^{H8581} **branch**,^{H5342} as the garment^{H3830} of those that are slain^{H2026} who are thrust through^{H2944} with a sword^{H2719} that go down^{H3381} to^{H413} the **stones**^{H68} of the pit^{H953} as an idolatrous image of a man^{H6297} trodden under feet.^{H947}

Lucifer is called the ABOMINABLE BRANCH or the Abominable Netzer/Nazerene. Remember, Lucifer desired to **become** 'Elohim' or, a Son of Elohim, who desired ascension into the sides of the North, which is the Supporting Branch - 'Alef Tav' - of 'The Heavens or Congregation'. This is why the Prophet Daniel speaks about the man of sin who comes to change times and seasons/Mo'edim (Daniel 7:23-25). The numerical value of this Hebrew phrase: Abominable Branch, is the same for the Hebrew phrase, '**Elohim Et HaShamayim**', which is the Altar which is the High Priest Altar of Genesis 1:1 - the Elohim Altar of Genesis 1:1.

If Lucifer was able to obtain these three Altars, it would have been a different Creation as we know it, but this was an impossibility Satan desired as High Priest status. He desires to sit as God/Elohim and He Desires to have his own Altar system on Earth, which would be his own lower Heavens system, as 2 Thessalonians 2 speaks of!

Here is an additional remark regarding the year 2020, this entity Lucifer is being embedded inside the COVID Vaccine as the Luciferase Dye I mentioned earlier this year. It is also interesting that the Luciferase Dye makes a Greenish Light Color. Isn't it interesting that Death rides on a 'PALE/CHLOROS/GREEN Horse according to the Book of Revelation? Horse can be symbolic of delivery and the transporting of things. The Altars are before everyone this day, which altar will you hold fast to? Also, it is believed that in March of 2020, (Passover Season) Bill Gates patented a microchip which is inserted into the body, which will digitalize the body of people in order to interact with the now accelerating Crypto Currency. This is also a branch of Artificial Intelligence.

This Patent number is numbered just like Bar codes as well as the DNA codes – 060606!! This will alter the 'Altar' of man's soul, which will make him the product of mRNA Chimera evolution! The same thing was happening in Noach's days – Genesis 6-9. This is the soul trafficking the enemy has been operating in, which is here, on Man's door step or, can I say, The Altar threshold?!

It has always been a battle between Altars since Lucifer/Satan, who is the counterfeit, fell from his Heavenly station! He wanted the Crown and the Congregation in the North!! He wanted the Kingdom of Heaven, which is the Adorned and Crowned Bride of Mashiach the King!! Yahshua Crowns Her Head with the Scepter of Righteousness by the Seal of His Priestly Service! Satan wants the Bride who contains the ability to carry the Cause which produces the Effect! Yahshua empowered The Bride as The Kingdom according to what is written - Luke 10:19!! We are representatives to the Crowned Altar of The Kingdom of Heaven!! We have a King Enthroned on our behalf, where we don't need to beg for the blessing, protection or deliverance! We do not need to beg for our breakthrough, neither for our healing!! We thank Him because He has already bestowed upon us, the Righteousness of His Kingdom, as His Scepter of The Altar Throne of the Heavens!

The Seven Altar Thrones of Genesis 1:1

Authority Concepts, the Power Surge

> **Luke 10:19** Behold,^G2400 I give^G1325 to you^G5213 the power^G1849 to trample under foot^G3961 on^G1883 serpents^G3789 and^G2532 scorpions^G4651 and^G2532 over^G1909 all^G3956 the^G3588 power^G1411 of the^G3588 enemy^G2190 and^G2532 nothing^G3762 in any way^G3364 injure^G91 you.^G5209

*Tread – from the LXX Hebrew connection - this word is translated from the Hebrew word: **HaDerekh/The Way**! Mashiach said He was The Way – The Way is The Walk of Authority, which crushed the kingdom of darkness. He is the Way of ascending the Altar, who is the Throne, the Door to Power!! The Way are the legs and feet of His Altar manifestation, and it is time we put boots on the ground!

Power#1849 – *exuosia* means: the magistrate, kingly authority! The Kingdom of Heaven, which was what Yahshua came preaching according to Matthew 4, is the delegated Power to overthrow ALL the functioning power of the enemy!! The Shamayim Altar is the point of contact, which The Priesthood unties to ensnare the enemy. The Priesthood of Mashiach is the actual Scepter of The Kings Throne!! *Exuosia* is the Greek concept for Magistrate, who is the one that operates with a higher level than a court system. The Magistrate is the Chancellor INSIDE the realm of Chambers.

Chambers are where all petitions are answered, not discussed. The Courts of Heaven deal with the petitions and pleas of the people, the Outer Courtyard! The Chambers is where Magistrates Decree and Establish the standing of what was petitioned for without hells rebuttal, this is The Inner Sanctum! The Altar of Heaven or Shamayim Altar is the Magistrate, the Royal Determination, who stands against the explosive power of the kingdom of darkness! *Exuosia* Power or, Magistrate Royal power, is He who holds the Power to Pardon all accusations –

> **Matthew 9:6** But^G1161 that^G2443 you may know^G1492 that^G3754 the^G3588 Son^G5207 of man^G444 has^G2192 power^G1849

on^{G1909} **The Earth^{G1093}** to forgive^{G863} sins,^{G266} (then^{G5119} he said^{G3004} to the^{G3588} sick of the palsy^{G3885} Arise,^{G1453} take up^{G142} your^{G4675} bed,^{G2825} and^{G2532} go^{G5217} into^{G1519} your^{G4675} house.^{G3624}

The **power**/*exuosia* ON Earth because He is speaking from The Heavenly Altar.

> **Matthew 10:1** And^{G2532} when he summonsed^{G4341} his^{G848} twelve^{G1427} disciples,^{G3101} he imparted^{G1325} to them^{G846} **power^{G1849}** over unclean^{G169} spirits,^{G4151} to^{G5620} cast them out,^{G1544} ^{G846} and^{G2532} to heal^{G2323} all manner^{G3956} of sickness^{G3554} and^{G2532} all manner^{G3956} of disease.^{G3119}

The Delegation from the Highest Altar to the Shamayim Altar was now activated here. Yahshua delegates this same Royal Priestly Power to His Disciples, for one reason – to CASTOUT Unclean spirits, and to Heal all manner of sickness! These are hinderances to The Shamayim Altar Crowning through the lives of every believer. These are also responses from the Tohu V'Bohu this world is enveloped in. Unclean Spirits are parallel to Tohu, which is Chaos that tries to manifest in the life of a believer. Sickness is the Void of Shalom and Life, which these two are enemies of The Kingdom of Heaven Altar! *Exuosia* Power is the 'Casting Out' Power that should be demonstrated with each encounter!! This Authority displaces the *dunamis* or, explosiveness of the enemy's altar!

Power#1411 – *dunamis* means: explosive power when attached to the kingdom of light is orderly, but when connected to the enemy its destructive.

Serpents – from the Hebrew word Nachash. We have authority over all the Divination, deception, cunningness of the enemy. The phrase 'To tread upon all these' means: we are from a higher place. This is Altar language!!

Scorpions – this is defined from the Hebrew word Aqrav/עקרב.

The Seven Altar Thrones of Genesis 1:1

This could compare to the deceit of religious leaders as this word is used in Ezekiel 2:6, which is made up of the 13 scrolls. In Ezekiel 2 we have this word attached to these leaders that are like scorpions!! Yahshua gives us Authority over all the words emanating from the evil deceptive words religious leaders may speak, especially the prostituting prophetic words, we hear today from some renown names people are too afraid to speak up about. Why? Because they have been stung by these scorpion kings and now sit paralyzed and hypnotized by their spells!!

The Shamayim Altar crushes all of these areas of the kingdom of darkness, all of them!!

> 🔴 **Luke 10:20** Rather[G4133] in[G1722] this[G5129] don't,[G3361] rejoice[G5463] that[G3754] the[G3588] spirits[G4151] are subject[G5293] to you;[G5213] but[G1161] rather[G3123] rejoice[G5463] because[G3754] your[G5216] names[G3686] are <mark>inscribed[G1125] in[G1722] The Heavens.[G3772]</mark>

Our names are written/inscribed **in** the Shamayim Altar, which is The Kingdom of Heaven!! Yahshua was pierced in three places – **His Feet (The Altar of the Earth - הארץ), His Hands (The 6ᵗʰ Altar that is pierced between Heaven and Earth - ואת) and, His Side (The Altar of the Heavens, which He sits enthroned by The Father's Side – אלהים את השמים**). This gives us the total of the last Three Altar Thrones and He being that 4ᵗʰ Altar of Genesis 1:1 – The High Priest-King **Alef Tav - את**. The Altar represents The Kingdom because the Altar becomes The Throne of Power!! Our names are engraved inside this Kingdom that is a living Throne! Our names are written as part of the Shamayim Miz'be'ach/The Altar of Heaven which is constantly pulsating the Life source of its Dominion! This is most likely the reason why we are given a white stone, which has our new name engraved into it, as our key of Access to the Altar of Heavens Dominion!!

> ➤ **Revelation 2:12** And[G2532] to the[G3588] angel[G32] of the[G3588]

congregation^G1577 in^G1722 **Pergamos**^G4010 (Pergamos, comes from the same Hebrew idea given in the LXX, as The Tower of Babel, which the rest of these verses declare the seat of Satan is in the midst of. Satan desired to alter the Sides of the North into ancient Pergamos legs for his Kingdom. This is one of the seven assemblies of The Kingdom the book of Revelation was also written about! This was the gateway Satan would come through. Today, we see this same insight in Jerusalem and Saudi Arabia – Manmade stone temples with the black stone of influence!) write;^G1125 These things^G3592 proclaims^G3004 he who holds^G2192 the^G3588 sharp^G3691 sword^G4501 with two edges.^G1366 **2:13** I know^G1492 your^G4675 works^G2041 and^G2532 where^G4226 you sit,^G2730 where^G3699 Satan's^G4567 seat^G2362 is and^G2532 you esteem^G2902 my^G3450 name,^G3686 and^G2532 have not^G3756 denied^G720 my^G3450 faith^G4102 even^G2532 in^G1722 those days^G2250 wherein^G1722 ^G3739 **Antipas**^G493 (**Antipas** is a compound word – **Anti,** which means: against; and **pas** - from peter or father. This hints to the Catholic Church system. A group who opposes the Catholic religion as well as two other religions, which are mentioned here. The Kingdom of Heaven is breaking forth from the chains of these world altar religions! The Kingdom can't be held down by chains and fetters of man's control! The Kingdom is a Heavenly Altar of Power that tramples over all the power of the enemy as we have read!!) my^G3450 faithful^G4103 martyr,^G3144 who^G3739 was slain^G615 among^G3844 you^G5213 where^G3699 Satan^G4567 sits.^G2730 **2:14** But^G235 I have^G2192 a few things^G3641 against^G2596 you,^G4675 because^G3754 you have^G2192 them there^G1563 that hold^G2902 the^G3588 **doctrine**^G1322 **of Balaam,**^G903 who^G3739 taught^G1321 Balak^G904 to cast^G906 a **hinder stone**^G4625 before^G1799 the^G3588 children^G5207 of Israel,^G2474 **to eat**^G5315 **things sacrificed unto idols,**^G1494 and^G2532 to **commit fornication.**^G4203 (The Doctrine of Bilaam was and is an altar influence embraced by many to this day. It causes people to defile themselves with that which Elohim hates!! We see this especially during Halloween, Christmas and Easter holidays. It seems innocent, but these have their roots in fertility rites, blood sacrifice and soul trafficking!

When YHWH Elohim said 'be Qadosh' He meant it because it's what He is! The Altar Throne of Heaven is one of Cleanness, Purity, Integrity and Holiness! Did you know, even the things you eat can play a part in your walk of holiness!? When Yahshua said, "…it's not what goes in the belly that defiles a man…" He was not focused on what was food or not food, but focused on the word's men speak.

Religion will still indulge in all manner of uncleanness, not realizing that their physical temple is getting sick! Not realizing that the Earthly Tabernacle is weighed down with other idolatrous altars! You wouldn't catch Yahshua eating any such unholiness neither indulging in such practices with all their perverted dainties.)

➢ **Revelation 2:15** So^{G3779} you^{G4771} also^{G2532} have^{G2192} them that hold^{G2902} the^{G3588} doctrine^{G1322} of the^{G3588} Nicolaitans,^{G3531} (The Doctrine of Nicolaitans was that of adultery, fornication and witchcraft. These were spiritual descendants of Jezebel.) which thing^{G3739} I hate.^{G3404} **2:16** Repent^{G3340} or else^{G1490} I will come^{G2064} upon you^{G4671} quickly,^{G5035} and^{G2532} will war^{G4170} against^{G3326} them^{G846} with^{G1722} the^{G3588} sword^{G4501} of my^{G3450} mouth.^{G4750} **2:17** He that has^{G2192} an ear,^{G3775} let him hear^{G191} what^{G5101} the^{G3588} Spirit^{G4151} proclaims^{G3004} to the^{G3588} congregations;^{G1577} To him^{G846} that overcomes^{G3528} will I give^{G1325} to eat^{G5315} of^{G575} the^{G3588} hidden^{G2928} (^{G3588}) manna,^{G3131} and^{G2532} will give^{G1325} him^{G846} a white^{G3022} stone,^{G5586} and^{G2532} in^{G1909} the^{G3588} stone^{G5586} a new^{G2537} name^{G3686} written,^{G1125} which^{G3739} no man^{G3762} knows^{G1097} except^{G1508} the one who receives.^{G2983}

The hidden manna, when looking at the Hebrew language, has the numerical value connection to: **Melkhitzedeq Priesthood**!! The hidden Manna is The Bread of Heaven which is the strength of the manifested Adamah Altar, which is the Melkhitzedeq Priesthood that administrates these realities. The Kingdom of Heaven is The Altar of Heaven and the Altar of Heaven is the Scepter of Heaven!! The Scepter of Heaven is the Dominion, Authority, and the rule of The Kingdom or Altar of Heaven! The Scepter is the Voice for and of the Crown that is Enthroned on the Seat of Authority! The Altar Throne of the Heavens is the governing power on Earth that Leavens all it comes into contact with!

The Influence of Leaven

I was meditating upon the model prayer for the believer and this prayer Yahshua gave to us which is an actual Altar parallel with its entire lawful system of function. One of the keys within this Altar of prayer Yahshua taught us is a statement reflecting this Shamayim Altar – 'Our Father who is IN HEAVEN…' first off, Abba is **in** The Heavens or can we say He is upon the Altar Throne of Heaven as we have read many times in this chapter. He goes on to say, "Thy Kingdom come Thy will be done **on Earth** as it is **in Heaven**!"

The will of The Father is the Leaven of the Kingdom that influences all it comes in contact with! The Kingdom is the Throne extended to us here on Earth. The Throne is The Altar of Power!! In one sense, Yahshua was stating that when we pray ask for His Will/INFLUENCE/Leaven, which emanates from The Altar of The Heavens, this is His Altar to be enacted or, fully expanded here on Earth. Heaven is attempting to Influence the Earth so, that The Earth would reflect the Image of Heaven. When this happens, these two become One Flesh or, Basar Echad, which means: One Kingdom Message of Good News! This one united message brings together two Altar Worlds and Thrones making them Echad - The Heavens and The Earth. This is accomplished as the Book of Revelation says, 'He MAKES a New Heaven and Earth.' To 'Make' means: to fashion together as One!

~ **Leaven** – The Agent of Influence and Agent of impartation. The Leaven is The Agent of Power and Conquest! **Leaven** – שאר H7603 & חמץ H2557 - H2558 – **Se'or** and **Chametz**, both speak of process of Leaven, which is the Cause and Effect. The Hebrew word Chametz is also the word for Vinegar. Both, can reflect the Kingdom and its operation. This is now going to be one of the most powerful and influential finalities to this Altar revelation.

When the vinegar was offered to Yahshua as John 19:30 records, when He received this Chametz/Vinegar, it released the Voice of The Word from the Adamah Altar '**It is finished!**' This statement would be the hammer that nailed The Kingdom of Heavens recognition upon this Earth Platform. He was the Starter Agent of the Kingdom Leaven and now this was released as His last Breath was the initiation to this process. Lastly, the numerical value of these two Altar of Heaven initiators is 639, notice the numbers 6,3&9 or 3,6,9 - which contain secrets to the Creation account. These numbers are the same for the Hebrew phrase:

האדמה השמים מזבח

– **Ha'Adomeh HaShamayim Miz'be'ach**

= **"Behold I will resemble the Likeness of The Altar of Heaven, or The Kingdom of Heaven Altar!!"**

This speaks to us that we are a walking pattern of This very Altar which is Mashiach Yahshua! He is The Adamah Altar which is the revelation and purpose of all seven Altar revelations of Genesis 1:1 manifested in the flesh. Yes, When the Word was manifested so were all seven Altar revelations of Genesis 1:1. This is why He is worthy to wear MANY Crowns! He won't wear an earthly kings Crown; He overthrew that with the Crown of Thorns placed on His Head which qualified Him to activate

John-James of the House of Flores.®

the redemptive power of His Adamah Altar on Golgotha and Earth. He wears the Many Crowns of Genesis 1:1. We will examine this idea briefly later on.

Matthew 13 –

> ● **Matthew 13:33** Another^G243 parable^G3850 he spoke^G2980 to them;^G846 **The^G3588 Kingdom^G932 of The Heavens^G3772** is^G2076 like unto^G3664 **leaven,^G2219** which^G3739 a woman^G1135 took,^G2983 and^G2532 hid^G1470 in^G1519 three^G5140 measures^G4568 (Three measures of meal speak of three wombs or garments for The Heavens Altar Kingdom authority.) of meal,^G224 till^G2193 the^(G3739) whole^G3650 was leavened.^G2220 **Mat 13:34** All^G3956 these things^G5023 spoke^G2980 Yeshua^G2424 to the^G3588 multitude^G3793 in^G1722 parables;^G3850 and^G2532 without^G5565 a parable^G3850 he spoke^G2980 not^G3756 unto them:^G846

Let me expound on a powerful insight. First, this word for Leaven can be found in the LXX under Exodus 12:15 as well –

> ● **Exodus 12:15** Seven^H7651 days^H3117 shall ye eat^H398 unleavened bread;^H4682 even^H389 the first^H7223 day^H3117 ye shall **put away^H7673 leaven^H7603 out of your houses:^H4480 H1004** for^H3588 whosoever^H3605 eats^H398 **leavened bread^H2557** from the first day^H4480 H7223 H3117 until^H5704 the seventh^H7637 day,^H3117 that^H1931 soul^H5315 will be cut off^H3772 from Israel.^H4480 H3478

As we extrapolate these words from this verse, they can say something a lot more powerful, regarding Leaven and Man's Soul–

> ➢ **"Seven Days you shall CONTINUE to eat Matzot…"** **Matzot** is said to come from **Matzah** which means flat bread as well to drain something out. This gives us the analogy of actual bread being absent from the wind of the world. It is also used for draining the altar out from blood and water in Leviticus 1:15; 5:9. Israel was to continue

eating an actual flat type bread, but more than this the Altar of Pesach, this Nation was being prepared inside the Threshold of each living stone House of Goshen. Goshen, represented the actual Soul of all the Hebrews, which needed to be drained out of any Egyptian Leaven/Influence.

> "...**even the first day you shall put away leaven**... This is a bad translation. Look at what the actual Hebrew Language says – אַךְ בַּיּוֹם הָרִאשׁוֹן תַּשְׁבִּיתוּ שְּׂאֹר מִבָּתֵּיכֶם – Akh Ba'yom Ha'Rishon Tash'Bee'to Se'ore Mee'Ba'teikhem = "Truly in the first day continue to cause the **leavening agent** to find **rest** from your homes..." What is being communicated during this Passover Altar build up in Goshen, was The Leavening agent of Passover's Altar had to INFLUENCE needed to spread in each Goshen home before the judgements would hit Mitzrayim/Egypt. This sounds like something that needs to happen more than ever before in this day we live. Many have the Leaven of twisted religion and of false Temple dwellings! Many have the leaven of worldliness! Many have the leaven of Levitical hierchy priesthood imposition running rampant in our day! Many are presented with the leaven of forced Luciferic DNA manipulation banging on their door steps of their homes! We need the Influence of all The Lamb of Elohim represents, which is The Kingdom Altar Throne of Heaven here on Earth!!

This verse reiterates what was to be in their homes, which was **rest**/**Shabbat** from the Egyptian influence that had taken over. This was an Altar manifestation! The word communicates that this SABBATH LEAVEN or, SABBATH INFLUENCE was to be emanating from their homes! Religious men will get stuck in a traditional day that comes with different bias stands, which the Day is most definitely important but, so is the demonstration of this REST or, Sabbath Power!! This manifestation of Sabbath brings rest from all labor, rest from sin, sickness, dis-ease, and all the manner of fleshly struggles many tend to constantly engage!

Over the years, we have taken Sabbath with us throughout the week, demonstrating the Influence of its rest to all around us! Yahshua came demonstrating this Kingdom Leaven by what He did, giving us the example to follow! **Se'ore**, which was the cause of expansion, became The Head of The Body and His influence in each house! This idea of Se'ore also represents the Rosh or Head! The Soul of the Hebrews was now being DRAINED from the influence of Egypt, in order for The Altar of Heaven to settle in that area. The home MUST have the LEAVENING agents INFLUENCE of this Kingdom Altar first, which then makes room for the Altar of Heaven or The Kingdom herself to come. The Influence will push out the former influence! Ask yourself this question, what is your influence today? Is it the world or is it truly influence that comes from The Heart of The King Yahshua?!

> "…whosoever eats **leavened bread** that soul shall be cut off from Israel from the first day to the seventh day." Leaven here is **Chametz**. There should be no Chametz in the homes of the Hebrews here, if so, that was Egyptian INFLUENCE or The INFLUENCE of another altar. Two altars cannot share the same space, one will be destroyed. 'Whosoever mixes two Altars together shall be cut off'! You cannot claim to be serving Abba and believe in Yahshua, then go sleep with the enemy during other times of the year, this doesn't work! You will either serve the one and hate the other or be rejected by The King!!

Egypt's Altar and all its demonic gods were about to be pulverized by The Altar of The Lamb, who is the Ambassador of The Altar Throne of Heaven!! In John

1:29 it is written, "Behold, The Lamb of Elohim who removes the sin of the world."

In Exodus 12:15, Matzot was to be eaten for seven days. This is a mysterious Kingdom Word because it doesn't find a home as Matzot, but fits in as a picture of what the home should look like due to its leavening influence.

In Leviticus 10:12 this Hebrew word Matzot is found and it is more than bread. This Matzot is called something that we see in the Tabernacle and Temple.

- **Leviticus 10:12** And Moses[H4872] spoke[H1696] to[H413] Aaron,[H175] and unto[H413] Eleazar[H499] and unto[H413] Ithamar,[H385] his sons[H1121] that remain,[H3498] Take[H3947] (H853) the meat offering[H4503] which remains[H3498] of the offerings of Yahweh made by fire,[H4480 H801 H3068] and eat[H398] it without **leaven**[H4682] **beside**[H681] **the altar:**[H4196] for[H3588] it[H1931] **is most holy:**[H6944 H6944]

➢ "...eat the Leaven beside The Altar..." וְאָכְל֣וּהָ מַצּ֔וֹת אֵ֖צֶל הַמִּזְבֵּ֑חַ – Ve'eek'luha Matzot **Eitzel** HaMizbe'ach. The word **Eitzel** can be read as: '**I will protect**'. **Tzel,** is the Hebrew word for protection. There is protection beside The Altar Throne when the Bread of Heaven is eaten there! Your strength and Power and Protection sit upon this Altar Throne and speaks from this place! The Bread of The Kingdom is invoked when eaten beside The Altar Throne! This Hebrew word Tzel also means shelter, shade, shadow.

The book of Psalms speaks about having protection under the SHADOW/Tzel of The Almighty! The shadow of El Shaddai is the nourishing shadow! You find nourishment under His wings of Healing and Authority! This was written when king David lay beneath the wings of The Ark of the Covenant while the Sun cast the Shadow of those Wings from the Covenant Seat! There is shade from the blazing heat of life's travels when we are covered by

His Covenant promises! You find rest for your souls underneath The Shadow of El Shaddai! The Shadow is Mashiach Yahshua standing right beside you, who called you before you were in your mothers' womb!! When He calls you, respond and come close! When you come close, then, you become what He is at The Altar!

> "**…it is most holy**." This Matzot/Bread is actually called The Holy of Holies! **:כִּי קֹדֶשׁ קָדָשִׁים הוּא** – Kee Qodesh Qadashim Hee = **For He is The Holy of Holies**!! The Matzot is called **He** and **He** is the Holy of Holies!! When you eat the Matzot of unleavened Bread of The Altar it's as if you are partaking of the Qadosh HaQadoshim/Holy of Holies Altar of the King! The Leaven is the Influence of The Holy of Holies!!! When you Eat the Bread of Heaven, which is The Bread of The Altar of Heaven, you become a place of Holiness where His Presence dwells and sits. When the scriptures say 'He is inside of you and I' where do you think He is? None other than in the Bread of The Holy of Holies which is the seat of The Altar of Heaven!! You are more than you think you are and you can do more than you think you can! Greater is He that is in you, the Holy of Holies here on Earth, than He that is in the world or, the lower altar realm!

So, we can see the depths with one concept found in this Kingdom Parable, Leaven! Leaven is not a bad thing when we distinguish between kingdom leaven, which is being articulated. Just as we read in Exodus and Leviticus, we can see the distinctions between the <u>actual</u> Leavening Agent from that which <u>is</u> Influenced by The Leavening Agent! Yahshua also said to beware of the Leaven of the Pharisees:

- **Matthew_16:6** Then[G1161] Yeshua[G2424] said[G2036] to them,[G846] Take heed[G3708] and[G2532] beware[G4337] of[G575] the[G3588] **leaven**[G2219] **of the**[G3588] **Pharisees**[G5330] **and**[G2532] **Sadducees.**[G4523]

- **Mat_16:11** How^{G4459} is it that you do not^{G3756} comprehend^{G3539} that^{G3754} I spoke^{G2036} not^{G3756} to you^{G5213} concerning^{G4012} bread,^{G740} but you should beware^{G4337} of^{G575} the^{G3588} **leaven**^{G2219} **of the**^{G3588} **Pharisees**^{G5330} **and**^{G2532} **of the Sadducees?**^{G4523}

- **Mat_16:12** Then^{G5119} they understood^{G4920} how^{G3754} that he said^{G2036} to them not^{G3756} beware^{G4337} of^{G575} the^{G3588} **leaven**^{G2219} of bread ^{G740} but^{G235} of^{G575} **the**^{G3588} **doctrine**^{G1322} **of the**^{G3588} **Pharisees**^{G5330} **and**^{G2532} **of the Sadducees.**^{G4523}

- **Mark_8:15** And^{G2532} he distinguished^{G1291} them,^{G846} saying,^{G3004} Take heed,^{G3708} beware^{G991} of^{G575} the^{G3588} **leaven**^{G2219} **of the**^{G3588} **Pharisees,**^{G5330} **and**^{G2532} **of the**^{G3588} **leaven**^{G2219} **of Herod.**^{G2264}

- **Luke 12:1** In the meantime,^{G1722 G3739} when there were gathered together^{G1996} an innumerable multitude^{G3461} of people,^{G3793} so many that^{G5620} they trampled^{G2662} upon each other,^{G240} he began^{G756} to say^{G3004} to^{G4314} his^{G848} disciples^{G3101} above all else,^{G4412} you must^{G1438} Beware^{G4337} of^{G575} the^{G3588} **leaven**^{G2219} **of the**^{G3588} **Pharisees,**^{G5330} **which**^{G3748} **is**^{G2076} **hypocrisy.**^{G5272}

The Kingdom of Heaven is like Leaven that was hidden into three measures of meal, all from the hands of one woman. This is very interesting language here. The Kingdom of Heaven is Like Leaven/Se'or; The Kingdom of Heaven is Like a Woman who took; The Kingdom of Heaven is like three measures of meal and the Kingdom of Heaven is like the Whole that was Leavened. All four categories are intertwined. The Kingdom is the Leaven. The Se'ore or, Influential Power that must be accepted, which is concealed inside three places. In the process of time, it influences the entire spirit, soul and body of man. The leavening agent of The Kingdom breaks the entanglement of the serpent's kingdom seed off the Altar platforms of landing! It's a conquering strategy of our King executed by Yahshua through His Ruach HaQodesh!

As we journey through this 5th Altar, The Shamayim Miz'be'ach or, The Altar of Heaven. This Kingdom of Heaven's Influence or, can I say Leaven, will transform the Body. The Kingdom of Heaven was being infused by The Melkhitzedeq Leaven of Righteousness and Justice, which was absent from Israel during the 2nd Temple era because the Presence went with the tribes into Exile!! Yahshua came unlocking the mysteries of the Beginning, which were scattered abroad! He came in the power of the Ruach HaQodesh as High Priest of the Highest Order, Influencing the wayward kingdom back into preparation for empowerment! John was the first Measure we see, which he 'prepared The Way' for the Righteous King Yahshua to come. Yahshua came and ministered as Melkhitzedeq Kohein HaGadol, Heavens Agent of Influence/Leaven! He came and began to untie the knotted fate of a lifeless kingdom filled with the bones of dead men, dead religion, dead rituals, dead influence. The Leaven of Heaven had come to infuse the Life of Heavens Altar people!!

1. The Leaven is The Kingdom Influence.

2. The Woman speaks of Israel as a whole – In Jeremiah 6:2 Israel is seen as a delicate woman. In Jeremiah 3:6-11, 20; Ezekiel 16 & 23 Israel is seen as two women who have become Harlots. In Ephesians 5 we have the Mystery of Yahshua and His Bride and the power of The Words influence of washing!

3. The three measures of Meal is a mystery. Yahshua is seen as the seed or, meal where all things begin. The beginning stages of this Mountain top 2nd Temple era was a Harlot. The Shkinah had departed leaving an empty place in need of repentance and Heavens Influence. This Nation had accepted another seed of influence, which corrupted the region and irrigated the people with deception.

   The manifestation of the Seed, which was in Jerusalem, was now breaking up the ground of this corrupted religious system! The three measures of meal prophetically communicate all three Temple revelations up to this time.

This was the second Temple prostitute with two upgrades making Her a Third type Temple. What men have done, over time was to assume Ezekiel speaks of a Third Temple when all along all this happened already. What will happen in our time is a Hybrid Chimera type Temple system filled with Genetically Modified animal sacrifices and priesthood. It's as if the Nephilim influence of Nimrod will be present on the Temple Mount proper!

The 3 measures of meal are the MelkhiTzedeq Order, which has come to expand the three measures of priesthood inceptions and shatter this once and for all Nephilim system. The MelkhiTzedeq Order comes in the face of the Anti-messiah, the false prophet and the man of sin, which all three are being shadowed across religion today.

When you see the spike in the prophetic word and there is the absence of obedience to The Written Torah of our King, you better believe the system has been set in place and in plain sight and its leavening influence complete. It happened three times in Biblical History beginning with: Nimrod, Antiochus Epiphanes and todays Empire Global Elite system. This one will introduce <u>itself</u> before all men as the Hybrid Chimera King and emergence of the Nimrod of old, the Antichrist himself. This man of sin has his blood transfusion ready for all mankind called the Luciferase Gene! If I may add to this amazing insight we have been addressing:

> **Hosea 13:12** The iniquity[H5771] of Ephraim[H669] is bound up;[H6887] his sin[H2403] is **hid.**[H6845] **13:13** The sorrows[H2256] of a laboring **woman**[H3205] will come[H935] upon him. He[H1931] is an unwise[H3808 H2450] son;[H1121] for[H3588] he should'nt[H3808] stay[H5975] long[H6256] in the place of **the crowning**[H4866] **of children.**[H1121] **13:14** I will **purchase**[H6299] **them from the power**[H4480 H3027] **of the grave;**[H7585] I will **redeem**[H1350] **them from death:**[H4480 H4194] O death,[H4194] I will be[H165] your

plagues;^{H1698} O grave,^{H7585} I will be^{H165} your devastation,^{H6987} repentance^{H5164} will be hid^{H5641} from my eyes.^{H4480 H5869}

This whole section identifying the children, who are breaking forth is powerful language of the Altar Kingdom! This Hebrew word is Mishber/משבר, which means: the womb ready to Crown the baby inside. This comes from the Hebrew word Shabar/שבר giving us the meaning of: Breaking, Crushing. It is used to represent what happened with Israel as they came out of Egypt! The Crowning of The Kingdom Crushes the kingdom of darkness without even trying. Could the silence in the Heavens the book of Revelation speaks of be The Crowning of The Kingdom in Her New Birth? Isn't it interesting these same Hebrew letters are the word for Good News as well as The Body of Light reference of Adam?! (בשר שבר)

To be redeemed and ransomed from the grave and death is the rescinding and revoking of Tohu V'Bohu from Heavens Courts! The ending here sounds like 1 Corinthians 15:50-56. The word for hid in the Parable of the Leaven Yahshua is used is the same for this word here in Hosea who speaks of so much regarding The Bride and The King Redeemer. The word 'hid' is: צפן – Tzaphan, yes, the very word Job used to describe the layer or Parable Enigma that was stretched out OVER Tohu V'Bohu that Job spoke of!!

This Parable, this Kingdom Parable, with all other Kingdom Parables, are keys Yahshua is teaching, which piece the Tzaphan, The Parable, The Enigma, the protective Threshold between Genesis 1:1&2 back together again! This Tzaphan was shattered illegally by Lucifer, as we read in Isaiah 14, as if he raped the protected place like the violation of a virgin, in order to ascend INTO the sides of the North, the place children come through! This Tzaphon or Tzaphan is the word used for the Influence or strength of a Parable and Enigma.

This Parable language Yahshua was using became that protective layer He once laid between the Tohu V'Bohu and The Earth, which was the Threshold of The High Priest of Genesis 1:1! It would take the Altar of HaShamayim to enter the Realm of HaAretz, in order to restore the Order of all things as they were in Genesis 1:1!

Israel was in Egypt for a total of 210 years and those were years of bondage. The count began with Isaacs birth and the promise given to Abraham about the descendants was phrased as such, "A land not of their own" (Genesis 15:12-13) speaking of Egypt. Then Jacobs birth takes place when Isaac is 60 years old, the 60-fold revelation. Jacob was 130 years old when he arrived in Egypt. He spent his last 17 years with Joseph, who was ruler, and then died at the age of 147. 60 plus 130 is 190. 400 – 190 gives us 210! The enslavement of the children of Israel was 210 years! They were a shattered enigma among the altars of Egypt!

The enslavement was a picture of nakedness first revealed between Genesis 1:1&2. To be naked is to be removed from where you are supposed to be! This powerful Parable Yahshua is speaking about is the Kingdom of Heaven Leaven or, Influence that is inside each one of us, which shatters the layer of enslavement! When you came to His Altar, the shattering began, which is why you felt the brokenness and relief of a hidden burden weighing you down! The Kingdom of Heaven Altar is the Leavening Agent, who pieces together the shattered nation and cleanses the spotted Bride who went wayward!

When Jacob first instructed his sons to go down to Egypt to buy food, that Hebrew word is רְדוּ - Ra'do, the same numerical value of 210! To descend FROM the place where you are supposed to be is like descending into the Tohu V'Bohu also known as Mitzrayim or Egypt! 210 is also the numerical value of a word found in Genesis 2:23 regarding Adam, "Now this time she is bone of MY BONES..." **My Bones – עצמי – Etz'mei!** The Altar Throne of the Heavens is the Expanding and Influential Leaven of The Royal High Priest of Heaven emanated through the Ephod Stones of prophecy! He came to clothe His Bone of

Heaven with the Garment of His Kingdom, by way of His Parable Language. The Keys that unlocked the wardrobe of The Heavens becomes the emergence of the Ephod Stones of Genesis 1:1! He wasn't teaching perse, but He was making a statement. He was saying in a sense, "I have come to put you back together my beloved and clothe in the Garments of the Ephod Altar Stones! I have come to Heal your wounds my beloved! I have come to cleanse your blood flow! I have come to forgive your sins! I have come to wash you clean! I have come to breathe upon you again! I have come my Bride for you with a matchless power and remove from within the influence of Harlotry by the Influence of My Altar of Heaven!! I came down to bring you up!!"

He came to stretch out the Heavens here on the lower realm! Yahshua came as High Priest of Israel, High Priest of The Kingdom and High Priest of The Altar of Heaven to bring Tikkun to the damaged Garment!

Leaven Distinctions

The Kingdom Leaven comes to dismantle the leaven of the kingdom of Darkness in several specific areas where it was hidden:

1. **The Leaven of the Pharisees** – Yahshua said these men were like whitewashed tombs filled with dead men's bones. They lacked the substance and Royal influence on many levels. They were not true sons of Aaron. They paid their way in through their ancestors when Antiochus Epiphanes 4th came in on the scene and changed things. They represented unrighteousness and the opposing side to the Righteous Priesthood of Mashiach Yahshua.

2. **The Leaven of the Sadducees** – in Acts 23:8 we have the reference that these men denied the superiority and supranatural power of the Melkhitzedeq Himself. **Act 23:7** And^{G1161} when he^{G846} had^{G5124} said,^{G2980} there came^{G1096} a disruption^{G4714} between the^{G3588} Pharisees^{G5330} and^{G2532}

the^{G3588} Sadducees:^{G4523} and^{G2532} **the^{G3588} multitude^{G4128} was divided.^{G4977}** (Paul was walking after the order of Melkhitzedeq and The Altar of Heaven authority!!! The Altar of Heaven will dismantle the religions and doctrines of the world! The multitude was divided!) **23:8** For^{G1063} the^(G3303) **Sadducees^{G4523}** say^{G3004} that **there is^{G1511} no^{G3361} resurrection,^{G386} neither^{G3366} angel,^{G32} nor^{G3383} spirit:^{G4151}** but^{G1161} the Pharisees^{G5330} confess^{G3670} both.^{G297} **23:9** And^{G1161} there arose^{G1096} a great^{G3173} cry:^{G2906} and^{G2532} the^{G3588} scribes^{G1122} that were of the^{G3588} Pharisees'^{G5330} part^{G3313} arose,^{G450} and strove,^{G1264} saying,^{G3004} We find^{G2147} no^{G3762} evil^{G2556} in^{G1722} this^{G5129} man:^{G444} but^{G1161} if^{G1487} a spirit^{G4151} or^{G2228} an angel^{G32} had spoken^{G2980} to him,^{G846} let us not^{G3361} fight against God.^{G2313} **23:10** And^{G1161} when there arose^{G1096} a great^{G4183} dissension,^{G4714} the^{G3588} chief captain,^{G5506} fearing^{G2125} unless^{G3361} Paul^{G3972} should have been **pulled in pieces^{G1288}** of^{G5259} them,^{G846} commanded^{G2753} the^{G3588} soldiers^{G4753} to go down,^{G2597} and to take him by force^{G726 G846} from^{G1537} among^{G3319} them,^{G848} and^{G5037} to bring^{G71} him into^{G1519} the^{G3588} castle.^{G3925} **23:11** And^{G1161} the^{G3588} night^{G3571} following^{G1966} the^{G3588} Master^{G2962} stood by^{G2186} him,^{G846} and said,^{G2036} Be of good cheer,^{G2293} Paul:^{G3972} for^{G1063} as^{G5613} you have testified^{G1263} of^{G4012} me^{G1700} in^{G1722} Jerusalem,^{G2419} so^{G3779} must^{G1163} you^{G4571} bear witness^{G3140} also^{G2532} at^{G1519} Rome.^{G4516} Paul represented The Kings Throne and Altar Throne of The Heavens!!

3. **The Leaven of Herod** – Mark 8:14-21 we have Yahshua saying beware of the Leaven of the Pharisees and Herod. Herod was after sensuality, sexual perversion, lust and Harlotry. He represented the goat head of the Temple mount area! The Leaven of Herod was worldliness. The Altar of Heaven, not the Altar of the World, came to smash this entity behind Herod!! It would be right after

this that Yahshua would heal the blind man, we spoke of last time, in Bethsaida or, the House of Entrapment! Between Herod and this House stood The Bread of Heaven, The true High Priest of Israel and Altar High-Priest King of Genesis 1:1! Between the Leaven of Herod now stood the High Priest and King of War! Leaven is a form of an altar that expands what is brought to its mouth, which is breathing.

4. **The Leaven of Corinth** – 1 Corinthians 5 – the Corinthian church was one of sensuality and deep carnality seasoned with major disorder. Paul came to flip this Altar system over! He came with balanced Power and revelation of The Altar of Heaven. Paul began to reveal to this group the way The Kingdom of Heaven was to function and then He taught them! Each one of these leaven revelations are types of altars. Leaven works silently, secretly, steadily, gradually spreading the power of its influence through what it was invited into. All these areas were brought in and not born in! You MUST be <u>born</u> into this Kingdom Leaven and revelation in order to function in due season as the Altar of Heaven. This is a gradual work to get things out and it is a gradual steadfast work to germinate and pollenate the Influence of The Kingdom of Heaven that is inside you!

5. **The Leaven of Galatia** – The Leavening pressure of going back under the system of sacrifice that had been laid to rest. Also, the burdens of the pharisaic traditions known as: Takanot and Gezerot or the re-enactments of the religious system which would have been against what Deuteronomy 4:2 and 12:32 says,

    ➢ **Deu 4:2** You will not add unto the word which I command you, neither shall ye diminish from it, that ye may keep the commandments of YHWH your Elohim which I command you.

> **Deu 12:32** What thing soever I command you, observe to do it: you will not add to, nor diminish from it.

There was also Ma'asim or the deeds from the religious groups not written in Torah. The entire Epistle of Galatians was born because of Acts 15. A very stunning verse in Galatians says much pertaining to the difference between the power of The Altar of Yahshua, which contains the Leavening power of Heavens Altar of HaShamayim Mizbeach, which is found in Galatians 3:19 –

- **Galatians 3:19** Wherefore^{G5101} does^{G3767} serve the^{G3588} law?^{G3551} It was **added**^{G4369} because^{G5484} of **transgressions,**^{G3847} until^{G891 G3757} the^{G3588} seed^{G4690} should come^{G2064} to whom^{G3739} the promise was made;^{G1861} ordained^{G1299} by^{G1223} angels^{G32} in^{G1722} the hand^{G5495} of a mediator.^{G3316}

This is a loaded statement pertaining to The Law being ADDED because of TRANSGRESSIONS. Let us examine this concept of 'transgression' first. What transgressions are Shaul/Paul speaking about? In order to discover this, we would have to journey back to Exodus 32, where the Golden Calf system or, another altar system of worship was first instituted. Transgression, in Hebrew is: Pesha/**פשע** – and means to revolt against the Most-High. It also means to step away or to be one step away from death or cut off. The Golden Calf system of rebellion or, Pesha gave birth to a Certificate System of Law. This gave birth to a Certificate system of priesthood that was subject to death. The Levitical priesthood that was instituted was the result of the Transgression of Israel. Here in Galatians, Paul addresses this Pesha sacrificial system of worship as something temporary, which was not an original intent:

~ **Added** – The Greek word for 'added' is G4369 προστίθημι - prostithēmi, where another related word that is very telling comes from: Prosthesis or Prosthetic limb. The entire sacrificial system was and still remains as a Prosthetic Limb Israel was never intended to walk by. It is an altar system that was never pleasing to The Most High Yah as the prophets speak of:

- **1Sa 15:22** And Samuel said, Has Yahweh as great delight in burnt offerings and sacrifices, as in obeying the voice of Yahweh? Behold, to obey is better than sacrifice, and to hearken than the fat of rams.

- **Psa 40:6** Sacrifice and offering you did not desire; my ears have you opened: burnt offering and sin offering have you not required.

- **Psa 51:15** O Master, open my lips; and my mouth will show forth your praise. **Psa 51:16** For you desired not sacrifice; or else would I give them: you delight not in burnt offering. **Psa 51:17** The sacrifices of Elohim are a broken spirit: a broken and a contrite heart, O Elohim, you will not despise. (Notice it is Elohim who desires these. Elohim is that Altar King of Genesis 1:1 who is giving passage to ascend when these are given.)

- **Isa 1:11** To what purpose is the multitude of your sacrifices unto me says Yahweh: I am full of the burnt offerings of rams, and the fat of fed beasts; and I delight not in the blood of bulls, or of lambs, or of goats. (Referring to the sacrificial system as Sodom and Gomorra!)

- **Hos 6:6** For I desired mercy, and not sacrifice; and the knowledge of Elohim more than burnt offerings.

    (**Compassion,** Mercy – Rachamim/רחמים which also means lovingkindness. Knowledge – דעת/Da'at. The ordinal value difference between sacrifices and burnt offerings **from** Mercy and Knowledge in Hebrew is: 50. The number 50 is the same numerical value of: "HaAdamah" or, The Adamah Altar of Yahshua HaMashiach. 50 is also the number for Jubilee/Freedom in Hebrew.

(Please examine diagram below as well as Hebrew Number Chart in the back of the Book:)

Hidden Truths of The Adam
(Diagram 16)

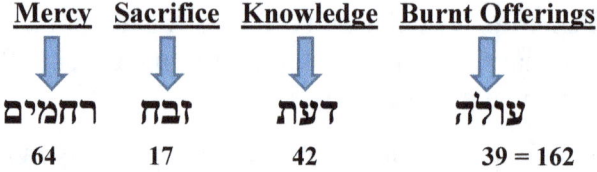

Mercy	Sacrifice	Knowledge	Burnt Offerings
רחמים	זבח	דעת	עולה
64	17	42	39 = 162

- 162 = בְּצֶלֶם – Be'tzelem which means: In The Image (Genesis 1:27)

When we remove that which Elohim never desired, we are left with the actual Image we are to be like and resemble:

- **162 – 56 (Mercy and Knowledge minus Sacrifice and Burnt Offerings) = 50, the numerical value of:** אֲדָמָה – **Adamah, the very Altar of Mashiach Yahshua who is** הָאָדָם **– HaAdam – The Adam of our Redemption!**

- **50 is also the numerical value of:** דָמוֹ **– Da'mo which means: His Blood! We put on Mashiach Yahshua who is The Image and Likeness we are to become. This is true freedom in Him. By His Blood we have changed our appearance before The Altar of Throne of Heavens!**

When the animal sacrificial system is removed, then the image we are to be like is manifested. The blood of bulls and goats <u>NEVER</u> pleased The Father and never produced His image in us, but the blood of His Son did. Why would anyone want to lower the standard to animal blood when we have the Atoning Blood that speaks for us at The Shamayim Altar?

> **Amos 5:21** I hate, I **despise** your feast days, and I will not **smell** your solemn assemblies. **5:22** Though you offer me <u>burnt offerings</u> and your minchah/grain offerings, I will not accept them: neither will I regard the <u>peace offerings</u> of your fat beasts.

True shalom is only found from Yahshua HaMashiach's Altar. The desire has always been for The Kingdom of Heaven, which are His enthroned people here on Earth! The Throne of this Kingdom is The Altar of The Heavens and His Throne is IN THE HEAVENS!!

> Psa 103:19 Yahweh has prepared his **throne** **in** **The Heavens**; and his **Kingdom** rules over all.

In Hebrew it is written like this: "YHWH In **The Heavens** has set up His Throne and His Kingdom over all from ruling." His Throne is The Altar of Heavens!! His Throne is that which is seated in the Highest Heavens!

The Prayer of the Altar Throne

We were given what is known as the model prayer from Yahshua, which is the Altar Kingdom example on how to access the Throne of Abba, who is seated in the loftiest Heavens far above all powers and dominions that may be! Let's contemplate this in conjunction to **The Altar of Heaven** –

Yahshua gave us the most profound, the most well-orchestrated pattern on how to pray. I like to pen this statement as an original, **'The Tabernacle Pattern of Prayer'**! This prayer is a pattern to answered prayer. Yahshua is The Word manifested here on Earth and the Tabernacled Word, who took on the flesh of man. Since He is the Tabernacled Word made flesh, then, His very words are cloaked as an enigma with keys of repairing the areas of man's shattered life and shattered foundation. This prayer is a Kingdom remedy to a fractured people. This patterned prayer is the antidote of man's relationship with Abba and his ascent back to Royal Dominion!

Our Father

~ Our **Abba** who is **in The Heavens**, Qadosh/Holy is your Name… The Father is in The Heavens. He sits or can I say He is Enthroned upon The Altar of the highest Heavens:

- **Abba**, this lets us know that we belong and that we are a part of something real. This reminds us that there is a family connection. This lets us know that we have access to what is on the inside and not just what is on the outside. **Abba** in Hebrew means: **Source, Holder, Origin**. What Yahshua is connecting us to is the Source of all things, which He came representing! Abba lets us know; we are no longer orphans distant from His House because The Door has come. The Door has manifested when there was no access to the Source of all life and blessing. Abba is man's greatest revelation of Elohim because it is the one term, we all can relate to no matter where we come from. We all come from a father. We can all relate to this one fact, which there is a Source place, which we are all intended to arrive to. This Altar Throne of The Heavens is His place where He is known.

- **Rom 8:15** For ye have not received the spirit of bondage again to fear; but you have received the Spirit of adoption, whereby we cry, **Abba, Father**. Two different Greek words are used here. Abba meaning Source and πατήρ - patēr which is the natural realm of fathers. So, we cry Father of all fathers or Source of all entrusted fathers.

- **Gal 4:6** And because **you are sons**, Elohim has sent forth the Spirit of his Son into your hearts, crying, **Abba, Father**.

- **1Co 8:6** But to us there is but one Eloah, the **Father**, of whom are all things, and we in him; and one Master Yahshua HaMashiach, by whom are all things, and we through him.

When Yahshua said call no man Father… What was He really

saying? Call is the Hebrew word קרא/Qara, which the entire book of Leviticus/Vayi**qra** is named after meaning: it is dealing with **drawing close** to The Source. Call no man the Source of what is from The Heavens! No earthly man is the Originator of life and blessing only a Representative and Ambassador entrusted with your soul. To call, also means: to pull out that from within. The Source of your origin is found only from Abba who is the Source of all life!

> **Ephesians 1:17** That the Eloah of our Master Yeshua Messiah, **the Father of glory**, may give unto you **the spirit** of **wisdom** and **revelation** in the **knowledge of him**: Eph 1:18 The eyes of your understanding being enlightened; that you may know what is the hope of his calling, and what the riches of the glory of his inheritance in the anointed ones, Eph 1:19 And what is the exceeding greatness of his power to us who believe, according to the working of his mighty power, Eph 1:20 Which he manifested through Messiah, when he raised him from the dead, and set him at his own right hand in the heavenly places, Eph 1:21 Far above all principality, and power, and might, and dominion, and every authority that is named, not only in this world, but also in that which is to come: Eph 1:22 And has put all things under his feet, and gave him to be the head over all things to the assembly, Eph 1:23 Which is his body, the fulness of him that fills all in all.

> **Eph 4:6** One Elohim and **Father** of all, who is above all, and through all, and in you all. The Source of The Kingdom lives inside of you this day!!

In The Heavens

> **Psalm 2:4** He that **is Enthroned** in **The Heavens** will laugh: Adonai will have them in confusion.

> **Psalm 11:4** YHWH is in his Sanctified Temple,

Yahweh's Throne **is in The Heavens**: his eyes behold, his eyelids try, the children of men.

- ➤ **Act 7:48** Howbeit the Most High dwells **not** in Temples made with hands; as the prophet said, Act 7:49 **The Heavens is My Throne**, and **The Earth** is My footstool: what house will you build Me? says Yahweh: or what is the place of My rest?
- ➤ **Psalm 103:19** Yahweh has prepared **His throne in The Heavens**; and his kingdom rules over all.
- ➤ **Psalm 115:3** But our Elohim is **in The Heavens**: he hath done what he has desired.
- ➤ **Psalm 123:1** Unto you I **lift up** mine eyes, you that **is enthroned in The Heavens**.
- ➤ **Hebrews 8:1** Now of the things which we have proclaimed this is the purpose: We have a High Priest, who is set on the right hand of **The Throne of the Majesty in The Heavens**.

His Throne is upon and in The Shamayim Altar Throne, which these verses say. The Altar of The Heavens is the place where prayer arrives to. It is from this Altar of The Heavens, we are heard, far above the chaos and emptiness of life situations. Abba hears your cries, your pain, your struggles, your hurts and even the words sealed in tears. Abba has a place for you here at this Kingdom Altar of power and might! Abba is that Source of mercy, forgiveness, healing, love. He is the Source of the restoration of all things!

His Kingdom has Arrived

~ Your **Kingdom** come your will be done **on Earth** as it is **in Heaven**… What it sounds like here is that Yahshua is giving us a key that allows The Altar of The Heavens, the Power of Heaven to invade this Earth realm that has many altars who oppose The Kingdom of Heavens Altar system. This Tabernacle Pattern of

Prayer gives us the keys, which release the supranatural here on earth! Yahshua said 'The Kingdom of Elohim was inside of you and I and that Kingdom is waiting to burst forth'. There is no reason to wait for this Kingdom to come man or woman of Elohim, you, who are reading this right this second! The Royal Dominion has already arrived, let it come forth from the depths of your belly?! Yahshua came preaching what was inside of you and I all along, which is The Kingdom of The Heavens!! The Kingdom speaks of Dominion, Rulership, Royal Power and Favor. You must work that Kingdom from within!! Your true essence has always been hidden inside of you. To work out your own salvation with fear and trembling, can also mean to birth this concealed Dominion!

- Kingdom – מלכות = The Place where The King Rules from. The Altar of The Heavens is The Kingdom Altar that Yahshua said was inside of the believer. The Place of Dominion is where The Kingdom is. 'Your Kingdom come...' This is invoking The Kingdom's manifestation, which reveals the Dominion man once had. Man was instructed to have Dominion over all that is upon The Earth or Altar of Earth.

Our Daily Bread

~ Give us this day our daily Bread...

Bread is symbolic of strength, endurance, longevity throughout Scripture. It is also symbolic of the expanding power of covenant as seen through the Leaving process discussed earlier. The first time Bread is mentioned in Scripture is Genesis 3:19 and the next time is in Genesis 14:18. Adam was commanded to eat Bread or, the strength that would lead him to The Highest Altar on Earth, which we will mention in the 6th Altar. He is the Adamah Altar, who sits above The Altar of Earth, who connects the Heavenly Altar with The Earth Altar because of His Enthronement:

> **Genesis 3:19** By the sweat of your face shalt you eat

bread, until you **return to the ground**; for out of it were you taken: for **dust you are**, and to **dust** will you return.

It was from this place of the Adamah, which Adam was forged from, which manifested that The Dust or, particles of Light from the Altar Adam was fashioned out of. The Quantum dimensions contain glimpses of this truth when speaking of Quarks and the rainbow with its spectrum light and color emanations, constantly vibrating from this place of One dimension.

This phrase '...**eat bread till you return to the ground**...' can be read in a more profound way because of the Hebrew language it was scribed from and first spoken as:

תֹּאכַל לֶחֶם עַד שׁוּבְךָ אֶל־הָאֲדָמָה – To'khal Lechem Ad Shoov'kha El-HaAdamah - which can be read: "...**you shall become The Bread of witness as you return to The Adamah/Altar**..." There is a numerical revelation connected to HaAdamah Altar that I have not mentioned. This is that the Ordinal value of this word HaAdamah which is 28, the number of Hebrew letters once again that make up the seven Hebrew words of Genesis 1:1 or can I say that make up the seven Altar revelations of Genesis 1:1?! The Adamah Altar is more mystical and powerful than we would ever fathom! The Adamah revelation is the Image and Likeness Altar, which the Seven Altars commune from. He is The Table Altar as well, who is Bread that the Heavens bring fellowship to. It is where the mind of The Creator allowed the Creation to see and hear His Majesty from!

The Hebrew words Son, The Altar, To Build, come from same numerical equivalency – 57. This tells us they are Divinely interconnected and inseparable. The Altar Empowers the Mission of The Son and the mission of The Son was to Build or, Rebuild The Kingdom that had fallen!

The Son said something powerful –

- **John 6:26** Yeshua answered them and said, Truly, truly, I say unto you, you seek me not because you **saw** the miracles, but because you did **eat** of the **Bread loaves**, and were **filled**. **John 6:27** Do not labor for the meat which perishes, but for that meat which endures to everlasting life, which the Son of man shall give to you: for him has Elohim the **Father** sealed.

The Bread of Heaven will cause you to seek The Son. Yahshua said, "Seek FIRST The Kingdom and His Righteousness and all these other things will be added unto you." Seek first The Bread of The Kingdom!! The Bread is The Righteousness that influences all it is invested into! This is the Bread that endures unto everlasting life. As the chart above shows, there on one side of The High Priest-King of Genesis 1:1 is the Eternal Realms and on the other side is the Everlasting Realms. He desires for us to ascend to this Heavenly Place and Order.

> ● **John 6:31** Our **fathers** did eat manna in the desert; as it is written, He gave them bread from heaven to eat. **(Notice Yahshua didn't say the Bread OF Heaven, but from Heaven. There is a difference to ponder.) Joh 6:32** Then Yeshua said unto them, Truly, Truly, I say unto you, Mosheh gave you **not** that **bread from heaven**; but my **Father** giveth you the **true bread from heaven**. **Joh 6:33** For **the bread of Elohim** is **He** who **comes down from The Heavens**, and giveth life unto the world.

The Bread of Heaven is The Word who came from the Throne of The Altar of The Heavens, who is The Shamayim Miz'be'ach or The Altar of The Heavens manifested!! The Hebrew word Adomeh means: I will resemble! He manifests all Seven Altar Thrones and He resembles all Seven of them.

> ● **John 6:34** Then they said to him, Master, please give us **this bread**. **John 6:35** And Yeshua said unto them, **I am the bread of life**: he that cometh to me shall never hunger; and he that believeth on me shall never thirst.

Why are so many so hungry even after being in religion for so many years? Why do so many return to the same sinful practices even though they have been in religion for so many years? Why are some of the people of the Kingdom empty? Because they have been in religion eating man's bread and not the Bread of Heaven, who came down from The Altar Thrones of Heaven. Yahshua said you will not hunger if you eat The Bread from Heaven. Having said that, there is no way you should be practicing your old life style if you have eaten this Kingdom Bread because this Kingdom Bread is Explosive, it is Expansive, it is Dominating, it is a Territory Conquest by Dominion Power! The Bread of Heaven is The Altar of Heaven's Leaven that takes over all it comes into contact with!

Forgiveness Produces Freedom

~ And **forgive** us our Trespasses as we **forgive** those who Trespasses against us...

Trespass speaks of a threshold breach, a relationship compromise. The threshold had been breached back in the Garden. A debt transfer took place in the Sacred Place. The Altar of Heaven comes to smash this debt transfer and bring about a Release and Overruling Authority against the kingdom of darkness and its Creditor called Death! Remember, Abba **Fore-**Gave His Son as a guarantee, which He has **For**given us our Trespasses before the foundation of the World! A Trespass is always against The Throne and Altar of The Heavenly Domain.

~ And **lead us** not into temptation but **deliver us** from the evil one... The Altar of The Heavens holds the power of deliverance from the grips of the evil one.

~ For yours is **The Kingdom**... The Altar of The Heavens with our King and High Priest Melkhitzedeq Yahshua HaMashiach enthroned upon it is alive!

~ And the **Power**... Exclusive, matchless, unrebutted, Royal, Kingly, Demonstrative Power over all and this is available to us as His Kingdom Altar of The Heavens representative here on the Altar of Earth!

~ And the **Glory** forever and ever... The weightiness of this truth rests inside and upon us. Yahshua said to take upon us His Yoke and His Burden which is easy and light. The weight of His Kingdom removes the burdens and darkness of the enemy kingdom! His Glory or Kavod in Hebrew shakes the Earth giving notice to all others that He is here.

The Altar of The Heavens is the Altar of MelkhiTzedeq, the One who is higher than any other who is YHWH in the flesh! This Altar of The Heavens is waiting to be seen throughout Creation itself especially you and I. This Altar needs something it can manifest through, which becomes the legal bridge, which gives access to Him, making way into the world of Creation through the manifested High Priest-King Altar of Genesis 1:1 – Yahshua HaMashiach. This is where we connect our next Altar revelation. The one who represents Heaven on Earth is the manifested High Priest and King of all, Yahshua HaMashiach The Word made flesh. The Waters of the Heavens have now given the place of Crowning into the next Altar Throne of Power, The Va'Et Altar King – The Word.

Chapter Seven

Sixth Altar:
The Altar Throne of Dominion, Royal Power on Earth –
The Earth's Loftiest Altar, The Adamah Altar

Miz'be'ach Va'Et –
The Ephod Throne of Creation continued,
The Manifested Royal High Priest:

ואת

I pray you are enjoying the revelation so far. What brings the revelation of this 6th Altar to manifestation is one Hebrew letter of connection, the Hebrew letter Vav. Vav is the 6th Letter and is the letter used in the Tabernacle revelation for the nails that secured the wood together. The number 6 is commonly agreed to as the number of Man. he was created on the 6th Day of the Creation week. Man was and is the closest to the Sabbath Day – The Crown of Creation.

The Hebrew letter vav is used to bring manifestation of the High Priest of Genesis 1:1 Altar between The Heavens and The Earth. This Hebrew letter vav sets the premise for The Word who became Flesh and Tabernacled among His people. In the

Tabernacle are 7 Power structures, which 3 of them are Crowned with the Seal of the Nazarene Himself!

In Exodus 38:28 we have this Vav being used as Security to ensure this Skin structure called the Tabernacle would stand up against the Earth interferences of nature. Let us look at this verse in Hebrew as it reveals more than meets the eyes –

> 🌑 **Exo 38:28** And of the thousand[H505] seven[H7651] hundred[H3967] seventy[H7657] and five[H2568] **shekels he made[H6213] hooks[H2053] for the pillars,[H5982]** and overlaid[H6823] their heads,[H7218] and joined/*loved*[H2836] them together.

1,775 shekels of weight was the weight for these 'hooks' used to join together the 'pillars.' The Hebrew rendering: "... וָוִים עָשָׂה לָעַמּוּדִים..." This can be read as: "...he made the hooks for the standing ones..." The hooks in Hebrew have the same numerical value as our entire subject in this book, The Altar. Va'vim equals 62 which is the same for: HaMiz'be'ach or The Altar in Hebrew. See chart below regarding this. Now, the 1,775 shekels of silver connect us to another telling Hebrew phrase fastened to The Covenant. This phrase is found in Exodus 19-24:12 and discussed further below in the diagram – va'vim – nails:

The Seven Altar Thrones of Genesis 1:1

Altar Connections
(Diagram 17)

וָוִים = 62 numerically, the same as: הַמִּזְבֵּחַ – **HaMiz'be'ach** – **The Altar**, not any Altar but The Altar of The Word, The Adamah Altar who is The Image of all seven Altar Powers of Genesis 1:1!

1,775 is the only thing mentioned, not any 'shekel', that part is inserted. These Va'vim/Hooks/Nails hold the weight of something that secures the Platforms of standing ones. Paul said in Ephesians 6:13 STAND! The numerical value for **1,775** is: היכל עצם

השמים – Hei'kel Etzem HaShamayim which means: **'The Temple of the Body of The Heavens'**. The hooks or Va'vim carried the weight of The Temple or Body of The Heavens. The Security on The Earth is The Body of The Kingdom of Heaven which is the people of The Kingdom; who are The Body of The King – 1 Corinthians 6:19; 12:26.

(Diagram 18)

Vav is the clothing to The Alef Tav or Word! This Altar is seen twice in Genesis 1:1 and manifested as the **6th Altar**. We will engage in this as we move through the revelation.

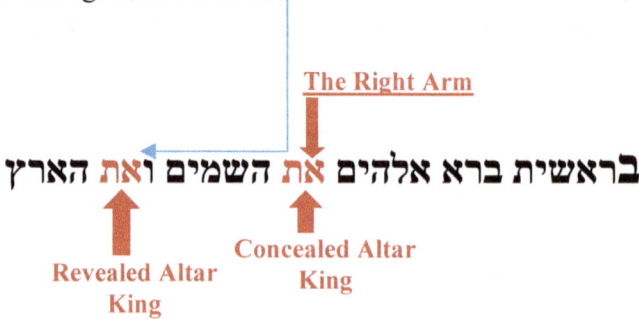

From the HaShamayim to the HaAretz Altars is what I call the Ephod of Genesis 1:1. Some might ask, what is an Ephod? The Ephod is what was worn by the High Priest Aaron and each born son afterwards, who would take the role of his father Aaron. The

Ephod details can be found in Exodus 25 and in detail in chapter 28. The Ephod was the resting place of the twelve stones named after the nation of Israel. This Ephod is also known as the Breastplate of Righteousness. Remember, the fourth Altar was also connected to the Urim and Thummim that was placed behind this Ephod Stones setting, illuminating the rest of the stones when Elohim YHWH would speak to Aaron on Yom Kippur. Let us look at a verse in Exodus 28:6 from its Hebrew origin:

"And they will make The Ephod..." – **וְעָשׂוּ אֶת־הָאֵפֹד** – Ve'Asoo ET HaEphod. This can be read another way that connects this 6th Altar. Remember, in the original Hebrew scrolls there were no spaces or chapter breaks, it was one thread of letters that was unbreakable. You had to know your Hebrew to find a specific section. This phrase can be read as: **וְעָשָׂה וְאֶת הָאֵפֹד** – Ve'asah Ve'Et HaEphod which reads: "And he made the Altar's Ephod!" Ve'Et is our Altar revelation. The last three Altars of Genesis 1:1 is a mystical picture of an Ephod, containing 12 Hebrew letters as well. Aaron's Ephod was an earthly image of the Eternal one. "And will make The Alef Tav The Ephod!

This Ephod revelation is connected to the Genesis 1:1 revelation of the seven Altars.

Sounds too farfetched, but if you look at the structure, the meaning, the countless words in this first verse, you will discover this to be no shorter than the truth. This first verse of Genesis One will leave the hungry student speechless and amazed! The power of these Altar revelations should astonish the minds of everyone, and I pray it is to you the reader as well.

Let's take a look at this verse again for a moment. As you can see, there are 12 Hebrew letters (going right to left) which parallel the Ephod of Aaron, being a pattern of the Greater Ephod. The one worn by our High Priest Yahshua HaMashiach The Word is seen in Genesis1:1! I can't get this out of my mind that these seven Altars of Genesis 1:1, or Hebrew words, form an

The Seven Altar Thrones of Genesis 1:1

actual Menorah! The center of these is the Alef Tav or The Kohein HaGadol – The High Priest who is at the right Hand of Elohim. Not only that but, each of these I believe are the embodiment of as seven Altar Songs.

The Song of Creation vibrates from these Seven Altars, which are Seven Altar Songs, composed of Seven Altar Notes like a Seven Stringed Harp. The center of these is our Kohein HaGadol who orchestrates the Genesis 1:1 Altar Song! This is a huge revelation. Seven Altars each containing a Song that would be seen in each of the seven days of Creation. Later in the sacrificial system, the Levites would sing the Sabbath Songs of Ascent (Psalm 121-134) connecting the seven categories of animal sacrifices! There are so many revelations regarding this thought, this would require another Book of it's own!

The Scripture says when Yahshua rose, He ascended to the Highest of the Heavens and sat down at the Right Hand of Elohim. This 6th Altar Throne is the very Earthly manifestation of that Altar Dominion! Read these scripture connections when you can as we build to this Altar revelation – Luke 22:69; Acts 2:33; Acts 5:31; *Acts 7:55; Hebrews 10:12; Hebrews 12:1 Peter 3:22 also, take note of Isaiah 41:10.

(Diagram 19)

- **Luke 22:69** Hereafter shall the Ben Adam **sit** on the right hand of the power of Elohim.

- **Acts of the Hebrews 2:33** Therefore being by **the right**

hand of Elohim exalted, and having received of Abba the promise of Ruach HaQodesh, he hath shed forth this, which you now see and hear.

- **Acts of the Hebrews 5:31** Him has Elohim exalted with his **right hand** a Prince and Savior, to give repentance to Israel, and forgiveness of sins.

- **Heb 10:11** And every priest stands daily ministering and offering daily the same sacrifices, which can never take away sins: **Heb 10:12** But this Adam, after he had offered **one** sacrifice for sins forever, sat down on **the right hand of Elohim**. *(The Epistle of Hebrews comes to life looking at these diagrams.)*

- **Heb 12:2** Looking unto Yeshua the author and finisher of faith; who for the joy that was set before him endured the cross/tree *(His Adamah Altar on Earth)*, despising the shame, and is sat down at **the right hand** of **the throne** of Elohim. *(To **sit** in Hebraic thought is to be **enthroned**. Kings are enthroned! Yahshua is Enthroned at the Right Hand of Elohim. He is our Enthroned Royal High Priest. The Enthroned King in the beginning was standing in Genesis 1:1 only to return seated or Enthroned as before!)*

- **1Peter 3:22** Who is gone into **The Heavens**, and is **on the right hand** of Elohim; angels and authorities and powers being made subject unto him.

Why does the verse say ON the Right Hand? It's because it is about covenant seed promise! Why? Because His Throne is The Altar and stands as the High Priest King of Genesis 1:1 overseeing all created things in Heaven and in Earth. This same Altar King is seen in our study now as the Adamah Altar of intervention and Dominion between the Heavens and The Earth! We will see this truth now.

Yahshua's whole premise of coming in the likeness of fallen man as flesh was to reconnect us to His Abba which is now our Abba. We briefly saw this with the Tabernacle Prayer, which I truly believe is one of the Most profound pattern of prayer Yahshua instructed us to follow. As a matter of fact, there is the pinnacle of all prayers within Judaism known as the Amidah Prayer, which is equivalent to the Our Father prayer. Amidah means Standing or The Pillar of Prayers, attaching this idea back to the hooks of the Tabernacle parallel.

Yahshua is recorded as standing one time from His seated position in The Altar Throne of the Heavens, when a man called *Stephanos* (whom I believe was James/Yaacob, his brother) was stoned. Stephanos means a **crowned** one. The brother of Yahshua was the first martyr, therefore Yahshua stood on his behalf. Standing is a metaphor of acceptance. Acceptance in His standing is the Scepter of The King being extended to James/Yaacob for passage into the Heavenly Presence of Abba. His brother was crowning the Presence upon his life. This is why Yahshua stood, He saw Heavens Altar seal on the life of man, His brother James/Yaacob.

In fact, this revelation goes very deep. The Hebrew letters that make up Genesis 1:1-2a reveal a branch to this Kingdom prayer, holding the keys of Mashiach Yahshua's redemptive work to restore all things back, as they were in Genesis 1:1. This connection is called the Ana Ba'Koach prayer. The Pillar of Words that unties the knotted fate of all creation. This Altar of the Manifested Word, or our 6th Altar, holds the keys to undoing the breach between The Heavens Altar and the Earth Altar of Genesis 1:1.

When we read through the pages of Genesis 1:2-2:25, this is a record of what was, and what came to be due to a breach, followed by the establishing of The Kingdom. Chapter 3 forward is the record of deception, man's fall and the restoring process of Heaven on Earth with the heartbeat of these Altars as seen in The Garden of Eden where the Tree of Life was and will be again.

When we look at this revelation of Genesis 1:1 and the 7 Altars that are there, we discover that The Kingdom Message Yahshua came preaching would come through The Word made flesh. Just by looking at the structure of these Altars, or seven Hebrew words of Genesis 1:1, the message is hidden in plain sight when the Hebrew scriptures are read.

Let me ask a question before we enter the next Altar, which holds the keys of Righteousness and Justification. This Altar serves to connect The Heavens and The Earth as one flesh, or more precise so I don't confuse, as Basar Echad/בשר אחד meaning: 'The One Kingdom Message of Good News'. Why did Yahshua come? Yes, many know Him as Jesus Christ, but I am asking a universal question so I don't lose anyone, why did He come?

First, we can read in John –

> 🟤 **John 20:19** Then[G3767] the[G3588] same[G1565] day[G2250] at evening,[G3798] being[G5607] the[G3588] **first**[G3391] of the[G3588] **week,**[G4521] (This is not a Sunday as western religion has butchered for hundreds of years. The word for Week here is Sabbaton, one of 7 weeks of counting as is found in Leviticus 23. This is the counting of the first weekly cycle leading up to Shavuot or Pentecost. The Master Yahshua is about to show Himself as The Master of Time by doing a Shavuot thing upon His Disciples. They are about to graduate from Disciple to Apostle or Sent Ones.) when[G2532] the[G3588] doors[G2374] were shut[G2808] where[G3699] the[G3588] disciples[G3101] were[G2258] assembled[G4863] for[G1223] fear[G5401] of the[G3588] Jews,[G2453] in came[G2064] Yeshua[G2424] and[G2532] **stood**[G2476] in[G1519] the[G3588] midst,[G3319] and[G2532] said[G3004] to them,[G846] Shalom[G1515] be unto you.[G5213] (Shalom will cast out all fear, especially from religious men who try to dictate and lord over the people their manipulative control. These religious men then took the livelihood of the people, in the end making Rome's pockets fat and the people begging for their basics. We see this happening today, leaders getting rich while the people are dictated over as humbled servants to some manmade control system indoctrinating the church!)

🟤 **John 20:20** And^G2532 when he had^G5124 spoken,^G2036 he revealed^G1166 to them^G846 his hands^G5495 and^G2532 his^G848 side.^G4125 Then^G3767 the disciples were glad,^G5463 G3588 G3101 when they saw^G1492 the^G3588 Master.^G2962 **John 20:21** Then^G3767 Yeshua^G2424 said^G2036 to them^G846 again,^G3825 Shalom^G1515 be upon you:^G5213 as^G2531 my Father^G3962 has <mark>sent^G649</mark> me,^G3165 even so I send^G2504 G3992 you.^G5209 **John 20:22** And^G2532 when he had said^G2036 this,^G5124 <mark>he breathed on</mark>^G1720 them, and^G2532 said^G3004 to them,^G846 Receive^G2983 the Holy^G40 Spirit/Breath:^G4151

(First, this word used for 'breathed on them' is the same word found in the LXX back in Genesis 2:7 –

Va'yee'pach/וַיִּפַּח = '**And he breathed**' when YHWH Elohim filled the first Adam with a piece of Himself and the sacred souls of mankind. Yahshua breathed a piece of Himself into the Disciples and now they became Apostles of The Melkhitzedeq Priesthood Altar Order. The Apostles were now marked as the foundation stones of the Born again Qahal/Ekklesia/aka Church! The Apostles became the beginning process of that enigma, or this Parable Threshold construct, for a wayward nation about to be united as one Kingdom! Shalom creates an environment for complete rest.

Isn't it interesting the numerical value of this Hebrew phrase Va'yee'pach is the same for a word in Genesis 8:9? **"But the Dove could not find a resting place for its foot…"** Two things, the Dove is symbolic of The Spirit. When Yahshua came out of the Jordan waters the Spirit descended upon Him AS a dove. The word for resting place is: מָנוֹחַ – Ma'Noach. The resting place is the wild branch grafted back into the Tree! The Spirit or Ruach/Breath rests upon the place of Peace. Also, the Ark Noach built was as an Altar. This Altar or Ark was the landing strip for Divine power!! The Ruach symbolic of *the Dove finds its place of Shalom upon those who have become a mobile Altar of Shalom or Peace!)*

Let's continue with a couple more verses regarding WHY Yahshua was Sent and then let us look at some verses which have been misunderstood for hundreds of years due to Roman manipulation that crept into the first century believers during the 4th century C.E.

We just read from His own words that Abba sent Him. Just a side note, the word sent is where we get the word Sholiach or Apostle from. A true Apostle or sent one will ALWAYS have their roots in Abba and All His ways and Word. The Apostle is the first shoots out of **the ground** or **The Adamah**. Yahshua is the Adamah Altar and the Apostles are brought forth from Him. If an Apostle is not rooted and grounded in The Truth, not his or her own truth, but The Truth then something is out of place. Please read: Psalm 57:3; 85:10; *Psalm 89:14; *Psalm 119:142 with Proverbs 6:23.

- **Luke 4:43** And^G1161 he^G3588 said^G2036 unto^G4314 them,^G846 I^G3165 must^G1163 preach^G2097 **The^G3588 Kingdom^G932 of Eloah^G2316** to other^G2087 cities^G4172 also:^G2532 for^G3754 therefore^G1519 G5124 **am I sent.^G649**

- **Matthew 15:24** But^G1161 he^G3588 answered^G611 and said,^G2036 I am not^G3756 **sent^G649** but^G1508 unto^G1519 **the lost^G622 sheep^G4263 of the house^G3624 of Israel.^G2474**

- **1John 3:8** He that **commits^G4160 sin^G266** is^G2076 of^G1537 the^G3588 devil;^G1228 for^G3754 the^G3588 devil^G1228 **sinned^G264** from^G575 the beginning.^G746 For^G1519 this **purpose^G5124** the^G3588 Son^G5207 of Elohim^G2316 was **manifested,^G5319** that^G2443 he might **destroy^G3089** the^G3588 **works^G2041** of the^G3588 Devil.^G1228

Basically, the MANIFESTATION of The Son of Elohim was to destroy the works of Satan or the Devil and restore The Kingdom. This is bigger than we thought though. This word for 'commits' is the Greek word ποιέω - poieō - *poy-eh'-o* and means to create by way of the mind first. It is a unique thing no one has ever done before. Yes, all have sinned and have fallen short of The Glory of Elohim, but this Greek word speaks of making something or bringing something into existence from you that had never been before. It is used in the LXX for the Hebrew word ONLY used in conjunction with Elohim – Bara – ברא –a simple definition meaning to create or to inflate something.

So, when someone willfully commits a sin, it's a creative power like the inflating of what was dead, bringing that thing back to life. The word for 'SIN' means to miss the mark. If you had an opportunity to hit the mark with a guarantee because someone else favored you to win the grandest prize you didn't deserve, who would want to forfeit that? So, to willfully commit sin is like creating a blow-up version of the first sinner called The Devil. The same inference is like when the construction of the Tabernacle was being built up. To willfully sin is to erect a forbidden Tabernacle and this happened through Satan first. Yahshua came to destroy the forbidden Tabernacle works of the Satan itself.

So, we can see Yahshua's manifestation was to destroy the works of the devil aka Satan. Notice the language says The Son of Elohim. Why? Because the creative power Satan wanted was man to give birth to an invitation to a Godlike standing Satan desired. Satan wants to be the manifested **Altered** King to oppose the Manifested Altar King of kings Yahshua HaMashiach! The Son came to rebuild that which had fallen and that which had become unrighteous and fractured. There is a verse that most in religion don't realize has a powerful connection to the biggest problem seen today and that is idolatry and unfaithfulness to Elohim. The Son came to pay the price no one could ever pay –

- **Matthew 20:28** Even as^{G5618} the^{G3588} Son^{G5207} of man^{G444} came^{G2064} not^{G3756} to be ministered to,^{G1247} but^{G235} to minister,^{G1247} and^{G2532} to give^{G1325} his^{G848} life^{G5590} a ransom^{G3083} for^{G473} many.^{G4183}

John-James of the House of Flores.®

He ransomed his wayward Bride. Her garments were filthy. What does this mean?

- **Isa 64:6 But we are**[H1961] **all**[H3605] **as an unclean**[H2931] (unclean – טמא – Ta'mei means ritually disqualified for service. This comes through touching what was dead or being touched by the same.) **and all**[H3605] **our righteousness**[H6666] **as filthy**[H5708] **rags;**[H899] (Our **righteousness** or our own ability to try and obtain a seat in royalty is like filthy rags. **Filthy Rags** – בגד עדים – **Beged Adim** – The Garment of Harlotry! Beged from **Bagad** means: to act unfaithfully to your spouse breaking the Covenant. Jeremiah 3:20; 12:1; Malachi 2:14 - **Jeremiah 3:20** Truly as a wife unfaithfully departed from her husband, so have you dealt treacherously with me, House of Israel, proclaims YHWH. **Jeremiah 12:1** Righteous you are, YHWH, when I petitioned with you: yet let me talk with you of your judgments: For what cause does the way of the wicked prosper? wherefore are all they happy that deal very unfaithfully?

    Beged is the action of unfaithfulness in a marriage.

    Also, the word Beged, which conveys garments and unclean coverings, is amazingly used with the coverings of the Tabernacle vessels, each is a revelation of Yahshua. Even the Tabernacle was not good enough for the abiding Presence! Even the Temple was not good enough for the abiding Presence! All these pointed to the one who would come. The Tabernacle pointed to The Word made flesh while the Temple symbolized The Bride. The Temple became the Harlot.

    Interesting that Elohim in bringing Israel out of Egypt could have given them all they needed to build an actual Temple, but chose a Skin Tent first. Why? Because it was all prophesy about The Son who would come as The Lamb slain BEFORE there was a foundation of a world and redeem His Temple Bride who would go whoring after other gods. In doing so she would exchange the wardrobe of Righteousness and Beauty for the Beged Adim, Filthy Rags!!

Yahshua would come clothed in the skins that looked like the Harlotry garment or fallen man. Adim from Ad/עד which can mean several things such as WITNESS, ETERNITY, etc., but used here is the word for the menstruation cycle of a woman. **Filthy rags** and **wrinkled clothes** are Hebrew idioms for an unfaithful bride and a bride who is in a state of ritual impurity also known as Niddah/Separation. We have been separated from our Creator and through the Son of Elohim our unfaithfulness, our uncleanness, our sin, our unrighteousness is all absorbed in Him, the High Priest and Apostle of our soul! He put on the flesh garment of sinful flesh in order to redeem us back into right standing with Abba and this is called Righteousness! Not ours, but His!

and we all[H3605] do fade[H5034] as a leaf;[H5929] and our iniquities,[H5771] like the wind,[H7307] have **taken us away.**[H5375] (If we miss the truth that we all have went astray we will miss the revelation of the true power of Redemption and Righteous Enclothement!!)

- **Isaiah 64:7** And none[H369] that calls[H7121] upon your name,[H8034] that stirs up himself[H5782] to take hold[H2388] of you: for[H3588] you have hid[H5641] your face[H6440] from[H4480] us, and have consumed[H4127] us, because[H3027] of our iniquities.[H5771]

- **Isaiah 64:8** But now,[H6258] Yahweh,[H3068] you[H859] are **our father;**[H1] we[H587] are the clay,[H2563] and you[H859] our potter;[H3335] and we all[H3605] are the work[H4639] of your hand.[H3027] (The Our Father Prayer Yahshua gave us was a vault of keys to give access into The Kingdom of Heaven

John-James of the House of Flores.®

which is what we are to become sons of – John 1:12. In this verse, we can see a revelation of this Tabernacle of Prayer. It reveals that when we are redeemed back by the blood of Yahshua, we are then placed in the Father's hands for remolding and reshaping due to the cracks, scrapes, bruises of life and sin that are now in need of transformation!! We become the work of His Hand, His Right Arm.)

Let's engage in a small subject matter that this Altar revelation demands to be investigated. What was nailed to the Tree or Cross of Yahshua aka Jesus?

First off in Colossians –

> 🔴 **Colossians 2:6** As^{G5613} you have therefore^{G3767} received^{G3880} Messiah^{G5547} Yeshua^{G2424} the^{G3588} Master,^{G2962} **walk**^{G4043} in^{G1722} him:^{G846} **Col 2:7** Rooted^{G4492} and^{G2532} **built up**^{G2026} in^{G1722} him,^{G846} and^{G2532} established^{G950} in^{G1722} the^{G3588} faith,^{G4102} as^{G2531} you have been taught,^{G1321} abounding^{G4052} therein^{G1722} ^{G846} with^{G1722} thanksgiving.^{G2169} **Col 2:8** **Beware**^{G991} unless^{G3361} any man^{G5100} **spoil**^{G4812} (Spoil in Greek here means to strip away. Don't let any man strip your covering away through their own interpretation and philosophical beliefs.) you^{G5209} through^{G1223} philosophy^{G5385} and^{G2532} vain^{G2756} deceit,^{G539} after^{G2596} the^{G3588} tradition^{G3862} of men,^{G444} after^{G2596} the^{G3588} arrangements^{G4747} of the^{G3588} world,^{G2889} and^{G2532} not^{G3756} after^{G2596} Messiah.^{G5547}
>
> **Col 2:9** For^{G3754} in^{G1722} him^{G846} dwells^{G2730} all^{G3956} the^{G3588} fullness^{G4138} of the^{G3588} Divine Seat^{G2320} bodily.^{G4985}
>
> **Col 2:10** And^{G2532} you are^{G2075} complete^{G4137} in^{G1722} him,^{G846} which^{G3739} is^{G2076} the^{G3588} head^{G2776} of all^{G3956} principality^{G746} and^{G2532} power:^{G1849}

On His Altar something very powerful took place –

> 🔴 **Col 2:14** Blotting out^{G1813} the^{G3588} **handwriting**^{G5498} **of**

ordinances[G1378] that was **against**[G2596] **us,**[G2257] which[G3739] was[G2258] contrary[G5227] to us,[G2254] and[G2532] took[G142] it[G846] out of[G1537] the[G3588] way,[G3319] **nailing**[G4338] **it**[G846] **to his tree/cross;**[G4716] **Col 2:15** Having spoiled[G554] principalities[G746] and[G2532] powers,[G1849] he made an open spectacle[G1165] of them,[G1722] [G3954] triumphing over[G2358] them[G846] in[G1722] it.[G848]

Handwriting of Ordinances was of a religious decree according to Thayer's dictionary. This handwriting was something AGAINST us that stood as a WITNESS. This was something we did. It was something we broke. It was a handwritten ordinance that only an Altar could destroy. There was something we did long ago that was recorded as a witness against us. It is actually written in a song long ago by Moses. It was a song sung by Moses through the Ancient Solfeggio Scale seen in the Genesis 1:1 Seven Altars, prophesied to be destroyed.

Remember, each Altar is also a Song constantly vibrating with creative and matchless power. This Altar of the Manifested High Priest of Genesis 1:1 came with a new song restoring and removing the death penalty. He came restoring Order back and removing the penalty of this handwritten song placed in the mouths of the people. No wonder Revelation speaks of a New Song – Revelation 15, the Song of Moses and the Song of the Lamb. Moses' song found in Deuteronomy was a prophetic song concerning what would happen, and the Song of the Lamb is what unties this fate –

- **Deuteronomy 31:16** And YHWH[H3068] said[H559] unto[H413] Moses,[H4872] Behold,[H2009] you will sleep[H7901] with[H5973] your fathers;[H1] and this[H2088] people[H5971] will rise up,[H6965] and go a **whoring**[H2181] after[H310] the gods[H430] of the strangers[H5236] of the land,[H776] where ever[H834] [H8033] they[H1931] go[H935] to be among[H7130] them, and will forsake[H5800] me, and **break**[H6565] **(**[H853]**) my covenant**[H1285] which[H834] I have made[H3772] with[H854] them. **Deu 31:17** Then my anger[H639] shall be kindled[H2734] against them in that^{H1931} day,^{H3117} and I will forsake^{H5800} them, and **I will hide^{H5641} my face^{H6440} from^{H4480} them**, and they shall be^{H1961} consumed,^{H398} and many^{H7227} evils^{H7451} and troubles^{H6869} will overtake^{H4672} them; so that they will say^{H559} in that^{H1931} day,^{H3117} Are not^{H3808} these^{H428} evils^{H7451} that overtake^{H4672} us, because^{H5921 H3588} our Elohim^{H430} is not^{H369} among^{H7130} us? **Deu 31:18** And I^{H595} will completely hide^{H5641} my face^{H6440} in that^{H1931} day^{H3117} for^{H5921} all^{H3605} the evils^{H7451} which^{H834} they have made,^{H6213} which^{H3588} they are turned^{H6437} toward^{H413} other^{H312} gods.^{H430} **Deu 31:19** Now^{H6258} therefore **write^{H3789} (H853) ye this^{H2063} song^{H7892}** for you, ('write this song' in Hebrew has a Ordinal value of 141, which is the numerical value of the word: הַקּוֹל – HaQol = **The Voice**. The cure is in The Voice and by The Voice. The Word manifested as The Walking Mobile Altar on Earth, who became the walking Song of our Redemption!) and **teach^{H3925} it^(H853) to the children^{H1121} of Israel:^{H3478} put^{H7760} it in their mouths,^{H6310}** that^{H4616} **this^{H2063} song^{H7892}** may be^{H1961} **a witness^{H5707} for me against the children^{H1121} of Israel.^{H3478}** ....**Deu 31:22 Moses^{H4872} therefore wrote^{H3789} (H853) this^{H2063} song^{H7892} the same^{H1931} day,^{H3117}** and taught^{H3925} it^(H853) to the children^{H1121} of Israel.^{H3478} **Deu 31:23** And he gave^{H6680} (H853) Joshua^{H3091} the son^{H1121} of Nun^{H5126} a charge, and said,^{H559} Be strong^{H2388} and of a good courage:^{H553} for^{H3588} thou^{H859} shall bring^{H935} (H853) the children^{H1121} of Israel^{H3478} **into^{H413} the land^{H776}** which^{H834} I swore^{H7650} unto them: and I^{H595} will be^{H1961} with^{H5973} you. (**Into the land** is the revelation of His Kingdom on Earth. The 6th Altar brings the song of redemption and restoration, brings the Kingdom Message, brings the people into the promise! The Adamah Altar, revealed through this 6th Altar, brought the song of Heaven's Throne. Remember, each Altar is seen in the Ancient Solfeggio musical scale as well which are the vibrations of restoration, healing and undoing fate!) **Deu 31:24** And it came to pass,[H1961] when Moses[H4872] had made an end[H3615] of writing[H3789] [(H853)] the words[H1697] of **this**[H2063] **law**[H8451] **in**[H5921] **a book,**[H5612] (What Law? The Law or, Governing Voice to this Song, which was the witness against Israel! The power of music is a law of its own. It holds creative power and can attach you to what it references! The Law here was the Law of this song, not the entire Law of Elohim as many religious men have said.) until[H5704] they were finished,[H8552] **Deu 31:25** That Moses[H4872] commanded[H6680] [(H853)] the Levites,[H3881] which bare[H5375] the ark[H727] of the covenant[H1285] of YHWH,[H3068] saying,[H559] **Deu 31:26 Take**[H3947] [(H853)] **this**[H2088] **book**[H5612] **of the law,**[H8451] **and put**[H7760] **it into the side**[H4480] [H6654] **of the ark**[H727] **of the covenant**[H1285] of YHWH[H3068] your Elohim,[H430] that it may be[H1961] there[H8033] **for a witness**[H5707] **against thee**.

The handwriting of ordinances written against us as a witness was a song and an unfaithful decree from Heaven's Courts. Moses was probably crushed as he heard this for the first time. After two whole generations and still they did not get it! After all the miracles, Hearing **The** Voice, after all the provision they still would rebel. It would take a recorded song, an altar song that would stand as an abiding law with The Law as the witness against a delivered nation in bondage to their own generational iniquity and fleshly appetites.

So, in Colossians when Paul was speaking about the Handwriting of Ordinances against us, this was an ancient Altar Song. This Altar song altered our destiny and ushered in other governing powers from an Altar manifested. The Altar Song can be a cure or it can be a disease depending on the words or can I say the Ordinances written. This Handwriting from the Altar song of judgment and prophecy was nailed to The Highest Altar on Earth!! From this manifested Priest-King Altar a song was vibrating throughout the Heavenly dimensions.

The Loftiest and most powerful Altar on Earth contained another song that was the hammer to destroy these ordinances against us. This song was the song of unfaithful Israel who became a harlot to many that was now crushed. She took in the seed of other doctrinal empires and produced elite generations that would be out to destroy mankind. It was on the top of a small mountain where a bright light would shine. It was upon the Tree that a song came forth from The Voice of innocent Blood. It would be from the loftiest Altar that stood between The Heaven's Altar and The Altar of the Earth with a Song of Redemption, who satisfied the payment.

He consumed the song of prophetic judgment against a wayward wife called Israel. The Altar of Dominion, Royal Power on Earth – The Earth's Loftiest Altar, The Adamah Altar caused the healing frequencies of forgiveness, acceptance, justification, sanctification, deliverance, adoption, to be sung for the first time on Earth over His beloved.

From the highest Altar on Earth is where the Divine met with man that all other sacrifices only pointed to. This is where each of us must come to in order to meet our King for the first time. (John 14:6) From here your name is not only known in the Heavens but your name is now mentioned and you are rejoiced over, Haleluyah!! From this Altar, Earth becomes witness to you as the New Creation in Yahshua HaMashiach according to 2 Corinthians 5:21!

It was at this HaAdamah (ואת) Altar between The Heavens and The Earth Altar's; the speechless animal sacrifices were given an answer of! At this place all debts are cancelled, all sin is paid for, all claims against your soul are undone by and through the power of the Blood of Yahshua HaMashiach! At this Altar there was a WARSHIP that took place, knocking out the battleships of satanic principalities and powers spoiling them making an open embarrassment of them, transferring our naked condition upon them! (Colossians 2:14-15)

The seven Altars of Genesis 1:1 are revelations of their own, but collectively because of the manifested Word, the manifested Royal High Priest of Genesis 1:1 this Ephod of His in Genesis 1:1 is a symphony or Heavenly unified Orchestra sustaining all things as One by vibrational unity. It is believed that Elohim sang all Creation into existence as the Hebrew text records, "ויאמר" – Va'yomer - 'And He said or and He sang into existence.' Amar is also the idea of activation and vibration as a frequency. The Creator used the vibrational power of worship and song when creating all things.

There is the Seal of Elohim upon every created thing because of this truth. There is a song that comes from these Altars of Power and Revelation just for you and I. There is a song of rejoicing in the Heavens still to this day since the day you were connected through Repentance/Teshuvah. There will come a day the Song of the Lamb will be introduced to His Bride as Zephaniah prophesied about –

- **Zephanyah 3:14** Sing, O daughter of Tzion; shout, O Israel; be glad and rejoice with all the heart, O daughter of Yerushalayim. **Zep 3:15** YHWH has removed your judgments, he has cast out your enemy: the King of Israel, YHWH, is in your midst: you will not see evil any more. **Zep 3:16** In that day it will be said to Jerusalem, Fear not: **and to** Tzion, Let not your hands be empty. **Zep 3:17** YHWH your Elohim in your midst is mighty; he will save, he will rejoice over you with joy; he will rest in his love, he will **joy over thee with singing**. (To twirl around and above you with vibrations and utterances is how these phrases of singing can be translated! This twirling is like a DNA Helix picture. What a powerful thought! Recreating through the Ancient Song of Joy and love for His world and people!)

- **Revelation 15:1** And I saw another sign in **The Heavens**, great and marvelous, seven angels having the seven final plagues; for in them is filled up the wrath of Elohim.

> **Rev 15:2** And I saw as it were a sea of glass mingled with fire: and them that had received the victory over the **beast**, over his **image**, over his **mark** and over the **number** of his name; stand on the sea of glass, having the harps of Elohim. **Rev 15:3** And they **sing the song of Moses** the servant of Elohim, and **the song of the Lamb**, saying, Great and marvelous are your works, Yahweh El Shaddai; just and true are your ways, our King of sacred ones.

Can you hear the word here? Zephaniah/Tzaphan Yah. Yes, the Healed Enigma because of the Song! The Song of the Lamb, the Song of The 6th Altar, is sung over all of Israel over all of Tzion. No longer can Tohu V'Bohu, the Void and Emptiness, have its place over us because the protective Threshold is the restored Song! The vibrational layer stands between the Altar of the Earth and Tohu V'Bohu. This is powerful because Lucifer was composed of musical instruments with the understanding of how to unlock the Enigma. Yet, he would never gain insight how to piece the Song together. This was the assignment of the Lamb slain BEFORE the foundation of the world!

The manifested Altar of Royal power, our 6th Altar intercepted the vibrational altar system of Lucifer and man's judgment. This is called Justification or Just-if-i-ed never sinned! Let us read a few verses on this Justification none of us deserved:

- **Romans 3:20** Therefore^{G1360} by^{G1537} **the deeds**^{G2041} of the law^{G3551} no^{G3756} ^{G3956} flesh will^{G4561} be justified^{G1344} in his sight:^{G1799} ^{G846} for^{G1063} by^{G1223} the law^{G3551} is the knowledge^{G1922} of sin.^{G266}

- **Romans 3:21** But^{G1161} now^{G3570} **the righteousness**^{G1343} of Elohim^{G2316} **without**^{G5565} **the law**^{G3551} is manifested,^{G5319} being witnessed^{G3140} by^{G5259} the^{G3588} law^{G3551} and^{G2532} the^{G3588} prophets;^{G4396} (There is the animal sacrificial system of self-works or deeds done to gain right standing and there is the right standing THROUGH The Son who is The Lamb slain before the foundation of the world.) **Rom 3:22** Even^(G1161) the righteousness^(G1343) of Elohim^(G2316) by^(G1223) faith^(G4102) of Yeshua^(G2424) Messiah^(G5547) to^(G1519) all^(G3956) and^(G2532) upon^(G1909) all^(G3956) them that believe:^(G4100) for^(G1063) there is^(G2076) no^(G3756) difference:^(G1293) **Rom 3:23** For^(G1063) all^(G3956) have sinned,^(G264) and^(G2532) come short^(G5302) of the^(G3588) **Abiding Presence**^(G1391) of Elohim;^(G2316) **Rom 3:24** Being **justified**^(G1344) freely^(G1432) by his^(G848) grace^(G5485) **through**^(G1223) the^(G3588) **redemption**^(G629) that^(G3588) is in^(G1722) Messiah^(G5547) Yeshua:^(G2424) **Rom 3:25** By who^(G3739) Elohim^(G2316) has seated^(G4388) to be a **Mercy Seat**^(G2435) (Yahshua is our Mercy Seat, outside of all animal sacrifices, which were unable to extinguish our sin or reconcile man back to Elohim. There is never one time through the animal sacrificial system where it says man was reconciled back to Elohim through animal bloodshed! The entire system was the school master system pointing to The Master of masters.) through^(G1223) faith^(G4102) in^(G1722) his^(G848) blood,^(G129) to declare^(G1519 G1732) his^(G848) righteousness^(G1343) for^(G1223) the^(G3588) forgiveness^(G3929) of sins^(G265) that have past,^(G4266) through^(G1722) the^(G3588) foreknowledge^(G463) of Elohim;^(G2316) **Rom 3:26** To^(G4314) proclaim,^(G1732) at^(G1722) this^(G3568) time^(G2540) his^(G846) righteousness:^(G1343) that he^(G846) might be^(G1511) just,^(G1342) and^(G2532) the justifier^(G1344) of him^(G3588) which believes^(G1537 G4102) in Yeshua.^(G2424)

This Altar revelation from the Shamayim Altar to the HaAretz Altar or The Altar of The Heavens and The Altar of Earth, is powerful with our HaAdamah Altar standing between the two unifying the distance through reconciliation! The Adamah or The Altar of **The Place** is the only access and threshold for the two to become Basar Echad or One Flesh! When you hear Flesh, you might think of natural flesh and bone, but far be it from the truth! Basar is also Besorah which means The Good News of The Kingdom! The very mission Yahshua our HaAdamah Altar came preaching!

The Shamayim Altar is parallel to the Holy of Holies. Having said that, this means within this Altar dimension are the revelations of The Ark of His Presence or where The Elohim of all Creation sits–

- **Hebrews 8:1** Now^{G1161} of^{G1909} the things which we have spoken^{G3004} behold the completion:^{G2774} We have^{G2192} such^{G5108} a High Priest,^{G749} who^{G3739} is enthroned^{G2523} on^{G1722} the right hand^{G1188} of **the^{G3588} Throne^{G2362} of the^{G3588} Majesty^{G3172} in^{G1722} the^{G3588} Heavens;^{G3772}** (Refer to the diagram with the Right hand of Abba) **Heb 8:2** A tiller of the people,^{G3011} of the^{G3588} Sanctuary^{G39} and^{G2532} of the^{G3588} true^{G228} Tabernacle,^{G4633} which^{G3739} the^{G3588} Master Adonai^{G2962} stretched out^{G4078} and^{G2532} not^{G3756} man.^{G444}

- **Psalm 11:4** "…Yahweh's Throne is in **The Heavens**…"

- **1Ki 22:19** And he said,^{H559} Hear^{H8085} you this,^{H3651} the word^{H1697} of Yahweh:^{H3068} I saw^{H7200 (H853)} Yahweh^{H3068} enthroned^{H3427} on^{H5921} His Throne,^{H3678} and all^{H3605} the host^{H6635} of **The Heavens**^{H8064} standing^{H5975} by^{H5921} him on his right hand^{H4480 H3225} and on his left.^{H4480 H8040}

- **Act 7:49** '**The Heavens is My throne**, and **The Earth** is My footstool. What house will you build for Me? says יהוה, or what is the place of My rest? **Act 7:50** 'Has My hand not made all these?'

- **Psalm 45:6** Your throne, Elohim, is forever and ever; The sceptre of Your Kingdom Is a sceptre of Righteousness. (Kingdom and Righteousness together give us: Melkhitzedeq!)

- **Psalm 103:19** Yahweh has prepared His Throne **in The Heavens**; and his kingdom rules over all. **Psa 103:20** Bless Yahweh, all his angels, that excel in strength, that do his commandments, listening to **The Voice** of his word.

The Heavens are the seat of His Throne. The Altar of The Heavens is His Throne. This is the Holy of Holies of the three Altars! And in this Place is a Crowned One! The Ark was Crowned. The Crown is the Hebrew word for Nazerene!

The next area is the Sanctuary or inner Sanctum or Sacred Space. This is where The Priesthood of Royal Power is connects two worlds as one, which he absorbed the sting of death! Yahshua absorbed our death penalty position. He canceled the death edict that was against us through the dogma and writ of men! He nailed it to the tree! (Notice the vav of this 6th Altar – Va'et/ואת)

He is the Crowned King of Heaven and Earth! The Sent One who brings Tikkun or, Repair to the Breach! The Breach was the shattered Tzaphon or Enigma Parable Layer of Genesis 1:1-2a.

The next Altar will be the HaAretz Altar or The Earth Altar. The place of the Outercourt where accusations are brought to the courts of Heaven. The Courts of Heaven are here. Heaven uses the Altar platform of Earth to settle accusations and sin debts! This is accomplished by the mediator of the New Covenant also reflected in our 6th Altar revelation, Yahshua HaMashiach!

The 6th Altar revelation, which is The Word made flesh, holds the only authority and power to function upon this Earth. The Word came clothed as the living man who is The Living Word in order to destroy the death decree against the people of Elohim. This Outercourt place if I may, is the place where accusations are all brought. This is the place where Satan will be cast down to as he is suspended between the Adamah Altar and the Earth Altar. He roams to and fro across this Altar of Earth but, never settles here.

He brings all accusations to the Bench Platform of this Altar of Earth and this is where Heaven hears from. This Altar of Earth area is like the clerk's office of the Courts. He has been submitting all his accusations against mankind from the Mountain of Moriyah UNTIL the High Priest after the order of

Melkhitzedeq came in on the scene! Satan can go no further from this place unless invited in. This Altar of Earth or Outercourt area of the 7 Altars of Genesis 1:1 is where all the accusations and edicts against you and I are overturned and overruled because of the Adamah Altar of Yahshua HaMashiach!

This Outercourt area of the Earth Altar is the final attempt by the hordes from hell to alter your confession. This is the battle ground between the Kingdom of Light and the Kingdom of Darkness.

There is a powerful verse that was changed revealing this Altar of Redemptive Power and Kingship, however, it was changed. Psalm 96:10 says from the older scrolls, "YHWH reigns from The Tree", revealing the Crowned Nazarene on The Tree. In my study series of the Crowned Kings of the Tabernacle, we have seen that the Ark, Shewbread Table and Incense Altar, had Golden Crowns called Nazarene in Hebrew – נזר. The Nazarene was sitting Enthroned upon each of these vessels of the Tabernacle as the Crowned King-Priest or, MelkhiTzedeq!

A side note, the numerical value of this word is 257, the same for Vayomer/ויאמר – **And He spoke**. Vayomer comes from the word Amar in Hebrew. Amar is where the Greek translation gets Rhema from. Yahshua said man shall not live by bread alone but by every word/**Rhema**/**Amar** that proceeds out of the mouth of Elohim. Yahshua was battling on the legal planes of the Outercourt Altar of Earth. He overcame Satan from the Outercourt as The Adamah Altar Man! He was the manifested Tavneet or Pattern Moshe saw in Exodus 25.

Ancient Solfeggio Voices

Amar is the vibrational movement music rides upon called airwaves. Even the airwaves will be healed as satan who is the Prince of the power of the Air will be evicted. The airwaves will be filled with the vibrational power of the 6th Altar's Song, which is the song of the Lamb. The High Priest of Genesis 1:1 is the

The Seven Altar Thrones of Genesis 1:1

Center Branch to this Mystical Menorah Altar scale. Six ancient notes that hold a frequency setting of: 396, 417, 528, 639, 741 and 852. Each number frequency is a hidden mystery to the Altars on each side of Genesis 1:1's High Priest Altar, which we are seeing manifested through this sixth Altar Throne revelation. Here is how this would seemingly look and how this can be read:

(Diagram 20)

בראשית ברא אלהים את השמים ואת הארץ
852　741　639　**528**　417　396

"In the Beginning Elohim Created the ancient solfeggio scale of music and vibrational power." These numbers reduce down to 369, which happen to be what science claim to be the secret numbers to the 'World of Creation'. 369 is the numerical value of: עולם הבריאה – Olam Ha'Briah which means: **'The World of Creations!'**

The B'resheet Altar or, the first Altar, is the multidimensional Throne that reveals all other six Altars. Yet, none have a beginning, as they are revealed through the Beginning. B'resheet can be read as **'Through the Beginning'** in which all things are revealed! Each one of these Solfeggio Vibrations is a song that creates. Each of these are an entire book of their own, but notice the 528 frequency is connected to the 4th Altar, the High Priest-King of Genesis 1:1. 528 is an actual Healing frequency. Now when we add up each number as a single digit, we have 90. The numerical number 90 presents another revelation that connects us to the previous point of this study:

90 = האפד – HaEphod – **The Ephod**. The Ephod is the Breastplate of The High Priest that sings on Yom Kippur, and how much more The Great Atonement of Yahshua HaMashiach. King David understood the significance of the Breastplate through the revelation of The Melchizedek High Priest. The last three Altars of this Genesis 1:1 revelation contain 12 Hebrew

letters, which allude to the 12 stones of the Ephod, and the 12 Gates named after the 12 Tribes of Israel in the book of Revelation. The ancient solfeggio scale contains the revelation of The Ephod that is worn by The One who restores all things. This brings me to our next revelation of the number 90.

90 = מֶלֶךְ – Melekh – King.

The numbers associated with the Altars here in Genesis 1:1 reveal the power of The King's Ephod or, the Ephod of The King. Each of these are a revelation of The King of all Creation's Ephod and Throne. When you get some time go to the internet and check out the Ancient Solfeggio Scale, it will blow your mind how they are all connected to this Altar revelation.

When Yahshua was here, everything He did when it came to the miraculous was a vibrational manifestation of The Beginning. His touch caused the physical bodies to sing again! Blind eyes became a song when opened, deaf ears became a song when opened, lame legs became a song when healed to walk again, leprous conditions reversed became the cry of a musical symphony when touched by this mobile Altar King Yahshua, the dead raised to life became a new song, blood flows dried up became the song of rivers of life, forgiven sins became a new song of deliverance and freedom causing angels that surrounded the Altar of Heaven to rejoice – Luke 15:10, demonic possession became songs of deliverance and healing! The Loftiest Altar on Earth was the Adamah Altar, who is the manifested King of Israel - Yahshua HaMashiach, our 6th Altar manifested!

Isn't it interesting that the Ancient Solfeggio Scale also parallels the vibrational scale of the colors in the Rainbow? The Rainbow, given to mankind and all living things in Noach's day, was a Song in the sky, that only those in Covenant were allowed to hear its musical genius. The rainbow stood as a silent Harp whose strings were waiting to be strummed by the hands of the Redeemed. The Rainbow is an untouchable reflection through water vapor of The Tree of Life that is on either side of The River of Life now as Revelation speaks of – Revelation 22:2.

The Seven Altar Thrones of Genesis 1:1

Seven Altars, Seven days of Creation, Seven colors in the Rainbow and the 7 Celestial Bodies in the Heavens with the Sun of Righteousness at the center. All functioning in agreement. Each pointing to the greater of them and all culminating into the 7 Altars of Genesis 1:1.

~ Rainbow in Hebrew is: קֶשֶׁת – Qeshet. This is first found in Genesis 9:13, after the flood of Noah's day. This might be far fetched for many, but in my study of the Scriptures, I have discovered there are no coincidences. Genesis '9:13', which happens to be the numeric connected to the first Altar Throne of Genesis, בראשית/ B'reshith – ת = 400; י = 10; ש = 300; א = 1; ר = 200; ב = 2; Total: **913**! This is an enigma of its own to ponder. In Genesis 9:13, the Hebrew phrase is scribed as such: אֶת־קַשְׁתִּי נָתַתִּי בֶּעָנָן – 'Et Qash'tee Na'ta'tee Be'anan: "My Rainbow I have set inside the clouds…" This verse has the same number system, which is connected directly to the first Altar Throne as stated above. The first phrase written here has the Ordinal value of 207. This value is equivalent to two key Hebrew words: אין סוף – Ayin Sof, or The Infinite One; and אור – Ore – Light. This Rainbow prismed the Color Candelabrum Songs of The Altar Throne Songs! The 6th Altar Throne manifested all these revelations, which were kept secret and concealed inside the first verse of our Scriptures! The number 207, also equals the Hebrew word: רז – Raz, which means Secret! When read the opposite way, we have: זר – Zeir, which means an edge, or crowned bordering; a Face. The Crowned molding, which surrounded The Ark of The Covenant, The Altar of Incense and Table of Bread. The Zeir, or Face, of the Altar Thrones was seen in the 6th Altar King, Yahshua HaMashiach. He was the Crowned One!

Our 6th Altar of Genesis 1:1 – וְאֵת – Ve'Et means '**And**' in Grammatical Hebrew. This word stands between The Heavens and The Earth. It is the connector between the Heavens and The

Earth!! When looking at this Hebrew word, we get a glimpse of past, present and future. You might ask, How so? This 6th Altar revelation is the One who transcends time and space. Let us examine this for a moment: **ואת** – The Hebrew letter Vav teaches us of the revelation of the past, things from the past being connected with the now, hence, the word 'And'. **אות** – Ote, A sign, and Enigma! An enigma or Parable becomes a sign in this present time. The Vav inserted in the midst of the Altar unites what was in the prophetic past with the prophetic fulfillment of present time. The 6th Altar is in the prophetic past, manifested in the prophetic present and waiting in the prophetic future! **אתו** – Ote means Him. He is concealed in the past, prophetically operating in the present and manifested in the future. Throughout all history we can see the past, present and future all intertwine with each other. The 6th Altar revelation is the governing seat of past, present and future.

When we really think about this 6th Altar, the number 6 should ring a bell because 6 is the number connected to mankind. Man was Created on the 6th Day without getting too mystical. What comes to mind regarding this Altar is that it represents the manifested High Priest-King on The Earth. What is the one thing aside from destroying the works of the devil, that The Son of Elohim, who is The Word, who is Kohein HaGadol (The High Priest after the Order of MelkhiTzedeq) come for? To Atone for His People!

Atonement and Redemption can be found all the way back in the beginning from this Altar revelation!! Atonement and Righteousness cannot be separated. Atonement can mean: At-One-Ment or to be with. It also means to be of one mind:

- **Philippians 2:5** (G1063) Let this **mind** be^{G5426 G5124} in^{G1722} you,^{G5213} which^{G3739} was **also**^{G2532} in^{G1722} Messiah^{G5547} Yeshua:^{G2424} **Php 2:6** Who,^{G3739} being^{G5225} in^{G1722} the image^{G3444} of Elohim,^{G2316} thought^{G2233} it not^{G3756} robbery^{G725} to be^{G1511} equal^{G2470} with Elohim.^{G2316}

Atonement also will change the way you think. Your mind which is the seat of the soul is impacted by the unseen power of atonement –

- **Leviticus 17:11** For[H3588] the **life/soul**[H5315] of the **flesh**[H1320] is **in the blood:**[H1818] and I[H589] have given[H5414] it to you **upon**[H5921] **the altar**[H4196] to make an **atonement**[H3722] for[H5921] your **souls:**[H5315] for[H3588] it[H1931] is the blood[H1818] who makes an atonement[H3722] for the soul/nefesh.[H5315]

Life is the word for Soul here – נֶפֶשׁ/Nefesh. This is saying that 'His Soul or life is inside the Blood'! The He is This Altar revelation. The phrase in Hebrew is this:

- כִּי־נֶפֶשׁ הַבָּשָׂר בַּדָּם הִוא – Kee Nefesh HaBasar Ba'Dam Hee = "For the Soul of His flesh is in the blood." The soul speaks through The river of life that is flowing in the veins! We have a deep revelation here. The Soul of His Flesh speaks THROUGH His Blood. The Soul is the platform of exchange between the spirit and flesh dimensions. The Blood of Yahshua is the blood that would speak on our behalf from the Highest courts of Heaven that we are redeemed and we are Atoned for!!

Now I need to mention something that I have expounded on in depth before. This is a sensitive subject matter for some, and highly misinterpreted verse of Scripture:

- **Gen 3:21** Unto Adam[H121] also and to his wife[H802] did Yahweh[H3068] Elohim[H430] **make**[H6213] **coats**[H3801] **of skins,**[H5785] **and clothed**[H3847] them.

The preaching that has come from this section of Scripture is powerful, beautiful and insightful but far from the truth of what is written. Many, including myself, have said this was the first blood sacrifice that took place which would seem to make sense, but nevertheless is not what the text says. In Adam's fall he initiated the manifestation of what we have engaged in when it comes to the 6th Altar revelation – The Va'et or HaAdamah Altar.

It reads in Hebrew –

וַיַּעַשׂ יהוה אֱלֹהִים לְאָדָם וּלְאִשְׁתּוֹ כָּתְנוֹת עוֹר וַיַּלְבִּשֵׁם:

Hebrew read right to left – **Vaya'as YHWH Elohim Le'Adam Ool'ish'to Kat'note Ore Vayal'beeshem.**

There isn't an indication of animal sacrifice or bloodshed, this is assumed by most. What we have here is an eisegesis of the text or, forced meaning of interpretation read into the text. The is the first time this Hebrew word for flesh is mentioned, referring to what can be touched, our tangible bodies. Never before mentioned until **after** the fall of Adam. Adam was clothed as a **Skin Altar** or man of the Flesh.

The Hebrew word Ore/עוֹר is cognate to Ear in sound. The word for clothe them is **Labash** and means to clothe oneself or cover one's nakedness. Adam refused to Hear from a spiritual level so Adam became a flesh man with flesh ears which are the scales of his life, mozenim. When we read **Labash** the other way it is the word for the ears of corn – Sha'beil, which are the coverings of corn, as well as the train of a robe. Man was now the garment, an Altar of Earth, that all Creation would depend upon to Hear the Voice.

Just like Aaron when he went into the Holy of Holies once a year to 'HEAR' what The Voice was speaking. The entire sacrificial system culminated to the Eternal Realms, and yet in a brief moment, The Voice would speak through the **Ephod** by The Alef Tav, which it rested upon. The power of The Altar of hearing!

The flesh of man now would have to be governed by what He heard from the Altar of Sacrifice. Man's ears became flesh gateways to the Altar. This is why we see the strongest force with man commanded to Hear. The Shema of Deuteronomy 6:4-9 is the declaration that connects us to the Altar Throne of Yahuwah or The Name. Hearing is vital throughout Scripture and Hearing, or the Ears, contain a very powerful revelation connection with the Altar!

It gets more interesting because the way these Seven Altars of Genesis 1:1 are placed, which is right to left. The High Priest Altar of Genesis 1:1 just happens to be at the Right Hand of Elohim!

(Diagram 21)

The Ordinal value of this entire phrase from Genesis 3:21 reveals to us this very truth of who the Blood for Atonement comes from which will connect us to its origin found in Genesis 1:1:

- The Ordinal value is 152 which equals: בנימין/Benyamin or Son of The Right Hand!!

- **Psalm 110:1** Yahweh[H3068] said[H5002] to my Yahweh,[H113] Sit[H3427] at **my right hand,**[H3225] until[H5704] I make[H7896] your enemies[H341] your footstool.[H1916 H7272]

- **Hebrews 1:13** But[G1161] to[G4314] which[G5101] of the[G3588] angels[G32] did he say[G2046] at any time,[G4218] **Sit**[G2521] **on**[G1537] **my**[G3450] **right hand,**[G1188] until[G2193 G302] I make[G5087] your[G4675] enemies[G2190] your footstool?[G5286 G4675 G4228] **Heb 1:14** Are[G1526] they not[G3780] all[G3956] ministering[G3010] spirits,[G4151] sent forth[G649] to minister[G1519 G1248] for[G1223] them who shall be[G3195] **heirs**[G2816] **of salvation/Yeshua?**[G4991]

The Right Hand is none other than the Son of Elohim, who tabernacled among man, in the Garment or Coat of Skin!! His Garment of unbreakable Skin and Crown of Thorns were the Declaration of The manifested Altar King of Earth now. In the Melkhitzedeq Psalm and in the Melkhitzedeq Epistle to the Hebrews we have two witnesses to this fact!! He was sent forth to Atone for those who would be heirs of this great salvation by His Blood!! We have another key to this truth found in the Ordinal value of Genesis 1:1 which contain our seven Altar revelation – the Ordinal value is 298, the same for a few Hebrew words that are very telling:

- חצר – Chatzeir – Courtyard area. The place of sacrifice and blood speech. Blood speech is a term I penned meaning when you can't speak the blood will speak for you. The only voice with the authority to speak on our behalf is The Blood of Yahshua HaMashiach!

These two areas – the Outer Courtyard and Inner Sanctuary are designed like the levels of Courts with the Supreme Court or the SCOTUS (Supreme Court Of The United States) which deals with cases brought and cases appealed. This Outercourt Area is the place of Accusation and where the accused can confront their Accuser. When Mashiach Yahshua was crucified this took place in the face of The Accuser of the brethren and this Has.a.tan with all his accusations day and night (day and night speak of the Outercourt area not the inner Sanctum where there was just the seven-tier revelation spectrum of Light emanating from The Menorah).

This took place in the Courts of Heaven, which is the Supernatural place where blood speaks. It is where The Altar and Waters of Immersion both constantly functioning. This place will condemn or give passage for enclothement. It was from this place the Earthly sacrifice of Yahshua impacted this mystical place in the courts of Heaven. (Read Exodus 27:9; 35:17; Isaiah 1:12; 62:9; 1 Kings 6:36; 7:12; 2 Kings 21:5; Ezekiel 40:14)

The next Chatzeir/Courtyard, would be from the revelation of the inner sanctum, what is known as the Chambers or, The Sanctuary. It is where accusations have no passage because the Blood overturned the accusations and Heaven's Courts overruled the verdict of the enemy. In this place are three revelations of Chambers seen in The Menorah, The Table and Altar of Incense. There is the Court area and then there is Chambers where kings speak with kings and priests speak with priests. There is so much to speak on here that it would be a whole other book. Let's look at the other words that equal 298.

- חצר – **Chatzar** – To sound a Shofar or Trumpet. Think about this for a second! The sound of the Shofar is like creating the entire atmosphere of the Heavenly Court room!

- רחמים – **Rachamim** – Mercy, Lovingkindness. It was from the Courtyard where we were all accused and found guilty that Mercy was extended by the Scepter of The King. By the Blood Atonement of Yahshua HaMashiach our guilt and well-deserved penalty was placed upon Him in exchange for His forgiveness and acceptance in the beloved. Mercy given for those who deserved none! His Blood spoke from the Outer Court on behalf of you and I.

- רחץ – **Rachatz** – To wash, to bathe or cleanse. It was from this place we were washed and cleansed from the old garments of sin and death. When Lazarus walked out of the tomb, Yahshua said, "Remove and free him up of those grave clothes!" Why? Because the Living Water had cleansed Lazarus from Death's hold! The Outer Courtyard area contained keys of entry and passage. One had to experience these levels for themselves in order to go to the next level in holiness.

There are keys that unlock certain doors and there is one key that unlocks the Door to The Kingdom and that is The Blood of The High Priest Yahshua after the order of Melkhitzedeq that speaks! The manifested Royal High Priest is seen in this first verse of our Scriptures as The Center Altar or, the 4th Hebrew word as I have mentioned. Then we see Altar King, The Word manifested in this 6th Hebrew word or the 6th Altar we are now unpacking.

The Hebrew letter Vav, or 6th letter of the Hebrew Alef Bet, is a picture of a nail and represents man. The Nail is what fastens two things and makes them one. This letter connects two worlds together just as it connects two thoughts in a sentence together. This Hebrew letter reveals the mystery of The High Priest of Genesis 1:1! This 6th Altar is the revelation of The Word, who would put on flesh in order to Redeem man. He is 100% YHWH Elohim inside a 100% Flesh Body which Heaven ordained and called The Bread of Heaven! This Bread of Heaven is the expanding influence that colonizes all its surroundings because it is the Leavening Agent Himself.

This revelation is seen throughout Scripture and constantly overlooked by many Christian expositor. Here is a key verse where this manifested High Priest who stands between The Altar of Heavens and The Altar of Earth as the manifested High Priest and King. This verse was hidden in plain sight, but missed by religious men as it was passed by the deaf ears and blind eyes of the pulpits in the English world of today –

> 🏵 **Leviticus 4:1** And YHWH[H3068] manifested the Word[H1696] unto[H413] Moses,[H4872] saying,[H559] **Lev 4:2** Speak[H1696] unto[H413] the children[H1121] of Israel,[H3478] saying,[H559] If[H3588] a **soul**[H5315] **sins**[H2398] through ignorance[H7684] against any[H4480] [H3605] of the commandments[H4687] of Yahweh[H3068] which[H834] should not[H3808] be done,[H6213] and will **do**[H6213] against any[H4480 H259] of them:[H4480] (The word do here is Asah in Hebrew and means to make. So, to do what Abba says not to do is to alter a part of creation. We hold power by the choices we make to create through the altar of speech and thought!) [H2007] **Lev 4:3** If[H518] **the priest**[H3548] **that is anointed**[H4899] does sin[H2398] according to the sin[H819] of the people;[H5971] then let him bring[H7126] for[H5921] his sin,[H2403] which[H834] he sinned,[H2398] a **young**[H1121 H1241] **bull**[H6499] **without blemish**[H8549] unto Yahweh[H3068] for a sin offering.[H2403] (The Priest that is anointed in Hebrew is:
>
> הַכֹּהֵן הַמָּשִׁיחַ – HaKohein HaMashiach means: The Priest who is The Messiah! This is The High Priest-King of the House of Altars or our Seven Altars. The numerical value of HaKohein HaMashiach is 443, the same as: בית

אֵל – Beit El or House of El/God! The High Priest who is The Messiah is the House of Elohim, our Ambassador and King-Priest. He is The Representative of The House of Altars – The Seven Altars of Genesis 1:1. Notice the following Diagram:

(Diagram 22)

In these verses from Leviticus are deep revelations of two ideas. First, The First Adam, who was The Priest and Anointed One, who sinned. Second, we see a hint to this 6th Altar revelation, communicated to us as the Manifestation of The Word, who put on flesh and Redeemed the fallen Adam – the man who first sinned! Next, we have 'a young bullock without blemish'. What stands between YHWH and This first Adam is a young bullock without blemish.

Let us examine the Hebrew text as we are still focused on the Altar revelation: פַּר בֶּן־בָּקָר תָּמִים – **Par Ben Baqar Tamim** means more than a young bull because Ben in Hebrew means a mature son. This is a hidden prophecy now revealed about The Son of the Morning or, the Son who scatters the darkness at His coming! **Baqar** means: to cleave to, to split or bring distinction and Tamim means to be perfect or unmixed. The revelation that stands between the fall of the first Adam who sinned and Yahweh is The Son who scatters the darkness at His coming, who is the Son that came to cleave fallen man to PERFECTION and to make mankind unmixed with the sin of the fall! Powerful revelation here!)

Lev 4:4 And he shall bring^H935 (H853) **the Bull**^H6499 **to**^H413 **the**

door[H6607] **of the tabernacle**[H168] **of the congregation**[H4150] before[H6440] Yahweh;[H3068] and will lay[H5564] (H853) his hand[H3027] upon[H5921] **the Bull's**[H6499] **head,**[H7218] (The Bull's Head is read as: רֹאשׁ הַפָּר – Rosh HaPar. This is why we MUST learn the Hebrew language because we can see what the English fails to pick up. When this Bull's Head CARRIES the sin upon Himself, a transfer takes place, a Healing is administered from the Heavenly Courts and Heavenly Altars to the Altar of the Earth where transactions between flesh and spirit are legally and lawfully executed. When the transfer is accomplished then the blessing of this Bull's Head is given to all who come to the Door.

Reading this Hebrew phrase Rosh HaPar in reverse gives us the Blessing: רֹפֵה שְׂאֹר Ro'feh Se'or which means: The Leaven agent of Healing or curing! The Agent to curing the impact of sin is found in and through The Manifested High Priest Yahshua HaMashiach who is concealed in the 4th Altar revelation and this 6th Altar revelation! The Power of this Redemptive Transaction healed the sting of death, breaking its curse of the Law off the Congregation and Bride!) and kill[H7819] (H853) the Bull[H6499] before[H6440] Yahweh.[H3068] **Lev 4:5 And the priest**[H3548] **that is anointed**[H4899] shall take[H3947] of the bull's blood,[H4480 H1818 H6499] and bring[H935] it to[H413] the tabernacle[H168] of the congregation:[H4150] ('And' is the 6th Altar revelation of the clothing for The High Priest of Genesis 1:1. He unites together, the two by the sacrifice of Himself. Here we have the Last Adam who is The Priest after the order of Melkhitzedeq and who is The Mashiach! Only the Mashiach can Redeem the fall of the first Mashiach who came from the Garden of Eden! The Power of the work of restoring all things back as they were intended was placed at the Door of the Congregation 2000 years ago. The Repairer of the Breach is The Son

The Seven Altar Thrones of Genesis 1:1

who Heals this fall of man and the Breach of Genesis 1:1-2! The Bull in Hebrew speaks of the Power of The Son's Resurrection. Paul/Shaul desired to experience this as he mentioned in Philippians 3:10!)

Let's seal up this Altar with a revelation conveyed to Earth from Heaven. This is also a revelation of its own, which a Book could be written about. This HaAdamah Altar in word form alone holds revelations just by looking at Him. Yahshua HaMashiach is this Adamah Altar who stands as the Ladder of ascension between the Heaven and The Earth Altars.

(Diagram 23)

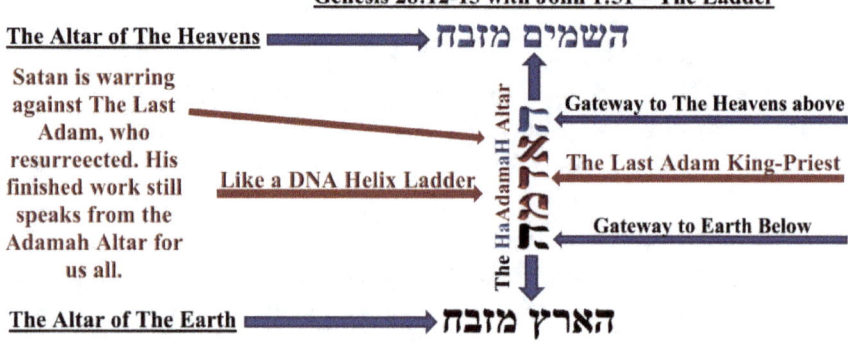

This first verse can be seen as the Body of what is known as Adam Kadmon or the Eternal Adam. I give you this thought to just think upon. The idea of 'The Adam', is more than some information about a man in a Garden. This idea is about a Power that can restore all things back to The Garden of Eden! Altars are lawful and legal doors between spirit and flesh. In a sense, the soul of man is his altar of operation between the spirit and the flesh. Man became a living soul, a speaking spirit – Genesis 2:7 – וַיְהִי הָאָדָם לְנֶפֶשׁ חַיָּה: – Va'yehi HaAdam Ke'Nefesh Cha'yah – And The Adam became a Living Soul or Breathing speaking soul. The only creation that can transport words into the future. The only creation that can create the platform of an Altar

John-James of the House of Flores.®

where his very words become the atmosphere of the courtyard or courtroom arena! Adam or the first man was given the platform bridge and threshold preeminence since Genesis.

In Genesis 1:26-27 we have something not talked about, but I will address this truth right here and right now. This is going to bless your heart and encourage you by letting you know your words and prayers and cries are never forgotten.

The Crowning of Remembrance

- **Gen 1:26** And Elohim[H430] said,[H559] Let us make[H6213] **Adam**[H120] in our **Image,**[H6754] after our **Likeness:**[H1823] and let **them** have dominion[H7287] over the fish[H1710] of the sea,[H3220] and over the fowl[H5775] of the air,[H8064] and over the cattle,[H929] and over all[H3605] **The Earth,**[H776] and over every[H3605] creeping thing[H7431] that creeps[H7430] upon[H5921] **The Earth.**[H776]

- **Gen 1:27** So Elohim[H430] Created[H1254] (H853) **The Adam**[H120] in his Image,[H6754] in the Image[H6754] of Elohim[H430] He Created[H1254] him; **male**[H2145] and **female**[H5347] He Created[H1254] them.

(Diagram 24)

(Right to Left in Hebrew)

Va'yivra Elohim ET HaAdam Be'tzalmo Elohim Bara Oto ZAKAR OO'NEQEIBAH Bara Otam.

As you will read in this book, what connects the two here is the

Hebrew letter **Vav** which is another hint to our 6th Altar of Genesis 1:1, our Altar revelation at hand. Adam was **created** from the place called Bara, that 2nd Altar revelation we covered already. There is a transition with the 6th Altar here, it goes from the connecting symbol to the connecting man – Oto meaning Him! The Adam was Created **Zakar** and **Ne'qeibah**. This is much deeper than we think, for the sake of this section here I will focus on the concepts of **male** and **female**:

- **Male** – זָכָר – also pronounced as Zekhar predominately means remembrance, to remember.

The Male and Female descriptions in the sense of English denotes an animal nature which we all do have one. In Hebrew thought this means to speak and act on behalf of another. This concept also connotes the ability to carry the origin of a thing. This speaks of the Source Holder. One who is first in line and time. He is the seed carrier. So, the Adam holds the ability to send forth something into the future by way of words that will speak and act on behalf of those it was sent for. The Source Carrier positions himself in the future of today.

Zakar becomes the demarcation point of something that has always been. Connection to this Adamah Altar which is Yahshua HaMashiach, He was SENT forth from Eternity into the moment of time when man needed bridging. He came around the 4th millennium from Adam's fall which is parallel to the 4th Altar who is the High Priest King Altar of Genesis 1:1.

Remembrance was sent to the future. You and I hold the key when we **become** prayer, as Psalm 19:4b says –

> "…and I *give myself* to prayer." The italicized part is an insert. The Hebrew actually says this: וַאֲנִי תְפִלָּה – Va'Ani Tefillah which means: And I am Prayer. We must BECOME in order to BE.
>
> We become the Altar bridge of communication here on Earth, and therefore the ability to position words, prayer

in the future to meet with us or our generation blood line.

- **Female** – נְקֵבָה – **Ne'qeibah**, the Place of gestation. Where what enters will expand and accelerate to its fullest potential.

This can be pronounced as **Niq'bah**, which means: a passage way granted. So, the **Zakar** combined with **Ne'qeibah** we have the Source of life sent forth and granted passage to be revealed. These two terms are prophetic terms to ponder because they tell us about the Word that was Sent and manifested through the womb of a woman. Embedded in Adam was the ability to send forth the promise that would speak on your behalf and the behalf of your generational line.

Adam and the Wife were to be the walking Altars who would 'Remember' – Speak and act on behalf of the Altar Thrones, and, to 'Manifest' what was delegated – Zakar and Ne'qeibah! They were supposed to manifest all 7 Altar Thrones throughout all Creation.

We can make this personal as we pray, we send forth words on behalf of ourselves and loved ones etc. BECAUSE we have become the pillar of prayer or can I say, The Altar Platform. These words enter the safe place granted until the appointed time to be manifested. There are words waiting in your future and mine that we will meet with one day. There are words that were prayed over us without us knowing that met up with us. I can tell you this, there were prayers sent forth for me and at 16 years of age those words and prayers met up with me at the appointed time and transformed my life. The same has happened to you all.

Communication became the medium between Heaven and Earth. These Hebrew terms are poorly translated as Male and Female, Zakar and Ne'qeibah. This is why The Word Himself took on the flesh and Tabernacled (John 1:14) among man of this dimension in order to proclaim The Kingdom that is not of this world.

- **John 18:36** Yeshua answered, My Kingdom is not of this world: if my Kingdom were of this world, then would my servants fight, that I should not be delivered to the Jews, now My Kingdom not from THIS PLACE. **18:37** Pilate therefore said unto him, Are you a king then? Yeshua answered, you say that I am a king. To this end was I born, and for this **purpose** I came into the world, that I should bear witness to the truth. Every one that is of the truth hears My Voice.

Scripture reads:

- 🟥 **Psa 119:89** For ever,H5769 Yahweh,H3068 your **word**H1697 is **settled**H5324 in **The Heavens.**H8064

Word in Hebrew is Dabar/דבר, when translated to the Greek language it is Logos. Logos is the term used in Greek to describe The Word in John 1:1-3, 14 who is Yahshua the Son of Elohim manifested in the flesh.

The word for SETTLED in Hebrew is Natzab/נצב, which means to be stationed or Appointed and be established. The Word is Appointed in The Heavens or Stationed WITH the Altar of The Heavens – In Heavens/בשמים – With the Heavens pointing to The Genesis 1:1 Altar! The Word has been Appointed to this Altar Throne because He is the One who has joined together through Himself as Basar Echad/One Kingdom Message, The Heavenly Altar Message the Altar of Earth has now received. The two have become One! This Settled Word is still speaking. The Eternal Word was sent to Earth to Communicate the Finished Work of The Beginning which is the declaration of The End! The Word is the settlement of The Kingdom! The BAR in Aramaic is the Son who is the Gateway, the Door!

- 🟥 **Colossians 1:13** Who has delivered us from the power of darkness, and has transplanted us into the Kingdom of his dear Son: Col 1:14 In whom we have redemption through his blood, the forgiveness of sins: **Col 1:15** Who is the Image of the invisible Elohim, the firstborn of every creature: **Col 1:16** For by/through him were **all things**

created, that are **in The Heavens**, and that are **in The Earth**, **visible** and **invisible**, (The Ladder or Sulam effect here – Heaven means Invisible, The Earth means visible that which is tangible and temporary.) whether they be **thrones**, or **dominions**, or **principalities**, or **powers**: **all things were created by him, and for him** alone. (Hebrew 1:1-3) **Col 1:17 He is before all things**, and by him all things **consist**. (The word **consist** comes from the word that means to glue together, to attach as one, to be commanded together. The Highest Courts of Heaven have filed the Decree for this truth, it cannot be undone or over ruled or over turned by any kingdom, throne, dominion, principality, power of any sort.)
Col 1:18 And he is the head of The Body, (Note Exodus 24:10 – The Bone/Body of Heaven) the called-out ones/aka Church: who **is The Beginning**,

(The Son who is The Word who is The First Altar King of Genesis 1:1, who is the Altar King-Priest between Heaven and Earth. He is also said to be The Beginning as well, or The Altar of called B'resheet/בראשית, The Crown of all other Altars, The House of The Altars!) the firstborn from the dead; that in all things he might have the **superiority**. (superiority means Superiority in all excellence. This is Creative Power and original Rule. Death could not hold back or hold down the King of Life. He contained the words of Eternal life that caused all graves to release the firstfruits He came to resurrect! Eternal Life is the manifestation of our first three Altar revelations of Genesis 1:1 as shown in above diagram.)

Col 1:19 For it pleases the Father, The Source of life that in him should **all fulness dwell**; (**all the fulness dwell can be defined as:** all the weight be enthroned upon. He entered this world as the Leaven of The Altar Thrones the Leavening Agent of The Kingdom and in doing so, He caused the Kingdom to burst forth from within. I can paint a picture of this from the Matrix movie part one at the end after Neo/One gets shot by the Agents in black coats/Dark kingdom, he resurrects from the dead touches the holes in His body then as he stands, the agents throw all they have at him and He proclaims, "NO!" He runs towards them and penetrates the depths of this dark kingdom and the Light of The Kingdom causes the agent to explode and Neo left Stationed, Appointed in the face of all others.)

- **Colossians 1:20** And, having made peace through the blood of his Tree/cross, (The Peace or Shalom came through The Blood from His Altar of Enthronement as He was suspended between Heaven and Earth. He was suspended as The Last Adam, The Adamah Altar King extending redemption and the forgiveness of sins to all who would approach the foot of This Altar Throne! His Blood had a Chambers conversation on your behalf.) by him to **reconcile** all things to himself; by him, I say, if they be things in earth, or things in heaven. (The power of Reconciliation through this Adamah Altar holds the only key to unlock the Enigma, the Parable or Kingdom Code putting all things back together.)

I have mentioned for years we can see the Kingdom revelation of The Jacob Ladder prophecy in Philippians 2:6-8

The Stairway of Heaven and Earth

1. Php 2:6 Who, being in the form of Elohim, (**Crown of all seven Altars of Genesis 1:1. This is the top of the Ladder Jacob saw in Genesis 28. Jacob saw Him there enclothed as all Seven Altar Throne revelations. Jacob calls this Place The House of Elohim. The House is the very first Hebrew letter that begins our Scriptures. Jacob called all seven Altar Thrones The House of all Eternity and everlasting dimensions.**)

2. thought it not robbery to be equal with Elohim: (**This is**

Enthronement. Seated at The Right Hand, stationed as that 4th Altar revelation of Genesis 1:1 who is King Priest of the seven Altars. He was equal in essence because he and Abba are Echad/Unified.)

3. Php 2:7 But made himself of no reputation, (**As He was Passing through the Altar Thrones from above making His way through The Heavens as The Connecting Altar and upon The Earth Altar.**)

4. and took upon him the **form** of a servant/Tiller of The Ground/Altar, (**The incarnation of manifestation of The Adamah Altar walking between the Heavens and the Earth Altars! This flesh is what touched this Earth while His Spirit was ever present on The Throne Altar of the Highest Heavens! He came and overcame the flesh with flesh!**)

5. and was made in the **likeness** of men: (**The likeness of men.** (The very opposite of Genesis 1:26-27; 2:7. The likeness, similitude, embodiment of a man. This is the 5th step. Each step is the seven-tier revelation of the Altar Thrones back in Genesis 1:1 as well as each day of Creation. These are revelation rings of the prophetic ladder of the seven days of Creation which we are living at the end of day 6. When Scripture says Yahshua is the Master of The Sabbath it infers more than a Day. This directs the listener to the Crown of many crowns Altar King who wears all seven from Genesis 1:1. Likeness comes from an interesting Hebrew word –

Tamunah/תמונה – etymologically it relates to Moon or Man in sound. The heart of this Hebrew word is Man. as you can see, the Vav at the center is the connecting revelation of our 6th Altar of Genesis 1:1 – Va'et or HaAdamah Altar!

The Hebrew word Moneh/מוֹנֶה, contains another Hebrew word which speaks of the electrical current that brings things to life. The Likeness was The Electrical current of The Altar Throne that would bring man back to the Life in The Garden!

The Numerical value of this Hebrew word Tamunah is 501, the same for three specific Hebrew phrases: **ארשׂ** – **Aras** which means: To Betroth, To be engaged. The Goal of this was the

Betrothal. Also, the Hebrew word phrase – דצכ עדש באחב – **De'tzak Ad'ash Be'achav** which means: The 10 Plagues that were unleashed on Egypt. These were the dilating Crowning positions of The Kingdom bursting forth out of the womb of Egypt!! The last numerical connection we have is: שאר – **Se'or** which means: **Leavening agent**. The Adamah Altar is the Head of The Kingdom who is also the Leavening Agent that colonizes this entire region. Once He arrived, there was no stopping this Kingdom takeover! When we read Se'or the other way, it's the Hebrew word Rosh which means Head or The Crowning of an era, the Crowning of The Altar King's Dominion! Rosh is who Crowned, or revealed the Altar revelations of Genesis 1:1, through House or Hebrew letter Bet/ב that was introduced.)

6. Philippians 2:8 And being found in likeness of man, he humbled himself, and became obedient unto death, even the death of the Tree/cross. (The pinnacle of the revelation or Crowning place of The Adamah Altar. He was crowned as King on this Altar over all The Earth! His Death was The Crowning of the Head of The Kingdom of Heaven. He said, "The Kingdom of Heaven has arrived!" - **Mat 4:17 From that time יהושע began to proclaim and to say, "Repent, for the Kingdom of The Heavens has drawn near."**)

7. Philippians 2:9 Wherefore Elohim also has **highly** exalted him, and given him The Name which is above every name: (**Seated at the Highest Altar Throne. The Name Yahshua is the Altar Name assignment given that connected The Heavens and The Earth! The Name Yahshua is the Garment of The Word who is now resurrected. The power of The resurrected Word is untouchable by Death, man's greatest enemy.**)

Philippians 2:10 That at the name of Yeshua every knee should bow, of things in heaven, and things in earth, and things under the earth; Php 2:11 And that every tongue should confess that Yeshua The Messiah is Master, to the glory of Elohim the Fathering Source.

(Diagram 25)

The loftiest and highest Altar on the Earth is this HaAdamah Altar who is Yahshua HaMashiach, The manifested Word. He was manifested to activate The Kingdom of Heaven on Earth. Now let me share something interesting regarding Ezekiel's Wheel.

- 🍎 **John 19:16** Then^{G5119} therefore^{G3767} he delivered^{G3860} him^{G846} to them^{G846} to be crucified.^{G4717} And^{G1161} they took^{G3880} Yeshua,^{G2424} and^{G2532} led him away.^{G520} **Joh 19:17** And^{G2532} he bearing^{G941} his^{G848} Branch/cross^{G4716} proceeded^{G1831} into^{G1519} **The Place**^{G5117} called^{G3004} the place of a ==skull,^{G2898}== which^{G3739} is called^{G3004} in Hebrew^{G1447} ==Golgolet:^{G1115}== **Joh 19:18** Where^{G3699} they crucified^{G4717} him,^{G846} and^{G2532} two^{G1417} others^{G243} with^{G3326} him,^{G846} on either side there was one,^{G1782 G2532 G1782} and^{G1161} Yeshua^{G2424} in the middle.^{G3319} **Joh 19:19** And^{G1161} Pilate^{G4091} wrote^{G1125} a title,^{G5102} and^{G2532} put^{G5087} on^{G1909} the^{G3588} Tree/cross.^{G4716} And^{G1161} the writing^{G1125} was,^{G2258} YESHUA^{G2424} OF NAZARETH^{G3480} THE^{G3588} KING^{G935} OF THE^{G3588} JEWS.^{G2453} **Joh 19:20** This^{G5126} title^{G5102} then^{G3767} read^{G314} many^{G4183} of the^{G3588} Jews:^{G2453} for^{G3754} the^{G3588} place^{G5117} where^{G3699} Yeshua^{G2424} was crucified^{G4717} was^{G2258} near to^{G1451}

the^{G3588} city:^{G4172} and^{G2532} it was^{G2258} written^{G1125} in Hebrew,^{G1447} Greek^{G1676} and Latin. ^{G4515}

First, the final manifestation of The Fathers Name was attached to this Tree. Over His Head was: יֵשׁוּעַ הַנָּצְרִי וְמֶלֶךְ הַיָּהוּדִים – '**Yeshua Ha'Natzri Ve'Melekh Ha Yahudim**', as you can see, we have the ultimate manifestation of The Father's Name here upon The Altar High-Priest, the Highest Altar ever to come in contact with The Earth. He is The Adamah Altar or The Manifestation of The Word united again with His Father's Name through Blood. The Altar gave access to man once again to come close through The Blood into The Most Sacred Space known, The Dimension of Altar Thrones!

This was the PLACE of the skull also called Golgolet in Hebrew. Let us unpack some of this revelation to this Highest and Loftiest Altar on Earth. Actually, this HaAdamah Altar was suspended **between** or '**Soned**' The Heavens and The Earth Altars! Yes, I know there is no such word, but I am using it to convey the revelation. What a mind-blowing thought! Golgotha in Hebrew: גלגלת – Golgolet, has the same numerical connection to what takes place again at this Loftiest Altar called the Adamah Altar or The Altar of The Ground, where man will return through as DUST or bodies of life! You and I must be rooted and GROUNDED in Him as the Scripture is written – Colossians 2:7.

Golgolet has the value of 466, the same as: Genesis 1:27 "...**The Adam in His image the Image and likeness of Elohim**..." – הָאָדָם בְּצַלְמוֹ בְּצֶלֶם אֱלֹהִים – HaAdam Be'tzalmo Be'tzelem Elohim. The Altar at Golgotha is the Altar where His Likeness and Image are born upon the life of the new believer. This is no small thing; it is actually a huge revelation! This is that original place Adam was to walk in and now through The last Adam who is the Adamah Altar we have this access and Scepter passage from The Throne!

When you read this in Hebrew there is an addition to the word 'The Adam' which looks like this – את־האדם – Et HaAdam.

Yes, this is the mystery of the High Priest Altar of Genesis 1:1 we covered already who manifested as The Last Adam. The one who stands between Heaven and Earth as The Kohein HaGadol or, Great High Priest! He is the Life-giving Spirit – 1 Corinthians 15:45.

As I mentioned manifestation, this Altar revelation is the One who would take what is from the Altar of The Heavens and make it so here on The Earth Altar! From dust you are Adam and to the Dust you will return. The dust is the spiritual body Adam once forfeited himself of by giving ear to the wrong voice. Dust in Hebrew is Aphar which finds its origin in the meaning of embers of fire. Now, when we look at this word, I have mentioned time and time again, HaAdamah from its Hebrew origin, the visual itself shows us that on either side of this word are dimensions leading to the previous and following Altars. Here is what that looks like:

(Diagram 26)

From this place of the manifested High Priest Altar of Genesis 1:1 we enter into our final Altar where things are tangible, where the battle is real and where the inheritance is given! On one side of this Altar, we have The Throne Altar of The Heavens and on the other side we have the Courtroom the Earth Altar. This **Va'et** revelation or, HaAdamah Altar, is Calvary - Golgotha. It is Mount Moriyah, where The King came to sing over His people with the vibrational music of Redemption that holds the power to split seas, crush other altars of generational iniquity and curses! This Vibrational Altar of the Redemption Song shatters the vessels of evil and repels the kingdom of Darkness.

The Seven Altar Thrones of Genesis 1:1

(Diagram 27)

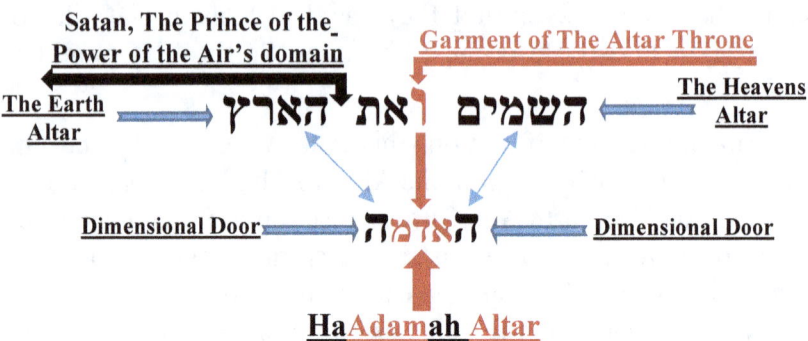

On either side of this HaAdamah Altar are dimensional doorways. Actually, one Main Door for those who are on Earth to ascend through **(John 10:7-9)**. The Door into The Adam Altar King known as Yahshua and through His Crowned finished work into The Heavenly Kingdom is our Heavenly Seated Place! He sits appointed as our Great Intercessor. He prays from the Loftiest Altar and those Eternal words impact us here like a vibrational Rainbow fixed Language. This Language of some sorts is what infuses the Trees or can I say The Bones of the believer. If the Bone of Heaven is mentioned as a vibrating Body then our Bones are the reflection to this truth.

Think about this, in Exodus 12 YHWH Elohim said when He sees the Blood, He would Passover the house that is marked by it. Blood speaks and blood vibrates. The Blood gives off the vibrational language The Altar only agrees with. The Altar will only be in agreement with The Blood that touches it. The Blood makes contact and from there The Altar is activated creating a language seen and heard by the Spirit realm, where The Altar of Thrones sit. Heavens Chambers are always speaking about you and I. We have The Voice that causes all in these dimensions to listen and accept who the Blood represents because the Truth speaks for us. The Truth is inside the Blood recorded. The Life is inside the Blood speaking. The Way inside the Blood that points to our life beyond this one.

> 🔴 **Psalm 141:2** Allow my prayer come before you as incense and the lifting up of my hands as the evening sacrifice. **Psa 141:3** Set a guard, Yahweh, above my mouth and guard the door of my lips.

Prayer is man's greatest weapon when coupled with The Word and a cry. We have been given something no other created thing has been given, the ability to pray from The Altar. We hold the power to send into the future words in the form of prayer because inside of us is this essence – Prayer:

> 🔴 Psa 109:4b "…but I *give myself unto* prayer." Bad translation. The Hebrew reveals to us the essence of this verse - ואני תפילה – Ve'ani Tefilah actually means: "<u>And I am prayer</u>".

We become prayer when we give ourselves continually from this place of prayer. We must BECOME the platform or Altar bridge between The Future and the now, Prayer. Stand as the vibrational ladder from Earth to Heaven. Every generation will have a Moses, a Noah, an Abraham, a David, a Samuel, an Elijah and Elisha, a John. Become that Ladder of vibration and power.

The HaAdamah Altar is a Prayer Gateway. This is what Yahshua did more than anything else. Everywhere He went, he connected The Kingdom of The Heavens here on Earth. All demonic forces knew He had arrived because His presence carried the fullness of the Godhead in bodily form. Look at this revelation for a second, the first Adam had Prayer built **into** him just by the style of His Name when expanded out:

The Impregnated Adam of Genesis
(Diagram 28)

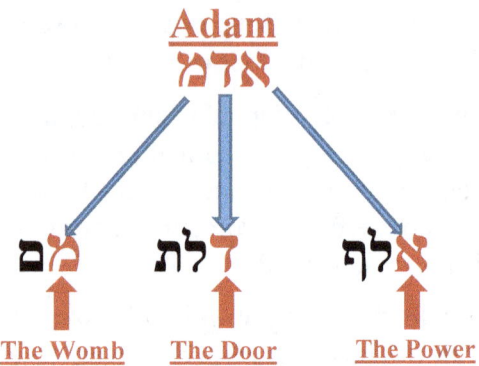

"The Power of Prayer is manifested through the Door of the Womb of Emunah/Belief!"

- **Mar 11:23** For verily I say unto you, That whosoever shall say unto this **mountain**, Be thou removed, and be thou cast into the sea; **(Micah 7:19)** and shall not doubt in his heart, but shall believe that those things which he saith shall come to pass; he shall have whatsoever he saith. **Mar 11:24** Therefore I say unto you, What things soever ye desire, **when ye pray**, (not if, but when) believe that ye receive *them*, and ye shall have *them*. **Mar 11:25** And when ye stand praying, **forgive**, if ye have **ought** against any: that your Father also which is in heaven may forgive you your trespasses. **Mar 11:26** But if ye do not **forgive**, neither will your Father which is in heaven forgive your trespasses.

The Mountain in the way of prayer is unforgiveness!

The remaining letters give us a Hebrew word which is mankind's built in Sulam/Ladder:

מתפלל

Mit'Paleil means: 'One who has BECOME Prayer.'

To become this bridge of prayer and platform of prayer is to be an activated Altar on the face of this Earth. In order to activate this which is on the inside, Elohim must cut open your side! There is a voice on the inside of you and I that is waiting to be revealed! There is a prayer language waiting to come forth! There is a freedom locked up inside of you that is pressing to be unlocked. You hold the key to unlock something in someone's life. The Word is waiting to burst forth from the inside of you. Prayer is the DNA Shofar Helix that releases what is in Heaven here on Earth. The numerical value of Mit'Paleil is 580, the same for the Hebrew word Shofar/שפר. The Shofar holds the voice of Jubilee or Freedoms. The sound that comes forth from the Shofar is called: Yobel – Jubilee which means freedom! Freedom comes when Prayer is unlocked. We are the communicating bridge now in Mashiach as He commissioned us or gave us one Common-Mission in Matthew 28:18-20

- **Mat 28:18** And Yeshua came and spoke unto them, saying, **All** power is given unto me **in The Heavens and in The Earth**. (He is the **AND** of this bridge or the Va'et of Genesis 1:1 who bridges the gap –

    השמים ואת הארץ ! He is the Adamah Altar that ALL Power is seen in Heaven and The Earth and in Hebrew is the 6th Hebrew word of Genesis 1:1 –

    Va'et/ואת:

(Diagram 29)

בראשית ברא אלהים את השמים |את הארץ

↑ The HaAdamah Altar clothed for The Earth

- **Mat 28:19** Now go forth, and teach all nations, immersing them into **The Name** of the Father, and of the Son, and of the Set Apart Spirit: **Matthew 28:20** Teaching them to observe **all things** whatsoever I have commanded you: and, behold, I am is with you always, into the end of the world. Amen.

The Name represents The Father, The Son and Ruach HaQodesh. The Name – HaShem – השם which has the numerical value of 345. The Hebrew word equal in value is: אל שדי – El Shaddai, the all nourishing One. The teaching and making disciples of all Nations is the promise given to Abraham as a Father of many nations. We nourish the nations with His Name. The Name is manifested when the Father, The Son and His Spirit are present and accepted. El Shaddai nourishes His people with the Name or The Authority of The Altar Thrones. We grow from Outer Courtyard struggles into Sanctuary maturity.

We can't stay in the Outer Courtyard struggling with the same fleshly setbacks, we Must ascend beyond the corridors of restrictions into the place of Sanctuary. Before this we must transition through this Outercourt area of The Altar of Earth, the final revelation of the Altar Helix of ascension! Let us enter past the gate of flesh into the Courtyard of The Earth Altar! The Earth Altar is the witness of the finished work of The Adamah Altar, who is the Platform, which the Heavens Altar decrees a thing and it is sent forth Through the Word made flesh.

This Adamah Altar is the speaking Altar. It is the Place where the Spiritual Dimension of Heaven meets with the flesh of man. This is the Place where exchange takes place for you and I that satisfying the judgement we all deserve as 2 Corinthians 5:21 says, "He has made Him to be sin who did not know sin that we might **BECOME** the righteousness of Elohim!"

The Adamah Altar is The Highest Altar and the only Altar that can travel from the Highest Heavens to this Earth Realm. This is the Only Altar that speaks, prays, walks through walls, cast out demons, heals the sick, heals the leprous, opens blind eyes, raises the dead, feeds the multitudes with supernatural resources while the desert laws stand contrary to such power. This Altar is the only Altar that can transcend time and space! This Adamah Altar is the only Altar that held the power to intertwine Heaven and Earth in one moment while nailed to The Branch from the Tree of Life! It was from this Altar of Adamah that Adam was once born out of through the womb of Bara.

This HaAdamah Altar is the only Altar that gives access through the Courts of Heaven as patterned in the Outer courtyard of the Tabernacle and through the Mystical Laver of the moving vibrating liquid Word Ephesians 5 speaks of that leads inside the Chambers.

In this Chamber area the Altar of Adamah is seen on multiple levels such as the Table of Communing. Intimacy and expansion where the Bread of Heaven is stationed breathing the life of Eternity into all who eat of Him. The Altar of Adamah is also seen from the eternal light and incense of The Highest Heavenly realms. This Adamah Altar is the only walking and mobile Altar that was appointed to walk with mankind and save mankind. This Adamah Altar is the Key of David, the Root of Jesse, the Rose of Sharon, the Bread from Heaven and The Lamb slain before the foundation of the world! This Adamah Altar was there when all was created because all came through and by Him as the vibrational frequencies and colors that also hold their own voices, were sung from off the Platform of this Adamah Altar.

The Adamah Altar is the standalone Interceptor of all and every accusation thrown at us like fiery darts. The Adamah Altar is our King Altar and High Priest Altar where the order of Melchizedek originated from! This Adamah Altar healed the Bride of her blood flow. This Adamah Altar was and always will be the demonstrative force to be reckoned with on our behalf in the face of every entity and power that might be. The Adamah Altar holds the new name that will be given to us! When we add the revelation from earlier regarding Zakar and Oo'Ne'Qeibah/ זכר ונקבה we have 390.

390 gives us the goal - שמים – Shamayim – Heavens; שמן – Shemen – Oil or fatness. The Adamah Altar brings to remembrance the expanding Power of the Kingdom of Heaven here on The Altar of Earth!!

Yahshua came and said, "The Kingdom of Heaven has arrived!" What was He saying to the people? He was making a Kingdom statement! He was saying, "I have come to make one, the Heavens and The Earth and bring my expanding influence of my Father's Altar of Heaven's Throne here on Earth! I have come to bridge the gap and heal the Breach of Genesis 1:1-2! I have come as The Adamah Altar to manifest my Father's Kingdom Reign here on Earth now watch me do what I was Sent to do!"

The Adamah Altar is a picture of two hands and Adam. The two Hebrew letters

'ה' at either side point to the two hands of this Adam as well as the open doors from The Earth Altar to The Heaven's Altar through HaAdamaH!

John-James of the House of Flores.®

(Diagram 30)

HaAdamaH

The Altar of Earth is witness of the witness sent from Heaven which is The Word who is The Adamah Altar. He connects the two in order to bring about The Decree of Heaven on The Earth. Earth becomes the final platform of elevation and ascension after the order of our Righteous King-Priest of Genesis 1:1. Who was manifested to make one new man by healing the breach and causing the Kiss of Heaven to manifest with the Earth.

- **Psalm 85:10** Mercy[H2617] and truth[H571] are come **together;**[H6298] (**Together** is the Hebrew word for Binding together or Bonding together by way of Covenant. Rachamim and Emet/Mercy and Truth are a picture of Heaven and Earth united. Rachamim is given on The Earth and Truth is established from The Heavens.) righteousness[H6664] and shalom[H7965] have kissed[H5401]. (Righteousness and Shalom have kissed, or attached, and are now inseparable! The Melchitzedeq Order is Righteousness and Royalty intertwined, that's called the Kiss of The Heaven's Altar! The Altar of The Heavens is The Throne of Elohim. So, His Throne has become bound together with all who come through The Door of His Son.)

- **Psalm 85:11** Truth[H571] shall burst[H6779] out of **The Earth;**[H4480 H776] and **righteousness**[H6664] will gaze[H8259] from **The Heavens.**[H4480 H8064] (Truth will burst forth from The Altar of Earth because the influence of The Heavens

> penetrated the darkness due to an invitation from the Earth Altar! Righteousness gazes from The Heavens because Heaven and Earth have become one body or Basar Echad - The Kingdom Message!) **Psa 85:12** Yes,[H1571] YHWH[H3068] gives[H5414] good[H2896] and our **land**[H776] will yield[H5414] **her increase.**[H2981] (Notice the Earth is referred to as **Her**. The Earth is a picture of the Bride, The Heavens as the Husband. But both separated because of the Genesis 1 Tohu V'Bohu breach. Yahshua is the Repairer of The Breach. He came to reconnect that which was separated. We see this throughout Scripture, the Husband and The Bride. Heaven is manifested through The Adamah Altar revelation! The King and High Priest of The Beginning has come and will come again one last time for His Bride! The word **Increase** is the word we get Jubilee from or Freedom – יְבוּלָה – Ye'boo'lah, the Bride's Overflow. It is the season of overflow! The Overflow is the Leaven of Heaven's Influence here on the Earth through the Adamah Altar who has Crowned. This Hebrew word is also the acronym for HaYobel/היובל – **The Jubilee,** or The season of **Release**. The season of release is the season of your increase!)
>
> **Psalm 85:13 Righteousness**[H6664] (Righteousness here speaks of the Tzadiq or The Righteous One. The Adamah Altar is the Righteous Kingly Altar between Heaven and Earth. The Adamah Altar is the Tzadiq Altar who has come to place us on the Narrow path of Righteousness which is the Melkhitzedeq Order of Heaven!) …

We now enter the place where all things are manifested and actualized. We have now stepped foot onto the Altar of Earth and we were born to be here! We were born for such a time as this. We are here to colonize this Earth with Heavens influential Kingdom Power. Yahshua said:

● **Matthew 18:19-21 19** Again I say unto you, if two of you will come into agreement **on The Altar of Earth** as **touching** anything that they shall ask, (The Earth is where the 'Touch' is ever present. The Woman gave birth to this Touch back in Genesis 3. When the Woman added to The Word and said,' …do not **TOUCH**…" This qualified Adam for the fall to the lower Altar called Earth. They were in The Garden or, Sacred Place, and fell into the Place of the Touch – Naga/נגע. This Hebrew word is found in Isaiah 53 regarding the Suffering Servant. This Hebrew word Naga is also connected to the worse disease of all – Leprosy. Yahshua is known as, The Leper Scholar of Israel. He is the One who came and absorbed Man's leprous condition of the fall. Satan even tried to Get the Last Adam, Yahshua to TOUCH a stone and turn it into Bread while He was walking on The Altar of Earth in the desert. The Adamah Altar didn't fall for this, no pun intended. Touch is the garment for this platform.) it shall be done for them of **my Father** which is **on The Heavens**. **20** For where two or three are gathered together in my name, there am I in the midst of them.

Yahshua said that agreement and touching, when established on The Altar of Earth as it is in The Altar of Heaven where His Fathers is Enthroned, it would be done for them because they are united and intertwined in His Name. The Name is in The Adamah Altar who connects Heaven and Earth. The Adamah Altar gives us Access into the Altar of The Heavens. This happens by and through the power of agreement!

So, let us agree together as we enter the Altar where things manifest and happen – The HaAretz Miz'be'ach – The Earth Altar! Remember, Yahshua didn't come to bring a religion as He was not part of one. He did not come to bring a Pharisaical Hierchy because He wasn't part of the one present. He didn't come to elevate a sacrificial system otherwise He would have been of the seed line of Aaron and Levi. He came clothed in flesh by way of the seed line womb of Judah of His Mother. He came to bring what man lost here on Earth's Altar Throne and that was The Kingdom Dominion reestablished for His people. He became the TOUCH the first woman gave birth to in Genesis 3, so let us make some declarations and confessions because of this touch that transfers!

The Power of a Decree and Confession

Let's make these confessions and proclamations together:

- I confess, decree and proclaim by unrebutted Covenant Right and come into the covenant of truth that The Adamah Altar of my righteous King Yahshua has set me free from all satanic altars that give birth to sin and death.

- I confess, decree and proclaim by unrebutted Covenant Right that every evil altar which accuses me and speaks contrary to The Adamah Altar of Yahshua where The Blood of The New Covenant is ever present, are silenced and over-ruled by The Voice from my King Yahshua's Altar.

- I confess, decree and proclaim by unrebutted Covenant Right that my victory is secured and cured in Mashiach Yahshua through and by His Adamah Altar which connects Heaven and Earth.

- I confess, decree and proclaim by unrebutted Covenant Right that any and all disease known and unknown to me is dissolved by the Adamah Altar of my Righteous King Yahshua.

- I confess, decree and proclaim by unrebutted Covenant Right that I am sanctified, justified, redeemed, reconciled, decreed innocent by The Power of The Adamah Altar of Yahshua HaMashiach my King.

- I confess, decree and proclaim by unrebutted Covenant Right that all other generational altars are mute and without voice. They hold no authority over my life or family bloodline anymore because The Blood of Yahshua Has spoken for me from The Heavens through The Adamah Altar on The Earth Altar!

- ➤ I confess, decree and proclaim by unrebutted Covenant Right that I am healed from every Soul injury and wound known and unknown. I am free by the Crowning of my new life in Yahshua HaMashiach my King of all kings and Crown above all crowns!

- ➤ I confess, decree and proclaim by unrebutted Covenant Right that I am victorious against every war and battle for my soul and the souls of my wife, children, grandchildren and future generations this day and future time. I send forth the power of my words and prayer into the future to await the generations that will come and to rendezvous with them at the appointed place and time.

- ➤ I confess, decree and proclaim by unrebutted Covenant Right that I am clothed with the Shadow of the Adamah Altar of Power and covered by The Blood of Yahshua HaMashiach.

- ➤ I confess, decree and proclaim by unrebutted Covenant Right that I am a joint heir with Mashiach Yahshua because of His matchless Altar that spoiled every principality and power publicly meaning on The Altar that Crowned at Golgotha!

- ➤ I confess, decree and proclaim by unrebutted Covenant Right that from this day forward I will no longer beg for or request what is rightfully mine, but I only praise you for what is finished in Yahshua HaMashiach because of His Adamah High Priest Royal Altar!

- ➤ I confess, decree and proclaim by unrebutted Covenant Right That I am forgiven and I walk in the Newness of Life this day by The finished work of The Adamah Altar of my King Yahshua Whose blood speaks for me.

➤ I confess, decree and proclaim by unrebutted Covenant Right that satan, you are a defeated foe. I don't challenge you but Yahuwah Gibbor rebuke you and you have no authority over my life, my spouse, my children or children's children. The Brakhah/Blessing overtakes me and the Kiss of Mercy and Truth are intertwined with my generational line!

Chapter Eight

Seventh Altar:
The Altar Throne of the Earth, Your Kingdom Reign

הארץ

What a journey it has been thus far. We have made our journey through the Ladder of revelation with the seven Altar Thrones of Genesis 1:1 and have come to the final Altar in this series, The Altar of The Earth – מזבח הארץ – **Miz'be'ach HaAretz** – Where the Kingdom will rule and reign, where The Kingdom of Heaven arrives to. In addition to all we will discover, the Numerical value of this Hebrew phrase is 351 (see numeric chart). There is a concept that is directly connected to this Altar of The Earth, which is: נשא – **No'se** which means: Forgiveness. This is given on this Earth Altar, but originates from the highest Altars of Genesis 1:1. Forgiveness is when the burden of sin is LIFTED off and a change of status takes place. **No'se** is also another Hebrew word – Na'sa which means to lift up or remove a burden. The Power of this Altar of Earth is where burdens are lifted and removed bringing true freedom and access into Eden. Who is this forgiveness for? It was for the fallen man known as, Enosh or, the Enash man. These same Hebrew letters are read another way are: **אנש** – Enash!

By now many of you reading this book have had your personal views 'Altered' because of the revelation of this 'Altar' paradigm shift because of one single Hebrew verse. The power of the Altar holds the ability and authority to alter an entire life. I made a statement in this book as well as on numerous occasions that The Loftiest and Highest Altar ever presented on Earth was the Altar on Golgolet where Yahshua HaMashiach was crucified for His people because of the sin of man. As a matter of fact, it was on a Branch that redemption would be accomplished. This Altar I have mentioned is the Adamah Altar.

HaAdamah, or as we see throughout Scripture – **The Ground** – is where Adam or mankind came from and MUST return to in order to receive passage back into the sacred place of The Garden which is called Eden, where the Tree of Life is. (Genesis 3:19)

This Tree of life is where a Branch was taken from, then passed down from Patriarch MelkhiTzedeq to MelkhiTzedeq UNTIL transplanted inside the Mountains of Moriyah, which means Yah is Teacher (Jasher 77). These Mountains became the historic Teacher no one really paid any attention to because they had no ears to hear His voice. Adam was commanded to till The Ground with this very Stick/Branch/Tree –

- **Genesis 2:5** And every^H3605 plant^H7880 of the field^H7704 before^H2962 it was^H1961 **in Earth,**^H776 and every^H3605 herb^H6212 of the field^H7704 **before**^H2962 **it grew:**^H6779 for^H3588 YHWH^H3068 Elohim^H430 had not^H3808 caused it to **rain**^H4305 upon^H5921 **The Earth,**^H776 and **there was no**^H369 Adam^H120 to **till**^H5647 (H853) **The Ground.**^H127 **Gen 2:6** But there went up^H5927 a mist^H108 from^H4480 **The Earth,**^H776 and watered^H8248 (H853) the whole^H3605 face^H6440 of **The Ground.**^H127

- **Genesis 3:19** In the sweat^H2188 of your face^H639 you will eat^H398 bread,^H3899 **till**^H5704 you return^H7725 **to**^H413 **The Ground;**^H127 for^H3588 out of^H4480 **him** were you received:H3947 forH3588 dustH6083 youH859 are and untoH413 dustH6083 you will **return.**H7725

Notice we have an interesting clue to something here that you can only see in the Hebrew. I am speaking about the words we see in English – **'till'**. Two different ideas in the Hebrew and yet the English seems to lump them both into the same boat. I must reiterate that I am speaking about the 7th Altar in this chapter and the revelation seen in the Adamah Altar that connects the Heaven and the Earth Altars with their Dimensions. Let us dive into these two verses and unpack the depths of a few concepts we can parallel to the work of our Altar King Redeemer Yahshua HaMashiach, but before we do here is a reminder of what Adam was supposed to be for this Garden INSIDE Eden according to Genesis 2:15 –

(Diagram 31)

(Reading from right to left in Hebrew)

- **Genesis 2:15** And YHWHH3068 ElohimH430 receivedH3947 (H853) the Adam,H120 and **put**H5117 him into the gardenH1588 of EdenH5731 to **dress**H5647 it and to **keep**H8104 *her*.

The Hebrew words with the arrows in **green** identify this sacred place in third person as the bride of someone, if I may, describing her with the words to serve cultivate or guard. Adam was instructed to guard the Sacred Eden while at the same time was given the ability to **cause** this Eden to produce - **effect**. Very interesting idea when we think about Marriage, but a totally different subject nevertheless well connected. The dot inside the Hebrew letters is not Dageshim but Mapik symbols used to identify the Bride throughout the majority of places in Scripture when dealing with the land and the people of Elohim.

The Hebrew word with the blue arrow comes from the word Nu'ach which means to cause a place to rest, to cause something to be settled and satisfied. In Genesis 8:4 the Ark '**rested** – Nu'ach' upon a place called Mount Ararat – הר אררט – Har Ararat which means to bring forth the rest from the curse and judgement. Har in Hebrew also means the nativity of a thing as well as Mountain or Summit. The Ark was 'BORN' and in its nativity came with the promise of the curse of the flood to recede! Sound familiar?

The Hebrew word Ark here is also a Hebrew word for The Word – Teivah/תבה. The Word in His nativity came with the promise to cause the curse of man to be lifted off of him. The curse of sin and death which was not scribed as such until the written Law of Elohim – Galatians 3:13.

Continuing in Genesis 2:5 – the seed of every plant of the field BEFORE it was inside The Earth (Altar) and the herb of the same field BEFORE it Grew (Tzamach) or burst forth from the Earth. The plant of the field, or Si'ach in Hebrew, infers more than just a plant, but the ability to communicate or articulate a language of Creation, revealing this is what The Plant of the field contained. Then the Herb of the Field before it Grew. The Earth was the place to reveal these two revelations of **Si'ach** and **Asav**/ שיח עשב.

No RAIN/מָטָר – Ma'tar was released because Adam was not brought forth to activate these dominions. Adam and the Rain worked in tandem. He was the original Rain Man! Ma'tar in Hebrew is also Me'ter where we get Meter for measuring from. Me'ter means the Poetic Rhythm of a thing. There was a vibrational song that was to be released from The Earth through the PLANT/Si'ach and Herb/A'sav! The Earth was inactive without the bridge, without the ignition control switch called Adam. Adam would come from HaAdamah's DUST when it would be stirred up or agitated by YHWH Elohim, from the DUST of this Adamah Genesis 2:7 says.

Then Genesis 2:5 would be fulfilled. Adam would orchestrate and regulate what would happen in the Heavens to manifest on the Earth Altar. He was this Connector Cable. That is why Genesis 2 begins with these are the Generations of the Heavens and The Earth. Adam was to give Heavens' Generations their Body here on this Earth Altar through a Poetical Rhythm and Song vibration. The Adamah Altar stands as the Connector Rod between The Heavens and The Earth Altars. This is what would happen in the future from this point forward to the last Adam Yahshuah HaMashiach. Adam was called to do the work of reconciliation because of what transpired in Isaiah 14 with Lucifer. We all have the same Work in ministry and that is called the ministry of Reconciliation. The power to reunite that which was separated!

(Diagram 32)

Scepter Granted, Dimensional Doors

➢ to till^{H5647} (H853) **The Ground**.^{H127} – לַעֲבֹד אֶת־הָאֲדָמָה
La'Abod Et HaAdamah.

The Adam, Heavens' Scepter

The **Blue Arrows** show the two-Dimensional Doorways or Bookends of man's beginnings (Last Adam) and man's beginnings (**First Adam**). While the **Red Arrow** shows **The Adam**, who is King of this place, connecting The Heavens and The Earth Altars as One. The **Adam**ah Altar becomes both Altars in one flesh and this is seen through The Royal Priesthood of

Yahshua HaMashiach. This Priesthood is the ONLY Priesthood with the authority to establish The Altar of Heaven's Throne here on The Earth. The Earth, has a numerical value of 296. This is the value of: במלכי־צדק – Be'MelkhiTzedeq which means: **Through The MelkhiTzedeq.**

Only through This Royal Priesthood are the Heavens brought here. He brings The Highest Throne of The Heavens here on The Altar of Earth!

Yes, you heard me correct, the Last Adam comes to bring us back into the Beginning because the First Adam had us removed from it. We went from Servants of this sacred place called Eden to being witnesses to this Kingdom place we long to return to. We now enter in Through the Royal Priesthood of The Mashiach Yahshua here on Earth. He didn't come dealing with Earth's affairs, but came and disrupted all of them. Turning over tables was a Kingly thing as well as a multilevel declaration of that time. He came to say, "I am here!"

Adam was the walking Altar between Heaven and Earth. Lucifer walked among the fiery stones while Adam was the Earthly King **OF** those stones until he forfeited them over! Adam was to produce Heaven on Earth as we read and can see within Genesis 2:5 with the Si'ach and Asav/Plant and Herb revelation. Adam is the only one with the authority to restore all things back as they are supposed to be. This is why you see Yahshua operating as High Priest and King, as The Last Adam. Only an Adam can do this. Satan wanted this position at Yahshua's temptation in the wilderness but couldn't cause the Bread Man from Heaven to budge OR Touch what was presented to Him.

This Altar of Earth is the final Platform of all battles and all victories. It is the place where things are planted and where things grow. It is the Courtyard dominion we see throughout the Tabernacle revelation as well as the Temple revelations. This is the place where Heavens' Courts function. The Courtroom of The Heavens isn't in The Sanctuary, no accusations can be brought there. This all takes place in the Outer Courtyard where Blood and Water speak.

On the Altar of Earth was where man was standing between the two in order for the HaAdamah to be tilled. Genesis 2:5 says Adam was to till the Adamah in order for the rain to touch the Earth. Man holds the key to the rain impartation. The Adamah Altar, which is connected to the Earth Altar revelation and the Heavens Altar, holds the disclosure of release. Adam was to till the Adamah, who was the image and Likeness revelation of Yahshua, before His arrival. From the Adamah Altar would come forth what He is. Till the Adamah not the Earth, two different places. You can't till the Earth because it is the Courtyard area where things are waiting to spring forth from.

The tilling of the Ground or Adamah Altar CALLS that which is seeded in the Earth to arise from the burial. The Adam holds the Authority to call those things that are not as though they were. The Adamah Altar has a voice and that voice is what unlocks the door from Earth to Heaven.

If you look at the diagram shown above the way this Hebrew word is styled you can see at the heart of '**HaAdamaH**' is **Adam** himself. At the ends of this Hebrew word are the letters '**Hei**' which mean behold or to give or bring forth something. These letters in Hebrew picture the access connection between two worlds or can I say two Altar Thrones. The Adamah Altar absorbed the collision course and healed the void, giving access and connection to Heaven and Earth. Remember, the revelation of Prayer is inside this Altar called Adamah. The Head of the Adamah Altar is in the Heavens while the Feet of the Adamah Altar are touching The Earth Altar, can you see this? Here is another Diagram with more detail as we connect this Altar revelation:

The Seven Altar Thrones of Genesis 1:1

(Diagram 33)

This revelation above shows us everything about Creation. Let us take a short detour into the Hebrew words for **'Cause'** and the **'Effect'** –

> - **Cause** – גּוֹרֵם – Go'reim = Cause, Source, Origin, Root, Multiplier, Mathematics. From the Hebrew word Garam or Gerem which means to be strong as a Bone. Something strong that can crush, or strong enough to withstand the crushing. Like the Coccyx bone also known as Luz in Hebrew. The name of the place where Jacob saw The Ladder that reach to The Heavens from The Earth. A perfect picture of what we are speaking about here. Bones are containers of vibration and frequencies. The Bones of Joseph were the final word leaving Egypt. The Bones of the Prophet brought to life a man in 2 Kings 13:21. The Bones carry vibrational power. The numerical value of 'Touch The Bones' – נגע העצם – Naga HaEtzem is 308, the same as: שוב – Shuv which means: to return or

Repentance. The promise of returning to our bodies of Light that we once had. Repentance is indestructible like a Bone. You cannot break Repentance, but the process of repentance breaks the resistance.

The Adamah Altar is The Last Adam who is this indestructible Bone of Heaven that was crushed in order to unite and restore The Heavens and The Earth. The Adam Altar Man stands between Heaven and Earth like the Leavening Agent of Expansion. Leaven causes the Bread to BURST forth beyond its borders and take over the territory known as The Earth Altar. This Influence is like Leaven or can I say the Cause of the Effect?!

> **Effect** – תּוֹצָאָה – To'tza'ah – Strong's #8444 = Effect, Result, Issues, Influence, Outcome, Consequence, *Gateway, Open Door of invitation. From the Hebrew root Yatza which means to Burst forth like a rushing river. First seen in genesis 2:10 with Eden, that Sacred Place we are to return to as I just mentioned earlier, where The River Burst forth into 4 riverheads. The Kingdom Heaven Burst forth on Earth because the Adam Altar had been received into this place causing that Leaven Effect to expand everywhere! It is a Kingdom Takeover!

Yatza/יצא and Garam/Gerem/גרם – The Cause and Effect of the Adamah Altar Influence, who is the Leavening Agent, bringing Heaven's Influence here on The Earth Altar like the Rain we read about in Genesis 2:5. The total value of these Hebrew words is: 344 which gives us: האדם מלכי־צדק – MelkhiTzedeq HaAdam = The MelkhiTzedeq Adam! Here is a revelation of this phrase, the first letters of this Hebrew phrase reveal to us the word – מַצָּה – **Matzah** meaning, Unleavened Bread! The MelkhiTzedeq Adam is The Bread Man from Heaven who comes to The Altar of Earth to set up His Kingdom! He is The Bread Altar from Heaven, we can all eat from, who is Unleavened from this world!! Our Yahshua HaMashiach The Adamah Altar is none other than The MelkhiTzedeq Adam! This Bread is unleavened, uninfluenced by the kingdoms of this world because it is the source of Leaven of Heaven's Kingdom. His Leaven is referenced in Matthew 13:33 – "The Kingdom of Heaven is like Leaven that a woman hid inside three measures of meal." Heaven's Leaven is manifested through the Adamah Altar High Priest and King here on the Earth Altar! Matzah also means to drain or squeeze something out of all its substance. This Melkhitzedeq Altar has come to dry up the animal blood of religion and squeeze out the impurities of the nation of Israel!

The Table of Yahshua was demonstrated through Bread. The Bread upon the Table before His crucifixion was a picture of this Earth Altar Platform. Yahshua being the Loftiest of all Altars can transcend through each mystical Altar of Genesis 1:1. He manifests on the legal platform of The Earth all seven Altars of Genesis bringing about the New Creation. Let me give just a few more numerical revelations of the number 135, the Bread Number of the Altar – 135:

מַמְלָכָה – **Mam'lakha** means: Kingdom, Dominion, Sovereignty, Rule and Reign. The Dominion of the Kingdom Authority is demonstrated on this Altar of Earth Platform. Earth is the final revelation before we return back to the beginning. The Altar of The Earth is the place where decisions must be made because it is the Audience area of the Courts of Heaven. The accusations and witnesses come from this place. This Altar of Earth has become the Platform Table of Yahshua who is the Adamah Altar that has come to take on the punishment for us. He has come to lift up a Narrow road, or can I say a Highway to Heaven? This is The Road of Righteousness most don't want to walk on! The Narrow path is between Heaven and Earth and that is Mashiach Yahshua Himself.

Earth is the legal platform for divine transactions to be made, then recorded in the Heavenly Chamber Vault called The Altar of The Heavens. The Altar of Earth is where the Kingdom Dominion is established and The Throne of Heaven's Rule is finalized for restoration. It's a Narrow path that leads to the Highway or Lifted up Place. 135 is also the value for:

מְסִלָּה – **Me'silah** means a Highway, a Raised up Place like Golgotha where the Adamah Altar was lifted up and drew all men unto Himself! Also, הָסֻלָּם – **HaSulam** means The Ladder. That same one Jacob saw back in Genesis 28. This Ladder was the Narrow Place, the Bridge between Heaven and Earth. The Narrow Place where that which is on this Altar of Earth is accepted into The Heavens through the Sulam or Altar Ladder which Yahshua said was Him in John 1:47-51. הסלם - HaSalam means to Modulate or Harmonize music. What we see happening with this revelation is the Harmonizing of Altars. The Altar of Heaven and The Altar of Earth come into harmony creating a unified symphony of music. Luke 15:10 says the angels of Heaven rejoice over one sinner that repents. The angels that surround the Altar of Heaven release a new song from the Altar of Earth around the Altar of Heaven because of Repentance. This Narrow lifted up Place is the Modulator of this truth!

The Altar of Earth is where the restoration of all things is executed. This Altar of Earth is the recording system of what is spoken from the Altars above it. Yahshua said He only came to say and do what He saw His Father do. The Altar of Earth is the Heavens' tangible Template! The Altar of Earth carried The Clothed Adamah Altar, who fulfilled His Divine Assignment of Tikkun, or Repair. When Yahshua came riding in on a donkey, that word for Donkey is Chomer/חומר which also means: This Natural world on The Earth. The Earth Altar is the Carrier of The Adamah Altar Himself. Earth gave birth to The Adamah Altar King! Chomer is also VeRachum/וְרָחֻם – 'And from the Womb'. The Altar of Earth is the womb that all things must come through in order to be legal on Earth. A spirit without a body of the womb is illegal on Earth. Angels that function outside a body while TOUCHING the Earth, not in the air, are illegal. Earth is the record of legalities. 135 is also the value of two specific words that are very telling –

צמה – Tzamah means a Veil that a woman wears before Marriage. This Altar of Earth is like the Veil that has hidden the Bride of The Husband. This Altar of Earth that bears the fruitfulness of The Seed of The Word of Elohim and produces its fruit is covered in a Veil that was never supposed to be. This Altar of Earth carries the Voice of The Creator within a people of flesh who have been called out of the shadows and darkness and ordained into something great! This Veil is to one day be removed as quick as our sin was removed from us at the Adamah Altar. 135 is the value of this last two words I will share for now:

קהל – Qahal means the called out ones also translated as The Church by western Roman mindset. The Called-Out ones are those who have split the Veil because they have heard the Voice. 135 is also the value of: הקל – HaQol means The Voice. Not any voice, but The Voice that has been speaking to Adam since the fall of man. The voice that walked with Adam, then came walking after him as to look for him. This Voice that every soul of righteousness hears when they split the veil of Earth's Altar Ears and ascends through the Narrow Place the Adamah Altar or The Word has made! The Voice that spoke to Noah, Enoch, Abraham, Isaac, Jacob, Joseph, Moses, Joshua, Caleb, Samuel, king David, king Solomon, the prophets and all the Judges of Israel! The Voice that spoke from atop the Mercy Seat from behind the Veil. Oh, the depths of this revelation we don't have enough paper to write!

The Voice that shook Mount Sinai, accelerated the gestation cycle of the cattle. This caused them to give birth as Time itself worm holed due to the manifestation of 'The Voice' on Mount Sinai. The Voice that Shattered mountains and split the cedars of Lebanon into toothpicks and caused the Cattle to instantly reach full gestation and give birth! The Voice that directed John the Baptist in the wilderness and gave him his platform to walk on! The Voice that visited a young virgin woman with an invitation which she said yes to! The Voice of all Altars of Genesis 1:1 came and put on the form of mankind and walked the streets of Jerusalem!

This same Voice, who was clothed in an Earthly Veil, summonsed the Disciples and molded them as that foundation, with the Prophets of old, for a called-out people! The Altar of Adamah or the High Priest of Genesis manifested caused this Earth Altar to be raised up in order to present the veiled people to His Father who sits above the Altar of Heaven! The Altar of Earth is the Earth womb we break out of like a virgin carrying a baby. We crowned coming here and we will crown leaving this Altar of The Earth.

Yahshua HaMashiach alone brings Reconciliation, Repair, Renewal, Freedom, Healing, Victory, Redemption, Justification, Sanctification, The Kingdom here on The Earth because He is The Adamah Altar, who stands between The Earth and The Heavens' Altar Repairing its Void! He was nailed as King of The Earth on The Adamah Altar of Golgotha with Arms stretched wide as if to pull together that which was separated in the beginning as Basar Echad – One Flesh or One Kingdom Body. The Basar of Adam was Heavens' Body on Earth, connecting them both! Think about this, they placed a Crown of Thorns upon the Head of The Adamah Altar. They surrendered the rights of rulership over to The King of kings and secured that on His Altar with Earth bearing witness to this closure!

Yahshua said in Matthew 11:12 –

- **Matthew 11:12** And[G1161] from[G575] the[G3588] days[G2250] of John[G2491] the[G3588] Immerser[G910] until[G2193] now[G737] **The[G3588] Kingdom[G932] of Heavens[G3772]** breaks forth,[G971] and[G2532] the breakers are expanding it.[G726][G846] **Mat 11:13** For[G1063] all[G3956] the[G3588] prophets[G4396] and[G2532] the[G3588] law[G3551] prophesied[G4395] until[G2193] John.[G2491] **Mat 11:14** And[G2532] if[G1487] you will[G2309] **receive**[G1209] it this[G846] is[G2076] **Elijah**,[G2243] which was[G3195] to come.[G2064] **Mat 11:15** He that has[G2192] ears[G3775] to hear,[G191] let him hear.[G191]

The Adamah Altar gave voice to The Earth Altar and we see this in this deep revelation Yahshua is communicating. Romans 8 says The Earth cries out… First it was all the prophets of old, whom the greatest of the prophets was – John The Immerser. He prepared the Way for The Adamah Altar, who would bear the Image of all 7 Altar Thrones on the Earth. We went from a crying voice **of** men to a Walking Voice **with** mankind.

The Earth could not release the revelation of the Plant or the Herb because it needed the Prophetic Voice to usher in the coming of the Adamah Altar known as Yahshua! John The Baptist was the Priesthood leader on Earth who submitted His Priesthood authority to The Greater Altar system known as The Melkhitzedeq Priesthood or can I say the Last Adam Altar?! The Earth Altar moans and groans waiting for the Adamah Altar to release its voice meaning, This Earth Altar was impregnated by The Seed of The Altar of Elohim who sits upon The Altar of The Heavens. (Romans 8:19).

The Revelation as we have seen in the beginning of this chapter from Genesis 2:5 and 3:19 –

- **Gen 2:5** And every^{H3605} plant^{H7880} of the field^{H7704} before^{H2962} it was^{H1961} in **Earth,**^{H776} and every^{H3605} herb^{H6212} of the field^{H7704} **before**^{H2962} **it grew:**^{H6779} for^{H3588} YHWH^{H3068} Elohim^{H430} had not^{H3808} caused it to **rain**^{H4305} upon^{H5921} **The Earth**^{H776} and there was no^{H369} Adam^{H120} to **till**^{H5647} (H853) **The Ground.**^{H127} **Gen 2:6** But there went up^{H5927} a mist^{H108} from^{H4480} the earth,^{H776} and watered^{H8248} (H853) the whole^{H3605} face^{H6440} of the ground.^{H127}

- **Gen 3:19** In the sweat^{H2188} of your face^{H639} you will eat^{H398} bread,^{H3899} till^{H5704} you return^{H7725} to^{H413} **The Ground**;^{H127} for^{H3588} out of^{H4480} Him were you received:^{H3947} for^{H3588} dust^{H6083} you^{H859} are and unto^{H413} dust^{H6083} you will **return.**^{H7725}

This can be revealed now! This Parable system can be explained and interpreted –

The **tilling** of Genesis 2:5 is **before** Adam's fall into the darkness and absence of Light which is different from the word for **Till** in Genesis 3:19. Let me explain if I can. There was no Adam on the Earth, yet according to Genesis 1:26-27 the first Adam was formed and fashioned after the Image and Likeness, which we will get into. This seems as if we have a dilemma, or maybe not.

The Adam of Genesis 1:26-27 was formed and the Adam of Genesis 2:5-7 is Activated and Infused with the Authority to be ON This Earth Altar!

Genesis 1:26-27 has no mention of the Altar **(HaAdamah – the ground)** which Adam would be formed and fashioned from, in other words activated from. The Adamah Altar is first revealed on this Earth Altar realm in Genesis 2:5-7. Did you hear this? The Adamah, or Ground as it is translated, is first mentioned here in Genesis 2:5-7. Adam, who was formed and Created after the Image and Likeness of YHWH Elohim, is now activated out of the Adamah Altar that was previously mentioned. He is now on His feet here on The Altar of Earth as the Father of all. He becomes the Authority to arouse the Altar of Earth, manifesting the blueprints to all four Earthly kingdoms - Mineral, Vegetation, Plant and Animal - which have been seeded there. **(See diagrams of this HaAdamah revelation above.)**

Notice the Order of Adam's Rule parallels the position of the Altars of Genesis 1:1, Genesis 1:27 –

וַיֹּאמֶר אֱלֹהִים נַעֲשֶׂה אָדָם בְּצַלְמֵנוּ כִּדְמוּתֵנוּ

(right to left in Hebrew and left to right in English)

Vayomer Elohim Na'aseh Adam Be'tzal'meinu Kid'moo'teinu

"And Elohim said let us make Adam in/with our image and as/after our Likeness…"

וְיִרְדּוּ בִדְגַת הַיָּם וּבְעוֹף הַשָּׁמַיִם

Ve'yeer'doo Beed'gat HaYam Oov'oof HaShamayim

"…and let them rule over the fish of the sea and over the birds of the air…"

Then, we have the categories of Earthly, or Land animals.

Notice, we go from the depths of The Sea to the heights of The Heavens and then it finishes off in the middle with The Altar of Earth. The Adam was to bring Kingdom rule that would restore what was above, below and in between as the Altar and bridge between Heaven and Earth. This Earth Altar is in between the two as this legal Platform. The Hebrew is also saying that the let 'THEM' is more than the Adam. The **Them**, is hinted at as The **Image** and **Likeness**, which are the two Throne Garments Adam wore, pointing to The Last Adam. These two speak of Kingly and Priestly. **Image** is The King of The Throne and **Likeness** speaks of a Representative. **King** and **Priest** or can I say **Melkhitzedeq** Altar King of Genesis 1:1 was now incarnate within Adam. We would later see this in The Son of Elohim, Yahshua HaMashiach.

Creation awaits the Adam of The Adamah Altar because this is the life source of the Altar of Earth. The Adam of Genesis 2:5-7 was instructed to modulate the movement within the womb of the Altar of Earth and bring forth the Kingdom Reign out of each kingdom. Adam, the **Tiller**, or as it is written in Genesis 2:5 from the Hebrew text:

לַעֲבֹד אֶת־הָאֲדָמָה: – Le'avod Et HaAdamah – To worship The Alef Tav of **The Ground**. The word 'Ground' in Hebrew alludes to a form of worship, the work of the Ministry, also known as – Reconciliation – 2 Corinthians 5:18. The animal sacrificial system was a type of worship system on Earth after the fall. Each hid the depths and mysteries of the service to The Adamah Alef Tav Altar King Priest! In our Altar of Earth, we have the manifestation of The Kingdom Reign which is The Worship of The High Priest and King of Israel seen in the HaAdamah Altar.

Let me conclude with these insights found in Genesis 2:5 with Genesis 3:19 -

In Genesis 2:5, the word used for 'till' the ground is: עבד — Ebed. This word for 'till' in Genesis is referenced as well to Adam's return BACK to this same Ground. Adam would now have to be a witness of the Testimony to the Adamah Altar he once operated and ruled from. The Hebrew word for 'till' in Genesis 3:19 is עד – 'Ad', which has many meanings. The dominate meaning is the word for 'Witness'. Adam and all those after him were to make the choice to come to the foot of the Altar system here on Earth and be a witness of it or have The Altar of Earth witness against you. The Earth Altar is The Heavens' Courtroom arena.

After the fall we see in Hebrew a Letter is removed from the word for 'till' or Service. In Hebrew and in all the Siddurs there is a Phrase called '**Avodah**' Worship. Avodah comes from this word Aved, which means to **till**, a form of worship. Worship is the act of tilling. (עבדה – Avodah & עבד – Eved) Adam was to till the Adamah Altar which the very Dust he was formed and fashioned after came from. To till the Adamah Altar is to become a part of it. What you worship is what you become a part of. To become a worshipper is to be connected to that focus of worship and detached from all else. This level of tilling/worshipping Adam was to bring about was to reattach all that had been impacted by the blow of Lucifer's fall hinted at inside Genesis 1:2 **("and the Earth became Tohu V'Bohu...")**.

We have another powerful truth here, and that is seen with the numbering system infused in this Hebrew word Eved:

- 76 = מול – Circumcised, the cutting away of flesh. To circumcise this flesh nature and garment and what follows is the crowning of His Kingdom Dominion.

Adam was given the authority to RULE/Radah/רדה meaning: to tread upon, have dominion over. In Luke 10:19 Yahshua gave the

Disciples, and us, POWER/Exuosia to tread upon serpents and scorpions, etc. Notice, Adam was to have Radah, treading Dominion over the Sea! When Yahshua was walking upon the waves of the Sea He was demonstrating what should have always been. Adam was given the authority to walk on water and rule over all within this kingdom of the marine world. Adam was given the authority to tread upon the birds of the air and the beasts of the Earth.

- 76 = חביון – Chev'yown means: Concealment, a Hiding place, covering.

Adam was the representative of The Adamah Altar on Earth and was given authority to cover, hide and clothe this Earth Altar with Dominion and Authority! Every kingdom and dominion that was from the Earth Altar was subject to Adam! Adam was from the Dust of the Adamah Altar which the English translates as The Ground. Adam, the first worship representative of The Adamah Altar Kingdom on Earth is where are being restored back to.

In John 4:23-24 Yahshua, our King, said that His Father is seeking something. I don't recall anything else Scripture says the Father seeks. Yahshua says The Father seeks those who 'worship' Him in Spirit and in Truth. Spirit and Truth are the witnesses for the Adamah Altar and witnesses for those who have come to this Altar to till it. To worship The One who sits upon the Throne of this Altar which is The King of Israel Yahshua HaMashiach.

The Earth Altar is where we demonstrate as witnesses the Majesty and truth of our King Yahshua. It is from this Altar that Heaven hears and takes note of. We as true worshippers of The King bear witness to His Priesthood and Kingship as Revelation speaks of **(Revelation 12:17 with 19:10)**.

Adam and the woman were sealed in and for this as they were the decree of Heaven on Earth. Eved is worship when the two become One Flesh or one Kingdom Message –

(Diagram 34)

If you remove the 'two/complete House which speaks of the Place' then worship becomes a distant witness who is in a bleeding out stage. When Adam and the woman fell, they both were removed and became the witnesses on Earth or The Earth Altar that they were in a place of what's called in Hebrew Niddah or Menstruation cycle. They began to bleed out which was something never seen before. Bleeding out means the entropy stage they now were clothed with.

The Word that remains when the House is removed is the word עד/Eid which means: **Menstruation Cycle**. Man has been bleeding out for 6000yrs and The Adamah Altar comes to heal the blood flow on The Earth Altar. The people of Israel were reminded to make an Altar of Earth according to Exodus 20 which was the bridge between Heaven and The Adamah Altar which would later manifest. Because of Exodus 32 the nation was given the Earth Altar where blood was to be shed and poured out upon. Yahweh Elohim saw what they were doing from the top of Mount Sinai. He then instructed Moses to build an Altar of Earth, as it was scribed at the end of the Covenant writings of Exodus 20. By reason of this Exodus 32 account, The Exodus 24:10 revelation – The Bone/Body of The Heavens, was rejected by The Nation for a Golden Calf.

The entire Earth is the Altar for this dimension of flesh, but

ONLY in the Place was The Adamah Altar to be lifted up in order to restore back those who would become witnesses to Him as the worshippers of and tillers of the Altar of Adamah!

When the House has become Basar Echad in and by The Adamah Altar, it is then the Heavenly Worship service is Restored, by way of the Earth Altar, who will put on Heavens' Bone or Body. Heaven will become the Garment of Earth as we read in Revelation – a New Heaven and a New Earth (Revelation 21:1-2). The New Jerusalem comes down out of Elohim's Throne called Heaven. The New Jerusalem comes through The King of that City and Bride of that City who is The Adamah Altar that has repaired the breach of Genesis 1:2.

As I mentioned, the woman and Adam fell, removing the House from being witnesses through worship. They gave way to sight instead of hearing the Voice of The Altar Throne. Together these two were united as a joint Witness/House to the Creative Power, Rule, Dominion and ability of clothing the Altar of Earth that was about to bleed out because of the fall. This is why the animal sacrificial system is a witness against us that The Altar of Earth is bleeding out.

Basar Echad has a numerical value of 515 which is the same for something that was built into Adam that would later be reflected as one who tills the Ground through Prayer. Man would be given the key to unlock what was in The Heavens here on The Earth Altar. Yahshua said He gave the keys and that upon The Rock of this Earth Altar, which is the Adamah Altar, the Gates of Hell would not prevail! The Rock is The Adamah Altar on Earth. Earth is the Legal Altar, upon which The Adamah Altar fulfilled the plan of the Restoration of all things. Basar Echad or One Flesh, One Kingdom Message **(Basar also means Good News or Gospel if you read the KJV)** has the same numerical value as: תפלה – Tefillah – Prayer. The one thing Yahshua did more than anything was Pray.

The Adamah Altar gives birth to that which is hidden in the Earth. Yahshua, with indignation, turned over the Moneychangers tables and said, "My Father's House shall be a House of Prayer!" The House is the People when they become Basar Echad. He wasn't worried about that Temple system there, as it was the Harlot on The Hill. Yahshua came declaring His mission! When the House is restored, the Eved revelation is complete and the witness finds rest.

Now, Adam and the Woman were removed from the Garden of Eden by a Tree Length, where the Adamah Altar was. In Jasher 75-77 we see Adam was given a sapphire Branch that would be passed down to MelkhiTzedeq Patriarch and end up transplanted within the Mountains of Moriah where The Adamah Altar would be lifted up and suspended between The Altar of Earth and The Altar of Heaven uniting the two making them both Basar Echad in the man Yahshua HaMashiach who is the Son of Elohim who is The Word made flesh (John 1:1-3, 14, 29). Adam, now separated by the length of a Tree, and it was through The Last Adam man was now reunited by the Length of The Tree. In the Last Adam all would be brought close by a Tree length of Hope! The Ad/עד is connected by the Unity of The Son on the Tree by His Adamah Altar – ב of His Father's House. We go from being distant witnesses/עד to the tillers of the Ground or Adamah Altar here on the Earth Altar – עבד – Eved. We go from being a witness '**TO**' The Truth to Worshippers '**OF**' The Truth! We go from a Mist of Sweat covering our face because of the fall, to the mist that comes from the Adamah Altar that covers the whole face of the Altar of Earth. Those who worship in Spirit and in truth hold the Kingdom Keys to unlock the mysteries of these seven Altar revelations of Genesis 1:1. It was from this place your life was always recorded and spoken about. It was from this place a plan was unveiled that would unfold throughout the ages. In every generation there is always a voice that rises up as a representative to the King who transcends all these Altar revelations.

In every generation there is always one, who has that fire in their soul and fire in their eyes because they have entered the corridors of true worship and power only known through the ascending order of the 7 Altars of Genesis 1:1. Is that you? This Mystery of these 7 Mystical Altars has one door of entry, that is through The Last Adam, The King of Israel, The Word made flesh, The Lion of the Tribe of Judah, the Rose of Sharon, the Balm of Gilead, The High Priest and Apostle of the soul of man, the Light of the world, the Voice that walked and communed with man, the Word that holds all things together, The Worthy One who opens the Seals of Revelation, The Mashiach and Anointed One who fills the cup that no man can, The Bread Man from Heaven, The Husband of The Bride, the Redeemer of the lost, the Resurrection and The Life, The Altar King of Heaven who ever sits enthroned to make intercession for the ones His Blood has spoken for.

Heaven and Earth now touch for the first time since The Beginning was. It is because of The manifested Altar King of Genesis. The Word that took on Flesh as The Adamah Altar which man was first created as light from the Dust of The Ground. The Adamah Altar is alive! The Adamah Altar bridged the Gap to this Altar of Earth and Heaven giving us access into the Throne room of Abba. You are chosen because you are sealed.

From the Altar of The Earth, ascending through the primordial ladder of the Altar of Beginnings, we have this Mystical Menorah constantly pulsating the ongoing Words of the Eternal Dimensions. It is up to you and I to be the Tillers and Worshippers of The Adamah Altar King, emanating the Songs once heard in the Beginning, from these Altar Thrones. We find our rest in the Bosom of The Altar King of kings, Yahshua HaMashiach, who has given to us a New Name, which comes with a New Song.

Hidden in the Numerical and Ordinal values of these 7 Altar Thrones, is the Secret to the Creation of The Adam, who conceals all revelations to them. This first Adam, as we read in this Book, who was formed from the Dust of the Adamah Altar and Created after the Image and Likeness of The Name of Elohim, concealed all Altar revelations in Genesis 1:1.

When we add up the Numerical values with the Ordinal values of Genesis 1:1, (2701+298 = 2999) we are given The Place that concealed all 7 Altar Throne revelations – Genesis 2:7:

וַיִּיצֶר יהוה אֱלֹהִים אֶת־הָאָדָם עָפָר מִן־הָאֲדָמָה וַיִּפַּח בְּאַפָּיו נִשְׁמַת חַיִּים וַיְהִי הָאָדָם לְנֶפֶשׁ חַיָּה:

- Va'yi'tzer YHWH Elohim Et-HaAdam Aphar Min-HaAdamah Va'yi'pach Be'apav Nish'mat Chai'yim Va'ye'hee HaDam Le'nefesh Ha'Yah.

- **Gen 2:7** "And YHWH Elohim formed the Adam from the dust of the Ground, and breathed into his nostrils the breath of lives; and the Adam became a living speaking Soul."

This verse has the Genesis 1:1 numeric system concealed and built into it. The first Adam contained in His entire being the secrets to the 7 Altar Thrones. From The Adam would come forth the Ezer K'negdo/Helpmeet of Genesis 2:21-22 or, The Woman, who was BUILT – Va'yi'ben/וַיִּבֶן. The woman had the Songs to the 7 Altar Thrones built into her. Together, Adam and The Woman were to demonstrate these revelations to all Creation, bringing Glory and Honor to The Name of Elohim! The Adam was to communicate the 7 Altar Thrones to all Creation. He failed, so, The Last Adam came and made these Altar Thrones known by what He did!

We read how He manifested all the Altar Thrones while here on Earth. Having said that, The Adamah Altar King has also manifested and Revealed the hidden mysteries to the Songs that emanate from these very Thrones which are hidden in the Womb of His Bride Israel. Stay tuned as the Altar Thrones of Genesis 1:1 open up the Eternal Orchestra to the Heavenly Dimensions by The Voice of Music. The Spirit and The Bride say Come, the Spirit and The Bride SING, come, and enter the place of Eternal Tranquility. Shalom

Hebrew Alef Bet
Numerical and Ordinal Value Chart

Letter	Numerical	Ordinal	Letter	Numerical	Ordinal
א – Alef	1	1st	ל – Lamed	30	12th
ב – Bet	2	2nd	מ – Mem	40	13th
ג – Gimel	3	3rd	נ – Nun	50	14th
ד – Dalet	4	4th	ס – Samekh	60	15th
ה – Hei	5	5th	ע – Ayin	70	16th
ו – Vav	6	6th	פ – Peh	80	17th
ז – Zayin	7	7th	צ – Tzadi	90	18th
ח – Chet	8	8th	ק – Qoof	100	19th
ט – Tet	9	9th	ר – Resh	200	20th
י – Yood	10	10th	ש – Shin	300	21st
כ – Khaf	20	11th	ת – Tav	400	22nd

John-James of the House of Flores.®

Glossary

Most of the words in this book will be defined or translated from the context thereof. Here are a few to keep in mind that are used throughout this book in place of what is commonly used.

Altar – Miz'be'ach
Christ – Mashiach
(The) **Earth** – HaAretz
God – Elohim
(The) **Heavens** – HaShamayim
Israel – Yisrael
Jesus – Yahshua
King – Melekh
Lampstand – Menorah
Lord/LORD – YHWH, Yahuwah
Melchizedek – MelkhiTzedeq
Peace – Shalom
Restore/Repentance – Shuv/Teshuvah

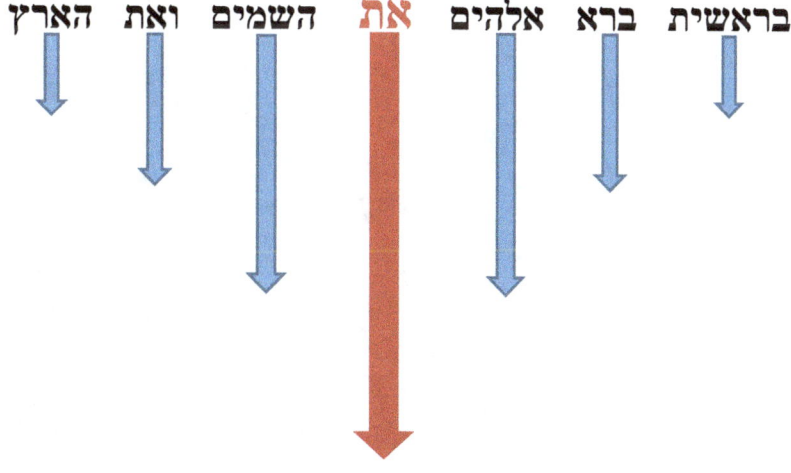

The Seven Altar Thrones of Genesis 1:1

About the Author

Pastor/Shepherd John-James is an adamant student and scriptural archaeologist of the written text in both the Hebrew and Greek languages, especially Hebrew. Pastor John-James is the founder of Remnant of Truth International and has a recognized voice Internationally by many ministries. Pastor John-James, not one who was raised in a Church setting until his late teenage years, had a spiritual awakening with The Messiah Yahshua, aka Jesus Christ by many. At that time, he was led on a Journey through the Scriptures from their Ancient Hebraic origins. Upon this Damascus Road Journey experience of his, the Voice of Elohim drew him closer to the depths and understanding of many truths concealed in the Scriptures. This would later mold and shape his character and mindset after the One who Authored the very Bible, we all read, Yahshua HaMashiach, aka Jesus The Christ. Pastor John-James is one of many who has been given the keys of unlocking the secrets and revelations most would have never known were hidden beneath the Hebrew language and that the Sages of old and rabbis today clearly know of. This work is compiled from years of research, study and meditation regarding the Hebrew Scriptures, especially the first verse of our Bibles. Pastor John-James is married to his beautiful Segullah/Treasure, Rochelle Denise Flores and has 3 beautiful children, two anointed grandsons and more grandchildren on the way as this is being written.

www.ingramcontent.com/pod-product-compliance
Lightning Source LLC
Chambersburg PA
CBHW051628230426
43669CB00013B/2216